BEHIND CLOSED DOORS

How The Rich Won Control of Canada's Tax System ...
And Ended Up Richer

Linda McQuaig

"She does a masterful job unleashing her fury at the inequities in Canada's tax system."
—*The Ottawa Citizen*

"Relentlessly convincing, revealing, entertaining and correct."
—*Perception*

"Courageous ... The brilliantly written chapter on Cohen is worth the price of the book by itself."
—*Books in Canada*

"A page-turner."
—*The Hamilton Spectator*

"Brutally honest ... This book should be read by everyone. Some may wish to dismiss it, but the truth is often hard to swallow."
—*Business & Finance*

"A lively, readable and infor mative book that successfully explains tax concepts c   well ... the book should be strongly recomme   dians."
—*Gordon Bale, pro   University*

PENGUIN BOOKS

BEHIND CLOSED DOORS

Born and raised in Toronto, Linda McQuaig graduated from the University of Toronto in 1974. In her fourteen years as a journalist, she has covered a wide range of subjects, from the revolution in Iran and the war in Lebanon to the political and financial dealings of Canada's establishment. She has worked for CBC radio, *Maclean's* and *The Globe and Mail*, where she is currently a national political reporter. In 1984, her articles in the *Globe* drew public attention to what later became a notorious scandal—the Scientific Research Tax Credit. She also exposed the fact that hundreds of rich Canadians paid no tax—a revelation that eventually pushed Ottawa to bring in a minimum income tax.

BEHIND CLOSED DOORS

Linda McQuaig

How The Rich
Won Control of Canada's
Tax System . . .
And Ended Up Richer

PENGUIN BOOKS

PENGUIN BOOKS
Published by the Penguin Group
Penguin Books Canada Ltd, 2801 John Street, Markham, Ontario, Canada L3R 1B4
Penguin Books, 27 Wrights Lane, London W8 5TZ, England
Viking Penguin Inc., 40 West 23rd Street, New York, New York 10010, USA
Penguin Books Australia Ltd, Ringwood, Victoria, Australia
Penguin Books (NZ) Ltd, 182-190 Wairau Road, Auckland 10, New Zealand
Penguin Books Ltd, Registered Offices: Harmondsworth, Middlesex, England

First published in Canada by Viking, 1987
Published in Penguin Books, 1988

Manufactured in Canada

Canadian Cataloguing in Publication Data
McQuaig, Linda, 1951-
  Behind closed doors

ISBN 0-14-010057-1

1. Income tax - Canada. 2. Wealth - Canada.
3. Income distribution - Canada. I. Title.

HJ4662.A6M38 1988   336.24'0971   C87-093552-6

To Audrey and Jack McQuaig
who, in very different ways, have been wonderful parents

ACKNOWLEDGEMENTS

Writing a book about the tax system, without a technical background in tax, has been a daunting project, to say the least. But I have been helped along the way by the kind efforts of a large number of people. Although their assistance was invaluable, none of them is in any way responsible for the book's tone or conclusions or, of course, any errors.

I was initially encouraged to embark on this task by Daniel Drache and Paul Hardman. Peter Livingston, my agent, had an immediate enthusiasm for the project, and went on to apply his marketing genius with remarkable skill. He remained a source of encouragement and friendship throughout.

In several years of writing about tax and tax policy, I have been greatly helped by numerous tax experts. Although this list is by no means complete, I would like particularly to thank John Bossons, Donald Brean, Kevin Charlebois, Irwin Gillespie, Francis Montreuil, Allan Maslove and David Perry. I am also grateful to the many other experts and non-experts who gave generously of their time in off-the-record interviews.

In addition, I am indebted to Leslie T. MacDonald, whose excellent thesis on the Carter report and its aftermath was extremely useful. I also benefited enormously from Mac McNair's thoughtful paper on the 1970 Senate Banking Committee hearings. Michael Wolfson helped me extensively on the difficult subject of wealth taxation; Richard Krever on the history of the income tax.

A number of journalists should also be mentioned: Jock Ferguson, Rod Mickleburgh, Christopher Waddell and, of course, my wonderful friend and colleague, Tom Walkom.

Geoffrey Stevens, managing editor of *The Globe and Mail*, was understanding enough to give me a year off to write the book, and to extend the leave when the project just kept growing. Dean Williams was a helpful and cheerful researcher. I am also grateful to many at the Canadian Tax Foundation for their assistance, including Douglas Sherbaniuk, Ron MacLeod, Zsuzsa Adlington and Pat Hillmer.

Penguin Books proved to be the ideal publisher. From the first time I walked in the door, I knew I had landed in the right place. President Morty Mint was unflagging in his support and excitement about the book. Debra Gallagher, Lorraine Johnson, Noona Barlow, Shannon Wray and Patricia Cooper were a pleasure to work with. Senior editor David Kilgour was every writer's dream editor. His excellent direction, patience and good humour kept me buoyant: even during marathon editing sessions that lasted until 4:00 a.m., I was still able to laugh.

One of the great things about writing a book is the opportunity to thank people who have provided special friendship during the project, and in life in general. Life just wouldn't be the same without: Leslie Elver, Mr B., Gene Allen, Jane Spanton, Linda Manzer, Anne Wordsworth, Rick Lynette and my many other friends associated with the Pit. David Graham, Ned Shorter, Gary Tenenbaum and my brother Peter offered timely and much-appreciated advice. Michael Code provided some excellent legal insights, as well as much fun and friendship. Bob Wise and his delightful son Brooker were always a welcome diversion.

Bruce Baldwin was a constant source of friendship and support, whether in providing special deliveries from Mr Pong or acting as my gentlest critic. His motto "No indulgence too absurd" took on special meaning in the final throes of getting the book done.

Gord Evans was always there, cheering me with summer tapes, late night cocktails and drives in the Volare. His loyalty and sense of fun could not have been more timely.

Finally, I would like to thank Neil Brooks, who teaches tax at Osgoode Hall Law School, for the endless hours he spent explaining to me the intricacies of tax law and going over the manuscript. But it would be wrong to imply his input was primarily technical. Far more important, he shaped the way I look at the tax system; his ideas permeate this book. Anyone who knows Neil Brooks knows that behind his playful exterior, there is a strong commitment to a fairer tax system. Over the years, he has taught thousands of law students the importance of approaching the tax system critically, of asking why the system is the way it is and who benefits from it. Neil Brooks is really the unsung hero of tax in Canada. He brings an intellectual rigour and a deep sense of justice to a subject too often approached in a purely technical manner. Like many who have been exposed to his ideas and his spirit, I have been deeply inspired. This book is a product of that inspiration.

Linda McQuaig
Toronto

CONTENTS

INTRODUCTION

"This isn't tax reform; this is tax deform."
—Neil Brooks, commenting on Michael Wilson's
white paper on tax reform

For many Canadians, the most lasting image of the June 1987 tax reform may be that of Mike Duffy.

On that warm June evening, the legendary CBC-TV reporter, probably the only Canadian reporter regularly asked for his autograph, was the one who really broke the news to the country about the government's tax reform proposals. Finance Minister Michael Wilson had officially unveiled them, before live television cameras, in a speech to the House of Commons earlier in the evening. Wilson's speech was one of the most crucial of his political career, and he had summoned up all the liveliness he could muster. But even at his liveliest, Wilson is leaden and flat, as exciting as a banker announcing a new convertible share debenture. This is a man who could make the play-by-play of a Stanley Cup hockey game sound dull.

It fell to Duffy to make the tax reform sound exciting. He noted that while the government was reducing income taxes for middle-income families, it was going after "the corporate welfare bums." Duffy added: "The financial, real estate and insurance industries, which in the past were able to organize their affairs to pay little or no corporate tax, those industries will be made to pay tax." And tighter rules on business lunches and other deductions "will probably cost the Conservatives some good will among their supporters."

This image of the Tories turning on their own friends in business and upper income groups was really the same message that Wilson had been trying to get across in his own wooden manner. But in the mouth of an animated Duffy, it sounded bold and dramatic.

As the evening wore on, however, a curious thing happened. Prominent business leaders—presumably the government's friends alluded to by Duffy—made statements indicating they were not displeased with the reforms. Business spokesmen, who have been ferocious in the past when faced with tax reforms they did not like, were mellow and even complimentary this time. John Bulloch, president of the Canadian Federation of Independent Business, was beaming as he announced: "I think they've got it right this time." Even Bill James, president of Falconbridge, seemed unconcerned by the apparent attack on the mining industry, speaking approvingly of the basic thrust of the reforms.

The day after tax reform, *The Globe and Mail* echoed Duffy's theme with front-page headlines: "Taxation overhaul hits business, gives a break to most families" and "Wealthy biggest losers in plan." But the *next* day, after the business community had had a chance to look over the proposals, the *Globe*'s "Report on Business" ran three pages of reporting and analysis that suggested a different interpretation: "Reflecting on package evokes sighs of relief," said the headline on the front of the business section. Inside there was more interesting news: "Banks escape unscathed from Wilson's tax reform moves." And as *The Financial Post*'s "Investor's Guide" noted in a headline: "It wasn't as bad as feared."

In the following weeks, a number of business spokesmen revealed their pleasure with the general thrust of the reforms. The Business Council on National Issues, whose members include some of the most powerful business leaders in the country, expressed some concerns about the yet-to-be-announced sales tax, but said: "We are generally satisfied with the overall direction of the personal and corporate income tax changes." Commented Anthony Hepburn, president of Vancouver investment dealer Odlum Brown: "I think by and large the business community applauds a lot of the things he [Wilson] is trying to do."

For a group that was supposedly being hit, the business and investment community was surprisingly full of praise for its assailant. The Conservative government of Brian Mulroney had discovered a whole new way to hit the rich—with a nice, soft punch.

There was some good news for low- and middle-income earners: their income tax bills would be coming down, just as Duffy had told them. But there were a few hitches. They would be paying more in federal sales tax, and a whole new sales tax lurked menacingly on the horizon. Indeed, a major sales tax hike apparently was scheduled for just beyond the next election as part of the second stage of tax reform.

And even considering the income tax reductions, any sense of gratitude had to be tempered with the knowledge that the Tories were only providing relief from tax increases they had themselves imposed. Since coming to power in September 1984, the Tories had raised taxes dramatically, hitting the poor and middle classes particularly hard. The tax reductions now proposed would still leave most of these people paying more than if the Mulroney government had simply left the tax system alone.

Take just one example. Government figures showed that this reform would result in an average tax saving of $90 for households with incomes below $15,000. But in 1985, this same government had removed a measure called the federal tax reduction, which had enabled low-income families to reduce their taxes by $100 a year. So even with the $90 saving Wilson was now proposing, a typical poor family would be $10 worse off than if the government had not tampered with the tax system. Needless to say, the massive information Wilson provided in his white paper on tax reform made no mention of the federal tax reduction—a measure that he clearly hopes Canadians have forgotten. When his other tax increases over the past three years are added in, the plight of the low-income family is worse still.

And what about the rich friends of the government, the ones Duffy singled out as losers? In fact, the government's own figures show that, on average, people with incomes above $100,000 will end up net winners. They will receive average tax savings of $1,615. As a percentage of income, this is a larger saving than the savings of those at the bottom end.

Furthermore, this $1,615 figure is misleading. The real tax savings that will be enjoyed by the rich as a result of this "tax reform" are actually greater. The government has calculated this figure in such a way as to understate the tax savings for those at the top.* This raises some serious questions about how honest the government is being in its massive effort to sell this tax reform package to the public.

Certainly, Wilson has made a point of stressing that the tax reform package will shut off some tax breaks enjoyed by high-income people and by large corporations. In fact, the package doesn't touch a number of the key tax breaks that have been the subject of bitter tax reform battles in the past; but, although many of these tax breaks remain intact, Wilson has dropped the tax *rate* for those at the top.

Indeed, Wilson's reform only consolidates the favoured tax position of the rich. Over the years, they have managed to reduce the tax burden officially imposed on them by winning more and more tax breaks. Under the current reform, some of these tax breaks will be eliminated or modified. But the rich aren't being asked to simply give these tax breaks up; they are being asked to *trade* them for lower rates. What the rich have been receiving through the back door—through special concessions and complicated shelters that protected their incomes from high tax rates—they will now receive directly and

*For more detailed discussion of this and other aspects of the Wilson tax reform, see Chapter Twelve.

simply in the form of lower rates. And, as we have seen, the trade is not just an even exchange; they will actually be better off as a result. Among those with incomes above $100,000, some individuals will end up worse off. But about 75 percent in this top income group—according to government figures—will actually pay less tax as a result of Wilson's reform.

If Duffy hadn't given the Canadian public the full picture, it certainly wasn't his fault. Like the rest of the media, he had been literally locked up in an Ottawa football stadium for ten hours prior to Wilson's speech.

These media lock-ups, which are customary before government budgets as well, are clearly designed to influence the media's reaction to government proposals. Journalists are allowed an advance preview of the tax changes in the lock-up, so that they can have their reports largely prepared by the time the government documents are officially released to the public. But the circumstances of this advance viewing are strictly controlled. Once they enter, journalists are not allowed to leave the locked area or communicate in any way with the outside world. Pay telephones are stripped of their outside connections. Guards patrol every exit with walkie-talkies. Inside, the journalists are provided with endless coffee and food—this time there was an elaborate roast beef dinner —and are surrounded by swarms of Finance Department officials, who readily explain and interpret the tax changes. Whatever the question—corporate tax, personal tax, sales tax, fiscal outlook, economic impact, fairness—there is a willing expert there, ready to sit down and provide private tutoring for the bewildered journalist. An aspiring cult leader could probably pick up a few useful ideas on mind-control methods from observing one of these lock-ups.

Certainly, all this gives the government enormous control over the crucial first batch of news reports and commentary. News organizations are permitted to bring in their own accountants, but Finance alone has access to internal tax data and has carefully selected which data to present and in what form to present them. So, although there are charts and statistics and answers to far more tax questions that any sane person would want to know in a lifetime, journalists are frustrated if they try to get simple information that the government has not chosen to make public.

For instance, the government proudly announced in its tax reform documents that the proposals would have the effect of removing 850,000 low-income Canadians from the tax rolls. This was indeed supposed to exemplify the theme of fairness that permeated the white paper. But when journalists asked how many of these low-income Canadians had only started paying tax since the Mulroney government's major tax increases in 1985, they were told the government didn't have this number.

Of course the government did have this number or could get it with a simple press of a button on one of its advanced computer systems. Without it, the 850,000 figure was meaningless. But without further information, journalists were forced to use the figure the government had provided. And so Mike Duffy and the rest of the press corps had no choice but to report the government's claim that the tax reform proposals would remove some 850,000 low-income Canadians from the tax rolls. It sure sounded fair. Later that evening, however, Ken Battle, spokesman for the National Council of Welfare, estimated that there had been about a million low-income Canadians added to the tax rolls since 1985, so that lopping off 850,000 now would still leave about 150,000 low-income people paying tax who had not been paying tax when the Tories came to power. But Battle's estimate of one million was not an official number and therefore was given far less prominence in the press coverage. It is the 850,000 figure which will be remembered.

Perhaps more than anything, the June 87 tax reform was an exercise in clever public relations. The government had gone to extraordinary lengths to make its proposals sound fair, holding back relevant information and even presenting the numbers in ways that diminished the gains to be enjoyed by the rich. The goal of fairness, which had ranked well below deficit-reduction in the Tories' earlier tax changes, had been elevated to the number one priority in the white paper. For months, the Finance Department and the prime minister's office had been focussing on ways to market the tax reform package, seeing it as a means to lift the Tories in the polls. One senior bureaucrat says that Mulroney himself probably spent more time on tax reform than on any other single issue since he became prime minister.

But if the tax reform was carefully dressed up to look like a boon to the lower and middle classes, this was by no means the original motive for embarking on the whole exercise. The roots of Wilson's tax reform had in no way come from a desire to redistribute the tax burden more fairly. Indeed, almost the opposite was true. For some time, the Mulroney government had been working on plans to redesign and move towards a greater reliance on the sales tax. This change promised to redistribute the tax burden far *less* fairly and, even in the early stages, the plan had caused considerable controversy. The government knew that it faced an almost impossible selling job.

But, inside the government, a clever idea was taking shape: if the move to a greater reliance on the sales tax could be made *as part of an overall package of tax reform*, then maybe it could be sold to the public. If income taxes were to be reduced now, most people likely wouldn't care or notice that they would end up paying more sales tax later—and more tax altogether. Tax reform became the vehicle to carry out what the government really wanted—to decrease its emphasis on income taxes and increase the emphasis on sales taxes. And that move, despite the dressing-up of the tax reform package, would have one clear effect. It would continue the trend of shifting the tax burden from the rich to the middle class.

To appreciate the nature and significance of this shift, it might be useful to briefly outline two schools of thought that have dominated the Canadian tax scene over the years.

The first was best articulated in the mammoth report of the

Carter Royal Commission on Taxation in the 1960s. The story of that ill-fated Commission—and the tragic personal story of Kenneth Carter—will be told in more detail later. But for now, it is enough to touch on the essence of Carter's philosophy.

At the heart of the Carter system was the idea that the tax burden should be distributed on the basis of ability to pay: the greater the individual's income, the larger proportion of it could be given up in tax. This wasn't a new concept at all. In the eighteenth century, British tax officials assessed tax burdens on the basis of the number of windows in one's house, this being considered a relative measure of the size of the house and therefore of the occupant's wealth. Although the system had its flaws—and perhaps had something to do with the popularity of dark, windowless mansions—it reflected the notion that the well-to-do could contribute a larger proportion of their resources to the national treasury than could the poor. This idea was not considered particularly radical. Even Adam Smith commented favourably on the concept of larger burdens on larger incomes in his *Wealth of Nations*.

Canada's income tax system has been built on this premise. It has always had a *progressive* rate structure; that is, tax rates rise as income rises.* This approach is based on the theory that the more income one has, the larger the surplus one generates. Since this surplus is not essential to meeting one's basic needs, it can be taxed at a higher rate than income which goes to cover necessities. Consequently, Canada's income tax system in the 60s had a steeply rising progressive rate structure, as did the income tax systems of Britain and the United States.

So in proposing a tax system based on ability to pay, Carter was hardly ringing any new bells. What did come as a shock

---

*Everyone pays the same low rate of tax on small amounts of income, but as income rises, further earnings are taxed at successively higher rates. These rates are known as marginal rates; any income above a set line or margin is taxed at a higher rate.

in the Carter report, however, was its insistence that individuals be taxed on the basis of their *true* ability to pay. Up until this point, the progressive ideal of higher tax rates on higher incomes had existed largely on paper. Few well-to-do individuals actually paid those dramatically high rates—which were as high as 80 percent—since the tax laws essentially allowed them to leave out large chunks of their income when they were calculating their total income for tax purposes. So the high rates remained largely mythical, something the rich could complain about without actually experiencing.

Carter wanted to change all this. He argued that all forms of income should be included for tax purposes, since they all increased the individual's ability to pay for goods and services. By recommending this "comprehensive income base," Carter was confronting the rich for the first time with the prospect of actually paying the tax rates that Parliament set down for them—a disturbing prospect indeed. He was proposing that the tax system be made progressive in fact as well as in theory.

Arrayed against the Carter principle of taxing individuals on the basis of their true ability to pay, we find another school of thought which would tax on a totally different basis. If the Carter philosophy can be described, with a little poetic licence, as "Make the Rich Pay," then this other school can be dubbed "Make the Rest Pay."

Rather than taxing individuals on their ability to pay, as measured by their *income*, the proponents of the make-the-rest-pay school often suggest taxing individuals on the basis of their *consumption*. Money spent is taxed; money saved is tax-exempt. At first glance this may seem fair; people who want to pay less tax can simply consume less. But an unmistakable fact quickly emerges: the rich are able to save more, which is what makes them rich. The poor and middle classes tend to spend the bulk of their income to cover fairly basic living expenses. Any tax based on consumption is bound to hit those who, by necessity, must consume almost everything they receive. A consumption-based tax then turns the ability-to-pay concept on its head: the heaviest burden falls on those least able to pay.

Consumption taxes can be structured to reduce this regressive effect by, for instance, providing tax credits for those at the lower end. Indeed, this is what Wilson is planning for his yet-to-be-defined sales tax, which will replace the current federal sales tax. He has admitted that the tax credits he has so far provided have not been adequate to protect those with low incomes. But he adamantly maintains that his new sales taxes will be accompanied by more generous credits that will more than compensate low-income people for the additional sales tax they will face.

Assuming that Wilson carries through with this commitment to protect low-income people, the sales tax will still be regressive for the rest of the population. Middle class people will pay a proportionately larger share of their income in sales taxes than will those with high incomes. Since Wilson has made it clear that the government will rely more heavily on sales taxes in the future, the regressive potential of this move is significant.

Indeed, the government is not denying that the middle class may emerge with a heavier overall tax burden. In an interview, deputy minister Stanley Hartt insisted that the lowest-income Canadians would be more than protected by the sales tax credit, but "after that, no promises." While there will be further income tax cuts in the second stage of tax reform, Hartt concedes that some middle class people will end up paying more tax overall. "In part, whether the burden is taken out or not will depend on people's spending patterns," said Hartt. "I can describe to you a person who I can guarantee will be a winner in the middle income. That person would be someone who lives very frugally and saves the maximum that one can conceivably save, whereas at the other end of the spectrum, somebody who spends a lot will not necessarily come out a winner in the middle-income brackets, even if they're middle-middle or lower-middle."

Hartt argues that this gives people a choice, and that people may learn to spend less under the new system. "You understand that spending patterns can change once people start thinking in those terms. Somebody might say: 'Well, if I buy that electric broom, I'm just giving the [government] back what they gave me. If I don't buy the electric broom and buy mutual funds, I don't pay the tax, and I'm saving and investing and participating in capitalism.'" Such a theory, however, ignores the fact that middle-income earners—unlike the rich—spend almost all of their incomes on basic daily living expenses, leaving little to invest in mutual funds. Rather than choosing between mutual funds and an electric broom, many middle class families may be faced with more difficult decisions—between mutual funds or a summer vacation or braces for their children's teeth. What is far more likely, however, is that they won't agonize over such choices. Rather, they'll continue to live as they've been accustomed to living, but they'll pay a great deal more tax.

Essentially, the government is saying that middle class Canadians can learn to do with a lot less. "Although you may consider that everything you do is absolutely necessary, you're defining necessary in terms of a standard and a lifestyle that you have set, and it isn't as necessary as live or die," said Hartt. "It's not eating and shelter and clothing. You're beyond that in the middle. You can buy a car or not buy a car, for example. That's a typical middle class decision."

While the Carter Commission's proposals would have pushed Canada clearly in the direction of Making the Rich Pay, Michael Wilson's two-stage tax reform package would push us in the opposite direction. Carter warned against the regressive effects of sales taxes. And he urged Ottawa to continue to rely heavily on the income tax, where rates rose in each income bracket. Now, Wilson is proposing not only to move towards a heavier reliance on sales taxes, but also to reduce the number of tax rates within the income tax system. Where the rich used to face marginal tax rates considerably higher than those in the income tax brackets beneath them, the rich will now find themselves facing the same marginal tax rates as some upper sections of the middle class.

With his proposal to reduce the number of tax rates from ten to three, Wilson is reducing the differences between the tax rates of high-income people and low-income people. He wants to reduce the top marginal tax rate from its current level of 50 percent to 44 percent, and he wants this top rate to apply to all incomes above $55,000. This means that many families with incomes just above $55,000 will face the same marginal tax rate as a family with an income of a million dollars— although the million-dollar family clearly has a much greater ability to pay.

Even more striking perhaps, many families with incomes of less than $30,000 will face a marginal tax rate of 39 percent— only 5 percentage points lower than the tax rate faced by the million-dollar family. Indeed, a secretary at Bell Canada could end up with a marginal tax rate only 5 percentage points below the rate faced by Bell Canada chairman Jean de Grandpré who earns a salary of $977,300. And the rates may well drop more as part of the second stage of tax reform. "I would like to see our top marginal rate come down further," said Hartt. "The idea is low, low rates." So with high-income people facing lower rates, who will make up the lost revenue? Presumably, middle class people who continue to spend as they have in the past.

What is really happening, then, is that the long-touted goal of a progressive tax system is being quietly abandoned, without the change ever really being debated. Did any finance minister ever stand up in the House of Commons and say that Ottawa no longer intended to tax Canadians on the basis of their ability to pay? Even Michael Wilson, who is busy dismantling what is left of our progressive rate structure, is not really identifying what he is doing. Rather, he says that he is reducing the number of tax rates in order to simplify the system. Yet reducing the number of tax rates won't do anything to simplify the system. The complexity of the system comes from the deductions and concessions that allow people to exclude or reduce income for tax purposes, and his changes won't simplify in these areas at all. Reducing the number of tax rates won't remove one single page from the Income Tax Act. But it will greatly diminish the progressivity of the rate structure.

In his tax reform documents, Wilson points out that the introduction of more and more tax breaks in the 70s and 80s had the effect of undermining the progressivity of the tax system. This is true. Although the top federal rate is 50 percent, many high-income people do not pay rates this high because they are able to use tax breaks and tax shelter schemes to shield part of their incomes from tax. But this raises an interesting question. If the rich have managed in this way to pay taxes below the prescribed 50 percent rate, why is the only option now to officially lower their tax rate? Why not close the breaks, cut off the shelters and make them, in fact, pay a top tax rate of 50 percent?

Such a question is clearly unfashionable in Ottawa. But would it be so unpopular with the general public? The Tories' own polling firm, Decima Research Limited, told them in the fall of 1984 that one of the few points of strong agreement among Canadians was a belief that the rich should pay more tax. According to the confidential Decima survey: "In only one of the six areas examined was one course of action clearly favoured over another—the vast majority (79%) believe there should be an increase in the amount of taxes paid by the rich." A March 1987 survey by the polling firm Environics reached similar conclusions: 85 percent felt the wealthy paid too little tax.

If that's any indication of public sentiment, then Canadians appear to favour a progressive tax system and, indeed, are frustrated that ours isn't more progressive. Yet the Mulroney government now plans to consolidate the low taxes of the rich into a new revised tax code. The small tax burden of the rich will now become official policy, not just the result of clever tax avoidance schemes.

Of course this is not the way the package is being sold.

Rather it is being presented as a fairer system that will reduce everyone's taxes. Since taxation is complicated and there are so many different taxes involved, the ordinary citizen might be forgiven for being a bit confused. But if a large majority of Canadians have felt in the past that the rich weren't paying enough tax, once the smoke and mirrors of the current reforms are removed these same Canadians may be surprised to find that the rich are paying even less tax.

In the debate between the two warring schools of tax thought, the contest has become badly one-sided. If the make-the-rest-pay school has been gaining the upper hand in recent years, the make-the-rich-pay school has been limping along with at least one hand tied behind its back. The public still seems attracted to the idea of the rich paying more, but the notion has lost whatever cachet it had with those in power. Consequently, what should be a lively scrap between the two sides has become an uneven contest in which the make-the-rich-pay school is barely able to mount a defence. This discouragement is perhaps not surprising, since the outcome of the debate already has been largely decided. It's as if the debate on capital punishment had started with the premise that there should be capital punishment, the only question left to resolve being a choice between the electric chair and the noose.

The possibility of shifting the tax burden up the income scale along the lines Carter recommended has already been removed from the political agenda. Thus, Jack McArthur, writing a column in *The Toronto Star* in April 1987, was able to argue that there is no way to relieve the heavy tax burden on individuals because there is nowhere to shift it. McArthur argued that corporate profits could not bear any greater tax burden. While this is a debatable point, what is striking is that McArthur never even considers yet another possibility: redistributing the tax burden *among* individuals.

It would have been one thing for him to raise this possibility, argue against it and eventually dismiss it; but he doesn't even acknowledge it as an option anymore. So unfashionable has the Carter view become that it is no longer even considered necessary to address it. It is dead, part of yesterday's hand-wringing about social justice, not in tune with the self-centred, fast-moving mood of the 80s.

But how has the progressive alternative been so definitively eliminated from the debate, without ever really being publicly repudiated by government or by the electorate? Even tax experts sympathetic to the Carter philosophy tend to scoff at suggestions of bringing back the estate tax or taxing capital gains at full rates. And to even suggest an idea like introducing an annual net wealth tax, modelled on similar European taxes, is to enter the world of pure fantasy. These notions, while technically sound, are *politically* impossible, the experts say.

What is never properly addressed, however, is why this is so. Essentially, they are considered politically impossible because the outcry has been so great whenever there has been any attempt to introduce them in the past. And who has the outcry come from? It has come almost exclusively from powerful special interest groups who have stood to lose from the changes. Meanwhile, the vast majority of taxpayers, who might have gained, have remained silent and uninformed. The notion of "political impossibility" takes on a slightly different hue seen in this light. We don't have a progressive tax system because the rich have indicated that they don't want one.

Indeed, even the Carter commissioners might not have waded into such treacherous waters had they known the sharks that awaited them. Douglas Hartle, a University of Toronto economist who served as the commission's research director, reports that he still has "scar tissue" from his days defending the report before irate business groups. He notes that the commission's willingness to embrace the equity and progressivity principles with such gusto sprang partly from inexperience. They simply didn't know the kind of torrent their proposals would unleash.

The notion that the progressive alternative is "politically

impossible" is a convenient one. If it is politically impossible it doesn't need to be discussed any more. It's just one of those things that's not going to happen, no matter how good an idea it might be or how appealing the public might find it. The powerful interest groups have managed to contain the debate. The Carter-style make-the-rich-pay approach has been quietly dismissed as impractical. So the focus has shifted to sorting out the possibilities within the make-the-rest-pay framework. Should there be a national sales tax or a federal value-added tax ... should there be a noose or an electric chair?

A crucial element in containing the debate has been limiting the participants. In order to qualify as a participant, one generally must have the credentials of an expert. This automatically eliminates just about everybody, and refocusses the debate as a technical one. As Hartle notes: "Equity issues are almost bound to be neglected in the welter of specialized opinion about the details." Ordinary taxpayers are not told that the long-touted principles of equity and progressivity are being abandoned. Rather, they are told the opposite; that these are the guiding principles of the current tax reform. So members of the public are inclined to bow out, trusting that value-free experts will take care of the technical details and ensure them a fair share of the national pie.

But of course ordinary people can't just be excluded from the debate. This is a democracy after all, and, even if people don't participate in debates, they still have to be convinced by those who do. Explanations have been offered, therefore, that have cast the make-the-rest-pay theory in an appealing light or, at least, an acceptable light. Thus, tax reductions for the rich have been advocated not on the grounds that the rich deserve a break but on the grounds that lower taxes will induce the rich to invest and investment is the key to creating jobs. The fact that, according to this theory, the public interest coincides with the interests of the rich is supposed to be purely accidental.

But, if we are approaching the subject intelligently, this coincidence may seem curious to us and lead us to question the sincerity of those claiming that the nation is best served by offering tax reductions for the rich. Perhaps, as the tax reform debate rolls on, a helpful rule for observing the process might be to react skeptically whenever a group argues that it is seeking a tax reduction out of concern for the national interest, rather than out of self-interest. Indeed, skepticism should probably increase in direct proportion to the lack of self-interest claimed. In this light, claims by the Business Council on National Issues that it is willing to sacrifice business interests for the good of the country should put our skeptical antennae on high alert.

Skepticism is, of course, a useful state of mind for approaching any request for a reduced tax burden. The late U.S. tax expert Louis Eisenstein deftly exposed the self-serving quality of most of the common arguments used to justify tax reductions. When examined closely, most of these arguments are revealed to be arbitrary and unconvincing. As the current tax reform debate heats up, there are a few popular ones to watch out for.

Take for instance the traditional plea for a low tax on capital gains. The investment community has often asserted that if the tax on capital gains is high, investors will hold on to their shares rather than sell them and receive a capital gain which will be subject to tax. This creates a "locking-in" effect, they say. Capital is tied up rather than being made available for other investments, and this hurts the economy. But although this "locking-in" argument is regularly used to justify low taxes on capital gains, it could equally be used to justify a tax measure advocated by Ottawa in 1969—a measure that received nothing but scorn from the investment community.

This measure would have imposed a tax on the increase in value of shares every five years, regardless of whether the investor cashed them in or continued to hold on to them. This would have clearly done away with any "locking-in" effect, since the shares would have been taxed no matter what was done with them. But investors were horrified at the concept of being forced to pay a tax like this every five years, and their previously stated concerns about capital being "locked-in" disappeared like ice cream left in the sun.

Another frequent complaint of investors is that they are taxed twice on their investments. This "double taxation" arises, they say, because corporate profits are taxed once in the corporation and again when they are distributed to shareholders as dividends. The dividend tax credit is designed to correct this "double taxation" problem by giving shareholders a tax reduction to compensate for the corporate tax already paid. It might seem logical, then, to expect that in situations where a corporation has paid *no* tax, its shareholders would not require a dividend tax credit. This simple logic has eluded the investment community, however, which has insisted on maintaining this compensation for double taxation even when there is no double taxation. The Finance Department toyed with the idea of correcting this anomaly in the current tax reform, but backed off out of fear of negative reaction from the investment community.

With similar vehemence, it is often argued that high marginal tax rates destroy the will to work in high-income executives and professionals. It is frequently asserted that, faced with substantial taxes, these high-income earners will lose their motivation to earn that extra dollar, since they know they will have to give up a large chunk of it to the government. Rather than spending that extra evening in the office working on a big deal, they'll go out drinking or go home to their families. Eisenstein collected all the grim predictions of what could happen to these executives, rendered aimless and despondent by high taxes. Some pessimists, he noted, even speculated that high taxes were driving perfectly capable businessmen into the priesthood.

This argument about the demoralizing effect of high taxes —like so many arguments used to justify tax reductions—is based on certain questionable assumptions about human nature. Clearly there are many other factors that motivate people —the desire for prestige, power, satisfaction, a corner office— besides the simple desire to keep a large percentage of one's income.

But even if we accept the one-dimensional view of human nature implicit in the argument, does the conclusion necessarily follow? In other words, if it's true that high-powered executives and professionals are really only spurred on to work more because of financial rewards, does it follow that we shouldn't impose high taxes on them? If we tax them heavily, won't this simply render them leaner and hungrier and make them have to work all the harder in order to receive a large financial reward? If we let them keep a big chunk of their income, maybe they'll become sated too quickly and no longer feel that compelling drive that keeps them late at the office. The point here is not to try to dissect the mind of a high-powered business executive. The point is that, once we enter into this realm of pseudo-psychology, we can speculate endlessly. One theory is as plausible as the next. Yet the one that is commonly advanced is the one that suggests an end to high taxes on high incomes.

Perhaps what should make us particularly skeptical is how quickly these arguments are reversed when it becomes convenient. The same people who argue that executives are only motivated to work when they receive large financial compensation will turn around and argue in the next breath that providing workers with financial compensation through the unemployment insurance system will destroy their will to work. Allowing executives to keep large amounts of money doesn't destroy their keenness to work—indeed it stirs them to work harder—but for some reason providing modest benefits to workers totally saps their drive, leaving them utterly content with their lot. So while workers must be left lean and hungry, executives must be generously fed—an appealing argument if you're an executive.

Couldn't we equally argue that cutting taxes on low-income earners might make them more productive? With less of a tax burden, they might feel more highly motivated on the job and less inclined to strike, saving the economy billions of dollars. After all, the size of financial rewards have a very direct impact on low-income earners. It may mean the difference between taking a vacation or not taking one, buying a new car or not buying one. Unlike high-income earners, who usually have more than they need, the material needs and desires of low-income earners are far from satisfied. Would their behaviour therefore not be at least as susceptible to the appeal of increased financial rewards?

Finally, before we leave these hard-working executives, maybe, just to be perverse, we might ask why we so badly want to keep them late at the office in the first place. Would it really be contrary to the public interest to have them go home to their families instead? Chances are they're working late on something of dubious public benefit anyway—a corporate takeover or a tax avoidance scheme. We might all be better off if they did just about anything else—went swimming or bowling or even carousing.

This book—written by a non-expert—is an attempt to take the subject of tax out of the technical realm and bring it into the popular arena. Although the tax laws are vast and complicated, the basic principles of taxation are not. And while the experts have a special knowledge of the details of tax, anyone can have an understanding of the underlying principles. The presence of non-experts could have a dramatic and beneficial impact on the current tax reform debate. Not only would it increase the number of participants, but it would almost certainly change the focus.

It could, for instance, lead to some fundamental questions about what our tax system is all about. In many ways, taxes lie at the heart of our political system. It is through taxation that we raise revenue to run the country, defend ourselves from outside attack and furnish the basic apparatus of our society.

While we all have our favourite examples of wasteful government spending, what seems useless and extravagant to one taxpayer may be an invaluable service to the next. Determining how much money the government collects and how it spends these funds is ultimately what the political process is all about. But if we want to live in anything resembling modern Canada, Ottawa must collect taxes. So the questions become: who will pay them? How will the enormous burden be distributed? Should everyone pay the same or should those who have more money pay more tax?

Those who oppose higher taxes for the rich sometimes argue that this amounts to a form of legalized theft, in which the rich are robbed so their resources can be transferred to less fortunate members of society. But in singling out taxes, these people often ignore the many other less visible ways in which governments intervene to juggle the nation's resources among different groups—often redistributing resources in ways that aid the rich.

When governments take public funds and build universities, for instance, they are providing far greater benefit to the children of middle and upper class families than to the poor, who also pay taxes but whose offspring rarely make it to university. Of course, we all benefit from living in a society with higher education, but the advantages are clearly much greater for those who actually receive university degrees and can use them to launch lucrative careers. Similarly, governments impose laws that give certain groups a monopoly over vital services. Lawyers and doctors, for instance, are allowed to restrict the number of people practising in their fields, thereby allowing them to command handsome fees for their services. Again, we all benefit from the services of these professionals, but individual doctors and lawyers—who rank among the highest-paid Canadians—obviously gain far more. And, in the case of lawyers at least, the benefits of their services are also heavily skewed towards the rich, particularly in such areas as tax law.

The point is that taxation is merely one way in which

governments aid some groups at the expense of others. (In fact, Canada's tax system does this far less than is popularly believed—a subject to which we will return later.) While a progressive tax system can be a highly visible mechanism for redistributing income from richer to poorer citizens, other government actions often redistribute funds the other way—although they do so less noticeably. Any meaningful look at who is winning and who is losing from government interventions would have to look much further than the tax system. Such a sweeping investigation is clearly beyond the scope of this book.

Furthermore, I do not attempt to offer here a comprehensive discussion of Canadian taxation. I have restricted my focus largely to federal tax.* And even in the area of federal tax, no single book could cover all the technicalities, and it is not my intention to try.

Rather, I have tried to give the public a peak at what's been happening behind the closed doors of the tax world. Behind those doors is an interesting, little-known world where rich individuals and large corporations have found ways to shift the burden of billions of dollars in taxes from their own backs—onto the backs of other Canadians. They have been able to do this by influencing Ottawa to put in place and keep in place tax laws that work to their advantage.

If this kind of talk leaves the impression that I am a flaming radical, let me state my biases up front. I confess. I do believe that we should have a progressive tax system and that the rich should pay more tax. But before I am dismissed as a Soviet

---

*Provincial tax, which varies across the country, is beyond the scope of this book. However, these provincial variations are relatively slight. The provinces largely piggyback on the federal income tax system, adding their own tax that usually amounts to about half of the federal tax. Quebec alone has its own income tax system and collects its taxes separately. But even in Quebec's case, the provincial income tax system mostly parallels the federal one.

agent, let me introduce a fellow-traveller, Finance Minister Michael Wilson. Here's what he said on the subject in his tax reform speech to the House of Commons in June 1987:

> We all know that the tax system allows many profitable corporations to avoid paying a fair share of tax, year after year. We all know that it allows some people with very high incomes to pay less tax than the average Canadian wage-earner, year after year. We all know that it allows those who are able to use special tax breaks to shift the burden to others less able to carry it.

I couldn't have said it any better. And Wilson's words are not out of line with the ideals espoused by Canadian politicians over the years. But it is important to look past the words, to judge politicians by their deeds. This book attempts to do just that, to look beyond the lip-service paid to the ideal of a progressive tax system by Wilson and others, and to see how their actions have matched their words.

In launching his tax reform, Wilson has followed in the footsteps of others who have sought to reform the Canadian tax system. Before him, Kenneth Carter spent five years in the 60s working on ways to improve the system, and Finance Minister Edgar Benson proposed some significant reforms in his 1969 white paper. Most recently, Finance Minister Allan MacEachen attempted a mini-tax-reform in his November 1981 budget.

Pundits and commentators have generally concluded that Wilson has succeeded where the others failed. Deborah McGregor, Ottawa columnist for the *Financial Times*, declared that Wilson had struck a two-base hit in the second inning. Continuing the baseball metaphor, McGregor argued that Wilson is clearly a better player than MacEachen, who was hit by the ball, or Benson, who didn't make it to first base.

Indeed, MacEachen, Benson and Carter all took a heavy beating for their tax reform efforts. None of them succeeded in

changing the tax system along the lines they originally envisioned. Commentators have been inclined to attribute Wilson's success to his greater political skills. We are told that he
learned the lessons of MacEachen's ill-fated effort, which was
sprung on an unsuspecting public out of the blue. Anxious to
avoid a repeat of the MacEachen disaster, Wilson prepared the
public for what was coming and consulted widely with tax
lawyers and accountants as the package was being prepared.

While all this is true, it misses the real difference between
Wilson's reform and the earlier ones. The reforms proposed
by Carter, Benson and MacEachen were genuinely progressive. They belong firmly in the make-the-rich-pay camp. In
each case, the proposals advanced would have significantly
reduced the tax advantages enjoyed by high-income individuals and large corporations. And it is precisely for this reason
that they faced such fierce opposition from powerful interest
groups.

Wilson's reforms, on the other hand, are mostly smoke and
mirrors. There is much talk about making the rich pay more
and helping those at the bottom end of the economy, but in
reality the reforms do almost nothing to achieve these ends.
Some well-to-do investors and corporations will pay more, but
most of these high-rollers will pay less. Business and high-
income individuals emerge largely unscathed. Deborah
McGregor noted that, while there was some complaining,
business reaction was generally fairly positive. Indeed, Wilson's reforms were so benign that within two weeks *The
Financial Post*, the *Financial Times* and the *Globe's Report on
Business* had virtually lost interest in them. Yet the business
press had been relentless in its opposition to the earlier reform
attempts of MacEachen, Benson and Carter.

The Wilson "reform" is a masterpiece of cunning. Wilson
has grasped two crucial points about the politics of tax. First,
he has noted that the polls consistently reveal the public feels
strongly that the tax system should be more progressive, that
the rich should pay more. Second, he has also noted that

making the rich pay more is political suicide. All attempts of this kind have failed, and their proponents have been eaten alive in the process. What Wilson has come up with, then, is a clever strategy that takes both these factors into account: talk about hitting the rich, but don't really do it.

Wilson has given a whole new meaning to the notion of tax reform. While previous tax reforms sought to eliminate the favoured treatment of the rich, this reform consolidates that favouritism. Whereas special privileges were once the antithesis of tax reform, now they are part of tax reform. In a brilliant public relations stroke, Michael Wilson has stolen the mantle of earlier tax reforms, but left behind their substance.

CHAPTER ONE
How The System Works . . . Against You

"In every community, those who feel the burdens of taxation are naturally prone to relieve themselves from it if they can. One class struggles to throw the burden off its shoulders. If they succeed, of course, it must fall upon others. They also, in turn, labour to get rid of it and finally the load falls upon those who will not, or cannot, make a successful effort for relief. . . . This is in general a one-sided struggle, in which the rich only engage and . . . in which the poor always go to the wall."
—Attorney James C. Carter in an 1895 address to the U.S. Supreme Court

"No conscription of men without conscription of wealth!"
—rallying cry of Canadian farmers and workers lobbying for an income tax during World War I

Sitting in a plush chair in the dark dining-room of a Toronto hotel, eating a lunch of fresh trout, the wealthy investor makes no bones about it: he doesn't pay income tax. Nor do his friends, he says. Why should they? The Canadian tax system provides plenty of opportunity for them to avoid tax, making any tax payment almost like a voluntary contribution. Indeed, he regards it that way. "I wouldn't mind paying tax if the government would spend the money properly. But they'll just waste it"—a sentiment no doubt shared by many other Canadians who would love to pay tax only if they felt so inclined.

The investor explains how he does it. No cumbersome tax shelters. No messy Swiss bank accounts. In his case, it's all done by borrowing. The interest on money borrowed to make investments is tax deductible, so he borrows large amounts of money. He can borrow $8 million, adding it to $10 million of his own. He can then invest the $18 million in a portfolio that will pay him $900,000 a year in dividends. This way, he can deduct the $900,000 interest cost from the $900,000 dividend income and end up with a tax bill of zero. Indeed, because of the way the dividend tax credit works, he is actually able to shelter more income than the $900,000 he receives in dividends. So if he has any additional income from another source—from employment for instance—he can reduce the taxes he owes on that income as well.

He may also take a small number of stocks out of his $18 million portfolio and cash them in for a profit of, perhaps, $50,000. This profit—or capital gain—is tax-free.* So he can live on this $50,000 of income without paying any tax. Meanwhile, his $18 million investment continues to grow in value over the years, giving him an increasingly large fortune. All this has been partly subsidized by the government which has allowed him to deduct his interest costs along the way. (Since part of these interest costs are purely inflationary, their deductibility provides him with a bonus beyond his real costs.)

"There's no question it's unfair," says the investor, a modest but distinguished-looking gentleman in his late 50s. "But every rich person does it to varying degrees."

He explains that he became interested in stock markets as a boy, listening to stock reports on the radio. At fourteen, he started investing the small amounts he saved from after-school jobs. Although he later became an engineer, he continued to take an active interest in the stock market over the years, making conservative, well-studied investments, particularly in real estate development companies, that have paid

---

*Up to a lifetime limit of $100,000. After that, he pays tax on it at a reduced rate.

off handsomely. "With a 14 percent return and no tax, you can double your money every 5 years," he says. He retired wealthy a few years ago.

While theoretically he could pay no income tax, he always pays a bit, maybe a couple of thousand dollars, "just so I won't have the bother of being audited [by Revenue Canada]," he explains. Although his scheme is perfectly legal and popular among the well-to-do, he believes that high-income taxpayers who pay absolutely no tax arouse the interest of officials in Revenue Canada's offices. He'd much prefer that the Revenue official handling his tax return simply yawn and move on to the next one.

Not all rich taxpayers are so concerned about appearances. In 1984, 287 Canadians with incomes above $250,000 blithely filed returns to Revenue Canada showing they owed nothing in income tax. And when the officials checked over their returns, they were obliged to concede that these high-rollers were quite right. Under Canadian tax law, some of the richest individuals in the country managed to pay not a penny of their income towards the national treasury.

Many of them were able to achieve this tax-free state by using the same methods as the wealthy investor in the hotel dining-room—taking advantage of special tax breaks on capital gains, dividend income and money borrowed for investment. They may have also resorted to retirement savings plans and more exotic tax shelters, such as the special deductions for investments in movies, certain kinds of buildings, and oil and gas, as well as more complicated stock manoeuvres. About one-third of the 287 had taken advantage of the Scientific Research Tax Credit, a risk-free financial transaction that saved many wealthy individuals large sums of money in a hopelessly ill-conceived attempt to stimulate research in the country. More on that later.

But the 287 are really just the tip of the iceberg. They are the ones who reported large incomes and still managed to reduce their tax. There are many, many others with large

incomes who do not show up in such statistics because they
have been able to arrange their financial affairs in such a way
that, on their tax returns at least, they appear to have small
incomes. They may have transferred some of their income to
their spouses or children, or placed part of it in personal
holding companies. They may have been able to reduce their
income from their businesses by charging large personal expenses—trips, entertainment and part of their car and housing expenses—to their private companies. Through these
kinds of mechanisms, all perfectly legal, they manage to
effectively hide their income from taxation. In the statistics,
they may appear as having incomes no larger than the typical
nurse or letter carrier.

Across the table in the hotel dining room, the investor
finishes his trout and orders a rich and creamy English trifle
for dessert. He is actually a nice man, thinks it's wrong that
the rich pay so little tax, but doubts the situation will ever
change. What about the new minimum tax? "It won't catch
the rich," he says confidently.*

Miles away, in the suburban sprawl north of Toronto, a
twenty-eight-year-old woman who works with handicapped
senior citizens in nursing homes confesses that she hasn't
really paid much attention to her tax bill. "I'm always pleased
when I do my taxes at the end of the year and get a little bit
back," she says.

While she hasn't given a lot of thought to her tax bill, she is
upset about how difficult it is to support herself on her salary
of $24,284. She lives a modest life, sharing a $416 a month
apartment with her boyfriend, who has recently gone back to
school after working for several years in child care. She is
currently $13,500 in debt for a loan that enabled her to buy a
new bottom-of-the-line car and pay off some old credit card

*Indeed, neither the minimum tax nor Michael Wilson's tax reform
proposals will destroy the tax avoidance methods of this investor, as
outlined above.

bills for furniture and clothes. Payments on the loan amount to $360 a month.

When she receives her paycheque every two weeks, $172 in income taxes has already been removed. Her total tax bill for the year: $4,472—more than the wealthy investor pays.

In theory, this doesn't happen in Canada. In theory, we have a progressive income tax system, which means that the more money people earn, the higher the portion of their income they pay in tax. The idea is that while ordinary people should contribute to the national treasury, the more affluent should contribute more, because they can afford to. The more the tax burden is shifted down the income scale, the more it interferes with people's ability to buy basic necessities. The more the burden is shifted up the income scale, the more its effects are restricted to the consumption of luxuries by those who already have plenty to consume.

Thus Canada's official tax rates rise with income. On a chart the tax rates form a gradually rising hill that becomes quite steep towards the top. The chart makes it look as if those with incomes above $200,000 pay a high rate of tax.

This is the official story; however, it's really just a pleasant fiction. There's another chart that is rarely shown—although it was released by the federal government in a rare burst of reform zeal in 1981—which reveals the actual rates of income tax paid. It tells quite a different story. This "hill," which represents the actual rates of tax paid, is much more gradual, without any steep part at the top. In fact, it stops rising and *drops off sharply after $200,000*.

Welcome to the real world of tax.

In November, 1967, Stanley Surrey, the U.S. assistant secretary for tax policy, made a speech that attracted little attention. Probably no one in the audience realized that Surrey had mentioned for the first time a concept that was soon to revolutionize thinking about taxation in most western nations. It was summed up in the expression Surrey introduced that night: "tax expenditure."

The expression, which sounds like something of a contradiction, sheds some crucial light on situations such as those outlined above. How can a tax system with a progressive rate produce such anomalies as a nursing home worker with a $24,000 income paying more tax than a wealthy investor with a large income? The answer, of course, is that the investor is able to take advantage of tax breaks that allow him to reduce his taxable income. Through a myriad of deductions and credits, a high-income person can reduce his or her taxable income so that it is lower than that of someone earning a tiny salary who is not able to take advantage of such special breaks.

All of this has long been clear. What Surrey added was the concept that these tax breaks are really "expenditures" made by the government. When the government allows someone to not pay tax that he or she would otherwise pay, the effect is the same as if the government had given that individual a grant for that amount of money. For all intents and purposes, the tax break amounts to a government expenditure, just as surely as a direct subsidy would. What I will call Surrey's law, then, goes something like this: "Giving someone a $100 tax break is the same as giving that person a $100 cheque."

The concept is simple, but it has some staggering implications. In 1985, the Reichmanns were able to win from Ottawa a $500 million tax break to facilitate their takeover of Gulf Canada Ltd. When the tax concession became public, it caused a minor stir in Parliament. Imagine, however, if the Reichmanns had come to Ottawa seeking a *grant* of $500 million to assist them in their takeover of Gulf. Imagine if the finance minister had had to stand up in the House of Commons and explain why it was in the national interest for the government to dip into the federal treasury and come up with a half a billion dollars to hand over to one of the richest families in the country, a family whose assets are valued at $6.2 billion.

Giving money in the form of a tax break and giving money in the form of a grant may result in the same money loss for the government. But there are some crucial political differences. The spectacle of a government handing over a cheque to an individual or a company causes the public—and consequently the press and members of Parliament—to ask all sorts of questions. Citizens want to know why their tax dollars are being given to this particular cause. Is it deserving or especially needy? Is it something that will contribute to the public good? Just how much does the government propose to give and what results can be expected in return? Taxpayers are naturally quite fussy about how the government spends their money.

Little of this kind of scrutiny applies to the billions of dollars the government gives away each year through the tax system. A tax break that drains millions of dollars from the treasury may never have been intended by government policy-makers at all. It may have originated in the minds of private lawyers or accountants looking for ways to spare their clients from a particular tax. These private tax practitioners are constantly scouring the tax map looking for little openings, for tiny flaws in the language of the legislation that will allow them to move millions of dollars of their clients' money into areas beyond the reach of the revenue department.

Yet tax breaks created in this way can exist for years without ever being official government policy. Take the bizarre example of tax breaks for yachts. Most people are surprised to discover that Canada offered a tax break to the purchaser of a yacht. But the truth is Canada never intended to offer such a tax break. It evolved and became popular with the well-to-do as a result of some clever work by tax lawyers and accountants in applying depreciation allowances in ways that were not foreseen by those who designed the laws. The spectacle of the rich receiving tax breaks for the privilege of sun-bathing on their yachts was too much for even Ottawa to take. Finance Minister Michael Wilson put an end to it, effective January 1986.

Even when a tax break is deliberate government policy, it receives none of the public scrutiny that direct government expenditures do. Any dialogue over the measure is almost always restricted to the narrow confines of the community of tax specialists. The government tax experts consult with private tax practitioners and often with their clients, usually businessmen and investors. Once a decision has been reached, the measure may be announced officially in government budget papers—in language so technical and obscure that it is largely ignored by the media, Parliament and the public. Generally, the only ones paying attention are those who will benefit from the measure. And they are paying very close attention.

The hidden nature of tax breaks has also allowed them to escape the scalpel of government restraint. While Ottawa has limited its direct spending on federal programs and crown corporations, it has done little to control tax expenditures. Under a program of restraint, government spending grew by 30 percent between 1976 and 1979. But, since no restraints were imposed on spending through the tax system, tax expenditures grew by 42 percent over the same period. By the 1980s, tax expenditures were costing Ottawa $36 billion a year —almost 40 percent of total government spending. Auditor General Kenneth Dye explained this lack of control over tax expenditures nicely in his 1985 report:

A cost-conscious Parliament is in the position of a team of engineers trying to design a more fuel-efficient automobile. They think they have succeeded, but the engine seems to go on consuming as much gas as it did before. They cannot understand the problem until they notice that, hidden from view, myriad small holes have been punched through the bottom of the gas tank. This is too often the way of tax expenditures. Revenue leaks away, and MPs do not know about it until it is too late.

The hidden, almost invisible nature of tax breaks is a boon to those receiving them. Since little attention is paid to the amount of revenue lost and little is known about what the measures are and who is benefiting from them, the subsidy is shrouded in a great deal of privacy. If the Reichmanns were receiving the money directly in the form of a grant, many less well-to-do taxpayers—a category which in the Reichmann's case includes just about everybody else in the country—might question what was going on. They might ask why they should be contributing their tax dollars so that the government can pay out $500 million to the Reichmanns. Ottawa would no doubt come up with an explanation of how the money will help build a brighter future for Canada. But ordinary taxpayers, seeing a direct connection between their taxes and government spending, would probably be skeptical and angry.

The beauty of tax expenditures, for those on the receiving end at least, is that this connection is rarely made. People rarely seem to see the link between their own tax bills and someone else's tax breaks. If the government announces a new tax break that, for instance, only benefits investors, the news is generally confined to the financial pages, as if it had no effect on the rest of the population. Indeed, non-investors generally pay little attention. But the fact that they won't benefit from the new measure should actually make them all the more attentive.

When the Reichmanns saved $500 million in taxes, it affected every taxpayer in the country. We will all have to pay a little more so the Reichmanns can get their money. Each taxpayer will have to pay about an extra $30 at some point to cover the cost of the tax break. In reality, some taxpayers will end up paying considerably more than $30, while others, who can shelter their income from Revenue Canada's grasp, will make a smaller contribution to the Reichmann cause. Yet this is hardly the way most Canadians want to spend their money. Needless to say, if the Reichmanns had instead tried to solicit donations from the public to help finance their takeover of Gulf, they would have had considerably more difficulty reaching the $500 million mark.

But the problem with tax expenditures is not just that they are hidden. The more serious flaw is that their benefits go largely to the rich. Allan Maslove, an economist at Carleton University, did a detailed study in 1979 of the dozens of tax breaks open to Canadians and reached the unsurprising conclusion that the benefits of tax breaks go disproportionately to the well-to-do. But what was surprising was just how great the disparity was. Maslove concluded that the benefits upper-income Canadians received from tax breaks were roughly one hundred times greater than what low-income Canadians received.

This enormous disparity exists because, although tax breaks are technically available to everyone, only the well-to-do are really able to take advantage of them. The vast majority of tax breaks only apply to people who run their own businesses or can afford to make investments. Therefore, millions of Canadians are excluded. But even some tax breaks that are widely used by ordinary Canadians confer far larger benefits on the rich. This can be seen best by looking at one of the most popular tax breaks of all—one that supposedly helps all Canadian homeowners.

When John Turner became Liberal leader in 1984, he sold his impressive Toronto mansion and moved to Ottawa. The fine, stately Turner home in the exclusive Forest Hill section of Toronto sold for more than $900,000. Turner had paid $265,000 for it eight years earlier. This left him with a $635,000 profit on the sale, making the transition to the chilly halls of the Opposition leader's house in Ottawa a little more bearable.

Turner was able to keep the profit on the sale of his house without paying tax on it—a privilege all Canadian homeowners enjoy. But while this tax break benefits millions of Cana-

dians each year, it benefits some much more than others. Few
Canadians will ever dream of making a $635,000 profit on the
sale of a house. Many homeowners, particularly in less developed parts of the country, would be glad to make one-tenth
that profit over the same period of time. But by providing an
open-ended tax exemption on the profits from selling one's
home, Ottawa is conferring a much bigger tax break on high
income earners like John Turner than it is on someone making a $60,000 profit. And both of them are getting a better
deal than someone who can't afford to own a home in the first
place.

The tax break on housing profits is clearly a popular one
that is rooted in the desire of most Canadians to own a nice
home. Typically, a family will buy a modest house to start and
then, with the tax-free profits earned on this first house, go on
to purchase a larger and more expensive home. But although
most Canadians would strongly resist the removal of this tax
break, few are probably aware of how unevenly housing tax
benefits are distributed. Figures released by the Finance
Department in 1981 show that for Canadians who earned
between $10,000 and $15,000, the average benefit provided
by housing-related tax breaks in 1979 was $314; for those with
incomes between $30,000 and $50,000, the average benefit
was $1,994. However those with incomes over $100,000 received an average benefit of $6,753—an amount more than
twenty times as big as the benefit received by the average
person in the low-income group.

The hidden nature of tax expenditures has kept these
disparities largely out of public debate. Instead of looking at
how unevenly the benefits of housing tax breaks are distributed or at how to correct this bias, restraint-conscious
governments have looked elsewhere to make cuts in Ottawa's
housing subsidies. Leaving the tax breaks intact, they've gone
after the direct spending programs for housing—even though
these programs distribute benefits far more fairly.

Ottawa's housing expenditures in fact provide a good

illustration of the pitfalls of making subsidies indirectly through the tax system rather than directly through spending programs. Ottawa's direct spending programs provide benefits to both low- and middle-income people through rental subsidies, public housing and mortgage assistance. These programs have been coming under intense scrutiny by the Mulroney government, which cut back spending in this area by $48.5 million almost as soon as it took office. Only four months after the new government came to power in 1984, Housing Minister William McKnight produced a consultation paper which suggested there was an urgent need to control Ottawa's spending on these social housing programs; that is, programs which provide direct subsidies for low- and moderate-income groups.

But what was far more significant was what the paper left out. In a tiny footnote below one of its tables, the paper noted that in calculating the benefits of its housing subsidies the government had not included tax subsidies. This is a little like preparing a study on Canada's climate and then mentioning in a footnote that winter had not been included. The government provides far greater housing subsidies indirectly through the tax system than it does directly through its social housing programs. In fact, for every $100 Ottawa spends *directly* on housing, it spends $200 to $300 *indirectly* through the tax system, according to David Hulchanski, a housing expert at the University of British Columbia's School of Community and Regional Planning.

This has some important implications since, as we've seen, the benefits of subsidies provided through the tax system are skewed in favour of the rich. The tax saved by John Turner on the $635,000 profit from his house far exceeds the money Ottawa pays out directly to any of the recipients of its federal housing subsidies. Indeed, as Hulchanski notes, a recipient would have to spend 118 years in a housing project to receive a benefit as large as the one Turner received!

Other housing-related tax breaks have been just as inequitable. One of the worst in recent years was the Multiple Unit Residential Building (MURB) program which provided a tax shelter for investors in apartment developments. By the mid-70s, there was an extreme shortage of affordable accommodation in many parts of the country, and Ottawa turned to the tax system for solutions. The Trudeau government figured that it could increase the supply of rental accommodation by offering tax breaks to those investing in the construction of new rental properties. The theory was that if the supply of rental properties could be increased, there would be more units available for those with moderate incomes. However, it didn't quite work out this way.

Most of the benefits ended up in the hands of the rich. To begin with, the rental properties constructed tended to be expensive luxury developments, since this market was more lucrative. In many cases, in fact, moderately-priced rental properties were torn down to make way for new, high-priced buildings erected with MURB tax breaks. The result was an actual decrease in the availability of affordable accommodation. Most of the benefits of the MURB program in fact seem to have gone to land-owners and developers. Little was passed on to tenants in the form of lower rents.

One 1982 study by George Gau, a professor of commerce and business administration at the University of British Columbia, found that the main beneficiaries of MURBs in the Vancouver market were those who owned parcels of land on which MURBs were built. "The MURB program has probably had little impact on rents and the long-run supply of apartment units," noted Gau. He concluded that the program was expensive and ineffective as a way to increase the supply of affordable rental units. By 1980, the program had resulted in a loss of about $670 million from the federal treasury. And although MURBs were discontinued in 1981, the existing MURB buildings will continue to qualify as tax deductions for their owners until 1991. Gau estimates that so far Ottawa has lost about $2 billion and is continuing to lose about $200 million a year as a result of the now-defunct and discredited program. Said Gau: "It's a loss that just hangs out there."

The Mulroney government's keenness to trim Ottawa's

direct housing expenditures, while turning a blind eye to the indirect expenditures delivered through the tax system, will only make the benefits of government largesse in this area all the more inequitable. Indeed, Ottawa's growing reliance on providing housing subsidies through the tax system over the past fifteen years has helped to move home ownership increasingly beyond the reach of low and moderate income Canadians. While 62 percent of the poorest Canadians owned their own homes in 1967, only 43 percent of this bottom group owned homes in 1981. Over the same period, however, home ownership among the top-earning Canadians actually rose from 73 percent to 83 percent.

Although these are government figures, produced by Statistics Canada, McKnight's paper on the urgent need to reform Ottawa's housing subsidies does not even allude to the problem the statistics illustrate. When asked if McKnight was aware of the trend, his office checked with him and reported back that he was. Johanne Godon, his press secretary, confirmed that McKnight was aware of the situation: "He regrets the trend to home ownership only in favour of high income groups of Canadians." But she said she did not know if the government planned to do anything about it.

Apparently it didn't, because the situation hasn't changed. And the new tax reform doesn't do anything to correct the problem.

The government might feel more impetus to do something if the minister responsible for housing had to defend tax breaks for housing in the same way that he has to defend direct housing expenditures. He might feel more than mere regret, for instance, if he had to stand up in Parliament and defend a tax break that Canadians knew provided a large benefit to the rich, a medium-sized benefit to the middle class and no benefit whatsoever to the poor.

These disparities are not widely appreciated by Canadians, who generally assume that the government redistributes wealth from the rich to the poor. At the heart of this assumption is the long-held belief that the income tax is truly progressive. This idea has become strongly entrenched since the 1960s, with the introduction of a more generous unemployment insurance system, enriched old age pension benefits and a new income supplement for the elderly poor. All this has left many Canadians convinced that Canada is truly a welfare state.

In fact, the real picture is somewhat different. Although it appears to be highly progressive, the Canadian income tax does little in the way of income redistribution. Prosperous Canadians have managed so effectively to avoid paying their prescribed rates of tax that they contribute far less than is generally appreciated. As a result, the income tax is only mildly progressive. Still, it is the only progressive tax in Canada; that is, the only tax that even attempts to put a proportionately larger burden on the rich. There was once another progressive tax in Canada—the estate tax on large inheritances—but it was abolished more than a decade ago (as we will see in Chapter Six).

The remaining taxes—sales and commodity taxes of various sorts—are clearly regressive. Since they impose a flat rate of tax on the purchaser, regardless of his or her income, the levy is felt more acutely by someone with a small income. Paying an extra $5 or $10 in tax on a $100 purchase is harder on the poor person than on the rich person. Furthermore, the poor must spend virtually all of their income just to get by, making them constant victims of sales taxes. The rich inevitably generate a surplus which they save and which, therefore, is not subject to sales taxes. According to government statistics, the lowest-earning 20 percent of Canadians spent 100 percent of their incomes in 1982, while the next lowest income group spent more than 85 percent of theirs. Yet the richest 20 percent spent only 57 percent of their incomes.

Indeed, when sales taxes are taken into account, the overall tax picture is actually regressive. Even the social welfare measures of the 1970s did little to alter the balance because as the government increased benefits to the poor and middle income groups, it reduced taxes for the rich.

In fact, contrary to popular belief, the big winners in the 1970s were the rich. In a study of the 1970-77 period, Carleton University economist Irwin Gillespie found that Ottawa's tax policies benefited the highest-income families the most and poor families the least. "Thus it was not the poor and needy who were protected from the 'ravages of inflation' during (John) Turner's tenure as Minister of Finance; in dollar benefits it was the richest 8 percent of families who were so protected," Gillespie wrote. "Budgetary policy during the 1970s has not been redistributive towards the poor and less fortunate members of society; rather it has provided larger benefits for the highest income families than for the poor." His study, sponsored by the mainstream C.D. Howe Research Institute, was called "In Search of Robin Hood." Gillespie concluded Robin Hood was nowhere to be found in Canada.

Nonetheless, the Robin Hood myth has lived on in the 1980s, despite the fact that the tax system has become even less progressive—considerably so in the first two years of the Mulroney government. As a result of the hikes in sales taxes and income taxes introduced in the Tories' first two budgets, just about all Canadians faced higher taxes, and the middle and lower classes definitely bore the brunt of the increases. Even the very poor, who are supposedly protected by the government's new system of more effectively targeting benefits to the bottom end, have ended up facing tax increases. But perhaps most alarming has been the substantial tax increases faced by those only slightly better off than the group at the very bottom. This next group of poor, many of whom are working full-time but remain below the poverty line, has not been singled out for any special protection and has been hard hit by the massive tax increases imposed by the Mulroney government.

The numbers are startling. A single person earning $7,000 in 1985—an amount well below the poverty line for a large city

—paid a total of $300 more in income taxes for 1986 and 1987. (If sales tax increases were added in, the additional tax burden would be much heavier.) This represented a tax increase of 145 percent for a person of clearly limited means. People living in real poverty like this were required to scrimp and do without so that they could save an additional $300—to give to the government. And they certainly didn't have the option of not paying if they happened to disagree with how the government was spending the money, if they didn't, for instance, feel inclined to help out the Reichmanns.

A single person earning $20,000 in 1985 paid a total of $445 more in income tax in 1986 and 1987. And those earning $30,000 had to hand over an extra $576 to the government in taxes.

But, oddly, the tax bite eased for those with larger incomes. Although the tax increases applied to all income levels, they were offset by other measures which decreased taxes for those in the higher brackets. With the introduction of more generous tax deductions for retirement savings and capital gains, a single person earning $50,000 in 1985 was only obliged to pay an additional $244 during the first two years of the Mulroney administration—a smaller increase than that faced by the person below the poverty line.

And single people earning more than $80,000 were actually able to *reduce* their tax bills. Over two years, they paid $706 less.

In effect, the tax changes introduced by the Tories actually redistributed money from the poor to the well-to-do. The stark reality was that, over its first two years in office, the Mulroney government ended up *taking* an extra $300 from someone earning well below the poverty line while *giving* an additional $706 to someone living in considerable prosperity. Under the Mulroney government, Robin Hood hasn't actually disappeared; he's working for the other side.

It was the winter of 1917, and the war in Europe had been longer and more devastating than anyone had dreamed. There were now more than half a million Canadian men overseas, and no end was in sight. With his mandate running out, Prime Minister Robert Borden knew he was in trouble. He still had the support of the manufacturing interests of Ontario, but just about everything else appeared shaky. Still, after a long and dreary exile in opposition, the Conservative government desperately wanted to avoid the debacle that seemed certain at the polls. Borden and his finance minister, Thomas White, a former trust company executive, slowly started to believe that they might have to give in to the pressure they had long resisted—the pressure *for* an income tax.

Perverse as this may sound seven decades later, there was a sizeable constituency during the First World War pressing a reluctant federal government to introduce an income tax for Canadians. It wasn't that Canadians then were any more generous or community-spirited. Rather, this apparently bizarre insistence on an income tax sprang directly from a desire, prevalent among western farmers and eastern workers, to redistribute the country's tax burden.

In fact, the farm and labour position was quite rational and helps illustrate a point we often lose track of today. Different taxes have different impacts on different groups in society. As we have already seen, income taxes, which generally have a progressive rate structure, impose a proportionately heavier burden on the rich—in theory at least. Sales or commodity taxes, which impose a flat levy on a product, place a proportionately heavier burden on those with low incomes. Most groups use whatever clout they wield in society to fight for relief from taxes that hurt their own interests, while being quite willing to accept taxes that hurt someone else's interests.

It is easy to see, for instance, why the original French settlers of Quebec, who relied heavily on hunting and on selling furs abroad, were displeased by the first tax imposed on the colony in 1650—an export tax that forced them to hand over half their beaverskins and one-tenth of their moose hides.

Clearly, if the French regime had decided instead to concentrate taxes on, say, luxury imported goods, the tax would have won more support among the modest-living *habitants*. But, of course, the colony didn't import much in the way of luxury goods. The French government was well aware that a tax on beaver and moose exports was one of the few ways it could hope to collect anything from its colonial subjects. A more advanced society clearly has more options.

Nonetheless, taxing business profits is no more popular with corporate owners today than beaver-and-moose taxes were with seventeenth century hunters. On the other hand, beaver-and-moose taxes would probably do little to upset the Canadian Manufacturers' Association or the Business Council on National Issues. While business groups denounce high taxes in general, they focus their efforts on reducing taxes that hurt them in particular, giving little attention to, say, taxes that affect the poor. When the Mulroney government's May 1985 budget removed the federal tax reduction, one of the few tax breaks for the poor, there wasn't a murmur of protest from business. Similarly, poor people are generally not upset by taxes that affect the rich, such as those on capital gains or estates.

Lobbyists seeking the ear of the finance minister are constantly coming up with reasons why the particular interest groups they represent should be spared some portion of the national tax burden that has been thrust upon them. The history of taxation is in many ways the history of groups trying to pass the tax burden onto the next group. The late Louis Eisenstein, a U.S. tax lawyer and Treasury Department attorney, once described taxes as the "changing product of earnest efforts to have others pay them." In this long-standing game of high-stakes pass-the-hot-potato, somehow it is always the lower classes that end up holding the steamy spud when the music stops.

As the statistics show, this has certainly been the case in Canada. And it will become even more the case here once

Wilson's tax reform is fully implemented. The emphasis placed on commodity-type taxes in Michael Wilson's proposed reforms reveals an intention to continue to move the burden away from those at the top. Indeed, it is a solid step backwards to the almost-forgotten days of the turn of the century when the extreme imbalances in Canada's tax systems led to political movements demanding tax reform—demanding specifically that commodity-type taxes be replaced with an income tax.

As has happened so often in Canadian history, the rumblings for change were first heard in the United States. The period following the Civil War had seen a burst of economic expansion as new railway lines crossed the country and new manufacturing concerns churned out goods for rapidly growing markets. But the benefits of the boom were very unevenly distributed. Enormous power and wealth, symbolized by the opulent lives of the Vanderbilts, the Rockefellers and the Astors, came to be concentrated in New York and the Northeast.

There had been less than twenty millionaires in the whole country in the 1840s; but by the mid-1860s there were several hundred in New York City alone. A.T. Stewart, the largest American retailer of dry goods, was reported to have a personal fortune of $50 million. New York's new breed of millionaires lived the life of kings, building ornate mansions along Fifth Avenue and throwing ever more lavish parties in an apparent attempt to make the ultimate splash on the city's social pages. At one party in the Vanderbilt's palatial Rhode Island summer home, all five hundred guests discovered a precious black pearl adorning their dish of pre-dinner oysters. At another, guests found diamonds at the bottom of their strawberry-and-ice desserts.

This kind of vulgar consumption stuck in the craw of many farmers and workers, who faced a rocky time in the post-Civil War boom years. The inflation of the Civil War period had driven up prices faster than wages, and a serious depression in the early 1870s led to an actual decline in wages throughout the decade. Bitter strikes, led by the Knights of Labour, pitted workers against owners and against the Republican administration, which sent troops in to suppress the rebellions on the owners' behalf. Meanwhile, a severe drop in farm prices left many farmers facing mortgage foreclosures and feeling deeply resentful of the power of the eastern banks. Farmers and workers and, to some extent, small merchants, came to feel they shared common ground in opposing the nation's powerful business and financial élites.

Radical organizations sprang up around the country, particularly in the Midwest. There were the Greenbacks, the Anti-Monopoly Party, the Grangers, the Farmer's Party, the People's Party and a number of others that strutted briefly across the political landscape. One of the common grievances was the high tariff, which was essentially a commodity tax on imported goods. It protected the manufacturing industries of the Northeast from foreign competition, but it drove up the cost of consumer goods. Increasingly, the radical parties pushed for a reduction in the tariff and an introduction of an income tax, which was seen as the only way to make the rich pay their fair share. By 1892, farmers and labour had come together to form the Populist Party, which, along with other economic reforms, proposed a graduated income tax.

In fact, the United States had had an income tax during the Civil War. Since the tax had only applied to incomes above a certain level, it had only affected the richest one percent of Americans. But while the income tax had seemed acceptable to this powerful élite when the future of the republic was at stake, it was less so when all that was involved was running the country and paying off debts from an already-won war. The business and financial interests used their clout within Congress to have the income tax repealed in the early 1870s, along with the inheritance tax, which they also disliked.

The fight to bring back the income tax in the 1890s was a bitter one, waged along distinct class lines. The movement won some adherents within the Democratic Party, and a coalition of Democratic and Populist congressmen fought to impose an income tax of 2 percent on incomes over $4,000—a substantial income in those days. The Republicans defended the cause of northeastern business and propertied interests, who were vehemently opposed to a return of the income tax. In emotional debates in Congress and the press, the income tax was denounced for being socialistic and "rank class legislation." "This attempt to array the rich against the poor or the poor against the rich is socialism, communism, devilism," said Republic Senator John Sherman. One Congressman opposed to the tax argued that, since it exempted the poor, the proposed income tax would undermine democracy because the poor would have no claim to control a government to whose upkeep they had not contributed.

In a highly charged counterattack in Congress, William Jennings Bryan pointed to the enormous tax burden the poor had shouldered due to the tariff: "If taxation is a badge of free men, let me assure my friend that the poor people of this country are covered all over with the insignia of free men."

Bryan, a powerful orator even though he was only thirty-four at the time, went on to denounce a group of some four hundred wealthy business leaders who had threatened to leave the country if the income tax was passed. "Of all the mean men I have ever known, I have never known one so mean that I would be willing to say of him that his patriotism was less than 2 percent deep. . . . If 'some of our best people' prefer to leave the country rather than pay a tax of 2 percent, God pity the worst . . . we can better afford to lose them and their fortunes than risk the contaminating influence of their presence . . . let them depart, and as they leave without regret the land of their birth, let them go with the poet's curse ringing in their ears."

In the end, after much stirring debate in Congress, the income tax passed in 1894, only to face an immediate court challenge. In March 1895, some of the nation's most illustrious lawyers faced off against each other as the Supreme Court pondered the constitutionality of the new tax. James C. Carter, widely considered the leading member of the American bar, defended the income tax, arguing that the Supreme Court had no right to interfere with the clearly expressed desire of the American people for such a tax.

Joseph Choate, a top corporate lawyer, countered that, even if it were true that "the passions of the people are aroused on this subject. . . . that sixty million citizens may be incensed by this [Court's] decision," it was the duty of the Court to strike down the income tax. Otherwise, he argued, there was nothing to stop the majority of Americans from imposing any tax they wanted on the wealthy. The majority could simply set the exemption level higher and higher and make the tax heavier and heavier. "There is protection now or never," Choate warned, in effect urging the Supreme Court to curtail the democratic impulses of the masses before they did something dangerous, like redistribute wealth in the country.

The Court ended up agreeing with Choate and ruled the income tax unconstitutional. One of the judges, Justice Stephen Field, revealed the extent to which he subscribed to the theory that the income tax was the poor man's foot-in-the-door to further wealth-snatching. "If the provisions of the Constitution can be set aside by an act of Congress, where is the course of usurpation to end? The present assault upon capital is but the beginning. It will be but the stepping stone to others, larger and more sweeping, till our political contests will become a war of the poor against the rich; a war constantly growing in intensity and bitterness."

Following the court's rejection, it took another eighteen years of agitation and pressure before the champions of an income tax were able to get their way. John D. Rockefeller summed up the sentiments of the rich when he lent his voice to the anti-income tax crusade in 1909. "When a man has accumulated a sum of money within the law, that is to say, in a legally correct way, the people no longer have any right to share the earnings resulting from the accumulation." In the hopes of staving off the growing pressure for an income tax, the Republican administration introduced a corporate profits tax that year. While the corporate tax infuriated the business community, it did little to quench the popular thirst for an income tax. Eventually a constitutional amendment was ratified by enough states to get around the Supreme Court's ruling, and in 1913 the United States got an income tax.

All this had not gone unnoticed in Canada. As in the United States, the tariff had long been the main source of government revenue, leading to grievances similar to those voiced in the United States: the manufacturing interests of central Canada were being protected from foreign competition, while the prices of imported goods were being driven up. These higher prices were particularly resented in the West and the Maritimes, regions which gained no benefit. But they were also resented by many in central Canada. While the tariff helped create jobs in Ontario and Quebec, the higher price of consumer goods was hard on the ordinary workers and farmers of the central provinces.

As in the United States, much of the original agitation in Canada came from farmers. *The Grain Growers' Guide*, a prairie farm journal, reported regularly on developments in the U.S. income tax fight and argued for a similar tax in Canada. Pushing for abolition of the hated tariff, the *Guide* pointed out the need for an alternative source of revenue: "Among the alternatives perhaps which appeals strongly to the majority of the people is the income tax." Throughout the West, farmers' organizations passed resolutions calling for an income tax, and similar demands were made by labour councils across the country.

For many farmers and workers, the income tax represented the best hope of passing some of the onerous tax burden onto the rich. This view had been popular for some time, but gained impetus during World War I, as the nation's financial needs increased dramatically and the disparities of wealth became greater and more obvious. The revved-up wartime economy had produced a great deal of wealth in Canada. Some 675 factories were working around the clock on government contracts, manufacturing vast amounts of weapons and shells for the allied war effort.

In Toronto and Montreal, the élites enjoyed an increasingly prosperous life. The turn of the century had seen the rise of some of the great dynasties in Canada. The Molsons, the Eatons and the Westons were already on their way to creating vast financial empires. Although Toronto and Montreal didn't have the opulent style of New York, the well-to-do built themselves substantial mansions along the tree-lined avenues of Rosedale and Westmount and set up private schools for their children. Millions of dollars of luxury goods—perfumes, fine clothing, crystal and cars from Europe and the United States—flowed into the country, prompting demands that this wasteful spending be diverted to war production.

To the workers and farmers, it seemed that hundreds of thousands of ordinary Canadians were risking their lives in the trenches of Europe, while the country's wealthy upper-crust was enjoying the fruits of war. As the Borden government toyed with the prospect of imposing conscription to meet growing military needs, a rallying cry rose from the ranks of labour and farm organizations: "No conscription of men without conscription of wealth!"

Opposition Liberals echoed this cry for an income tax, portraying the Tories as the party of big business. Michael Clark, a Liberal from Red Deer, Alberta, called for "a good fat tax upon incomes," and A.K. Maclean, a Halifax Liberal, called for a "broad system of taxation based upon income." Saskatchewan Liberal J.G. Turriff claimed the Tories' chief concern was "to place the taxation of Canada on the poor and the middle classes of Canada that the big business interests and the millionaires would escape." He denounced the business profits tax that the Tories had introduced in 1916 in the hopes of derailing demands for an income tax. Turriff claimed that the tax was so loosely designed that it failed to hit any of "the multi-millionaires sitting on the treasury benches." Corporate owners could escape its claws by simply withdrawing all their profits in the form of dividends. In a fiery speech in the House of Commons, the prairie populist noted that one company had remained tax-free by paying out dividends of 900 percent.

As the cry "No conscription of men without conscription of wealth!" echoed around the country, the Tory government stood firm in its refusal to impose an income tax. Instead, it opted to pay for the war effort by borrowing money and selling war bonds. Finance Minister White's staunch opposition to an income tax as late as the spring of 1917 had strong support from Toronto manufacturing interests and the Toronto press. The tax, it was argued, would discourage postwar immigration—a rather unlikely scenario, except perhaps in the case of the four hundred wealthy Americans who had threatened to flee the oppression of the U.S. income tax. Furthermore, White argued, the tax seemed unfair since many who would be affected by it had already made generous contributions to the Red Cross.

But by the summer of 1917, the unpopular Borden government was wavering. Keen to win Liberal support for its divisive conscription bill, the Tory government hinted it might be willing to consider introducing an income tax in exchange for support on conscription. On July 24, 1917, the conscription bill was passed in the House, with the support of many Liberals. The next day, White announced that the government would introduce an income tax. When the bill was presented to the Senate the following month, government leader Sir James Lougheed echoed some of the sentiments of income tax opponents south of the border. "This tax," he said, "is unquestionably the outcome of public opinion as represented by the most numerous class of citizens—a class which, in all probability, will have to contribute very little to the taxation provided for in the Bill."

How wrong he was.

In fact, of course, the income tax has not turned out to be the great soak-the-rich weapon that was once anticipated. The graduated rates that were designed to place a heavy burden on high income earners have turned out to be largely fictitious for many affluent individuals. Nor has the majority of ordinary citizens escaped the tax, as Sir James Lougheed predicted. The middle class has ended up bearing the bulk of the burden, and the poor have made a surprisingly large contribution as well. A family of four living at the poverty line paid about 11 percent of its income in income tax in 1986.

Still, despite the failure of the income tax to live up to the expectations of its champions, the fight to have it implemented is revealing. For both sides, what was at stake was the answer to the key question of who would bear the burden of taxation. Edwin L. Godkin, a prominent U.S. commentator at the turn of the century and fierce opponent of the income tax, clearly saw the whole fight as a class struggle. "The history of taxation from the earliest ages," he wrote, "has been the history of the attempts of one class to make other classes pay the expenses, or an undue share of the expenses, of Government." Godkin supported the wealthy classes in their belief that they should not be subjected to an income tax, and he denounced as Marxists those who favoured such a tax.

With such fundamental issues at stake, it's little wonder that the debates were so emotional. In one raucous session in the U.S. Congress, with the galleries packed, Democratic congressman William L. Wilson made such a moving, eloquent plea to shift the tax burden off the backs of the nation's poor that, when he finished, a group of wildly cheering congressmen lifted him onto their shoulders and carried him triumphantly down the aisle.

Needless to say, this kind of fervour is generally lacking from tax debates today. The annual conference of the Canadian Tax Foundation, for instance, has all the passion of a seminar on electrical wiring, even though the matters discussed at the conference bear directly on the same volatile question of who is to bear the tax burden. Of course the issues are never presented that way. Instead, the potentially emotional and divisive subject of taxation becomes buried in a mountain of legalistic language that reduces the debate to one of technicalities: how to design a better flow-through mechanism, how to distribute earnings on a corporate reorganization, how to handle non-depreciable capital property, how to deal with corporate dissolutions that do not qualify for rollover treatment, etc. Is it any wonder that no one gets carried on the shoulders of a hooting crowd at the end of such presentations?

The apparent dullness of tax issues is also reflected in the current fashion of banishing from the debate highly-charged words such as "rich," "poor," "wealth" and "class." Instead, politicians, commentators and the media use the more neutral concepts of "high-income groups" and "low-income groups," or, duller still, they adopt the statistical approach of dividing the population into five quintiles. Imagine how much less moving would have been William Jennings Bryan's impassioned defence of the income tax had he thundered in the U.S. Congress: "If taxation is a badge of free men, let me assure my friend that the bottom quintile is covered all over with the insignia of free men," or that "the poet's curse should ring in the ears of departing members of the top quintile." Certainly the old Canadian rallying cry would have had much less punch if reformulated in the language of today: "No conscription of men without conscription of the incomes of those in the top brackets."

If the expressions "rich" and "poor" are now passé, the word "class"—used by both sides in the turn-of-the-century debates—is downright taboo, a sign of raving Marxism. The only exception to the ban is the use of the expression "middle class," to which we all now supposedly belong. The truth is however that we don't all belong to the middle class. There is a sizeable number of Canadians—several million—who are too poor to be really identified in any meaningful sense as middle class, and there is a small but powerful segment—including the Bronfmans, the Batas, the Southams, the Irvings, and thousands of others—whose lives bear no more resemblance to those of ordinary Canadian workers than the lives of the hosts of the Vanderbilt parties did to those of their waiters. By wiping out all classes but the big one in the middle, we are suggesting that we all have the same basic interests. We are denying that some taxes hurt some classes more than others. We are denying what was painfully obvious to those on both sides of the great income tax debates at the turn of the century.

The point is not that tax should be exciting. The point is that tax issues, before the cold shower of technical, statistical language is applied, *are* exciting. At least, what is at stake—who should pay for what in society and, therefore, how society's wealth should be distributed—are vital, controversial, exciting questions. By disguising them behind the jargon of law and accounting, we avoid addressing these highly-charged issues. The language of Canadian budget night does its best to deny or obscure what is really going on: the pie is being redivided in a way that affects everyone, some oxes are being gored while others are being fattened.

This becomes all the more clear when considered in the light of James C. Carter's dictum that, in the ongoing effort by social classes to pass their tax burdens onto the next class, it is the poor who always "go to the wall." By steering clear of anything even vaguely hinting at different class interests, we make it harder to see whose ox is being gored and whose is feasting. Instead, contemporary TV audiences on budget night are treated to dull discourses by business leaders and economists on whether the incentives provided will stimulate the economy or whether the expenditure reductions will trim the deficit enough to restore business confidence.

In the turn-of-the-century debates over taxation, those on both sides knew what was being debated. John D. Rockefeller came straight out and unabashedly defended his right to hold onto all his accumulated wealth on the grounds that that was his privilege. Today, those with money—and their spokesmen —argue for tax reductions in a far more indirect way. Taxes on corporations and investors should be reduced, they say, not because of any basic moral right but because that's the best way to get the economy moving. Only by giving corporations a reduced tax burden will business confidence be restored and companies create jobs.

Put this way, the case for tax breaks for the rich sounds far more compelling than it did in the mouth of John D. Rockefeller. Under this modern scenario, everyone benefits when the rich benefit. Whether or not this is true is rarely even examined. It is held to be true, and the people on TV all treat it as if it were true.

Thus, the ability to package their case in an acceptable, even convincing, manner has made it far easier for the rich to sell their point of view. Indeed, in a sophisticated, modern democracy this effective packaging has been crucial. Only by moving the tax debate from class politics onto safer, drier terrain have the rich managed to avoid the fate prophesied for them by their predecessors almost a century ago. Then it was feared that if the majority was given the right to impose taxes as it wished, it would shift the burden from itself onto the rich. Yet this hasn't happened. And the clouding of the issues involved surely has a lot to do with this.

And so it is that the rich and the powerful resort to arguments about the need to stimulate the economy rather than trying to defend their low tax burden as a God-given right. Such arguments go down a lot better with ordinary folk in Spokane and Peoria and in Sudbury and Moncton.

In this book, I use expressions like "rich" and "poor," and will even, in a few isolated spots, risk talking about "classes." The point is not to inflame or incite, or suggest that rich people are bad and poor people are good. Rather the point is to try to identify more clearly to what extent certain groups or . . . dare I say it? . . . "classes" benefit from the Canadian tax system. There is a strong tendency these days not to see patterns of this kind, not to examine the bias towards the rich. Just why this ostrich approach is popular is not entirely clear. One thing that is clear, however, is that the silence helps perpetuate the situation.

CHAPTER TWO
Tax Haven In The Snow

"I am a brigand: I live by robbing the rich."
"I am a gentleman: I live by robbing the poor."
—from George Bernard Shaw's *Man and*
Superman

If the words "rich" and "poor" have become taboo, the reality of wealth and poverty in our country has not. We may not talk about it much anymore, but an enormous gulf remains between the rich and the poor. While there is plenty of data on the poor, there are few hard figures on the rich, who tend to be less forthcoming about their financial situations. From the data available, however, some striking discrepancies leap out. In this country there were an estimated 3,950,000 people living in poverty in 1985—one in every six Canadians. More than half a million people joined the ranks of the poor in the last five years in Canada. Meanwhile, at the very top, we have produced six billionaires—possibly more, depending on the measurement used—and dozens who count their fortunes in the tens of millions.

The tax system has played a role in perpetuating this situation. Even after Wilson's tax reform, many Canadians living below the poverty line will still pay income taxes, and many well-to-do individuals will continue to pay little or no income tax. Indeed, although few people are aware of it, Canada's taxation of wealth ranks among the lowest in the western world.

Every now and then statistics appear that suggest the size of the gap between the rich and the poor in Canada. In July 1986, for instance, Statistics Canada released a study of high-income families which revealed that the top 1 percent—some

63,250 families—earned an average of $212,000 a year (in 1986 dollars). *The Toronto Star* ran a banner story about the study across the top of its front page, noting that the remaining 6.3 million Canadian families had an average income of $39,626.

While the gap between $212,000 and $39,000 is obviously large, these figures actually misrepresent the real extent of the gulf. The $39,000 is particularly misleading in that it suggests this is the income of the average Canadian family. This may be true in a statistical sense, but not in any meaningful sense. The figure is derived from adding the income of all families in Canada and then dividing by the number of families. The very large incomes of those at the top distort the results, creating an "average" family income that is much higher than what is actually enjoyed by the majority of Canadians. More than half of Canadian families, for instance, have incomes below $33,000. Furthermore, the Statistics Canada study, in calculating the $212,000 figure, did not include a number of key sources of income for the rich, such as capital gains, which would have pushed up the average income for the top-earning Canadians even higher.

All this is very hard to visualize. In an effort to bring the picture into focus, Dutch statistician Jan Pen came up with the idea of presenting the distribution of income as a parade in which everyone in the country marches and in which everyone's size is proportional to his or her income. The taller the marcher, the greater the income. After figuring out the relative heights for a parade of this sort in Britain, Pen described it as "a parade of dwarfs (and a few giants)." Roughly here's what the parade would look like in Canada.

The whole parade is only going to take an hour, so everyone will be moving quickly, flashing by us as we stand watching at the side of the road. Like any school parade, this one will begin with the smallest marchers—that is, the poorest Canadians—and the heights will gradually rise until we see the tallest marchers—the highest-income Canadians.

As the parade begins, we notice some extremely tiny people

at the front. Masses of people less than a foot tall hurry past us. These tiny individuals are a mixed group of all ages. They include some welfare recipients, unemployed individuals, old age pensioners, part-time workers, struggling farmers—all earning less than $7,000 a year. Although they are moving quickly, it takes at least six minutes for this group of miniature people to pass.

For the next twelve minutes, we see a horde of very small dwarves, people less than three feet in height. Marching in this group are more people on public assistance; but we also now see a large number of full-time workers as well, people working at extremely low-paying jobs. There are building cleaners, day-care workers, bank tellers, salesclerks, etc. We can't help being struck by the preponderance of women in this group of very short marchers.

The parade has been going on for more than twenty minutes before we start to see taller dwarves who reach about four feet high. This group includes somewhat better-paid blue collar workers: parking lot attendants, maintenance and factory workers, as well as some individuals collecting unemployment insurance.

The parade reaches the halfway mark, and even at this point we are still seeing people only about five feet tall. Among them are skilled industrial workers, electricians, plumbers, as well as nurses and executive secretaries.

Another few minutes and adults of normal height start appearing. This group includes teachers, civil servants, computer programmers and factory supervisors. It is not really until the last twelve minutes of the parade that we begin to see business executives and professionals—doctors, lawyers, accountants, engineers. These people are really quite tall, well over eight feet.

As the parade nears its end, the marchers become ever larger. With about six minutes to go, we see more and more doctors, lawyers and business executives, all with incomes over $100,000. Fourteen feet tall, they tower over the dwarves at the front of the parade. There are some well-known faces in this crowd: Quebec Premier Robert Bourassa standing almost fifteen feet tall and Prime Minister Brian Mulroney, measuring more than nineteen feet.

In the last minute, the height of the marchers rises dramatically. With about 25 seconds remaining, they have reached 30 feet. Ian Sinclair, the retired president of Canadian Pacific Enterprises stands 37 feet tall—in retirement. Then, in the final few seconds, some real giants walk by. Among these, standing 75 feet tall, we will find J.L. Dunlap, president of Texaco Canada Inc. with a 1986 income of $538,308. Then there is W.W. Stinson, president of Canadian Pacific Limited, with an income of $677,418, measuring 96 feet tall. Looming in this crowd is Edgar Bronfman, chairman of Seagram Company, with a salary of $1.8 million and standing 257 feet high. But towering even above him is Frank Stronach, president of Magna International, with an income of $2.2 million and reaching a commanding height of 314 feet.

But this parade only tells part of the story, because these figures deal exclusively with *income*. In many ways, the more meaningful measure is *wealth*. When *The Financial Post Moneywise* magazine does its semi-annual survey of the richest men and women in the country, it isn't talking about their income. It is talking about their wealth—the real measure of economic power and command over the country's resources.

Someone could have significant wealth, for instance, in the form of stocks, bonds or land holdings, but receive relatively little in the way of income. This, in fact, would be the logical way for wealthy people to arrange their financial affairs, to minimize their income tax bills. Indeed, the men and women in *The Financial Post* survey employ some of the highest-priced talent in the country to come up with ways for them to avoid receiving huge incomes—incomes which would leave them vulnerable to substantial income taxes. By receiving only as much in the way of dividends as is needed for living expenses, a wealthy individual can keep the rest of the money tied up in ever-growing assets, where it is better sheltered from tax. But in the government income statistics, a wealthy person living on a dividend income, of say, $80,000 a year would resemble an employee receiving a salary of $80,000, even though the two individuals may have vastly different resources.

The gap between the wealth of the rich and the poor in Canada is far greater than the gap in their incomes. Consider the following statistics, all from Statistics Canada. In 1981, the top-earning 20 percent of Canadians enjoyed 45 percent of national *income*, while the bottom-earning 20 percent enjoyed a mere 4 percent of that income. But if one looks at *wealth*, the disparities grow dramatically larger. The wealthiest 20 percent of the population enjoyed a massive 68 percent of the national wealth. The bottom 20 percent owned less than 1 percent. Indeed, this bottom group owned less than 0, their debts being greater than their assets. The numbers are in some ways even more striking when one looks at the wealth of the top 1 percent or the top one-tenth of 1 percent, rather than the top 20 percent, since wealth is so heavily concentrated in a very small group. In Canada, the top 10 percent own more than half of the country's wealth.

Let's now watch the same parade of Canadians, this time with their heights reflecting their holdings of wealth rather than income.

This second time around, the parade has been going for about ten minutes before we realize it has even started. That's because, despite our rapt attention, we can't see anyone. The marchers who've gone by during the first ten minutes aren't just miniscule in size, they are actually underground. These underground people represent Canadians who own nothing of value, have no savings and are, in fact, overall in debt.*

*Most Canadians have debts, such as a mortgage on a house. But their assets, including equity in their homes, outweigh their debts.

They include university graduate students who have gone into debt to finance their education as well as young families with consumer loans.

At last, we start seeing the first signs of life above ground, tiny people a few inches high. They include the same low-income people we saw in the early stages of the last parade. It's not till fifteen minutes have passed that we begin to see dwarves—people about three feet high who have net wealth of about $18,000, mostly in the form of equity in their homes or savings that will be put towards buying a home.

The rest of the parade proceeds in much the same way as the first parade . . . until the end. By the last minute, we are encountering wealthy giants as large as Toronto's CN Tower.

But it is what happens in the last *second* which is truly astonishing. Indeed, with less than a tenth of a second left, some of the most prominent Canadian businessmen and investors suddenly appear, boasting assets of more than $100 million and ranging up into the billions.* These individuals are so tall that their heads disappear into the clouds. To mention only a few, there is Vancouver real estate developer Charles "Chunky" Woodward, a little over 3 *miles* high. Chatty Toronto financier Conrad Black, who, along with brother Montegu, has assets of $200 million, stands 6 miles high. There's even a tall woman—Mitzi Steinberg, heiress of the Steinberg grocery store fortune, 7 miles high. Calgary oil man Ronald Southern is more than 8 miles high; Toronto real estate magnate Robert Campeau, almost 12 miles high; Toronto shoe baron Thomas Bata, a little more than 12 miles high; Montreal entrepreneur Paul Desmarais, 18 miles high; Galen Weston, head of the Weston food empire, 29 miles high; Charles Bronfman, who inherited the Seagram's liquor fortune, 32 miles high; Paul Reichmann, 195 miles high; and

*This only includes assets they own. In addition, many of them control a far more extensive range of assets. For example, Peter and Edward Bronfman own $650 million worth of assets, but they control a corporate empire worth about $47 billion.

finally, the richest man in Canada, Kenneth Thomson, head
of the Thomson newspaper empire, 198 miles high.

Over the years, Canada has taxed people on the basis of their
stature in the income parade rather than their stature in the
wealth parade—a fact that has been enormously beneficial to
the giants in the wealth parade. Although the wealth giants
generally stand tall in the income parade as well, they stand
out less there than in the wealth parade, where they tower
miles above the dwarves running around below. If the tax
system were to concentrate more on taxing people on the
basis of their size in the wealth parade, we would have fewer
people with their heads in the clouds—and fewer underground.

It would be easy for Ottawa to tax people on the basis of
their wealth. This can be done directly through estate taxes
and annual net wealth taxes. Furthermore, the returns of
wealth can be taxed by including capital gains in income
under the income tax. When just these methods alone are
considered, Canada has surprisingly low taxes. Indeed, when
compared with the tax systems of twenty other western industrial nations, *Canada has the lowest overall tax on wealth.*

Actually Canada is tied for last place with Italy, behind all
the other European nations, the United States and Japan.
The heaviest taxes on wealth are found in Switzerland, Fin-
land and Norway. As a little-publicized 1980 study done by
the Canadian Finance Department noted: "The effective
rates of tax on wealth in Canada are already the lowest among
OECD [Organization for Economic Co-operation and
Development] countries." The paper, which was addressing
proposals from the investment community that Canada reduce its taxation of capital gains, went on to point out that any
reduction in the taxation of capital gains would only further
exaggerate Canada's light taxation of wealth. "Given that the
federal government and most of the provinces do not impose
any taxes on wealth or estates, exemption of capital gains

would leave Canada as the only industrialized country that permitted large amounts of wealth to be accumulated and to be passed between generations without any tax liability." The paper concluded: "Canada's extreme position may already be a cause of concern to the extent that it restricts the government's ability to promote a fair and equitable distribution of income and wealth in the country."

Unconcerned, the Mulroney government lessened Canada's taxation of wealth still further. In 1985 it exempted capital gains from tax, up to a lifetime limit of $500,000. This exemption meant that up to $500,000 worth of profits made on the sale of capital property—stocks, bonds, real estate, jewellery, etc.—would not be subject to tax, giving the small group of Canadians who owned this kind of wealth a lifetime tax saving of up to $125,000. The current tax reform proposes to cap the exemption at $100,000, reducing but not eliminating this special break for the rich.

In addition to the lifetime exemption, capital gains already enjoy special tax benefits. Currently, they are taxed at only half the rate applied to other types of income, such as income from salary. For someone paying the top marginal rate on $100,000 of salary income, the tax would amount to $50,000; on $100,000 of capital gains income, the tax would be about $25,000. Under the tax reform proposals, the tax on $100,000 of salary income would drop to about $44,000, while the tax on $100,000 of capital gains income would rise to roughly $33,000—still leaving in place preferred treatment for capital gains. And, when capital produces income in the form of dividends, these dividends are also taxed at a lower rate than regular salary income and will continue to be after tax reform.

Furthermore, as discussed in the previous chapter, the interest on money borrowed for investments that produce dividends and capital gains is almost always tax deductible. The lifetime exemption is really just icing on the already rich capital gains cake. All these factors combine to lighten the burden of taxation on those with sufficient funds to save and invest, or, in other words, to accumulate wealth. Of course, what is lost in taxation of wealth must be made up elsewhere, and so the burden on salary and wage incomes has become heavy indeed.

Canada's big move away from wealth taxation came back in 1971 when it abruptly abolished the federal estate tax. The estate tax had almost exclusively affected the well-to-do. Estates of less than $50,000 (equivalent to about $150,000 in today's dollars) were completely exempt. And for estates larger than $150,000, there were additional exemptions for spouses and dependents. What remained was taxed at gradually rising rates, starting at 15 percent and rising to a maximum of 50 percent on estates of more than $300,000 (or about $900,000 in today's dollars.) Only a tiny segment of the population was wealthy enough to be affected by the estate tax, and of those who were, a still smaller group faced taxes of any consequence.

But for this tiny wealthy élite the tax was significant. Its removal was generally regarded as a trade-off for the introduction of a tax on capital gains, which was brought in at the same time. But the trade-off ended up providing substantial benefits to those who already held wealth. Since capital gains were only to be taxed starting January 1, 1972, the tax would not apply to increases in the value of assets prior to 1972. These pre-1972 gains would normally have been caught in the net of the inheritance tax. Now that it was gone, though, all the wealth accumulated before 1972 was to escape taxation entirely—some $66 billion. John Bossons, an economist at the University of Toronto, calculates that the result was effectively a lump-sum transfer of $12 billion to the very wealthiest Canadian families. A bit like carrying coals to Newcastle.

But perhaps the most interesting of the taxes that affect wealth-holders is the one Canada does not have—an annual net wealth tax. This tax has existed for some time in a number of western European countries: West Germany, Austria,

Norway, Sweden, Belgium and Denmark. It has never been applied in North America, nor even really seriously considered here, perhaps because it might actually redistribute a small part of some of the great fortunes.

Basically, a net wealth tax imposes a levy on individuals on the basis of their total wealth, which includes the value of their stocks, bonds, real estate and, often, personal possessions such as yachts or jewellery. Since the tax is designed to hit the well-to-do, it only applies to those whose wealth is above a certain dollar value. Everything below is exempt.

The interesting thing about an annual wealth tax is that it can collect large amounts of revenue, even if the tax rate is set very low at only 2 or 3 percent. Its effectiveness lies in its frequency. Whereas the inheritance tax and the tax on capital gains allow huge accumulations of wealth to build up untaxed over a lifetime, an annual net wealth tax is there each year collecting a tiny portion of the increased value of the fortune. Michael Wolfson, an Ottawa-based economist who studied wealth taxation, found that a wealth tax with a top rate as low as 2.6 percent would have more impact than an estate tax with a top rate of 80 percent.*

Of course, a tax like this could become a powerful tool for gradually whittling away at some of the great fortunes, thereby creating the possibility of a redistribution of wealth. It all depends on what tax rate is imposed. Under our current tax system, with its light taxation of wealth, a properly-invested fortune can grow considerably each year, despite taxes and inflation. If a wealth tax with a high rate is imposed —anything above the real rate of return on investments—a fortune would be gradually reduced over time. On the other hand, a wealth tax with a low rate of perhaps one percent or less, would allow a fortune to continue to grow, but would

*In Wolfson's example, the tax was applied to wealth in excess of $75,000. Of course, exemption levels can be set much higher—at say, $200,000 or $300,000, so that only the truly affluent are affected. Assets include equity in a home, not its market value.

siphon off a small additional amount of that annual growth for the national treasury beyond what is currently retrieved under our income tax system.

This may sound punitive, since these same individuals are also subject to the income tax. But is it any more punitive than sales taxes, which are also in addition to income tax? The difference is that sales taxes hit lower and middle income groups much harder, while a wealth tax would hit only the well-to-do.

The Mulroney government has shown no inclination to consider any of these alternatives. In searching the tax cupboard for ways to reform the system, it has happily skipped over changes that could be made in the taxation of wealth—changes that would only bring Canada into line with some European nations. In its stated quest to make the tax system fairer, the government has ignored the large pools of potential revenue that could be reached through such changes. It has, for instance, overlooked the possibility of taxing capital gains at the same rate as other income, bringing back the estate tax or imposing a small annual wealth tax. Instead, the Mulroney team has opted for rejuggling the tax burden among the marchers in the income tax parade, leaving the much taller marchers in the wealth parade undisturbed.

Even though Canada imposes a relatively light burden on wealth, there are some who would like it to be lighter still. One of the ways the very rich can further reduce their taxes—and enhance their reputation in the process—is by establishing charitable foundations.

In Canada, as in the United States, some of the most prominent, wealthy families have set up foundations over the years, making sizeable bequests in the name of charity. Sitting on billions of dollars of untaxed assets, these foundations are subject to minimal regulation. The public knows little about them, except that they are synonymous with good works, an ongoing testimony to the decent, humanitarian intentions of the wealthy individuals who dominate the economic horizon.

In reality, of course, there's a bit more to the story. While private family foundations give out millions of dollars to charities in Canada each year, this represents a small fraction of their total assets, which almost certainly exceed $2 billion. (Nobody really knows the full value of their assets.) In many cases, the money given is just enough to meet minimum government requirements.

In the last decade or so, as Ottawa has endeavoured to impose some limited rules on foundations, the foundations have organized and fought vociferously. And what has the fight been about? Has the government been trying to make them pay tax? Have faceless bureaucrats been attempting to control which charitable causes the foundations support? Has Ottawa somehow tried to interfere with their ability to carry out good deeds? No.

Rather, what has made the wealthy benefactors of the foundations so hot has been the government's attempt to make them pay out more of their charitable foundations' funds to charity. But isn't this what they are there for? Isn't giving money to charity exactly what the foundations were set up to do? The spectacle of private foundations kicking and screaming as the government forces them to give a small portion of their money each year to charity does not reflect the public image these institutions enjoy.

The reason for the confusion lies in the fact that there are many reasons for setting up a charitable foundation, not all of them immediately obvious or particularly charitable. Ostensibly, a family sets up its own charitable foundation—rather than, for instance, just handing money over to an existing charitable organization—because it wants more control over which charitable causes will benefit from its largesse. It may also want to build up a large sum of money that will keep growing, allowing for an ongoing distribution of funds to worthy causes.

But a charitable motivation may be only one of several factors involved in setting up a foundation, and perhaps not the most important. There are also considerable tax, business and financial advantages to be gained in establishing a private foundation which can be controlled by the donor and his family. Arthur Drache, a prominent Ottawa tax lawyer who headed up the personal tax section in the Finance Department in the mid-70s, points to a number of reasons why a wealthy family would want to set up a charitable foundation, regardless of its charitable instincts. To begin with, donations to foundations are tax-deductible. So high-income people are able to reduce their taxes substantially by making donations. If they are in the top tax bracket, facing a marginal income tax rate of 50 percent, they are able to deduct half the cost of their charitable donations from their taxes. In essence, the government is picking up half the cost of the donations. This still leaves the donors putting up half the money, and once they have handed it over to the foundations, they cannot get it back. So what are they getting in return, besides a warm feeling about helping their fellow citizens?

One extremely valuable benefit is the opportunity for the donor to solidify his or her family's control over the family business. This is an absolutely crucial advantage. A wealthy family likely already has as much money as it currently can use. What it often wants is to be able to maintain control of the family company that generated the wealth. By controlling the company, the family is controlling a valuable asset, a present and future source of income. If it controls the company it can, for instance, decide when and how much dividend income will be paid out. It can also ensure that family members occupy desirable, high-paying jobs in the company or hold lucrative directorships on the company's board.

U.S. author Ferdinand Lundberg notes that control is the key objective of those who understand corporate power: "Asked whether he would rather have all the Ford Motor dividends or company control, the average man would probably choose the dividends. He would be mistaken, for those in control determine whether there will be any dividends at all. . . . Control is always the prime objective of the true leaders in all large organizations. . . . For control determines everything that is subject to the will."

But how can a private foundation be used as a vehicle for maintaining control of a family company? First, the family sets up a foundation and appoints family members to controlling positions on the foundation's board. It then donates a significant block of the company shares to the foundation. (The family of course receives a tax deduction for the shares donated.) Meanwhile, the family holds onto another block of shares outside the foundation and, together with the block inside the foundation, the family has enough to control the company. Since the shares inside the foundation technically belong to a charity, they cannot be purchased by an outsider. As Drache notes, this leaves the family protected from a hostile take-over bid.

With this set-up, the family can maintain control over the company from generation to generation. It can also avoid a lot of capital gains taxes. Consider, for instance, what would happen if the family had not set up the foundation. Let's say the father held the bulk of the company's shares. If he were to sell the shares, he would pay tax on any capital gains he made (above the lifetime exemption). But chances are he doesn't want to sell them; he wants to hold them and pass them on to his children, giving them control of the company after his death. The only problem is that, when he dies, his shares are automatically taxed as if he had sold them. If the father's holdings are substantial, his children could face paying a significant amount of tax at his death. Depending on the family's financial situation, the children might even have to sell some of the shares to pay the tax owing, possibly losing control of the company.

But with a foundation, these problems can be avoided. To begin with, charitable foundations are tax-exempt bodies, so shares held inside the foundation are never subject to tax. Thus, the foundation spares the family from paying the capital gains taxes they would otherwise have to pay as the shares passed into the next generation's hands. As a result, there is no danger that the family will have to sell any shares to pay the tax and no risk of losing control of the company. The foundation therefore offers the family the double-barrelled benefits of maintaining perpetual control and avoiding once-a-generation capital gains taxes.

And there are other advantages. Since the family controls the foundation, it can control what is done with the foundation's funds. Of course, there are limits to what can be done with these funds. They cannot, for instance, be handed back to the family. In fact, funds can only be *given* to charitable causes. But foundation funds can be *loaned* to anyone—including the family business and members of the family. These loans must be made at the government-prescribed rate of interest; but that rate is usually at least a couple of points below market interest rates.

A wealthy benefactor is thus able to make a donation to his family's charitable foundation, receive a tax deduction for the donation, and then arrange to have the money loaned back to himself or his company at a favourable interest rate. So while the family no longer has the money, it has the use of the money, sparing the family business from having to borrow from the banks or dilute the family's equity by raising capital from the public. Lundberg describes foundations as being "like closely held private family banks." One interesting effect of this is that the family business has a leg-up on its competitors, who presumably must borrow funds from banks at market rates.

In fact, it was this competitive advantage enjoyed by foundation-controlled companies that prompted a massive U.S. congressional investigation into foundations in the 1960s. The House of Representatives' Select Committee on Small Business uncovered the startling fact that many of the leading U.S. corporations—including Coca-Cola, Eli Lilly, Great Atlantic and Pacific Tea, S.S. Kresge, Kellogg, Midwest Oil, Kaiser Industries and Ford Motor Company—were partially or fully controlled by private charitable foundations. Even the Watergate complex in Washington—the sprawling multi-milliondollar office centre best remembered for its role in the downfall of Richard Nixon—was wholly owned by a religious order.

The select committee, headed by Representative C. Wright Patman, found that charitable exteriors masked the real business, tax and financial purposes of private foundations, and conferred on the corporations they controlled a distinct advantage over competitors. The Patman committee's findings clearly suggested that desire to maintain control of a familyowned company was the prime motivation behind the establishment of some of the major private foundations in the United States. The largest of all, the Ford Foundation, with assets today of more than $4.7 billion, was certainly not the product of any charitable motivations on the part of its chief donor, Henry Ford. Indeed, Ford was by most accounts a crusty, self-centred man, who spoke out against public benefactions.

Ironically, the Ford Foundation only came about because of Henry Ford's refusal to follow the normal tax-avoidance practice of passing some of his assets along to his children and grandchildren through special trusts before his death. Since Ford had insisted instead on hanging onto 55 percent of Ford Motor Company stock himself, his family would have faced a huge inheritance tax on his estate, valued at between $500 and $700 million. A last-minute decision before his death in 1947 placed the bulk of this stock in the Ford Foundation. Since his son Edsel also gave most of his fortune to the foundation, about 90 percent of Ford common stock ended up in the foundation. The family was saved from significant inheritance taxes and gained perpetual control over the company.

The Rockefeller family used an extensive network of private charitable foundations to operate their equally extensive network of private companies. These foundations played a crucial role in allowing the Rockefellers to maintain control over their

Standard Oil empire after a Supreme Court ruling ordered the empire dissolved in 1911. Through the use of a number of charitable foundations, the Rockefellers were able to sidestep the court order and maintain control of the same series of oil companies that they had been ordered to sell in 1911.

Howard Hughes also used foundations as an integral part of his corporate empire. The Hughes Foundation held $134 million in stock in Hughes's companies, but never received a penny in dividends. Assets were shuffled between the Hughes Medical Institute, another charitable foundation, and several large Hughes-owned corporations in ways that resulted in enormous tax savings. The charitable foundation also purchased $75 million in commercial assets and assumed liabilities of $56 million. Congressman Patman was moved to comment: "This sounds more like high finance to me than charity."

The sensational disclosures of the three-volume Patman report turned the little-known world of charitable foundations into a political issue in the United States in 1969 and sparked an interest in the subject in Canada. Despite the popularity of private charitable foundations among the wealthy in Canada—there are more than a hundred—almost nothing was known about them. Unlike the United States, Canada required very little disclosure of information, even to the government. Finance Department officials trying to gather some basic data about foundations quickly discovered just how secretive the private Canadian foundations were. As one Finance official wrote in an internal memo in 1976: "It would be naive to assume that the abuses which are taking place in the United States are not taking place in Canada or cannot take place in the future. The basic problem we have had is obtaining firm data."

What little information they could lay their hands on convinced Finance officials that some questionable practices were going on here. One foundation, which was the sole shareholder in a large Quebec textile operation, loaned the textile company $9 million interest-free. Since interest rates were running above 9 percent at the time, this firm gained a considerable advantage over competitors. In another case, a private foundation in Alberta with assets of $3.7 million had loaned $2.8 million interest-free to the donor's private company. In a third case, a foundation controlled by a family in the jewellery business held shares in the family business and it also apparently held a substantial block of shares in a major competitor. This raised the possibility that, as with the Rockefeller interest in Standard Oil, placing shares in a charitable foundation disguised a situation that was less competitive than the public realized.

The internal Finance memo described as "offensive" many of the practices uncovered in the limited investigation. As in the United States, these practices usually occurred in situations where a family used a foundation to hold a key block of the shares of its private business. "The major abuse, and we found quite a number of cases of this, was, through one method or another, extending interest-free loans by the foundation to the company," said the confidential memo. "Another was the holding of non-productive land . . . where the land was being utilized by family members for recreational purposes. A third situation was the utilization of control by the foundation to ensure large salaries and so forth be paid by the company to family members."

There were no laws governing these kinds of activities by charitable foundations. In fact, there was little to compel foundations to spend much of their funds on charitable causes. In the absence of strict requirements, some foundations were spending almost nothing on charity. A law requiring foundations to disburse 90 percent of their income to charity each year may have sounded strict, but it had little effect since foundations could—and in some cases did—structure their affairs so as to have little or no "income," while sitting on millions of dollars worth of capital. In both the Quebec and Alberta cases mentioned above, the no-interest loans not only spared the family companies from paying considerable amounts of interest, they also prevented the foundations from receiving any interest. This was important, because interest would be considered income for the foundations, and foundations were required to distribute 90 percent of their income each year to charity. But if the foundation had no income, it was under no obligation to distribute money to charity.

Ottawa concluded that the rules needed to be tightened. In a green paper in 1975, the Finance Department proposed a number of changes, including tougher disbursement and disclosure rules. The foundations, particularly the private foundations holding shares of family companies, protested strongly. An internal Finance memo warned the cabinet that, judging from the response to the proposed changes, the government should be prepared for considerable opposition. "This opposition will come from very influential sources including some of the most wealthy people in Canada," said the confidential memo.

The mild reforms Ottawa introduced in 1977 were designed to prod private foundations into giving more to charitable causes. The key reform was aimed at private foundations that held stock in family or non-arm's-length businesses. Henceforth, these businesses would be required to pay dividends to the charitable foundation equal to 5 percent of the foundation's stock. These dividends would therefore end up in the foundation as income, and 90 percent of them would have to be disbursed.

The changes were strongly resisted by the foundations. But the foundations eventually came to see that the new law wasn't really that harsh. It would still allow them to keep their capital base intact, since their capital would likely earn them 5 percent a year or more through proper investment. Furthermore, since it was up to foundations to report the value of their assets, they could place a low value on them and, therefore, only be required to pay out 5 percent of this artificially low value.*

---

*Technically, assets were to be valued at fair market rates, but with private company shares, which are not sold on the open market, it is often difficult to determine a market value. This gave the foundations considerable leeway.

Still, for the first time there was a law that would force foundations to distribute at least a small percentage of their assets. And, also for the first time, foundations had to reveal publicly a few minimal details about themselves: the value of their assets (perhaps not the full value, but at least part of the value), the amount distributed to charity and the names of their directors.

For Toronto's Weston family, which controlled the W. Garfield Weston Charitable Foundation, the new rules were excessive. The Westons, one of the wealthiest families in the country, decided to give up their foundation's charitable status in December 1976—just before the new rules were to come into effect the following month. However, the Weston foundation's assets were left intact and the foundation remained the kingpin in the Weston family's immense corporate empire of more than 250 companies. Today, the foundation still sits at the top of the Weston pyramid, holding large blocks of shares in the family's private holding companies, and ensuring that control of the $2.6 billion empire doesn't slip out of the hands of the Weston family.

As for the charitable side of things, the Weston foundation quietly dropped the word "charitable" from its title. Roger Lindsay, the foundation's secretary and the executive vice-president of the family's key holding company, Wittington Investments, said this was done to make it easier to fit the foundation's name on its letterhead. Lindsay insisted that the foundation continues to give money to charity even though technically it is not obliged to under the current tax laws. He refused, however, to give any details. He would not reveal the value of the foundation's assets nor the amount given out to charity, except to say that the foundation each year gives away virtually 100 percent of its *income*. But asked if the foundation gives away about 5 percent of its *capital* each year—as other foundations are now required to do—Lindsay refused to comment, saying that the requirement doesn't apply to the Weston foundation.

Lindsay argued that what the Weston foundation does with its money is nobody else's business. He said that he believed the Weston family did not claim tax deductions when the original bequests to the foundation were made thirty years ago, although he admitted that he did not know this for sure. He agreed that the foundation probably has records relating to the bequests, but said that he did not have "the time or the willingness" to check them. At this point there are no public records. Revenue Canada throws out its records six years after a foundation's charitable status is revoked. A Revenue Canada official confirmed that the Weston file was thrown out several years ago.

The revocation of its charitable status may have freed the Weston foundation of obligations under the tax laws, but charitable foundations are also subject to common laws governing trusts and charities. These laws, which ensure that charities operate in the public interest, require charitable foundations to disburse all their assets to charitable causes if they cease to operate as a charity. This raises the interesting question of whether the Weston foundation could have been required, under common law, to disburse its funds to charity when it ceased to be a charity.

When the Weston foundation gave up its charitable status in 1976 without disbursing its funds, the public trustee's office of the Ontario government looked into the situation to see if there were any violations of the common law. But the Weston foundation persuaded the Ontario officials that the province had no jurisdiction over it. Although the foundation operates out of Toronto, where the Weston corporate headquarters is located, the foundation is technically headquartered in Charlottetown, Prince Edward Island—beyond the reach of Ontario, the one province that actively enforces the common laws governing charities.

Even as the Westons had grown disaffected with the tougher rules, others were finding new reasons to resort to charitable foundations. Reader's Digest Magazines Ltd., which publishes *Reader's Digest* in Canada, quickly set up a charitable foundation when faced with a new law in 1976 requiring magazines to be Canadian-owned in order to qualify for special tax deductions for advertisers. While the new law prompted some U.S. magazines to simply close down their Canadian operations, opening up markets for a weekly *Maclean's* magazine, Reader's Digest figured out that a charitable foundation could provide a way around the new law. The Canadian subsidiary of Reader's Digest placed a block of its shares in the foundation, thereby meeting the new law's minimum requirement for Canadian ownership. This allowed advertisers in *Reader's Digest* to take advantage of the tax breaks, while real control of the magazine's Canadian operation apparently remained in the United States.

While the new rules would ensure that at least a small percentage of a foundation's assets went to charity each year, there was nothing to prevent many of the abuses that had prompted concern about foundations in the first place. The United States had banned non-arm's-length deals between foundations and those controlling them, but Canada continued to allow these cosy arrangements. And the practice remained fairly common among private foundations, giving the families controlling these foundations access to low-interest money for themselves and their companies.

In 1981, interest in the foundations surfaced again within Finance. In the spring and summer of that year, a rare reform zeal gripped the department as interest focussed on cutting off measures that helped the rich avoid tax. Among a long list that came under scrutiny were private foundations.

In his controversial budget in November that year, Finance Minister Allan MacEachen proposed upping the annual charitable pay-out requirement of foundations from 5 percent to 10 percent of the value of their stock in family-controlled companies. He also proposed that any capital gains received by the foundation be considered as income and, therefore, be subject to the distribution rules. This time the foundations were furious. "We were quite incensed the way it was sprung on us," recalls Arthur Bond, an accountant who runs the

Association of Canadian Foundations. "There was no forewarning. I got a copy of the budget papers ... and I couldn't believe what I read."

Bond and representatives from individual foundations, including the Molson family of Montreal, took their protests to Ottawa. They argued that what was really at stake was the ability of foundations to go on existing indefinitely. And, in that sense, they were right. The new rules were designed with the idea that foundations would have a long but limited life-span, distributing all their assets to charity over a number of decades. Foundations had come to be regarded as an ineffective, costly way to direct money to charity, a vehicle that over the years has been used for private gain as well as for public good.

But, as with a number of other items in that budget which the rich disliked, the tough measures for foundations were withdrawn. After extensive consultations with the foundations, the Finance Department worked out a deal in the spring of 1982 that promised to make the rules governing foundations even less onerous than they'd been before the budget. Under the new deal, the 90 percent pay-out rule would be scrapped. The new pay-out rules, Arthur Drache noted in *The Financial Post*, would actually require foundations to disburse less per year than they had been required to disburse in the past. Far from being forced to wind up over time, foundations were being given a new opportunity to grow and expand their capital base. The only losers, it seemed, were the charitable causes that were supposed to be benefiting from their largesse.

The point of all this is not to suggest the rich are uncharitable. More than one hundred wealthy Canadian families, including the Eatons, the Molsons and the Westons have set up private foundations which now hold assets believed to be well in excess of $2 billion. And no doubt these foundations have aided many good causes over the years. Much of this is undoubtedly the product of generosity on the part of those funding the foundations.

But the other side—the considerable financial advantages that the rich can and do derive from setting up foundations—should serve as a warning signal that perhaps we should approach the subject with a touch of skepticism. After all, donations are tax-deductible, which means that in most of these cases, the government—ultimately the Canadian tax-payer—has picked up half the costs.

When cast in this light, it seems reasonable to raise questions about whether we are getting our money's worth. At least some of the benefits are going to provide lower-interest loans for some of the wealthiest individuals and companies in the country, giving them an edge over less well-endowed competitors. Yet we are not entitled to know the details of such loans. Nor are we allowed to know if foundations are being used to provide cushy jobs for family members or to maintain family control of a company. Foundations are not required to report this kind of information on the public disclosure forms they now must file with the government.

Furthermore, despite the major public funding involved through the tax system, the public has little control over how the money is spent. The money must go to causes broadly defined as charitable or non-profit. But these include causes that are quite different from our popular understanding of charity as aid to the poor. The Griffith Foundation, which was set up by the McConnell family of Montreal—one of the largest fortunes in Canada—dispensed about $850,000 in 1985 to private schools. It also gave $100,000 to the Fraser Institute, an arch-conservative think tank. In fact, looking through the lists of gifts made by foundations, one is struck by how much of the money seems to go to the very established cultural and educational institutions and how little to anything directly helping the poor.

If the rich prefer to support their favourite cultural and educational activities, that is certainly their right. But when tax benefits are given to them in order to provide that support, the public surely has more than a passing interest. Again, it is useful to think of a tax break as a tax expenditure: if a wealthy family is able to reduce its tax by millions of dollars by setting up a charity, then that is equivalent to the government providing a grant for the same amount to the family's charity. But would we hand over a cheque for tens of millions of dollars to a wealthy family's charity and say: Here's the money; you choose your favourite causes.

This is basically what happens with private foundations. While grants given out by the publicly run Canada Council, for instance, are constantly scrutinized and criticized by the press and public—as they should be—there is virtually no questioning of grants given out by private foundations. The feeling is that they are private, that we should be grateful for whatever is given since it is their money. In fact, what they are giving is usually only half their money.

Private charitable foundations are an odd sort of creature. They are really a very roundabout, inefficient way to channel money to worthy causes. They divert funds that would otherwise end up in the public purse into privately controlled bodies where they are stockpiled for years on end and sometimes made available for private use. A small portion of this money ends up trickling out to causes that the wealthy donors choose to support, often a cultural activity or educational institution that particularly pleases the family. In the process, foundations enable some of the most powerful families in the country to quietly consolidate their economic power in the name of charity.

If charitable foundations aren't exactly what they appear to be, they certainly aren't alone in presenting a misleading image to the public. In the world of tax, things are not always as they seem. And nowhere is this more true than in the magical world of corporate taxation.

CHAPTER THREE
The Confidence Game

"If you ask me when we expect to pay these, I'll tell you never."
—**Consolidated Bathurst Limited controller Jean-Jacques Carrier commenting on the $218 million in taxes his company "owes" Ottawa**

The blank faces around the cabinet table expressed disbelief. It was not that members of the Trudeau cabinet were surprised to hear an outlandish suggestion from their colleague, Eric Kierans. Most of the ministers at the 1970 meeting already considered Kierans something of an oddball, who was given to diatribes on subjects outside his own territory. As postmaster-general, Kierans was supposed to run the post office. But his real interest was economics. He had taught economics at McGill University and had served as president of the Montreal Stock Exchange. And when economic subjects surfaced in cabinet, Kierans was not shy in offering his opinions, which were sometimes quite off the beaten track.

Still, this time he was going too far. Judging by the incredulous expressions of his cabinet colleagues, Kierans had just destroyed whatever minimal credibility he retained. He had made the outrageous suggestion that Ottawa should start charging interest on the more than $3 billion in taxes that corporations—most of them large and profitable—had deferred paying. "We should be charging them interest—at prime plus one," said the feisty postmaster. The sober group around the table showed little interest in the woolly scheme. Clearly this was Kierans at his wildest. Although nobody said it, the real question on many minds was: Why doesn't he just deliver the mail?

Kierans got nowhere with his exotic plan. Today, more than fifteen years after his repayment plan fell flat on the cabinet floor, the $3 billion in corporate taxes remains unpaid. Indeed, the bill has mushroomed as new unpaid taxes have accumulated over the years. Officially, corporations now "owe" Ottawa more than $30 billion in taxes they have deferred over the years—almost as much as the annual deficit. And no interest is being charged on the money. Ottawa isn't even sending out friendly reminder notices. And the corporations involved—which include some of the biggest in the country—aren't exactly scrambling to come up with the money. The truth is that the companies have no intention of paying these taxes, now or later.

While corporate officials, such as Jean-Jacques Carrier of Consolidated Bathurst, will usually admit this, casual observers might easily miss this simple fact in reading a company's annual report. Indeed, they might be left with the exact opposite impression: that the taxes have been paid. The 1982 Consolidated Bathurst annual report lists taxes of $28 million, which, it notes, gives the company a tax rate of 34.7 percent. But the surprising truth is that *none of these taxes were actually paid*.

Rather, Consolidated Bathurst "deferred" the taxes. This increased the company's tally of deferred taxes accumulated over the years to $218 million. Other major corporations in Canada have even bigger deferred tax bills: MacMillan Bloedel, $227 million; Stelco, $390 million; Bell Canada, $1.2 billion; Imperial Oil, $1.3 billion; to mention only a few.

Deferred taxes are a Bay Street fiction. They result from a series of corporate tax breaks that allow companies to depreciate their purchases of machinery, equipment and buildings at artificially fast rates. If a company purchases a machine with an estimated life of eight years, for instance, it might be expected to deduct the cost of the machine over that period, reducing its taxable income a little bit in each of the eight years. For accounting purposes, this is the way the machine is depreciated on the company's books, as specified by accepted accounting principles.

But companies actually keep two sets of books—one for accounting purposes and one for tax purposes. For tax purposes, the machine can be written off much faster, sometimes in as little as two years, even though the company is paying for it and using it over a much longer period. This provides companies right away with large deductions which allow them to significantly reduce their tax bills. Theoretically, the taxes they avoid paying are not actually eliminated, just deferred. But as long as the company keeps purchasing new equipment, it can keep deferring these taxes indefinitely. In practice, the taxes are almost never paid.*

Deferred taxes are really tax breaks Ottawa has provided to business over the years in allowing them to write off their plant and equipment at artificially fast rates. Since the taxes are almost never paid, the money amounts to an interest-free loan from Ottawa, without any collateral required or any due date.

But what is curious about them is their clandestine nature. Why are they called "deferred" when they are actually, in almost all cases, effectively "eliminated"? Finance Minister Marc Lalonde contributed to the public confusion on the issue in March 1984 when he was asked in the House of Commons about Carrier's reported comment that Consolidated Bathurst had no intention of paying its deferred taxes. Lalonde disputed Carrier's statement and suggested that Carrier might well end up fired. In fact, Carrier was not fired; he knew exactly what he was talking about.

Corporations also play along with the pretence. Corporate annual reports regularly fail to make a clear distinction between paid and unpaid taxes, leaving the erroneous

---

*They are only paid in cases where a company stops expanding but remains profitable. If it stops expanding and is not profitable, it would not have to pay tax in any event.

impression that all taxes have been paid. They even calculate their tax rates as if the deferred taxes had been paid, as we've already seen in the case of Consolidated Bathurst.

Or consider Shell Oil. In its 1982 statement, it reported income taxes of $152 million on profits of $302 million. This, the report calculated, gave the company an effective tax rate of 50.4 percent—a hefty rate by any standard. In fact, careful reading of the report reveals that Shell deferred $199 million in taxes that year through writing off investments in plant and equipment at an artificially fast rate. This wiped out the company's $152 million tax bill, leaving Shell tax-free that year. In fact, Shell actually ended up with a *credit* of $47 million, which could be used to reduce taxes in future years.

While this was clearly a much more pleasing picture to Shell's management and shareholders, this wasn't the story the company wanted to project to the public. By reporting a tax rate of 50.4 percent, Shell looked like it was making a sizeable contribution to Canadian society. Clearly Canadians would be much more inclined to regard Shell as a good corporate citizen if they believed the company contributed $152 million to the national treasury, than if they realized that the treasury ended up owing Shell $47 million.

This mistaken impression left by deferred taxes also helps business in its plea for more tax breaks. Business commentators frequently trot out statistics showing that corporations are saddled with too much debt, compared to their equity. But these numbers can be deceiving. Often included in these tallies of corporate debt are deferred taxes. But, as we have seen, deferred taxes are not really debt at all, in that money is not really owing. As the Finance Department noted in one study: "deferred taxes have the characteristics of a permanent source of financing without an attached interest cost, so that it is more appropriate to include these with equity than with debt." By adding deferred taxes to the corporations' debt, however, business commentators are able to make a strong—but false—case about how badly corporations need tax breaks to reduce their poor debt-to-equity ratios.

This Alice-in-Wonderland approach to corporate tax has played a key role in disguising the enormous erosion of the corporate tax base over the past few decades. In 1954, Ottawa collected almost as much income tax from corporations as it did from individuals. Today, more than thirty years later, the balance has shifted dramatically. In 1987, corporations shouldered only 20 percent of the income tax burden, leaving individuals to make up the remaining 80 percent. The current tax reform proposals will do little to redress this imbalance.

Over the years, the real rates of tax paid by corporations have plummeted. While corporations officially pay tax at a rate of 46 percent,* their real rates are much lower and in some cases non-existent. Yet this erosion has happened largely out of public view. No government ever came forward and argued that corporations should pay such low tax rates. And certainly, no government ever argued the inevitable corollary—that more money would have to be collected from other taxpayers. But over the years, Ottawa has brought in a series of technical measures under dull-sounding names— accelerated capital cost allowances, investment credits, five-year and two-year write-offs, etc.—that have effectively sliced corporate tax rates in half.

The process began in earnest in the late 1940s. Ottawa had provided some special corporate tax breaks during the war, as a way of enticing firms to invest in plant and equipment necessary for the war effort. After the war, these breaks were seen as a way of encouraging firms to convert from wartime production. When Ottawa undertook a major overhaul of the tax system in 1948, it enshrined a capital cost allowance as a permanent feature designed to stimulate investment in Canadian industry. Although corporations emerged from the 1948 tax overhaul with a tax rate close to 50 percent, relief was on the way. With the capital cost allowance, many future taxes

---

*This figure includes federal and provincial tax. Under the current tax reform proposals, the combined federal-provincial rate will drop to about 38 percent.

would end up "deferred." The new measure provoked little interest outside the business community, but it was the beginning of a trend of disappearing corporate taxes that would dramatically reshuffle the national tax burden over the next few decades.

More relief measures followed in the 50s, all aimed at enticing investment in Canadian production. In the early 60s, Liberal Finance Minister Walter Gordon kept up the trend, but added a new twist. Special tax breaks would be linked to corporate behaviour that the government, and particularly the finance minister, wanted to encourage. Gordon was a committed nationalist who was alarmed by the extent to which Canadian industry was owned by Americans. So when he introduced a generous new two-year tax write-off for purchases of manufacturing and processing equipment, he restricted it to firms with at least 25 percent Canadian ownership. Three other generous corporate tax measures introduced by Gordon also had strings attached—they were available only to firms locating in depressed parts of the country. The business community chafed at Gordon's blatant attempt to influence corporate behaviour. Most of all, businessmen disliked the finance minister's attempt to increase Canadian control over the economy.

By the time the Carter royal commission started examining the Canadian tax system in the mid-60s, major tax concessions for corporations had been quietly entrenched without provoking much public controversy or even discussion. Both Liberal and Conservative governments supported this approach, implementing their own corporate tax breaks during their times in power. Disapproval was confined to the CCF and, later, the NDP.

The Carter commission disrupted this peaceful mainstream consensus with some stunning recommendations in 1967. The lawyers, accountants and economists who devised the Carter commission's reform package were concerned about the way corporate tax breaks had destroyed the neutrality of the tax system, leaving companies making investment decisions on the basis of tax rather than business considerations. They also documented the extent to which certain industries, particularly in the resource sector, were receiving a free ride while others were bearing a heavy burden. The reforms they proposed would have increased the overall corporate tax burden by about 27 percent. About half of this increase would have fallen on foreign shareholders. Massive opposition from the business community killed most of the Carter reforms.

So fierce was the business response, in fact, that Trudeau's Liberal government, which had inherited the Carter report, went beyond simply killing the Carter reforms. Under Finance Minister John Turner, the government introduced several new tax measures that greatly enriched corporate tax breaks. Turner revived Gordon's incredibly generous two-year write-off, but without Gordon's Canadian ownership rider. This meant that some of the biggest and most profitable companies, whose foreign ownership had disqualified them from reaping the rich benefits of Gordon's tax break, were in a position to cash in this time. Not only had the foreign multinationals weathered an attempt by the Carter commission to increase their tax bills, but they also now found themselves receiving a whole new tax gift from John Turner.

By the time Turner quit the Cabinet in 1975, his new corporate tax breaks were saving companies close to $1 billion a year—on top of the tax savings they were already enjoying before Turner's stint at Finance. And the new measures were to go on saving corporations billions of dollars long after Turner's departure, helping to create a huge federal deficit.

In general, the benefits of corporate tax breaks have gone disproportionately to large, foreign-owned companies, since they can afford the cost of new plant and equipment and they have large incomes against which to deduct these costs. In 1980, some 13 percent of the 450,000 firms in Canada received 82 percent of the benefits of deferred taxes. An even more select group of 37 firms—less than .01 percent of the nation's total—received 12 percent of the tax savings.

But perhaps the most telling indictment of corporate tax breaks is not that they distribute benefits unfairly or unwisely, but that they don't seem to work. They are almost always given in the name of stimulating investment. But in reality they seem quite ineffective at encouraging this result. As Carleton University economist Allan Maslove has pointed out, if demand for a company's products is low, it is unlikely to invest even if there are special incentives to do so. If demand is high, then the company may be planning to invest anyway and the tax break is simply an added windfall.

Economists generally dismiss the notion that corporate tax breaks will do much for the economy. Douglas Auld, former chairman of the University of Guelph's economics department, compares the effectiveness of tax breaks in stimulating the economy to "stirring orange juice with a potato peeler." Richard Bird, an economist at the University of Toronto, is similarly unimpressed with the use of tax breaks. "It certainly is not going to stimulate the economy. Why on earth would it?" says Bird.

The pessimistic view of the economists is borne out by the evidence. Four major Canadian studies done in the last fifteen years all found that the amount of increased investment generated by tax incentives was actually *less* than the amount of money the government gave up in revenue.

In one study, Douglas May, an economist from Memorial University in St John's, found that for every dollar Ottawa gave up in corporate tax breaks to stimulate investment, it got about twenty-one cents of new investment—hardly an impressive return. (May also found that the tax breaks usually generated a certain amount of unemployment by encouraging companies to replace manpower with machines.) Two other studies by university-based economists put the amount of additional investment even lower—at fourteen and seventeen cents per dollar of revenue foregone. The fourth study concluded the investment generated was closer to thirty-five cents on each dollar—still only about a third of the revenue the government gave up in hopes of encouraging additional investment. The message is clear. Tax breaks cost more than they're worth.

This raises some disturbing questions. Almost every tax concession made to corporations—and to investors—is based on the premise that granting them a concession will induce them to invest more and that this will benefit the economy as a whole. But surely it is not enough to argue that tax breaks increase investment. We have to know how much additional investment is generated. And will that added investment be greater than the amount of revenue given up in order to achieve it? The studies mentioned above indicate it is not. And if this is true, then the economy ends up losing more than it gains. As we have seen, the hidden nature of tax expenditures has hindered us from making these calculations and drawing the simple conclusion that the country emerges with the short end of the stick. If we were handing over cheques for billions of dollars to entice corporations to make additional investments and then discovered that their investments were not even increasing by the amount we were giving them, we would realize that something was wrong. But, in the tax world, the true picture never clearly emerges.

Furthermore, how do we know that whatever benefits the economy derives from these investments are greater than the benefits that might be derived by passing the equivalent tax savings on to the wage-earning population, which would go out and spend the extra money? We are being asked to accept, as an article of faith, that giving money to corporations and investors is the most effective way to stimulate the economy.

Besides, there is much evidence to show that tax levels have little impact on the amount invested anyway. Indeed, when Ottawa moved to begin taxing capital gains in 1971, there were dire predictions that investment would dry up. In fact, no such thing happened. Investment levels, as a percentage of gross national product, have been remarkably stable before and after the taxing of capital gains. Indeed, private sector savings and investment rose throughout the 70s and 80s despite the new tax on capital gains.

Although tax breaks may not stimulate the overall level of investment, they do influence what types of investments will be most attractive. University of Toronto economist John Bossons argues that the capital gains exemption introduced by the Mulroney government in 1985 actually has the effect of discouraging investment in risky, start-up ventures because the exemption restricts the deductibility of capital losses. Without the opportunity to write off losses against other income, many investors shy away from ventures they might otherwise have been willing to gamble on in the past.

Bossons also notes that the capital gains exemption has the unfortunate effect of stimulating real estate investment, thereby leading to speculation. Indeed, there are indications that the exemption played an important role in sending the Toronto real estate market into a frenzy in 1986-87—a frenzy that placed affordable housing even further beyond the reach of many low- and middle-income earners. This should come as no surprise to Ottawa. The Finance Department has long known that more than half of all capital gains are made in real estate investments. Michael Halsall, a Toronto real estate broker, attributes a good deal of the recent market hysteria to the capital gains exemption. "All that did was help to drive what otherwise would have been an active sales market into one that's gone crazy," Halsall told the *Financial Times* in April 1987. "It simply encouraged speculation and speculators by the droves have been jumping all over it."

Still, whether or not tax breaks make sound economic sense, businessmen like them. And who can blame them? Tax breaks allow companies to dramatically reduce their taxes, something everyone likes to do. But neither businessmen, who seek tax breaks, nor governments, who dispense them, particularly like to admit that tax breaks are just a way of channelling money to business. That sounds a bit raw. Ordinary citizens might be left wondering why corporations—particularly big, profitable, foreign-owned ones—need handouts from the national treasury. Hence the need for a theory to explain what is going on in other, loftier terms. Enter the concept of "business confidence."

In its simplest form, the doctrine of business confidence goes like this: jobs are created when businessmen invest. Businessmen invest when they have confidence in the economy. They have confidence in the economy when the government creates a good investment climate. Many things contribute to a good investment climate, but perhaps the key is the tax system. Nothing buoys up confidence like low corporate taxes.

One of the delightful features of business confidence, to its proponents at least, is its vagueness. It can't be pinned down. It has all the substance and firmness of a mass of jelly. It's a state of mind, a way of feeling. And as such, it defies measurement or verification. Governments are asked to fork over billions of dollars without guarantees of anything. Just on the hope that the extra money will make businessmen and investors feel more confident. And what if they don't? No one is called to account. How can one account for a state of mind? So what if hundreds of millions of dollars of tax were avoided? Perhaps the businessmen still didn't feel confident.

It is this nebulous quality that makes business confidence such a powerful weapon. Since it can't be proven or disproven, it has a force all its own. It exists or does not exist to the extent that businessmen *feel* it. Are they thinking positively or are they not? Only they can tell what their mood is.

In 1984, the Canadian Manufacturers' Association argued for a package of $1.8 billion of new tax breaks on the grounds that businessmen's confidence had been shaken—"their confidence died"—by the removal of some corporate tax breaks in the November 1981 budget. In fact, many of the tax changes they complained about so bitterly in 1981 never materialized because the Liberal government retreated in the face of their opposition. Besides, the government had more than atoned for its sins in 1983 with a whole new package of corporate tax breaks, widely hailed for their confidence-building effect. This left business better off than it had been before the alleged catastrophe of 1981.

But businessmen still reported feeling a bit shaky in 1984. Were they going to be waking up scared in the middle of the night indefinitely? Would they never regain the will to invest? Would a clammy fear of government intentions continue to paralyse their keenness to create jobs? Apparently only one thing would convince them the government was not out to get them: more and more tax breaks.

Despite its vagueness, or perhaps because of it, the business confidence doctrine has proved extremely useful in explaining away evidence that might contradict some business positions. The deficit debate provides an interesting example. The business community claimed a severe lack of confidence in the mid-80s over the government's failure to trim the deficit by cutting back social spending. (Watching other groups in society receive too many benefits can apparently be as destructive to businessmen's confidence as not receiving sufficient benefits themselves.)

But while business was pushing for deficit-reduction, the Finance Department's own economic forecasting models were indicating that planned deficit-reduction measures would slow down economic growth, including employment. Asked about this, William White, a senior Finance Department advisor, dismissed the department's forecasts and invoked the doctrine of business confidence. "Any macro-model will throw out those sorts of numbers [showing] a slowdown in economic activity," he said. "That's what models will tell you, but the models are wrong.... They don't take into consideration the confidence effect." Confidence is difficult to measure, he noted, "but you know it's there."

But if you can't see it or measure it, how do you know it's there? Clearly, you ask businessmen. This is exactly what an interdepartmental government committee did when trying to assess the value of the corporate tax breaks John Turner had given out in the early 70s. The committee sent out a questionnaire to one thousand business executives about the impact the tax breaks had had on their investment decisions. The businessmen reported that, yes, the tax breaks had encouraged them to invest and then reported all sorts of investments that they said they would not have made otherwise. But then, would we expect them to say anything else? Imagine if the government had cut personal taxes in the name of encouraging citizens to buy more Canadian goods, and then sent out a questionnaire asking everyone if this is how they had spent the extra money. Would we be surprised if most replied, yes, they had spent the windfall exactly as the government had hoped? This might explain why the results reported by the businessmen themselves are so much more positive about the benefits of tax breaks than the results found in the economists' studies using less subjective criteria.

The vagueness of the business confidence doctrine also helps disguise its mean side. On the upbeat side, businessmen are asking the government to buoy up their confidence so they will think positively and feel like investing. But the flip side of this scenario is a threat: Give business what it wants—tax breaks, deficit reduction, whatever—or it will lose confidence, and no confidence, no investment. This is the implicit extortion business uses against all governments. But, to come out and express it directly, to actually flash sharp teeth or unsheath long swords, would make businessmen look like bullies in the public eye. Instead, they simply refer to the need to maintain business confidence. The threat remains unspoken, but the government gets the message and usually responds with more tax breaks.

When labour resorts to its ultimate weapon—withdrawing its services in a strike—the public generally blames labour, rejecting the element of extortion in the situation. But business has the power to threaten something far more serious—the withdrawal of its capital. It is the genius of the business confidence doctrine that it can dress up this most powerful intimidation of all in the harmless lingo of a positive-thinking slogan.

But things are supposed to be different now. The benefits of tax breaks have become so unequally distributed that even business and government—the duo that created the situation —have grown concerned about their handiwork. The disparities between the tax rates of the resource sector and the service sector have been noted and even documented by the government. Business commentators now complain about the lack of neutrality in the tax system, noting that investment decisions are made on the basis of tax rather than market considerations. These kinds of arguments were advanced twenty years ago in the Carter report, only to be fiercely rejected. Now they have become fashionable in business circles.

A number of factors may be responsible for this change in attitude, but one stands out. When the Carter commission recommended taking away corporate tax breaks, it didn't advocate handing over anything else to business in return. In Carter's view, tax breaks had reduced corporate taxes too far— particularly in the resource sector—forcing the government to raise a great deal of revenue elsewhere. In urging the elimination of some important tax breaks, Carter hoped to restore corporate taxes to their intended, higher level.

The tax reform proposed by the Mulroney government is very different. While Ottawa is now suggesting the reduction of many corporate tax breaks, it is offering business a substantial *quid pro quo*. In exchange, Ottawa proposes reducing the general corporate tax rate from 46 percent to 38 percent. This is a highly significant reduction. Under this new system, some corporations will pay more tax, some will pay less. The tax burden will be shifted somewhat within the corporate world, reducing the bias in favour of certain industries. But overall, the changes will do little to reverse the long slide in corporate tax revenue.

For almost forty years, business has fought for and won a long series of tax breaks. As we have seen, this has left corporations shouldering a much smaller portion of the national tax burden than they did thirty years ago. As a result, when the government has moved to reduce the deficit, it has raised the bulk of the additional revenues from taxes on individuals. Corporations have largely escaped the burden of deficit-reduction.

This favourable treatment perhaps explains how the business community's ferocious opposition to the Carter reforms or to the mini-tax reform attempt of November 1981 has given way to a helpful co-operativeness with the current tax reform exercise. It's not that businessmen have mellowed over the years or given up in despair. It's that this time they have little to complain about. If anything, they are leading the government cheering team. Tax reform never looked so benign.

Even for those sectors that may face higher corporate taxes in the future, the new package consolidates many of the benefits of tax breaks accumulated over the years, but removes the riders that were originally attached to them. It should be remembered that tax breaks were almost always introduced as a way of enticing companies to do something that was deemed helpful to the economy: to invest, expand, locate in undeveloped regions, carry out research, convert to Canadian ownership, etc. Generally, companies had to accomplish one or other of these socially desirable goals in order to qualify for a tax reduction. Now, however, due to the lower rates proposed, the business community will continue to bear a low tax burden—with no strings attached.

Furthermore, once the current tax reform exercise establishes a lower corporate rate, business will still be in a good position to reduce its taxes further by pressuring for new tax breaks. Politically, it is probably more difficult to win an overall rate reduction than to win individual tax breaks. Rate reductions are highly visible and obvious. Even someone with little knowledge of the tax system can see that a rate reduction means a reduced tax burden. So it is more difficult for the government to sell the public on the idea of a corporate rate reduction when many of the beneficiaries are big business enterprises. Tax breaks, on the other hand, are technical and complicated and, therefore, largely invisible.

Here, then, is a possible scenario: Once the lower corporate rates are in place, the business community will start pressuring Ottawa for new tax breaks. There will be much talk of business confidence, international competitiveness, etc. And the government, in an effort to entice corporations to invest, expand, locate in underdeveloped regions, etc. will be tempted to offer new tax incentives to encourage these valued activities. After all, business will make its case forcefully and the government's fear of a collapse of business confidence will be great. Jobs will be said to be at stake. And since new tax breaks will appear to be mostly technical, the public won't really notice anyway. The new measures will be given dull names and their arrival will be noted only on the business pages.

Those who favour low corporate taxes often argue that tax increases are really borne by consumers, since corporations pass their tax hikes along in the form of higher prices. The extent to which this is true is difficult to measure and the question has baffled serious tax scholars for years. Certainly corporations are more likely to raise their prices in situations where a few large firms control the market and there is little price competition between them.

Some argue that, because of this corporate tendency to pass tax hikes on to consumers, corporate profits should only be taxed when they are distributed to shareholders, not while they are in the corporation. While this makes sense in theory, in practice there would be many problems. To begin with, corporations could then become perfect vehicles for storing profits tax-free indefinitely. Furthermore, the government would have little power to tax corporate profits distributed to foreign owners—a serious problem for a country that is as foreign-owned as Canada.* Essentially we would lose much of our power to tax the profits of most of the major corporations in the country. The result would be a staggering revenue loss making it necessary to raise taxes on everyone else. Imperfect as the corporate tax is, it is the best of a bad set of options.

Perhaps the most popular argument these days for keeping the corporate tax low, however, is that the U.S. corporate tax is low. If Canada doesn't respond with low rates, it is often argued, capital will flow out of the country and into the United States.

Corporate spokesmen refer to this under the general heading of "maintaining international competitiveness." While no one would argue against Canada being internationally competitive, the full implications of what is meant by the phrase should be recognized. In the tax sphere, international competitiveness means keeping rates low for the highly mobile—that is, for high-income professionals and for corporations and individuals with capital. Since ordinary workers cannot easily find work in the United States, we don't need to worry about them being driven south by high Canadian taxes. Taxes can be safely shifted from the highly mobile rich to the largely immobile middle and lower classes, without any consequences for international competitiveness. It can even be done in the name of patriotism.

Lower U.S. rates, therefore, are grounds to drive down Canadian rates. It's all part of a downward spiral. Any country that wants to attract or hold on to capital must get into an international bidding war, offering lower and lower taxes. Many Third World countries, of course, are so desperate to attract anything in the way of investment they have made

*Although Canada has a withholding tax that applies to foreign shareholders, its use is restricted by our international treaties.

themselves tax-free havens for corporate and individual capital. The fact that countries are willing to engage in this kind of international bidding war is of course highly beneficial to the owners of capital. Indeed, they are often the ones reminding us of the need to compete in this international game.

One solution might be to refuse to participate in the bidding war, to set corporate tax rates in Canada at the levels where we feel they should be set. This might not be as idealistic and naive as it sounds. A number of studies have found that tax considerations are relatively low on the list of reasons determining where corporations locate themselves. Far more important, for instance, are factors such as access to markets, transportation and skilled labour.

While corporations may be unlikely to withdraw large amounts of capital, they may well be tempted to transfer a greater portion of their profits to the United States if they operate in both countries. In the case of Canadian companies owned by U.S. parent firms, this can be done by adjusting internal payments. If a Canadian subsidiary imports a product from its U.S. parent or it pays a management or royalty fee to the parent, those payments could be adjusted upward so that more of the firm's profit ends up in the United States, where it would be subject to a lower rate of tax.

This could result in a major tax drain for Canada. There are roughly $24 billion worth of these sorts of transactions annually between U.S. companies and their Canadian subsidiaries. If these U.S. firms attempt to reshuffle even 10 percent of their profits from Canada to the States, this could remove more than $2 billion a year of corporate income from the reach of Canadian tax authorities.

All this is part of much broader problem, and one that Canada has shown little interest in tackling. Unless we match the low tax rates of the United States—or the even lower rates of a number of Caribbean tax haven countries—companies will transfer profits out of Canada. In fact, this has been going on for years with tax haven countries, resulting in the loss of hundreds of millions of Canadian tax dollars. "We do think we're being hosed," said James Gourlay, director of taxation for Revenue Canada in Victoria, British Columbia.

This is roughly how corporations make use of tax haven countries. Let's say that a Canadian company usually buys a product abroad for $1.00 and then sells it on the Canadian market for $1.80, generating an 80-cent profit in Canada, which is subject to Canadian income tax. If that company wanted to transfer the profit out of Canada, all it would have to do is set up an affiliate in a tax haven country and route the product through the affiliate. This way, the affiliate would purchase the product for $1.00 and then sell it to its Canadian parent company for, perhaps, $1.70. The Canadian company would still sell it in Canada for $1.80, but only 10 cents of the profit would end up in Canada. The other 70 cents would be in the company's affiliate in the tax haven, where it would escape tax.

The same principle can work in reverse for exports. In both cases, products pass only briefly through the tax haven affiliate, which is really a "sales corporation," set up to act as a middleman operation where profits can be accumulated. These sales corporations are usually little more than corporate shells that do only the most minimal processing or packaging. (In one U.S. case, a large pharmaceutical company was routing its drugs through a tax haven affiliate that just consisted of "seven guys and a blender," according to a Treasury Department report.) And in some cases, the product doesn't even pass through the sales corporation at all—except on paper. "The shipment goes directly from Prince Rupert to Japan," explained Gourlay. "But the paper work goes from Prince Rupert to the Bahamas or the Dutch Antilles to Japan." Needless to say, the benefits for the tax haven countries are limited.

But at first glance, the benefits to the corporations using tax havens might seem limited too. What's the point of accumulating profits in the tax haven? They will be taxed at normal

Canadian rates the moment they're brought back to Canada.
But companies can get around this by having the tax haven
affiliate "lend" the money back to the Canadian parent with
no interest charge. This "loan" can amount to a permanent
transfer of the funds back to Canada, tax-free.

Since 1972 there have been Canadian laws designed to
prevent companies from setting up tax haven affiliates for tax
avoidance. But the Canadian restrictions only apply to affiliates used to shelter investment income; companies cannot, for
instance, place stock in affiliates and allow the dividends to
accumulate tax-free. The Canadian tax laws do not, however,
apply to sales corporations, which are ostensibly set up to carry
on business activities as opposed to merely receiving investment income. In the absence of any tax laws to limit the use of
these sales corporations, Revenue Canada has had little success
in trying to collect taxes on profits accumulating in the sales
corporations. When the cases have ended up in court, Revenue
Canada has usually lost.

In one dramatic case, it failed in its attempt to prosecute
Redpath Industries Limited for tax evasion, despite clear
evidence at the trial that the sugar company had set up an
affiliate in Bermuda strictly for purposes of avoiding Canadian
tax.* Quebec Sessions Court Judge D'Arcy Asselin accepted
evidence that the Bermuda affiliate was just a tax vehicle
which took its orders directly from Redpath's head office in
Montreal. The Bermuda affiliate had no employees, no warehouse, not even a telephone. Still, Judge Asselin ruled in a
1982 decision that there was no tax evasion and said that
Redpath owed no tax—a decision that has dampened the
enthusiasm of prosecutors contemplating court actions in similar situations.

---

*A confidential memo produced at the trial indicated that Redpath's
officers were advised that similar activities were carried out by such large
corporations as Canadian Pacific Railways, Melchers Distillers and Canada
Steamship Lines.

Although the use of tax havens has grown in recent years and has become considerably more sophisticated, Canada has failed to take steps to effectively deal with the problem. There have been no moves to clamp down on these kinds of tax avoidance schemes by, for instance, following the U.S. example and extending tax laws to cover sales corporations operating in tax havens. Although the United States still has tremendous difficulty policing the use of tax havens, it at least has laws that address the problem.

But if Canada has taken few steps to get tough on the use of Third World tax havens, it is showing a similar lack of interest in taking action to stop the transfer of profits to the United States. In proposing to lower our corporate tax rates to keep pace with those in the United States, the Mulroney government is giving up revenue we can ill afford to lose. Instead of simply giving up like this, we could strengthen our tax laws to deal with the problem. But not only have we failed to move in this direction, we actually tried to kill a California system that could have served as a model for Canada. The California system taxed multinationals operating inside the state on the basis of how much of their worldwide sales were made in the state. This eliminated the incentive to transfer profits out of the state, since sales—not profits—became the key factor in determining their tax bills. Unlike profits, sales cannot easily be moved. Under the innovative California law, corporations were facing an extra $500 million a year in taxes.

Multinationals took California to court in 1983, but lost in a bid to stop California from imposing such a tax system. Alcan Aluminium of Montreal, which along with other multinationals faced higher taxes on its California operation under the new scheme, tried to appeal part of the ruling to the U.S. Supreme Court. Canada actively intervened on behalf of the Canadian company. The Finance Department notified the U.S. Treasury Department that Canada supported Alcan's position. Since then, California has largely abandoned the tax, under pressure from multinationals.

If Canada wanted to get serious about the problem of multinationals transferring profits out of the country—whether to tax havens or to the United States—it could have easily supported California's bold initiative, with an eye to adopting a similar system here. But instead of going that route, Ottawa has opted to reduce our corporate tax rates to bring them closer to U.S. rates. In the process, Ottawa is letting corporations escape with hundreds of millions of dollars in taxes—revenue that will have to be made up from those whose familiarity with tax havens is more likely to come from travel posters.

It was a warm summer night and the garden glittered with twinkling lights and pale pink azaleas. On terraces overlooking a deep ravine, guests dined under transparent tents, drinking fine wine and feasting on shrimps, clams, mussels and lobster. Below, a live orchestra played and guests danced on top of a lighted swimming pool covered with clear Plexiglas. The spectacular party, at the sprawling chateau-style Toronto home of Loblaw's senior vice-president Brian Davidson, was to celebrate Richard Currie's tenth anniversary as president of Loblaw's. Among the three hundred guests were many prominent, well-to-do Canadians, including billionaire Galen Weston. And although the public wasn't invited, it shared in the experience indirectly.

Like many lavish indulgent events, the Loblaw's party in September 1986 was conducted in the name of business. It therefore would qualify as a deductible business expense. With the catering, the orchestra, the serving staff, the liquor and the flowers, the party would easily cost $50,000. By reducing Loblaw's taxable income by that amount, this soirée would reduce the company's tax bill.

Despite calls for national restraint and deficit-reduction, business entertainment budgets are booming. American Express Canada Inc. reports that business entertainment has been rising significantly in recent years. Indeed, 25 percent of the $8.5 billion worth of meals consumed in licensed establishments are on business expense accounts, according to the Canadian Restaurant and Food Services Association. And though the national treasury subsidizes these events, Revenue Canada makes no attempt to control the costs or even monitor them.

Over the years, business entertainment costs have largely escaped the scalpel of tax reformers. Except for a few changes in the 1970s, when companies were denied the right to deduct the cost of a yacht purchased for business entertainment, there has been no attempt to control this burgeoning expense. Despite the Mulroney government's claims that it is closing tax breaks for the rich, the current tax reform only trims modestly in this area, limiting entertainment deductions to 80 percent of their cost. While many of the guests at the Loblaw's gala would undoubtedly be keen supporters of Ottawa's deficit-reduction strategy, their event would largely avoid the new belt-tightening measures.

Business entertainment is an exotic area that includes everything from lavish parties to expensive dinners to private boxes at sports events. Canadian tax law allows entertainment expenses to be deducted as long as they are a reasonable part of the process of earning income. But that process can be fairly long and convoluted.

Consider the private box. While ordinary baseball fans sit pressed together in the stands below, the élite crowd in the private boxes at Toronto's Exhibition Stadium can sit on swivel chairs, stretch out on plush couches, nibble shrimp and canapés, watch television, make phone calls, observe themselves in full-length mirrors, heat food in microwave ovens, wash dishes in a dishwasher or use their own private bathroom. The tab for this luxurious privacy right above home plate is considerable. The smaller private boxes—which include an indoor lounge area as well as a large outdoor balcony and which can accommodate about twenty people—are leased for about $50,000 a year. With the price of the tickets, catering and decorating, the bill easily reaches above $70,000 a year. But the cost is made a little lighter because the public is picking up part of the tab through the tax system.

Twelve of the fourteen private boxes at Exhibition Stadium are leased by corporations, including Labatt's, Dominion Stores and the Canadian Imperial Bank of Commerce. These corporations can deduct the cost of the boxes from their taxable income on the grounds that they use the facilities to entertain clients. One Revenue Canada official compared entertaining in private boxes to "going fishing—you put out the bait" in the hope of wooing a client into a sale. Are we to assume, then, that company executives are making sales pitches to their customers even as the ballgame progresses? Is a major deal interrupted each time a foul ball lands on one of the balconies? Probably not. In fact, the executives doing the entertaining don't have to try to make a sale or even discuss business at all. The whole evening may be just a way to induce a good feeling in the client. And if the executives also end up feeling good, then that's just part of the process of earning income.

Making a client feel good can include just about anything. While Revenue Canada auditors are fussy about receipts, they give companies a great deal of leeway in determining what is necessary to induce a feeling of contentment in a client. Restaurants, bars, private parties, theatres and sports events are popular spots for business entertainment. The services of "escorts" are also apparently acceptable, as long as receipts are provided.

The question is not whether business executives should entertain. Surely they should be able to enjoy as many lavish parties, expensive dinners and private recreational events as they choose. But why should they do so at public expense? It's nice that Loblaw's threw a party to honour its highly successful president, but does the public have to help out with the cost?

Surely no one would seriously argue that Canadian business

would suffer if these costs were not deductible. Business executives could work out deals in their boardrooms, or if entertainment was essential, they could go ahead and entertain, but strictly at company expense. No competitive advantage would be lost, since the same rules would apply to all firms.

Companies competing in international markets argue that it is necessary for them to entertain foreign clients to keep up with foreign competitors. Fine. Canada could easily adopt the British practice of only allowing companies to deduct their entertainment costs when they are entertaining foreign clients. The British law even applies to the ubiquitous business lunch. Since the law was enacted more than twenty years ago, British firms have continued to entertain local clients at restaurants, theatres and sports events—even in private boxes—but the costs are no longer passed on to the public.

Perhaps the most common argument for the deductibility of business entertainment costs, however, is that it props up the restaurant and hotel industry. Without the regular patronage of corporate clients, some of the fanciest restaurants and hotels in the country would go under, it is argued. Restaurant owners, and even waiters and waitresses, are made to appear the victims of any attempt to shut off the tax deduction.

This is a very interesting argument. Are we to believe, then, that the real reason for the business entertainment deduction is the need to subsidize the restaurant and hotel business? Because if subsidizing these industries is really what we want to do, then why don't we just do it directly? Why don't we give out special grants to restaurants? Or, if the point is to help out waiters and waitresses, why don't we give them a special subsidy?

Or, if we want to keep the restaurants full of customers, why don't we spread the benefits around more evenly? At least the pleasure of eating all those publicly subsidized meals could be shared by a wider cross-section of Canadians. How many janitors or construction workers or parking lot attendants ever have the opportunity to enjoy a meal at a nice restaurant or the best seats at a sporting event, subsidized by the government? How many Loblaw's cashiers get to eat shrimp and dance on Plexiglas-covered swimming pools at Loblaw's parties? If we're going to give out these kinds of perks through the tax system, why should they be restricted to well-to-do business executives and their clients? How about a private box for the unemployed at ball games or a special table for welfare mothers at Winston's?

This brings us to the corollary to Surrey's law.

In almost every area of public life, myths and confusions abound. Nowhere is this more true than in the domain of tax. Despite its public nature—all tax laws are written down—the tax system provides a wonderful opportunity to obscure what is really going on, namely, who is receiving what benefits and who is paying what costs.

We may know what we're paying, but we don't know what our neighbour is paying. And, often more important, we don't know what he or she is *not* paying. Hence the enormous appeal of receiving benefits through the tax system. They can be delivered so privately, so quietly, so discreetly. The whole experience is so intimate.

The late Stanley Surrey, former assistant secretary for tax policy in the U.S. Treasury Department, fought vigorously to destroy all this intimacy. He made a compelling case against delivering public subsidies through the privacy of the tax system. He argued that subsidies should be made explicit so we can see how much we're spending, who's benefiting and whether we're getting our money's worth.

Surrey's law, as outlined in Chapter One, stated: Giving someone a $100 tax break is the same as giving that person a $100 cheque. The corollary is as follows: If we want to give someone $100, it's better to do so by cheque, because that way we can at least see what we're doing.

There's a certain compelling logic to all this. If we are going to subsidize something, doesn't it make sense to be clear about what we're doing. Would we rather not know what we're doing? But if Surrey's corollary seems eminently reasonable, it is a far cry from what actually happens. In reality, we give out subsidies—enormous ones at times—in ways that obscure the fact that they're subsidies. And we invoke all sorts of reasons to justify these subsidies, reasons that are often irrelevant, dishonest or downright silly.

Following Surrey's corollary, then, would mean extricating subsidies from the tax system. If we want to give a person or a corporation a benefit, let's hand it out directly in the form of a grant or loan. Then we can all see it. If there are to be any conditions attached, we can set them down clearly. It will soon become evident if the money given out doesn't lead to the results we want or if the whole thing just gets too expensive.

Probably nowhere in the area of tax policy is this kind of approach more urgently needed than in corporate taxation. However, Surrey's corollary would not be a hit in the business community. While businessmen have demanded a great deal of assistance over the years, they have generally preferred to receive this assistance unobtrusively, through the tax system. What corporate executive wants the public to know his or her company is receiving a $10 million grant if the firm could receive the same amount without anyone being the wiser? This discretion can be particularly attractive if the company is not planning to create jobs or do other things the public might expect in return for handing over public money. Ottawa has generally acquiesced. Consequently, in 1984, corporations received $18 billion in subsidies from the federal government—$7.4 billion of it in direct grants and supports and about $11 billion in tax concessions.

The tax system not only offers discreet delivery of benefits, it also allows business executives to perpetuate one of their favourite myths: they desperately want to be free of government intervention. While they clearly don't like some forms of government intervention, it's obvious that they're hopelessly addicted to other forms, i.e., subsidies. With those subsidies well hidden in the tax system, the business community can continue to rail against the evils of big government while quietly pocketing billions of dollars of government largesse.

When right-wing crusader Colin Brown died in March 1987, the organization he founded, the National Citizens' Coalition, took out a full-page advertisement in *The Globe and Mail* highlighting Brown's self-proclaimed fight for "more freedom through less government." One of Brown's biggest fights, however, was his battle in the late 60s and early 70s against reforms aimed at removing some of the tax subsidies traditionally enjoyed by corporations and the rich. More freedom through more government money.

With most corporate subsidies hidden in the tax system, we face a daunting task in trying to figure out who is benefiting and by how much. Then, as if the problems weren't forbidding enough, we have to wade knee-deep through language that is, at best, confusing and unhelpful. For example, we are told that billions of dollars of corporate taxes are "deferred" when every accountant in the country knows that they are, in any meaningful sense, "eliminated."

And signs in liquor stores in British Columbia notify customers that prices include a "social services tax." This no doubt leads B.C. consumers to conclude that the province's social security system is driving up the cost of liquor. Not mentioned at all are the millions of dollars in subsidies British Columbia provides business, both through the tax system and through grants and loans. By labelling the tax on liquor a "social services tax," the B.C. government is focussing public attention on the high cost of maintaining social services—a message the government very much wants to communicate as it continues to trim social spending. Imagine if the signs in the liquor stores notified consumers that the cost of their purchases included a "business welfare tax."

The business entertainment deduction is equally surrounded by confusion. Are we, for instance, trying to maintain the international competitiveness of our firms, are we subsidizing the restaurant industry, or are we providing an additional set of perks for those already wallowing in them? If the answer is the last option, then the deduction is clearly unfair and objectionable. If it is either of the first two, then the mechanism we are using is a hopelessly inefficient, clumsy and expensive means of achieving these goals and is creating an unnecessary windfall for the well-to-do.

As for the business confidence doctrine, here we are in desperate need of a little clear thinking. Claiming a failure of confidence is really just a businessman's way of saying: I want more. But if businessmen feel they need more from government, let them say so. Only when we accurately see how much they want, can we assess whether they should get it. Perhaps their grievances are real. Maybe they've been losing ground, letting too much of the national pie slip out of their hands. If so, they can make a case that the pie should be recut. Once we can see what their requests are, we can weigh them against competing requests and decide what to do.

But let's not resort to some silly argument about business confidence, which has all the clarity of finger painting. If there's some compelling reason why Consolidated Bathurst should pay no tax, then let's hear it. If there's a good argument why the national treasury should owe Shell Oil $47 million, let's have it laid out for us. Without a little more clarity, how can we differentiate between what businessmen need and what they simply want?

To test Surrey's corollary—that it's better to hand out subsidies in the form of cheques than in tax breaks—let's look at what actually happens in the case of one of the largest and most popular subsidy programs, the small business tax credit.* To properly assess its merits, we should first figure out what we're trying to accomplish and then figure out whether

---

*For an excellent discussion of the problems of the small business tax credit in Canada, see Neil Brooks' article "Taxation of Closely-Held Corporations" in the *Australian Tax Forum*, Vol. 3, Number 4, 1986.

we can accomplish that objective best through a tax break or a grant.

The small business tax credit has the effect of cutting corporate taxes in half on small businesses—a cut that costs the treasury more than a billion dollars each year. The rationale for the tax credit is that it helps compensate for the discrimination small businesses encounter when they try to borrow money. The argument goes as follows: Since banks often refuse to extend credit to small businesses or will only do so at a high rate, small business is operating at a disadvantage and, therefore, should receive tax relief.

In fact, the argument has merit. Banks do discriminate against small businesses, and it may well be socially desirable to correct that imbalance. But is the tax system the best way to do so? If our goal is to give small, struggling firms access to capital to help them grow, the tax system is a horribly clumsy instrument. To begin with, in order to benefit from the small business credit, a firm has to have a taxable income. But the most needy firms—the ones just starting up, facing enormous overhead costs and tremendous difficulty raising money—don't have anything even vaguely resembling a profit. Thus our billion dollar subsidy program to aid small business utterly fails to help these struggling entrepreneurs in their moment of greatest need.

Furthermore, while the net doesn't extend to the most needy, it unfortunately takes in some of the least needy. All kinds of businesses taking advantage of the small business credit are neither small nor in any way struggling. This is because, due to the difficulty of targeting tax subsidies, the credit has been left wide open. Small firms with huge profits are able to claim its benefits, as are firms owned by wealthy individuals and firms that have no need or desire to raise money for expansion. And, to top it all off, since changes were introduced to simplify the credit in 1985, the tax benefits have been available to any privately owned Canadian firm on the first $200,000 of income. Thus we have the absurd spectacle of

Ottawa offering the likes of Eaton's and Birks the advantages of a program designed to help struggling entrepreneurs.

Consider, instead, if we were to simply correct the bias against small businesses by extending government loans to them or guaranteeing bank loans. We already have such programs, but they could be greatly enlarged and could actually replace the small business credit, providing more accurately targeted benefits at a fraction of the cost. Suggestions of this sort regularly prompt scorn from those who believe grant programs involve excessive government intervention. They argue that delivering subsidies in the form of grants or loans gives too much power to governments and creates bureaucratic red tape and complexity.

Of course a little more government monitoring and control might not be such a bad thing, considering the number of freeloaders who have taken advantage of the small business tax credit over the years.* But even if we accept the argument that more government intervention is automatically bad, this doesn't explain why we should deliver subsidies through the tax system. If we want to give the private sector more rein, we can design our grant programs more loosely, place fewer requirements on those applying for grants. Ultimately, if we want to make our grant programs as wide-open as our tax programs, we could just turn them into automatic cheque-writing operations. You're a small business? You want some money. Here's a cheque for $50,000.

But such a wide-open grant scheme is unthinkable, even if it's not far from what we do through the tax system. The public would quickly see the opportunities for a raid on the national treasury and call for a halt. The abuse would be so much more visible if bureaucrats were sitting there actually writing cheques. When Ottawa introduced the Scientific Research Tax Credit in 1984, it predicted the program would cost

*For more on the abuses of the small business tax credit, see Chapter Seven.

about $200 million in lost revenue. In fact, it drained about $3 billion from the national coffers before Ottawa finally moved to stop the deluge of government funds flooding out to rich investors, middlemen and hucksters involved in some of the least worthy research ever conducted in this country. It is less likely that the government would have issued cheques totalling more than $3 billion before noticing that something was amiss.

As for allegations of complexity, no amount of complexity in the grant programs could possibly match the complexity of the tax laws that have grown up around the small business tax credit. Although Ottawa has bent over backwards to simplify the credit—thereby making it available to all sorts of companies that certainly don't need it—there is one complexity that is almost impossible to avoid. Since the credit is so generous, larger businesses are often tempted to split themselves up into a series of smaller businesses in order to qualify for the credit a number of times, instead of just once. This has led to the evolution of one of the most complex areas of tax law—the laws limiting the use of the small business credit by associated companies.

But even complex laws can do little to limit the abuse of subsidy programs delivered through the tax system. Abuse is almost inevitable because of the wide-open nature of the tax system and our attitudes towards it. We attach almost no social stigma to those who set out to exploit the tax system. Indeed, no matter how absurd a tax shelter scheme—tax breaks for buying yachts, for instance—there is rarely much social disapproval of those who dream up the schemes or take advantage of them. It is considered only reasonable for everyone to avoid paying as much tax as possible and to concoct whatever financial scheme is necessary to accomplish that end.

Compare this attitude for a moment to the immense social disdain we have for those who abuse direct spending programs. The incredible tax avoidance schemes indulged in by the rich are just as damaging to the nation's finances as any efforts by the poor to cheat under the welfare or unemployment systems. Indeed, in sheer dollar terms, the social security abuses pale into insignificance compared to the billions of dollars lost in clever manipulation of tax programs. But while tales of cheating the social security systems have produced a highly vigilant set of bureaucrats monitoring the most personal aspects of the lives of welfare recipients—including surprise inspections to make sure women on welfare aren't secretly living with men—little of the same scrutiny applies to the devious taxpayer.

Indeed, one of the most highly paid professional groups in the country—tax lawyers and accountants—dedicate themselves to the task of aiding the well-to-do in their attempts to exploit the loopholes in the tax system. Imagine the outrage if a set of bright activists dedicated themselves to devising elaborate schemes that would allow the poor to exploit the loopholes in the welfare system. Yet tax professionals move about freely in respectable society without even the slightest tinge of shame or embarrassment! In fact, we train them at great public expense in our universities and law schools. The very presence of this huge group of clever, well-paid tax professionals—and our implicit approval of their activities—is a virtual guarantee that any tax program will be scrutinized from every angle for possible exploitation. If the government makes one false move in designing our tax programs, some of the brightest minds in the country are sitting there ready, waiting to pounce on the flaws. It is to these tax predators that we now turn.

CHAPTER FOUR
The Cosy World Of Tax

"What do you guys tell your kids you do for a living?"
—**Neil Brooks, speaking to a conference of tax lawyers and accountants in Toronto in October 1985**

In the spacious boardroom of one of Toronto's ritziest law firms, senior business executives and tax lawyers were sipping cocktails, nibbling on hors d'oeuvres and talking about a subject dear to their hearts: the contents of the upcoming budget. Brian Mulroney's Conservative government was to present its first budget on May 23, 1985. With only two weeks to go, the anticipation was almost palpable that evening in the McMillan, Binch boardroom. Situated on the thirty-eighth floor of the gold-tinted Royal Bank Plaza, easily the most extravagant-looking in the parade of Bay Street bank buildings, the McMillan, Binch offices provided an exclusive setting for this most exclusive meeting. The gathering included a number of important businessmen, tax lawyers and the finance minister's special advisor, William Mackness. But the most interesting participant was Conservative Finance Minister Michael Wilson himself, who, in the middle of one of the busiest weeks of his life, had taken the time to attend.

The meeting only came to light accidentally. W.A. (Bill) Macdonald, a senior tax lawyer at McMillan, Binch, who is well connected in both the Liberal and Conservative parties as well as in business circles, became evasive when asked about it. Macdonald attended the meeting himself but would not reveal the identities of the other participants, except to say they were business executives from across the country.

According to Richard Remillard, Wilson's press secretary, the meeting was part of the pre-budget consultation process —which is odd considering that Wilson had consulted extensively with the business community for months and his budget was at that point in the process of being printed.

What, then, was the meeting all about? One could suppose that, without giving away any details, Wilson was providing only the broadest outlines of his budget, trying to ensure that these key business leaders would support his budget when he presented it to the country two weeks later.

There was much in that budget that business would like— notably, the fact that the middle and lower classes were to bear the brunt of the government's deficit-reduction. But the finance minister could hardly come out and say that publicly. It might be desirable, therefore, to privately signal to members of the business community that, if they studied the budget closely, they would see it was very much in line with what they had been requesting. If the key business leaders got that message a couple of weeks in advance, the government could count on having this important group onside on budget night.

Perhaps the most interesting thing about the McMillan, Binch meeting was the fact that Wilson was there. No matter what was said, and no matter whether Wilson was primarily talking or listening, his attendance indicates the importance he attached to the opinions of the men in that boardroom. In many ways, the gathering is a nice metaphor for the cosy world of tax. Right there were key representatives of the business community, the tax community and the government: the three major forces in the formation of tax policy all meeting behind the closed doors of the McMillan, Binch boardroom.

Would the finance minister have been as likely to take time out, virtually on the eve of his first budget, for a special confidential meeting with, say, labour leaders or heads of social welfare organizations? What is it about a group like this that commands such singular attention from the finance minister?

Perhaps this is merely raising the obvious. If the minister of finance is more interested in the views of businessmen than labour leaders, does that come as a surprise to anyone? Probably not. But sometimes the obvious bears stating. If we are to understand how Canadian tax policy is formed, we must look at who the finance minister is talking to—not just in the well-publicized formal "consultation" meetings he holds with a wide range of interest groups, but in the more informal, confidential meetings he goes to some trouble to attend.

This chapter, then, is about the obvious, about the close relationship between the worlds of business leaders, tax practitioners and government. It is also about how that close relationship affects Canadian tax policy, often to the detriment of those whose only view of the McMillan, Binch boardroom is from the other side of the gold-tinted glass, thirty-eight floors below.

In talking about these close relationships, one encounters two kinds of arguments. The first, as mentioned, is that the situation is so obvious it hardly bears mentioning. To mention it is to be trite. The second, ironically, is almost exactly the opposite: that to suggest the existence of a business-tax-government clique is to engage in a conspiracy theory. According to this argument, suggesting that the tax system favours the rich and then noticing that the rich have considerable access to the designers of tax policy is equivalent to suggesting that there is a plot, a nefarious scheme of some sort.

In case there is any doubt, let me state that, as far as I know, there is no such plot. While it is not clear what was said behind the closed doors of the McMillan, Binch boardroom, it is pretty clear what was not said. I am convinced that at no point did anyone lick his lips and say: "To hell with the ordinary wage-earner!" or "Aha, now we finally have control of Canada's tax system!"

But it can also be said with some certainty that, at this meeting and others, businessmen and their tax spokesmen would advocate measures that would improve their financial situations in ways that would inevitably pass the tax burden on to others. And the presence of the finance minister indicated his inclination to pay more attention to these individuals than to others. Certainly the budget he presented two weeks later was more pleasing to those gathered at McMillan, Binch than to most other groups around the country.

For Aideen Nicholson and the other MPs on the committee, the whole thing just didn't make sense. How could any government department possibly design a program that bad? The Finance Department had definitely set a new standard with its Scientific Research Tax Credit (SRTC) program, which drained $2.8 billion from the government's coffers in 1984-85. As the morning session wore on, Nicholson and her fellow MPs on the parliamentary public accounts committee were getting more and more exasperated in their attempt to get to the bottom of the fiasco. The Finance Department officials appearing before them kept replying to their queries, but never satisfactorily answering the basic, underlying question: how could you guys let this happen?

Again and again, the MPs were told that the problems had simply not been anticipated. But what were officials paid for if not to anticipate problems like this? By the end of the morning, it was clear that the MPs considered the Finance officials to be incapable of supervising the passing of a church collection plate, let alone the handling of the government's multi-billion dollar budget. Committee chair Nicholson summed up the lack of faith in the judgment of those officials when she pointedly asked: "Why did the Department of Finance officials not also check with accountants, with tax lawyers, with investment dealers, to see what snags there were in their model and what the risks were of abuse?"

Nicholson's question, which was expressed in various

forms by a number of committee members, had a certain logic to it. If Finance officials were so dozy they couldn't spot the avalanche ahead, why had they not at least consulted with a more alert group that could have tipped them off? After all, the community of tax practitioners includes some of the brightest individuals in the country—lawyers who try to figure out ways to get around tax laws and accountants who apply this information in actual tax calculations. These individuals often earn hundreds of thousands of dollars a year figuring out the intricacies of the tax system. Here was a group of exceptionally smart, well-informed experts, whose wisdom could perhaps enlighten the more lowly-paid tax experts in the Department of Finance. But if Nicholson's question was logical, it betrayed an immense misunderstanding of the ways of the tax community.

Nicholson and her parliamentary colleagues were expressing the naive view that one could turn to tax practitioners and receive completely objective advice about tax measures. Given their training, their background and their clients, they tend to develop a certain orientation. Consulting with them would be equivalent to consulting with chiropractors to determine whether they approved of a scheme to provide subsidies for back treatments. One would hardly be surprised if the chiropractors considered such a subsidy program ideal. Tax practitioners are not fundamentally different. They too can spot a soft pitch when it's coming their way. Indeed, contrary to the understanding of Nicholson and her colleagues, the community of tax practitioners *had* been consulted on the SRTC scheme. As one former Finance official privately noted: "I can't think of any tax provision on which we did more outside consulting."

Indeed, the consultation over the SRTC program included some of the most highly respected tax lawyers and accountants—a fact that has gone largely unnoticed.

In fact, by 1982, when Finance was devising the SRTC program, the department had become almost obsessive about consulting the tax community. Only a year earlier, in November 1981, the department had been badly burned when it attempted to reform the tax system on its own, without consulting outside tax practitioners. Having received nothing but abuse for that 1981 budget, the department was bending over backwards, virtually letting the tax community help write the legislation. "By that time we were open house, in terms of discussing tax legislation," said the Finance official. "We hired people, we went out with a paper ahead of time showing how we'd structure it, we went out with draft legislation. . . . and before that there was all kinds of discussion."

And what did Finance gain from this massive consultation? The tax community greeted the proposed measure with a great deal of enthusiasm, assuring the government it was on the right track. Not a word of caution. "Everybody had a crack at it. All the tax professionals had a crack at it. Nobody pointed out the problem . . . of people taking the money and running," said the official.

This is not particularly surprising. The measure was enormously appealing to the tax community. Tax professionals generally represent investors, and the SRTC program offered wonderful risk-free benefits for investors. Furthermore, the program was rich in benefits for tax practitioners themselves. It was structured in such a way that tax practitioners were necessarily involved, even though a far more sensible alternative would have left them out of the picture entirely, allowing research and development companies to collect their tax benefits directly from the government. The SRTC fiasco is dealt with in greater detail in Chapter Nine.

But the tax community not only failed to tip off the government in advance about the dangers ahead, it maintained a steely silence throughout the whole sorry two-year affair. It is not sufficient to say that tax practitioners stood by and watched as more than $2 billion was legally raided from the national treasury. That grossly understates their role. They were right there assisting, filling out the papers, arranging the deals and reaping huge fees for their efforts.

Many of them were privately disgusted by what they saw. "I don't think it was a particularly glamorous period for any involved," says Wolfe Goodman, a dignified senior lawyer with a reputation for being a brilliant tax practitioner. "I remember how amazed my partners and I were when we heard the government had approved [these deals]. . . . if that's what Finance had in mind, they ought to hang their heads in shame." But did Goodman and his colleagues protest? No. Rather, they moved to ensure their clients could take full advantage of the government's stupidity.* "Once we knew [these deals] were possible," said Goodman, "we moved to assist our clients to get the best tax treatment possible."

Goodman's comments, although more candid than most, reflect the way many tax practitioners regarded the SRTC program. And yet the protests of the tax practitioners against the program were so quiet one could have heard a pin drop on Bay Street. The silence is particularly striking since it comes from a group not known for its shyness in expressing criticism of the tax system. The Canadian Bar Association and the Canadian Institute of Chartered Accountants frequently prepare detailed joint submissions for the government on what they see as problems with the tax system. Yet, no joint submission was prepared to draw attention to the ravages of this enormous draining of tax revenue.

If the tax community has been slow to blow the whistle on tax scams, it has also been resistant to important new ideas in the tax field, such as the tax expenditure concept. As we have seen, the concept—that a tax break is equivalent to a direct subsidy—was developed in the late 60s by leading U.S. tax expert Stanley Surrey. It quickly became a vital tool in the United States for analysing the extent of the subsidies different taxpayers receive through the tax system. But it is interesting to note that the concept only really entered the Canadian scene when it was introduced here in November 1976 by the National Council of Welfare, a government-

*Indeed, a lawyer's code of ethics requires her or him to take full advantage of all laws available to a client.

funded citizen's advisory body that reports to the Health Minister on the problems of the poor. The council applied the tax expenditure concept to the Canadian situation, did some calculations and came up with a punchy little critique called *The Hidden Welfare System*, which provided some striking evidence that tax breaks favour high-income groups. That led to a conference on tax expenditures at Osgoode Hall Law School, which, in turn, prompted the Finance Department to begin preparing a tax expenditure account—a vital document detailing the billions of dollars of revenue lost through tax subsidies. It is interesting to note, however, that when *The Hidden Welfare System* first appeared, many tax practitioners scoffed at it and dismissed the tax expenditure concept. Today, the concept has become widely accepted even in tax circles.

Letting the tax community shape tax legislation is a bit like getting the fox to build a safer henhouse. And yet this is exactly what we have done with our tax system. We have given the community of tax practitioners—a highly clever and inventive group if ever there was one—surprising input into designing our tax laws. Although they almost always represent clients with business or investment interests, not to mention their own interests, we have ignored the obvious bias this creates and treated tax lawyers and accountants as if they are all objective experts, value-free foxes striving to build the perfect fox-proof henhouse. The fact that we've lost a few chickens over the years shouldn't surprise anyone.

By looking at the role of the tax practitioner in shaping tax policy, we are raising an important question. To what extent are tax practitioners able to advise the government objectively about tax policy when the financial interests of their clients— and sometimes themselves—are at stake?

To a surprising extent, we seem willing to overlook this apparent problem. Indeed, the world of tax has been interconnected with the world of business for so long that we take it for granted. Thus, when Bill Macdonald from McMillan,

Binch wrote an article, published in *The Financial Post*, arguing against the removal of capital cost allowances in April 1987, he didn't even bother to point out that he is on the board of directors of Imperial Oil Limited, a company that benefits enormously from capital cost allowances. Apparently nobody raised an eyebrow.

There was also no comment about the dual role played by Robert Brown in providing input into Michael Wilson's tax reform proposals. Brown, vice-chairman of Price Waterhouse and one of the most respected tax practitioners in the country, was retained by the Business Council on National Issues to help with the preparation and presentation of its brief to Ottawa on tax reform. Yet Brown also served on a committee of 36 tax specialists that Ottawa assembled and consulted with regularly as it prepared its tax reform package. Brown, then, was representing the major business interests of the BCNI and also advising the government on the same subject.

There was a brief stir in Parliament when *The Globe and Mail* revealed that members of this group of 36 had been allowed to see the final package the day before it was released, thereby giving these individuals an apparent advantage over others in the investment community not privy to such information. But the concern may have been misplaced. The technical advisors had been sworn to secrecy, and no doubt obeyed their oaths. What *is* of concern, however, is that Ottawa was relying on technical input from a group that is closely tied to one segment of the taxpaying public—as Robert Brown's relationship with the BCNI illustrates.

And in their submissions to the government, the Canadian Bar Association and the Canadian Institute of Chartered Accountants regularly call for changes that will aid their clients; that is, they call for changes that will aid the business and investment community, whose members they tend to represent. Tax lawyers dismiss the notion that there is anything improper here. They insist that they are arguing for measures that will aid the business community in general, not any company in particular.

This may be true, but there is a world beyond the business and investment community. What about the 90 percent of Canadians who are neither businessmen nor investors? Tax practitioners have done little to champion their interests over the years. In fact, by helping business and investors find ways to avoid tax, these practitioners have done a great deal to shift the tax burden onto the rest of the population.

Indeed, tax practitioners are so closely allied with the world of business and investment, they are really a part of that world. Not surprisingly, then, the overlap between the worlds of business and tax could be readily observed at the 1971 hearings of the Commons finance committee examining the Liberal government's tax reform proposals. In a doctoral thesis in political science at Carleton University, Leslie MacDonald noted that the committee was inundated with 524 briefs from corporations and business organizations. The briefs were often written and presented to the committee by tax practitioners. McDonald identified 152 tax lawyers, accountants and business executives in a group he labels "tax advocates"—those who appeared at professional meetings discussing tax reform and who also made presentations before the Commons committee. These tax advocates represented some of the largest and most important corporations in the key sectors of the Canadian economy, from mining and oil to heavy machinery and banking, and in some cases also sat on corporate boards themselves.

The tax specialists at the big legal and accounting firms almost inevitably become intertwined with large corporations. The tax issues involved in a major corporate reorganization can keep a tax practitioner busy full-time for weeks or months. The same issues may be involved in the reorganization of a smaller company, but the cost of the practitioner's time is simply too great to justify coming up with complex tax-avoidance solutions. As a result, the most prominent and influential practitioners spend much of their time working for major corporations and are closely tied in with them.

It could be added that the big legal and accounting firms place a high value on tax practitioners who can bring in corporate clients, frequently basing a practitioner's remuneration to some extent on the amount of business he or she attracts. Consequently, connections to major players on the corporate scene are highly prized among tax professionals, who often mix socially with the corporate élite at private clubs and functions. Is it any wonder that tax practitioners become convinced of the need for more tax incentives for business, of the dangers of an overly progressive tax system, of the desirability of minimizing taxes on those whose business they would very much like to have?

There is nothing particularly evil in all this. But what is questionable is the extent to which Ottawa has chosen to ignore these connections, treating tax practitioners as independent experts rather than as the technical arm of the business and investment community. And so the Finance Department constantly consults with these experts, sometimes by setting up special committees, sometimes by commissioning studies. One practitioner reports that he often receives phone calls from Finance Department officials wanting his opinion on a tax change under consideration.

When Glenn Jenkins arrived as assistant deputy minister for tax policy in August 1981, he insisted on a $2 million annual budget to pay retainers and commissions to outside tax experts for consulting purposes. Indeed, at any given point there are always tax experts from private law and accounting firms on the payroll of Finance, or even serving right within the department on interchange programs.

Tax professionals move easily between the worlds of private practice, business and government. When Jenkins, an academic economist, left the department in 1984, the key job of supervising tax policy was handed to an accountant, David Weyman, from the major accounting firm of Peat Marwick.

When former finance minister Marc Lalonde retired from politics, he joined the prominent Montreal law firm Stikeman Elliott. Not long after, another Stikeman Elliott lawyer, Stanley Hartt, left the firm to become deputy finance minister.

But perhaps nobody's career illustrates the cosiness of the world of tax better than that of Mickey Cohen. Cohen has glided smoothly from private tax practice to the top ranks of government service and on to one of the most powerful jobs in business. Starting out as a tax lawyer in Toronto, Cohen went to Ottawa where he quickly became assistant deputy finance minister in charge of tax policy and, later, deputy finance minister. When he left the department in 1985, he was catapulted to the top ranks of the business world as president and chief executive officer of the Reichmanns' Olympia and York Enterprises Limited. In this latest incarnation, Cohen now sits alongside other CEOs on the Business Council on National Issues, an important lobby group, whose members he used to deal with as deputy minister.

A number of factors have led to even more intense co-operation between government and tax professionals in the last few years. The hostility which greeted the November 1981 budget had such a demoralizing impact on the department that anything associated with that budget became taboo. There was a feeling that lessons had been learned the hard way. And the most basic lesson, it seemed, was that Finance officials should not go concocting tax reforms without the guidance and blessing of Bay and St James streets. In the bloody aftermath of November 1981, consultation became a religion within the department.

Indeed, as business opposition to the 1981 budget grew, the department quickly set up a committee of outside practitioners to examine a controversial measure which restricted the tax benefits in corporate reorganizations. The committee, which included tax practitioners Tom McDonnell and William Strain, looked at the situation and concluded that the new rules were too tight. Shortly after, the new rules were withdrawn. Interestingly, what went on in that committee was almost an exact replay of what had happened nearly ten years earlier, after the government had tightened the tax benefits for corporate reorganizations in its 1971 tax reform package. In response to business protests, Ottawa had set up a committee of outside tax practitioners, including Bob Dart and Arthur Scace. After examining the situation, the committee had concluded that the rules should be loosened and they were.

Another committee set up in the aftermath of the 1981 budget looked at the controversial proposal to limit interest deductibility—the scheme used by the wealthy investor mentioned in Chapter One. That committee, which included leading tax practitioners David Timbrell and Ed Harris, concluded that the old, looser rule should be re-instated. It was.

With the help of those two committees, some of the key reforms in the 1981 budget were quietly rolled back. Yet the same budget included a significant drop in the top tax rate—a measure that clearly benefited high-income people. No committee was set up to look into that change.

The arrival of the Tory government in September 1984 only reinforced the trend towards greater consultation with tax practitioners. Suspicious of the bureaucracy after long years of Liberal administrations, the Tories were only too keen to consult more actively with the outside business and tax communities, whose members were more likely to share the philosophical bent of the new Tory team than the tax experts already within Finance.

When Michael Wilson took over the Finance portfolio, he brought in as his special advisor William Mackness, a vice-president of the Bank of Nova Scotia and a very conservative economist with a keen interest in tax matters. The idea was that Mackness, a representative of the business community, would serve within Finance temporarily. He was to be followed by an advisor from the ranks of labour. Without explanation, the program was discontinued after Mackness's departure.

More crucially, the government has relied extensively on tax experts from the private sector in its current tax reform. The department turned to individual practitioners as well as to the joint committee of the Canadian Bar Association and the Canadian Institute of Chartered Accountants to help it devise the reform package presented in the June 1987 white paper. In addition, the select group of thirty-six tax practitioners— including David Timbrell, William Strain, Robert Brown and Robert Lindsay—met regularly in Ottawa for the eight months prior to the release of the white paper. Their role was to advise the department on its reforms. Prior to that, a smaller group of six, including David Timbrell and H. Heward Stikeman, had held a number of meetings with Michael Wilson and deputy minister Stanley Hartt. This time, the government wasn't taking any chances.

It was a delicate problem that confronted the gathering of tax practitioners at the Windsor Hotel in Montreal. The several hundred lawyers, accountants and businessmen who gathered at the annual conference of the Canadian Tax Foundation in 1951 were clearly disgruntled by the government's failure to develop what they saw as a reasonable tax system. Only a few years earlier, there had been high hopes that, with the war now over, the government would reduce the heavy tax burden on business and high-income groups. With rates as high as 80 percent for those in the top income bracket, the best hope of avoiding a scalping from the tax authorities lay in receiving income in the form of capital gains, which were not taxed. But this created great uncertainty for investors, since they couldn't always count on convincing the national revenue department that profits from various business ventures constituted a capital gain rather than regular income.

Dissatisfied with the situation, a small group of lawyers, accountants and businessmen had come together in 1945 and organized the Canadian Tax Foundation. The foundation, which would be run by tax lawyers and accountants, was to operate as an impartial body of experts, dedicated to the cause of helping the public and the government understand and improve the tax system. From the outset, however, the foundation had a clear business orientation. One of its founders was J. Grant Glassco, a well-known accountant who later headed up the Brazilian Light and Power Company. The foundation was almost entirely dependent on corporate sponsorship. From the beginning, then, there was a sense of a community of interests among the businessmen and the tax practitioners at the foundation.

Central to the concerns of the tax foundation members was the government's unwillingness to do something about the uncertainty of the tax laws. They figured that a group of outside experts might have sufficient stature to be able to influence government policy. By 1947 the foundation had grown to almost one hundred members, and it helped prod the government into a significant overhaul of the tax laws in 1948. From the perspective of those at the foundation, there was much in the 1948 changes to be pleased with. Yet even the overhauled tax system failed to deal with the pesky question: when is a capital gain not a capital gain? As long as this question remained unanswered, there could be no certainty for investors.

But the question was somewhat delicate, as the men gathered at the Windsor Hotel in 1951 well knew. What they wanted was a clear legal definition of when a gain could be considered a capital gain and therefore qualify for the tax exemption. And they wanted that definition to be a broad one, allowing as many types of gains as possible to qualify for tax-free status. Profits made through land speculation, for instance, were always a worry, since the courts had generally barred them from enjoying the favourable tax treatment of other capital gains.

But the men at the Windsor Hotel clearly knew there was a risk involved. In pressing Ottawa to define more clearly what a capital gain was, they chanced having Ottawa define it very narrowly. And there was the nagging fear at the back of some minds at the tax conference: what if the issue somehow caught the interest of the public at large? And what if the public started demanding that some kind of tax be imposed on capital gains? In March 1950, Finance Minister Douglas Abbott had stated clearly in his budget speech to Parliament that the government had no intention of taxing capital gains. Welcome as that statement was, it still left many in the business and investment community nervous. Finance ministers come and go. What was wanted was a law that would spell out the finance minister's commitment.

With all this to consider, the 1951 tax conference became the scene of some animated discussions about political strategy. The participants divided into four groups of about sixty each for more intensive debate. The big question was how best to entrench the tax-free status of capital gains—through the courts or through changes in the law? For years tax practitioners had relied on the courts to define when something qualified as a capital gain and when it did not. And for years, the system had worked quite nicely. After all, many of the judges were former lawyers who shared their point of view. Even so, in recent years the courts seemed to be defining capital gains more and more narrowly, causing concern in the business community. Many of these cases could still be appealed to higher courts and most participants in the 1951 conference argued that the tax community should follow this avenue as far as possible before resorting to the more treacherous route of Parliament. "It is preferable to have the cases in this twilight area decided by the recognized specialists in tax matters who constitute the courts rather than by an inexperienced Parliament," said a summary of the proceedings.

Clearly what the tax practitioners feared was that the members of Parliament, who were generally "inexperienced" in the ways of the tax world, might just do something foolish like come up with a very narrow definition of capital gains. This fear was fuelled by the fact that the booming postwar economy was producing some huge capital gains, particularly in land speculation. If Parliament started looking into the whole business, things could slip beyond the control of the courts. The tax practitioners even acknowledged that the courts were operating without the authority of any law in defining capital gains as exempt from tax. As the summary pointed out: "the courts have been giving the taxpayer protection to which he has not been entitled."

The dangers, then, of letting Parliament muck around seemed very real to the tax practitioners at the Windsor Hotel. ". . . if the taxation of speculative gains is brought to the attention of Parliament for debate, and particularly if the matter gets into the public limelight, then it might very well become a political football," noted the summary of proceedings. "Our expanding economy will soon make the receipt of large speculative gains glaringly obvious; it would be politically impossible to define such a large segment of economic gain and make it tax-free. But if you leave matters in their present state of ambiguity, *Parliament and the public may accept the present exemption of many gains because they are not aware of them*" (italics added).

What the tax practitioners were saying, in the privacy of their meeting rooms at the Windsor Hotel, was really quite revealing. Capital gains would remain tax-free only because the public had no idea what was going on. And since the capital gains windfall was expected to get bigger in the coming years with the growth of speculative profits, the situation would only look worse in the future. So how did the tax practitioners—supposedly impartial experts seeking to educate the public about tax—feel about the public being left in the dark? Did anyone at the 1951 conference suggest that perhaps someone should *tell* the public what was going on? No. Discussion centred on how to keep the matter safely within the cosy world of tax. The courts, it was decided, were the answer.

This desire to keep the public in the dark still exists today. Tax practitioners bristled in 1984 when brokerage houses and financial institutions took out full-page newspaper advertisements for their services in setting up tax avoidance schemes involving family trusts. Tax lawyers and accountants had been setting up these family trusts for their well-to-do clients for more than two decades, but the schemes were not widely known and were only used by a fairly élite clientele. The brokerage houses and financial institutions clearly saw a chance to market family trusts to a broader range of taxpayers, including some upper-middle-income as well as upper-income families.

But the tax community was not at all pleased by the sudden spotlight these full-page ads placed on one of their best tax avoidance schemes. In his column in the *Financial Times* in November 1984, accountant Don Beach predicted that all this attention would surely prompt Ottawa to cut off the tax advantages of family trusts. Beach noted with disdain that this would not be the first time indiscretions had led to the elimination of an effective method of tax avoidance. Canadian investors at one point had been allowed to put their money into tax haven investment funds, where the income would accumulate tax-free. But Beach said that as the method became more popular and investment firms took to publishing information about such funds, the government felt compelled to shut them down.

This raises a question for Beach. If family trusts are to be eliminated, who should be held responsible for their unfortunate demise? Beach argues that "blame" should fall on those foolish enough to draw public attention to the neat little tax avoidance schemes the rich were enjoying. He insists that while there's nothing wrong with offering family trusts to more taxpayers, the financial institutions should have done so in a "more discreet" way. For Beach, the intimacy of the tax world must always be preserved. If the public at large becomes aware of the extent of the tax avoidance carried on by the rich, the government will have no choice but to tighten the rules. Beach's column calls for silence in the art of tax planning.

But if there is an unwritten code of silence on certain

subjects, there are other subjects on which tax practitioners want to be heard. Here the tax foundation has played a key role. Although it takes no stands and has steered clear of direct political involvement, it has influenced the shape of the tax system significantly by providing a forum for tax practitioners to vent their opinions and emphasize their concerns. Since these practitioners have tended to favour generous tax breaks for investors, this pro-investor point of view has been given a regular and prominent platform through foundation conferences and publications.

At the 1961 conference, for instance, there was intense criticism of the concept of a progressive income tax. The three speakers on the panel—a consultant, a tax practitioner and a vice-president of Imperial Oil—all spoke strongly against a progressive tax system, on the grounds that high tax rates destroyed the will to invest. No other point of view was expressed. H. Heward Stikeman, founding partner of Stikeman Elliott, called on the tax foundation to play a central role in dismantling the progressivity of the tax system.

A colourful member of the tax community who was known for his ingenious tax avoidance schemes, Stikeman argued that it was up to the members of the foundation to put together a plan for a new tax system. "This plan could be accepted by any government without danger," he said, "because it would be sponsored by this Foundation in keeping with its tradition of objectivity which has kept it free from special pleading of the importuning of pressure groups."

Stikeman certainly had an interesting notion of "objectivity." In outlining the goals for the new tax system he envisioned, his concern seemed to dwell entirely on improving the climate for investors, along the lines long sought by business. Indeed, as one of the founders of the tax foundation, he believed that the purpose of the organization was to provide a way for tax practitioners to sell the business point of view to government. "The thought was to organize a forum at which professionals, basically accountants and lawyers, could winnow out the good thoughts from their businessmen clients and sit down with the government in an organized and research-oriented manner and try and develop a better system," he said in a recent interview. Stikeman apparently sees no conflict between the foundation's stated aim of objectivity and this role as a promotor of a more business-oriented tax system.

If the tax foundation has cloaked itself in objectivity, the tax community has been less coy in the joint submissions made by the Canadian Bar Association and the Canadian Institute of Chartered Accountants. These submissions, which take stands on tax measures, are designed to allow the professional tax community to communicate its collective concerns about the tax system to the government. In fact, they are little more than an annual pitch for loosening up the tax laws in ways favourable to business and investors.

One important exception was the tax community's criticism of the capital gains exemption introduced by the Mulroney government in 1985. Both at the tax foundation meetings and in the 1987 joint submission of the Canada Bar Association and the Canadian Institute of Chartered Accountants, the tax community criticized the capital gains exemption for the complexity it added to the tax system. This is laudable since the exemption undoubtedly benefits members of the tax community and their clients.

It should be noted, however, that in the 1987 joint submission the lawyers and accountants argue that the exemption be withdrawn *in exchange for* a significant reduction in tax rates. By this they undoubtedly mean there should be lower tax rates for those in the upper income brackets who would be foregoing the benefits of the capital gains exemption. In fact, there should be no need to trade anything for the exemption. The exemption was introduced in 1985, opening up a new, unnecessary tax break for the rich. Why should the rich get something in exchange for giving it up, if it should never have been there in the first place?

In arguing for looser tax laws on investment and business

income, tax practitioners have insisted that they are not addressing policy questions but confining themselves instead to the technical aspects of tax. As a result, their constant pleading for looser tax laws favourable to business and investors is seen as just sorting out the mechanics. But the amount of tax relief given to business and investors *is* a policy question. It limits how much relief can be given to other members of society.

The mystique of technical expertise, however, is powerful. Businessmen and investors may appear self-serving when they call for greater tax breaks; but when technical experts endorse that call with a mound of technical argument, it is more difficult to dismiss. Indeed, it is more difficult to see what is at stake.

Perhaps this wouldn't be a problem if the government and the public were getting as much alternative technical advice from experts representing non-investors. If labour groups or consumer groups had tax experts to put forward their point of view, the process would be a little more balanced. As it stands now, however, the business community has almost all the technical expertise on its side. This allows business to not only mount impressive arguments but also to monopolize the technical debate, leaving the impression that its arguments are the only technically sound ones. No wonder business so often gets its way.

The tax community has done nothing to draw attention to this fundamental problem. The tax foundation has been called upon by government on two occasions to suggest ways to reform the tax-making process. On both occasions, in 1977 and 1982, a committee of tax practitioners set up by the foundation ignored this problem of unbalanced input. Instead, they concentrated on proposing reforms that would provide greater tax certainty for those making investment decisions. They also argued for greater advance consultation before tax changes are made. While both these reforms may be desirable, they do nothing to address the more basic problem. Since the only technical input tends to come from the business community, more consultation simply means more input from this already well-canvassed group. Surely the tax foundation should be grappling with how to achieve more meaningful input from the other 90 percent of the population.

Obviously, governments should listen more to those outside the business community. Michael Wilson has made a point of meeting with social welfare groups, giving them greater access to him than they often had to earlier finance ministers. But meeting with these groups is not the same as heeding their advice or having a meaningful discussion with them. Patrick Johnston, former head of the National Anti-Poverty Organization, said that in meetings with social welfare groups before the May 1985 budget, Wilson never mentioned his controversial plan to limit the indexation protection on social programs. "[That] suggestion had not seriously been discussed as an option and made a sham of the pre-budget consultation process," said Johnston. Even if more interchange programs were set up, allowing representatives of labour, welfare and consumer interests to act as inside advisors, there would be no guarantee of results. If the government doesn't want to listen, no amount of consultation or advising will have impact.

A more effective way to provide clout to these less entrenched groups would be to give them an effective vehicle for questioning the government's tax agenda. What is needed is a forum where tax experts, retained by groups outside the business and investment community, can publicly challenge tax legislation. One such forum could be the House of Commons finance committee, which reviews proposed changes in the tax laws.

But as the system currently stands, the finance committee receives technical advice from mostly one expert, who is appointed by the committee. This key expert, advising all MPs on the committee, is selected by the party in power, since it generally controls the committee. That advisory role is currently filled by accountant David Weyman. One would hardly expect Weyman to be a fierce critic of the tax policies of the Mulroney government. After all, he was in charge of formulating its tax policies not so long ago when he served as assistant deputy minister for tax policy under Wilson until July 1, 1986. In that capacity, he oversaw the early stages of corporate tax reform—part of the package he is now advising the Commons committee about. Indeed, Weyman makes no secret of the fact that he is strongly committed to the basic thrust of Wilson's reform. "I think it's a very important thing for Canada," he said in a recent interview. "I think particularly we have to get the tax rates down. . . . I feel strongly we need a new sales tax system." Only in the clubby world of tax could such connections raise no eyebrows.

It would be useful to restructure the committee's review process so that each party could retain its own technical advisor. And it would be particularly desirable if these technical advisors—either academic tax experts or tax practitioners —were allowed to participate in the public grilling of Finance Department officials and businessmen appearing before the committee. This would let the public see that the business community's vision of a technically sound tax system is only one option, and one that tends to benefit some members of society far more than others.

Of course it would be wrong to imply that the cosy world of tax consists mostly of wheeling and dealing and secret cocktail parties with the finance minister. At the heart of even the most glamorous tax career is, unavoidably, the Income Tax Act— hundreds of pages of stultifying complexity. The day-to-day life of the tax practitioner is dominated by such mind-boggling notions as capital cost allowances on non-owned property, amalgamations 88(1) winding-up and Part II tax, adjusted cost base of capital interest in a trust, to mention only a few.

For the majority of tax practitioners the appeal of tax, if one can call it that, lies not in shaping the country's political or economic agenda, but in working out the world's toughest crossword puzzle. "I don't think any lawyers in the country have as much fun as tax lawyers," says tax lawyer and commentator Arthur Drache. Of all the areas of law, tax is the most purely analytical. While corporate or real estate lawyers find themselves buried in mounds of paper, the tax lawyer just sits at his desk and *thinks*. Drache compares solving tax problems to playing chess. Tax practitioners often bring up the chess analogy. Says Tom McDonnell of McMillan, Binch: "It's like playing chess. There are a lot of pieces, and once you get beyond the standardized opening moves, the interaction of the pieces is unique. It very quickly takes you in, in this very seductive way."

"Seductive" might not be a word most people associate with tax. In many ways, the tax world appears to be the very antithesis of seduction and sexuality. It seems appropriate, somehow, that the repressed young man in the 1986 movie *Something Wild* turns out to be a Wall Street tax consultant who resists the lunchtime advances of an attractive young woman because he has to get back to the office to complete a tax deal known as a commodity straddle.

But, if tax practitioners seem to be some of the greyest men in the country, one is quickly struck by the presence of sexual imagery in the tax world. In the midst of depletion allowances and annuities, we find an assortment of tax techniques dressed up in sexual lingo—strips, straddles, bumps and grinds, in and outs, and rollovers. The Little Egypt Bump, the tax avoidance scheme used by the Reichmanns in their takeover of Gulf, was named after a legendary Chicago stripper. There's even a tax planning technique known as the rhythm method.

Perhaps it is during the long hours of just sitting there thinking that the tax practitioner's mind turns to sex. Or perhaps it is the fact that the tax world resembles the world's biggest men's locker room. (Despite the increasing number of women in law and accounting, few have made it beyond the junior levels in the tax field.) But for whatever reasons, sex seems to lurk just beneath the surface in the tax world. In the end, the seductress in *Something Wild* succeeds in luring the tax expert into her car and transforming him into a carnal beast, who puts the commodity straddle on hold while he wiles away the afternoon handcuffed to a motel room bed.

What tax practitioners don't seem to be interested in is the big picture. They are oriented to solving a puzzle, winning at a very complicated game. If the process can be compared to a game of chess, then the tax practitioner is locked into a fierce contest with the tax experts inside government. They make their move to compel his client to pay tax, then he responds by trying to avoid their trap, deftly moving his king around the board behind an array of pawns and rooks and bishops.

In the tax world, then, the ultimate achievement is to figure out ever more clever ways to avoid tax. Members of the tax team at the Toronto law firm Davies, Ward and Beck won prestige among their peers after they successfully adapted the Little Egypt Bump for the Gulf takeover, saving the Reichmanns $500 million. Those who invent innovative schemes are said to be "working on the frontiers"—a kind of tax equivalent of pioneer trail-blazing. McDonnell talks about the professional jealousy that causes tax lawyers to keep their best tax avoidance schemes to themselves. "If someone's got a good idea, they don't want to sell it out too soon," he said. What's at stake isn't just money, but pride.

The bad guy in the game is always some faceless bureaucrat at Revenue Canada whose power seems unlimited. He can probe relentlessly into the client's most intimate financial details, demand endless documentation, reject expenses that may seem perfectly justifiable. His decision can be appealed to the courts, but that is such a tiring, expensive, unpredictable route and it leaves the taxpayer once again in the hands of an austere outside authority. It's not surprising that the tax practitioner comes to see his clients as victims and quickly sheds any moral qualms about doing everything possible to protect them from the heavy, omnipotent hand of the state.

Pat Thorsteinsson knows this process well. A Vancouver tax lawyer who belongs to the small old guard of lawyers who were practising tax before it became popular in the 1970s, Thorsteinsson still does nothing but tax. In fact, he notes his firm of some two dozen lawyers is still "virginal," by which he means it has been unsullied by other areas of law: they all do nothing but tax. Sitting back in his office with an impressive view of Vancouver harbour, the silver-haired Thorsteinsson notes that tax lawyers have always bristled—"the hair on the back of your neck goes up"—at the way economists tend to approach tax problems by searching for solutions that are in the public interest. "I think the reason is this: the economist is seeking the greatest good for the greatest number of people. So he says: 'I've got a theory or an approach here that will happily deal with nine cases out of ten.' And the lawyer invariably says: 'yeah, but number ten is my client'."

An army of bright, sophisticated tax practitioners have over the years carved out ingenious methods for protecting the tenth guy, who usually happens to be rich. In fact, a great deal of the complexity in the tax legislation springs from the insistence on the part of tax lawyers that tax laws be spelled out in detail, so that their clients can be protected from the arbitrary taxing powers of the state. Prior to the 1948 overhaul of the tax system, the government had far more discretionary power over when to tax and when not to tax. Capital cost allowances were granted to corporations at the discretion of the minister of national revenue. This left the tax burden of corporations very much up to the whim of the government. In one case, a company called Pioneer Laundry of Windsor, Ontario, was allowed only a $1 capital cost deduction.

This arbitrariness led tax lawyers to fight for—and win— the right to have the government's taxing powers much more clearly defined in law. What this meant, ultimately, was extremely intricate laws designed to cover all possible situations. With a clearly defined set of rules, the lawyers and accountants had a definite chess board to play on. Then every time they made a move to open up some clever tax avoidance scheme, the government would make a counter-move to shut it off.

The number of situations that had to be defined and brought into the rules just continued to grow and grow, making the laws ever more complicated.

This move away from the discretionary power of the state had some other important implications. Now that there was a minutely codified system of laws, tax lawyers were given endless new opportunities to fight for more rights for their clients through the courts. As a result, a huge body of jurisprudence has grown up to protect the rights of the taxpayer, who almost always is the tenth guy—the rich one who can afford a lawyer in the first place.

For the tax practitioner, wrapped up in his defence of the tenth guy, it is easy to lose sight of the other nine, whose interests might not even appear to be involved. Saving the tenth guy some tax seems harmless, even desirable, as long as you don't have to think about the other nine who will pay more as a result. And in the world of tax, which revolves around corporate boardrooms, Bay Street law firms and private men's clubs, the other nine become invisible. You don't encounter a lot of teachers or nurses or blue collar workers in the dining room of the National Club or the boardroom of McMillan, Binch.

All this has left many tax practitioners indifferent to the impact of what they are doing. "The truth is, a good number of us never think about it," says Tom McDonnell, who probably does think about it.

Perhaps it is not the job of tax practitioners to think of broad social policy, to worry about the other nine. But, whether or not they are to blame, the tax practitioners' indifference creates a gross imbalance in the system. Essentially, we have a system where a phalanx of lawyers and accountants are fighting to defend the tax interests of the tenth guy before the government and the courts. Arrayed against this impressive team of professionals are the other nine people, who naively appear in court and before the government without a lawyer. They have only the Crown to defend their interests. But the

Crown is an ambivalent defender at best. Half the time, it throws in its hat with the other side, allowing the tax concessions in the interests of avoiding a fight. Without someone specifically representing their interests, it is easy for the other nine to get lost in the shuffle, especially in such an enormously complex field as tax.

The advantage of having a tax practitioner defending one's interests is magnified when tax practitioners, individually and as a group, are called in to actually help formulate tax laws. By managing to greatly increase their role in the tax formation process since 1981, tax practitioners have enhanced their ability to protect the rights of their clients. Douglas Sherbaniuk, director of the Canadian Tax Foundation, concedes that tax lawyers and accountants may retain their biases towards the investment community when they are advising the government. But this isn't a problem, Sherbaniuk argues, because government officials take this into consideration when they are assessing the advice of tax practitioners. Unfortunately, some Finance officials are not as skeptical of the objectivity of tax practitioners as even Sherbaniuk is. One high-ranking official in tax policy insisted that good tax practitioners, on whom the government relies for advice, are above that sort of bias and look at the subject dispassionately.

In recent years, tax practitioners have insinuated themselves into the process of making tax laws, to an extent that the early members of the tax foundation could only dream of. Since the 1948 tax changes, they have had enormous impact by convincing the courts that the tax laws entitle their clients to engage in a variety of tax avoidance practices that were clearly never envisioned by those who wrote the laws. Furthermore, they have dramatically increased their influence over those in government charged with the creation of tax policy. The outcry that went up from the business and tax community when Ottawa attempted tax reforms on two previous occasions—in 1969-71 and in November 1981—has left politicians and Finance officials shaken and fearful of trying any further reforms without the blessing of the tax community. Thus, deeply enmeshed in the creation of new tax legislation, the tax practitioners are able to screen out laws potentially harmful to their clients before they are even introduced.

At the same time, the tax community has been changing in ways that has probably made it more impervious to the interests of the rest of society. As the tax community has blossomed and flourished in the last few decades, and particularly in the last fifteen years, the sheer number of practitioners has multiplied. Whereas there were only a handful of people practising tax law in the late 1940s, there are about 10,000 full-time practitioners today. This has meant that more and more exceptionally bright experts have been poring through the tax laws, looking for angles and openings. It has also meant increased specialization. Almost no one at this point has a handle on all areas of tax law. As the laws have grown more complicated, tax lawyers and accountants have increasingly sought out little corners of the tax puzzle in which to specialize. This only increases their tendency not to look at the whole picture.

As the tax community has grown, it has also undergone subtle changes. For example, in the 50s and 60s, many tax practitioners had qualms about surplus stripping, the popular tax avoidance scheme of the time which allowed owners of private companies to remove corporate surpluses as tax-free capital gains. For years, there was tension within the tax community as some practitioners indulged in these schemes and others refused to, partly out of fear that the courts would strike them down and partly out of simple repugnance at their gimmicky, morally dubious quality. Some firms, such as Price Waterhouse, were known to disapprove of them, while others, such as the Montreal office of McDonald Currie, were actively pushing them. Stuart Thom, a respected tax lawyer with the Toronto firm Osler, Hoskin and Harcourt, publicly opposed them, while Stikeman, another titan of tax, became an avid promotor of the schemes. The flamboyant Stikeman, who still flies his own plane at the age of seventy-four, earned a reputation in some quarters as "the magician of tax." He once laid out an assortment of methods for surplus stripping at a tax foundation meeting. One of his favourites was the "two-tiered tandem sidestep."

In many ways, it was the tension between these two camps that led to the establishment of the Carter commission. It was hoped that a royal commission could sort out the different points of view and get a uniform system in place. But if the surplus stripping schemes caused some angst in the tax community in the 50s and 60s, the far more dubious schemes dreamt up under the SRTC program apparently caused little soul-searching twenty years later. One senior Toronto accountant, who started practising in the 50s, argues that the SRTCs—and the government's willingness to go along with the wild schemes devised by the tax community—have destroyed whatever vestige of moral restraint there was in the tax world.

"The fact that the government condoned or encouraged [the SRTC schemes] pushed the mores into a different phase," said the accountant. "When tax practitioners first dreamed up [the SRTC schemes], they expected to be turned down. But Finance said, 'OK boys'. That undermined and destroyed a lot of whatever reticence there was among professionals to do really far-out tax planning. Now almost anything goes. Lawyers and accountants are more adventurous since then and less reticent to come up with what you could call unnatural uses of the tax system."

The distinguished, softspoken accountant added: "It's now just a money game with complicated rules."

But if there were disputes in the 50s and 60s over some of the more adventurous tax avoidance schemes, there was general agreement in the tax community about what the tax system should look like. Stikeman's view of a system built around the needs of the investor was an article of faith among tax practitioners and the businessmen they served. Certainly nobody in the tax community talked about the need to increase the tax burden on rich investors in order to provide tax reductions for the poor and middle class—nobody, that is, until Kenneth Carter.

CHAPTER FIVE

How A Nice Bay Street Accountant Ended Up Hated By His Neighbours: The Tale Of Kenneth Carter

"It is probably fair, rational and even inevitable. And yet —somehow it's rape."
—Montreal accountant Herbert Spindler commenting on the report of the Carter Royal Commission on Taxation

A shrill note had crept into the voice of the aging dowager as her gray eyes focussed on the man sitting across the wide oak table. Her evident emotion, as the lines hardened on her face, cut through the intimate atmosphere in a way that was almost unthinkable at a genteel Rosedale dinner party. "I want you to know, Mr Carter, that I won't have any government scoundrel laying his filthy hands on my jewels," she said, clutching her heavy diamond-studded necklace against her throat as if to suggest it would not be removed while she was still breathing.

Across the table, Kenneth Carter put down his fork on the dessert plate in front of him and sat momentarily stunned in disbelief. His dignified demeanour appeared ready to crack. "Madam," he said slowly, his voice betraying uncharacteristic agitation, "this is a gross misrepresentation." Around the table, the easy chatter of almost a dozen other guests stopped abruptly. Carter's petite wife Marshall, who was wearing an elegant little necklace herself, turned slightly red.

123

For Kenneth Carter, his little outburst had been oddly satisfying. It was not normally his style to respond with anything but respect to a lady, let alone an elderly widow. But then a great many things had happened recently that were not at all normal and that had left him frustrated and upset. As the managing partner in the Toronto office of Montreal-based McDonald Currie and Company, one of the nation's most prominent accounting firms, Carter had long been accustomed to the deferential obedience of those around him. He was, after all, a brilliant man who commanded respect in others and was used to having things as he wanted them. He belonged to the city's most exclusive clubs, counted among his friends some of the nation's most powerful businessmen and was married to a stunning woman, whose delicate beauty and southern charm had long made him the envy of many of his male friends. And if life had seemed generous to Kenneth Carter, never had it been more so than in the past few years, when, in addition to heading up his accounting firm, he had held the prestigious post of chairman of the federal government's Royal Commission on Taxation.

After five years of seemingly endless deliberations, the commission had finally and with much fanfare presented its report to the public in February 1967. But in the seven months since then, Carter had, to his astonishment, found himself the target of a growing amount of abuse. What was particularly galling was that he was coming under attack from ill-informed critics. Most of them—and the bejewelled dowager undoubtedly fit into this category—had not read the massive commission report, a compellingly logical prescription for a new tax system that was already winning extraordinary praise from economists around the world. But the ignorance of his critics didn't prevent them from slamming his entire report on the basis of brief accounts they had read in the newspapers. So, after four and a half years of strenuous work, when he surely deserved to be at the pinnacle of his career, Carter found himself insulted and ridiculed, scorned by friends and colleagues.

But if Carter felt shocked by their disloyalty, they were equally shocked by his. What the dowager was expressing, perhaps a little rudely, was felt to varying degrees by the assortment of business and professional people around the table. It was almost a sense of betrayal.

Ironically, these were the types of people who had been clamouring for tax reform. And it was the pressure exerted by just these sorts of people that had led Prime Minister John Diefenbaker to finally appoint the royal commission in 1962, in the hope that this would satisfy the business community's growing anger over high taxes. When Carter had been selected to head up the commission, there was general agreement—shared by the guests at the dinner party—that he was just the man for the job, an expert who grasped the highly technical aspects of the tax system and who also understood the needs of the business and investment community.

But Carter had ended up recommending a sweeping set of changes that would disrupt everything and would hurt many of them personally. They had long been convinced that they were paying too much tax, that successive governments of both political stripes had been robbing from the rich to finance the nation's increasingly generous welfare system. Now Carter was telling members of the nation's business and financial élite that, contrary to their firmly held conviction that they were paying more than their share of tax, in fact they were paying less. It was the lower and middle classes who were paying too much. The system as it now stood, Carter said in his report, was "grossly unfair."

This was not at all what the nation's élite wanted to hear. At that dinner table, almost everyone would face hefty tax increases if Carter's new system were made law—increases of ten or twenty thousand dollars in some cases. There might even have been some who belonged to the select group of 633 taxpayers, identified in Carter's report, who were making over $300,000 a year. For this tiny group at the top, Carter's reform would mean an average tax increase that year of $67,000. As far as the dinner party guests were concerned, this wasn't tax reform, this was communism.

There was nothing in Carter's background that would have suggested he would produce such a radical document. Born into a well-to-do family in Montreal in 1906, Kenneth Carter grew up very much a part of the English upper crust of Westmount. Although he was an only child through much of his early life—his sister Marion wasn't born till he was ten— he was raised mostly by a governess, an English woman who spent twenty-four years with the family, raising both children. The Carters had a comfortable life typical of an upper middle class Westmount family. Ken's father, George Carter, owned a leather wholesale business that prospered selling to the city's shoe manufacturers. The family lived in a tastefully decorated home that was maintained by a couple of servants, leaving Ken's mother Alice free to socialize with her friends in the afternoon and indulge in her passion for bridge. Ken attended grade school at Lower Canada College and high school at Selwyn House, both private schools favoured by Montreal's English élite.

When Ken was in his late teens, his father grew tired of the leather business, sold it abruptly, bought an apple orchard near Hamilton, Ontario and moved the family there. Ken remained in Montreal, acquiring a fair bit of independence at an early age. A handsome and successful young man, he excelled at schoolwork and athletics and was popular with girls. He had a slight stutter, which became more pronounced when he was nervous, but he never let it undermine his self-confidence. He enrolled at McGill at the age of sixteen, graduating with a degree in commerce and finance at the age of twenty. Three years later he became a chartered accountant and soon joined the Quebec City office of McDonald Currie.

It was while Carter was living in Quebec City that he met his wife. At twenty-four he had already had a string of girlfriends and was constantly warding off inquiries from his parents about his intentions of marrying. But in his seemingly long experience, he had never met anyone like the girl he first encountered at a party one summer evening at the home of a Quebec City friend. She was vivacious and feminine and pretty, with her dark hair, smooth skin and flouncy pink dress. Still, he was introduced to her only briefly that evening and didn't expect to see her again. But the next morning, as he boarded the train to go home for a weekend visit with his family, he was surprised to discover the southern belle from the night before already seated in an Ontario-bound car on the same train.

Her name was Marshall Rebecca Murdoch and she was from Portsmouth, Virginia, as her heavy southern accent attested. She had been in Quebec City visiting a cousin and was now on her way to visit other relatives in Guelph. Carter enjoyed her beguiling, theatrical manner, her lilting voice and her slightly unbelievable tales of growing up in a former plantation house and being the great-grand-daughter of former U.S. chief justice John Marshall (a story he later discovered to be true). But when the train neared Burlington, where Carter knew his father would be waiting on the platform, he came up with a mischievous scheme. Why not present this lovely southern creature to his father, who was always trying to set him up with local girls. Marshall agreed and the two got off to meet his father during the stop at Burlington. Before the train was ready to depart, Carter's father had convinced her to stay the weekend.

Ken Carter's eventual marriage to Marshall in 1933 turned out to be a surprisingly successful union, even though she was as indifferent to reason and logic as he was committed to them. "My father drew a sharp line between truth and fiction," recalls their son Tim. "With my mother that line was blurred. And I think my father came to realize that, in her case, it really didn't matter." Both Ken and Marshall shared traditional attitudes about the roles of men and women, however. When Carter came home one evening to discover that his ten-year-old daughter Linton had wrestled her six-year-old brother to the ground, he gave instructions to his wife that his son was to be enrolled immediately in boxing classes. He was the very next day, and the classes continued for ten years.

Carter meanwhile had already established himself at McDonald Currie as an ambitious and competent young man. He had a forceful personality and showed definite signs of leadership. In 1935, when he was still only twenty-nine, he was made a partner and offered the challenging task of opening a Toronto office for the well-established Montreal firm. Carter keenly accepted, and soon found himself in Toronto, operating out of half a room he sublet from a lawyer.

The Toronto branch flourished with the growing prosperity of the city's financial scene in the 1940s, and Carter's prestige and importance grew with it. He was elected president of the Institute of Chartered Accountants of Ontario, served as chairman of the Canadian Tax Foundation and by the early 50s was overseeing more than twenty high-priced accountants at McDonald Currie's penthouse offices at King and Bay streets.

As the managing partner in the Toronto office, Carter became close to many of the firm's clients. Cultivating social relationships with them and their friends was a key part of maintaining and expanding the firm's clientele, and Carter excelled at the task. He thrived in the clubby old boys atmosphere of Bay Street and soon counted among his friends some of the most prominent Toronto businessmen: Bud McDougald, the powerful mogul of Argus Corporation; Wally McCutcheon, a major Argus shareholder and the company's hatchetman; E.P. Taylor, the flamboyant entrepreneur; J. Grant Glassco, head of Brazilian Light and Power (and a former classmate of Carter's from McGill); and Sydney Hermant, who controlled Imperial Optical Company.

Carter mixed easily with this crowd at the Toronto Club, perhaps the most exclusive of the downtown businessmen's clubs; the Toronto Golf Club, a preserve of old Toronto families; and the York Club, where businessmen would dress in black tie for evening stag parties. (Black tie was for informal gatherings of men only; white tie for more formal events where ladies were present, Carter explained to his son.) There were also private cocktail and dinner parties, where he and Marshall were an animated and dynamic presence.

It is hard to imagine a much more conservative and establishment way of life. Carter flaunted his taste for the traditional, indulging his penchant for 1930s-style double-breasted suits long after they went out of fashion. The Carters lived in Toronto's exclusive Forest Hill, in a custom-built two-storey house on the shady street behind Upper Canada College, the Toronto equivalent of Montreal's Lower Canada College where Carter himself had been educated. Like his own father, Carter believed in the value of a private school education. He sent his son to Upper Canada and his daughter to Bishop Strachan School, the private girls' school only a few blocks away. He also relied on a governess to raise his two children. Throughout most of their early years, Tim and Linton Carter ate dinner alone each night with their governess, only dining with their parents once a week at the Sunday meal after church.

It was probably Carter's close ties with members of the Toronto business establishment, particularly Wally McCutcheon, that led to his selection as head of the Royal Commission on Taxation. McCutcheon played a key role in convincing the Diefenbaker government to set up an inquiry into the tax system. Like many Toronto businessmen, McCutcheon had long been pushing for an overhaul of the tax system, with the goal of making it more favourable to business.

According to McCutcheon and others, such as Imperial Oil President W. O. Twaits and Simpson's chairman E. G. Burton, the chief problem was that taxes on businesses were too high. The business community had a tireless spokesman for this point of view in *Globe and Mail* editor Oakley Dalgleish, who used the paper's influential editorial space to call repeatedly for tax reforms to aid business. "The importance of taxation policy in the business climate does not need to be established in this day and age," Dalgleish wrote in a 1962 editorial. "Everybody should know by now that high and ill-designed taxes cripple business, slow down growth and reduce the revenues available to government. That is the ailment Canada has been suffering from for years, and the ailment that a Royal Commission can go far to cure."

By the spring of 1962, the chorus of complaints about high taxes from business and the *Globe* was commanding the attention of the prime minister. With only a year left in his government's mandate, Diefenbaker was planning to go to the polls later that spring and was worried that business support for the Tories appeared to be flagging. One way to win brownie points with some key businessmen—without really offending anyone else—would be to give in to their seemingly harmless demand for a royal commission into the tax system.

Furthermore, the appointment of a commission would almost guarantee enthusiastic editorial endorsement in the *Globe*. Despite the *Globe*'s long-standing support for the Tories, Dalgleish had been very critical of Diefenbaker that spring for following through on his earlier election promise of increasing welfare payments. "Dief wanted to placate Oakley," recalled the late Donald Fleming, who was finance minister at the time. The prime minister figured that a keen endorsement from the *Globe* would help win wavering business leaders over to the Tories. Promising to deliver on Dalgleish's constant demand, a royal commission on the tax system, seemed like a small price to pay.

If there was any doubt in Diefenbaker's mind, Wally McCutcheon likely banished it. Diefenbaker wanted to appoint McCutcheon to the Senate. The idea was that McCutcheon would then join the Tory cabinet, thereby adding a prominent businessman with extensive corporate connections. (McCutcheon sat on the boards of a host of major firms: St Lawrence Corporation, the National Life Assurance Company of Canada, Canadian Breweries Limited, British Columbia·Forest Products, the Canadian Imperial Bank of Commerce, Dominion Stores, Massey Ferguson and others.) But McCutcheon virtually made it a condition of his joining the cabinet that Dief appoint a royal commission on the tax system. And McCutcheon knew who he wanted for chairman: his good friend Kenneth Carter.

It was McCutcheon, by this time minister without portfolio in the re-elected Diefenbaker government, who placed the call to Carter in August 1962 to offer him the job of chairman of the Royal Commission on Taxation. Carter had been on a fishing trip in northern Quebec with his son and was just stopping over in Montreal for the night before heading home.

"Where the hell have you been?" McCutcheon bellowed good-naturedly into the phone. He had finally reached Carter at the Queen Elizabeth Hotel after three days of impatiently trying to locate him.

Carter readily accepted the offer, welcoming the honour and the challenging work. His good friend Grant Glassco had just headed up the Royal Commission on Government Organization, which seemed to have only enhanced his prestige among their peers. Tackling the tax system was a somewhat more daunting task, but that made it all the more exciting. Carter certainly knew what the problems were; or at least, what businessmen and investors perceived the problems to be.

Apart from the general complaint that taxes were simply too high, there were a series of problems that continued to vex the financial community. Basically they all arose out of the same phenomenon: that there was no tax on capital gains, that is, profits made from selling property, whether land or stock or jewellery. Of course, investors weren't complaining about that; they were delighted there was no capital gains tax. What frustrated them was that they could not receive *all* their income tax-free or, rather, that when they received income other than capital gains, they were hit by the high tax rates.

This created a bizarre situation for high-income investors. They could be paying marginal tax rates as high as 80 percent on salary income. At the same time they could be receiving thousands—or even millions—of dollars in capital gains on which they paid absolutely no tax. One clear result of this discrepancy was that, understandably, they were keen to receive as much of their income as possible in the form of capital gains. Tax practitioners had built thriving practices coming up with ingenious ways of disguising all sorts of income as capital gains. And the courts had spent a great deal of their time trying to figure out the distinction. The riddle "When is a capital gain not a capital gain?" became the most heavily litigated issue in Canadian tax law. And still no clear and reliable definition emerged.

All this drove high-income investors to distraction. The uncertainty of the situation was annoying and made business decisions difficult. Yet they could hardly afford to ignore the whole thing, since the potential tax savings were enormous.

While this trying situation had led to many agitated conversations over lunch at the Toronto Club, the National Club, the St James Club and wherever else businessmen gathered, it was having virtually no impact on the general public. Indeed, many middle class taxpayers probably didn't even know what a capital gain was, let alone that it wasn't taxed. One had to have investments or own a business to be troubled by the problem at all.

The tradition of not taxing capital gains had its origin in the British aristocracy's approach to taxation in the eighteenth century. Property, the theory went, was like a tree, and the income or rent or harvest from that property was like the fruit of the tree. The tree itself should not be taxed, since it was only the source of the income and had to be retained intact in order to produce next year's income. Only the annual yield or fruit of the tree, which could be consumed, should be taxed. While the tree-and-fruit metaphor may have had a certain logic, it also had some interesting implications. The tree almost always belonged to the land-owning class. The peasants who worked on the land only shared part of the fruit. By taxing the fruit and not the tree, Britain was sparing the aristocrats the burden of taxes on their huge estates, allowing them to pass their family properties untaxed from generation to generation.

Furthermore, the tree-and-fruit metaphor was not nearly as apt when applied to the modern financial world. In the twentieth century, the tree was often stock or land holdings that could be turned over quickly for staggering profits. Nevertheless, the British courts continued to find that profits from selling property were beyond the grasp of the tax authorities. This created increasingly demanding legal gymnastics as the learned judges tried to define when a profit fit into the "fruit" category and when it fell into the luckier, tax-free "tree" column.

After decades of wrestling with the problem, they came to the conclusion that the key factor was whether the individual had planned all along to sell his property for a profit or whether the profit had simply come as an unexpected surprise. If the profit had been planned all along, then the individual was really carrying on a business-like activity and should be taxed. If, on the other hand, he simply stumbled unwittingly across a windfall when he sold his property and discovered that it was worth a great deal more than he'd paid for it, then he was just fiddling around with his capital and should not be taxed. The courts seemed to be encouraging people to behave as absent-minded boneheads indifferent to profit, and indeed many of them did their best to imply that

that's exactly what they were. In some particularly imaginative cases, individuals tried to convince the courts that they had bought everything from several tons of sewer pipes to box cars full of raw lead—even a warehouse full of toilet paper—without any intention of selling them for a profit.

The Canadian courts swallowed whole the British courts' view on the taxation of capital gains and proceeded to perform fantastic legal acrobatics of their own. There was perhaps less excuse however in the case of the Canadian courts. The British courts had essentially been given a free hand by British law, which failed to specify whether a capital gain should fall into the tax net with other income. This presumably left the courts free to define the issue as they saw fit.

But Canadian tax law was quite explicit on the subject. Its definition of taxable income specifically included a profit or gain made from an "undertaking of any kind whatsoever"—a definition so broad that an untutored observer might well have assumed it covered everything, including capital gains. Indeed, similar language in the U.S. tax laws had led the courts there to include capital gains as income. But the Canadian judges saw things differently. Ignoring what appeared to be the plain meaning of the Canadian law, they turned instead to the precedents set by the bewigged judges of Britain's upper courts.

Following the British example, the Canadian courts ended up debating such esoteric issues as: what if the investor had not bought his property *primarily* with the intention of selling it for profit, but this had been his *secondary* intention. In a famous case known as *Regal Heights*, a Calgary developer claimed that he had bought a piece of real estate with the intention of building a shopping centre, and had only ended up selling it for a profit when the shopping centre plans fell through. Since his primary intention in buying the land was not to sell it for profit, he argued, the profits of the sale should be tax-free. The Supreme Court said no to this. But any fear among investors that the courts were toughening up was quickly put to rest in 1962 when the Supreme Court appeared to open the floodgates even wider than the British courts had done. In a case involving a firm called Irrigation Industries, the Supreme Court of Canada said, essentially, that a taxpayer should be able to buy and sell stock without paying tax on the profit, even if the taxpayer had intended all along to sell the stock for profit as soon as possible.

Throughout all these cases, the lawyers and judges implied that they were strictly concerned with legal concepts. They all seemed to assume that the only problem was how to distinguish between different forms of income. Nobody ever mentioned that what they were talking about also had enormous impact on a major political question—how much of a tax burden would be borne by the small group of well-to-do people who could afford to invest and earn capital gains in the first place. While the lawyers and judges went on at length about primary intentions and secondary intentions and what someone really intended to do with a warehouse full of toilet paper, nobody ever acknowledged what they were really deciding: are the rich going to be made to pay more tax?

Judges of course aren't supposed to make political decisions. But what about their original decision to ignore the plain wording of the Canadian law, which would have hurt the interests of investors, and follow instead the two-centuries-old British precedent, which helped investors. When the judges made that decision were they really indifferent to what it meant to Canadian investors?

In addition to the high-wire acts performed by investors as they tried to convince judges that profit was the last thing on their minds—or at least not the first—owners of private businesses were busy devising ways to use the capital gains exemption to strip profits out of their companies tax-free. Normally, the owner of a privately held company could take accumulated profits out of his firm by paying himself a dividend. But this way he would have to pay tax. (Dividend income was taxed at a lower rate than salary income, but it was still not tax-free like capital gains.) The owner could try to sell his company, thereby realizing a tax-free capital gain. But there were several problems with this, including finding a buyer.

So inventive tax practitioners developed schemes to strip out surpluses without selling the company. These schemes took a wide variety of forms, and new ones surfaced as soon as the revenue department figured out how to outlaw the existing ones.

Basically they all revolved around the same principle. If the owner received a dividend from his company he would have to pay tax. To avoid doing so, he sold his shares to a dummy company that he controlled. The dummy company actually had no money to buy his shares, but it could "owe" him the money. The real company could now safely pay out a dividend to the dummy company, since dividends can pass tax-free between corporations. The dummy company could then use the dividends it received to pay the owner the money it "owed" him for the shares. By inserting the dummy company between the owner and the real company, the owner was able to take advantage of the law that allowed corporations to receive dividends tax-free.

As we have seen, some conservative practitioners were alarmed by the questionable schemes and refused to offer them to their clients. But these hold-outs found themselves under increasing pressure as more and more of the adventurous schemes went unchallenged by the Revenue Department, which simply didn't have the will or the manpower to police the situation. H. Heward Stikeman, the prominent Montreal tax lawyer, insists that the Revenue Department deliberately turned a blind eye to the schemes and in some cases would even give advance approvals to taxpayers seeking confirmation that their schemes were legal. "The government really condoned it." Stikeman said that the late Walter Gordon, who as finance minister put an end to the schemes in his 1963 budget, had done them himself in his earlier days as an accountant. "Walter told me how to do it one day in the Rideau Club," said Stikeman. Certainly, it became increasingly difficult for conservative tax practitioners to convince clients that the schemes were bad tax planning when so many people seemed to be using them effectively to avoid tax.

By the early 1960s, surplus stripping had become an epidemic. At one tax foundation conference in the early 60s, hotshot lawyers and accountants were actively trying to peddle their wares to the audience, offering to arrange surplus stripping deals for a percentage of the surplus. "The competition was so fierce, the rates were dropping," recalls Robert Brown, a senior Price Waterhouse accountant. "A fellow would give you a card and it had a fee of 10 percent on the back and he'd cross that out and put in 8, and then he'd cross that out and put in 5. So many people were in the business."

All this led to a feeling that the situation was out of control and there was a strong need to clarify the tax laws. At numerous tax foundation sessions, businessmen and tax practitioners pondered at length what should be done. Some of the finest minds in the country applied themselves to the issue. Strangely, none of them came up with the incredibly simple solution eventually put forward by the Carter commission: abandon the tax-free status of capital gains and tax all income in the same manner. This way, it wouldn't matter how a surplus was removed from a company; the tax bill would be identical.

Of course, it was no accident that the experts at the tax foundation meetings never came up with this obvious solution. The last thing they wanted to see was a tax on capital gains, since this would greatly increase the taxes of their clients and often themselves. At the 1960 tax foundation conference, Vancouver chartered accountant Denham John Kelsey suggested an entirely different solution: why not remove the tax on dividend income as well, thereby eliminating any advantage in disguising dividend income as capital gains—also, incidentally, sparing the rich even more tax.

Kelsey's idea was greeted with some serious interest by the assembled businessmen and tax lawyers. Stanley Edwards, a lawyer with the Toronto firm Fraser Beatty, told the meeting that he found merit in the idea but doubted whether the government would have the "political courage" to implement it. He pointed out that the existing tax on dividends didn't raise much revenue, but "the complexities of the law prevent this fact from being readily apparent to the general public." If the tax on dividends were entirely removed, however, the light tax burden on shareholders might become obvious to the public. "The abolition of all taxes on dividends would be easily understood," Edwards told the tax conference. Better to hold onto the existing situation with a slumbering public than risk attracting attention with a run at an even bigger prize. A tax break in the hand is worth two in the bush.

This fear of the public arena, as we have seen, was strong among businessmen and tax practitioners. So, as they pondered how to bring a little more clarity into the tax laws, there was agreement on one point: there was no need to drag the public into all this.

What was needed was an inside job. What was needed was a royal commission—a commission made up of trusted tax experts, who could operate like a subcommittee of the Canadian Tax Foundation. That was exactly what McCutcheon had in mind when he sold Diefenbaker on the idea of a commission. It was a brilliant solution really. Businessmen and tax practitioners had every reason to believe their problems would soon be sorted out by a carefully selected group of experts committed to furthering the needs of investment capital.

They made only one miscalculation. They underestimated the integrity of Kenneth Carter.

Although the problems that had led to the establishment of the commission had been quite specific, the terms of reference for the commission were surprisingly broad. It was called upon essentially to undertake a thorough examination of the tax system. But this seems to have had less to do with the wishes of the Diefenbaker cabinet than with the pique of officials in the Finance Department, who apparently felt snubbed because the department hadn't been trusted to handle the tax reform exercise. By making the mandate almost impossibly broad, the Finance officials seemed to be dooming the commission to a hopeless, thankless task.

When the commissioners were announced by the Diefenbaker government in September 1962, there was certainly no cause for alarm in the investment community. In addition to Carter, whose establishment credentials were impeccable, the other five were all associated with business in one way or another. J. Harvey Perry, a personal friend of Carter's, was to play a key role on the commission, effectively serving as its deputy chairman. An economist by training, Perry was perhaps the most knowledgeable man in the country on tax matters. He had spent sixteen years in the Department of Finance and nine years as the director of the tax foundation. Now, as executive director of the Canadian Bankers' Association, Perry was involved with some of the most powerful and élitist investment institutions in the country.

Two other commissioners were closely associated with the world of business and investment. A. Emile Beauvais, a prominent Quebec City accountant and tax specialist, was executive vice-president of Donohue Brothers and served on the boards of two companies, including the Quebec Savings Bank. Donald Grant was a Halifax lawyer, director and general manager of the Nova Scotia Trust Company, vice-president of the Yarmouth Building and Loan Society, and a director of two other companies. These four would certainly bring a strong business point of view to the commission.

The remaining two commissioners deviated somewhat from the strong business orientation of the first four, and were apparently meant to represent the rest of Canadian society. But in its choice of these last two, the government revealed just how little outside input it wanted. Both of them, while ostensibly representing regional and special interests, had a connection to the business world. Charles Walls of Victoria had been a farmer and was executive director of the Canadian

Federation of Agriculture, but he had also studied business at Alberta College in Edmonton, worked as a departmental manager at a western wholesale firm and as a provincial manager for an insurance company. For a farmer, he had a fair bit of exposure to the corporate world.

The final commissioner was actually a woman, a strange phenomenon in the almost exclusively male preserve of taxation in the early 1960s. Eleanor Milne, or Mrs S. M. Milne, as she's referred to in the official documents, was a Winnipegger who had served as a treasurer of the National Council of Women. But she too had some familiarity with business and tax matters through her involvement in her husband's accounting practice. She was appointed over the objections of Carter, who had urged that there be no women on the commission, perhaps because he assumed all women were as illogical as his wife. Carter may well have communicated this attitude to Milne who, through almost five years of commission meetings, sat silently taking notes, rarely breathing a word.

Notably absent from this team was anyone with even the vaguest connections to labour, a group that might have been considered to have a substantially different and even conflicting interest in the structure of the tax system. The public was so used to leaving tax matters to business and the professionals that this absence of labour representatives never even became an issue.

In addition to Carter and Perry, there were two others who came to play crucial roles: Jack Stewart, the commission's legal counsel and Douglas Hartle, its research director. Stewart, a highly respected senior tax lawyer with the firm Fraser Beatty, had co-authored the leading textbook on corporate law and had worked with Carter setting up a tax news service. His private school background, Bay Street experience and conservative views were very similar to those of Carter, who valued his judgment highly.

Hartle was the only one of these four key individuals who was in no way connected to the corporate world. A thirty-six year-old economist who had worked for the federal Labour Department before teaching economics at the University of Toronto, Hartle didn't know the other three men. Also, he knew little about the tax system and was selected to be research director after his name was put forward by the chairman of his department. Furthermore, it was not at all clear at the outset that Hartle would play an important role on the commission. Carter had chosen Michael Pitfield as commission secretary, and Pitfield was keen to have Hartle report to the commissioners through him—a system which would have greatly augmented Pitfield's role and greatly diminished Hartle's. After considerable manoeuvring, Hartle won the right to report directly to the commissioners. (Pitfield left his post soon after this and went on to wield considerable power in Ottawa as clerk of the Privy Council.)

Hartle's victory in his struggle with Pitfield placed him in a pivotal position for influencing the direction of the commission. This was significant since, of the four key players, Hartle was the most well disposed towards ideas of progressive reform and social change. Even so, his interests were primarily academic, and he had no strong feelings about the fairness of the tax system. "I don't think I had any predetermined point of view," he recalls. "I didn't know enough about the thing to have some predetermined view."

And if Hartle didn't envisage any massive change at the outset, certainly none of the others did. Perry, the most knowledgeable about tax, felt there was little seriously wrong with the system as it stood and thought the business community was getting overly exercised. "Why all this ferment was going on was beyond me," he recalls. Carter himself believed the system was basically sound. "The chairman made it very clear early on," says Hartle, "that there wasn't anything terribly wrong with the tax system. It wasn't going to take a monstrous great task to straighten it out."

Two years later, the situation looked very different. After massive research by a professional staff of accountants, lawyers and economists that had swollen to 150, the commission had abandoned any notion that it was simply trying to resolve a limited set of problems. Indeed, it had launched an examination of the very fundamentals of the tax system.

As it delved deeper, it discovered some disturbing facts. The sharply progressive rate structure of the tax system, which appeared to be placing an onerous burden on upper income groups, was largely a mirage. The rates were indeed high, but the tax system had become so full of special deductions and exemptions that many high-income individuals were paying effective rates less than half those prescribed. This revelation came as something of a shock to the commissioners. "I think we were naively assuming the graduated income tax took care of the progressive element," says Perry. "We began to see it wasn't all that progressive." In fact, the commission had access to confidential government tax data which revealed that some wealthy people were paying no tax at all. Yet when the commission searched for explanations to justify the special treatment, it could find little that was convincing.

All this had led Carter to begin questioning some of his long-held assumptions. After years of identifying with Bay Street investors and businessmen, he was coming to regard many of their arguments on taxation as self-serving. At one of the commission's public hearings in Ottawa, Carter surprised a delegation from the Mining Association of Canada with skeptical questions. Members of the delegation were outlining the importance of the tax break that spared new mines from paying tax in their first three years of operation. But what did Canada get out of it, Carter wanted to know. "The people from the mining association just sat there dumbfounded and speechless that anyone would question them like that," said a member of the commission research staff who attended the hearing. "It was like a Monty Python skit, the mining association up there in a castle and Carter shooting arrows up at them."

Carter's growing skepticism was fuelled by a lively and critical book on the U.S. system that he read while on vacation in Bermuda. Written by tax expert Louis Eisenstein, *The Ideologies of Taxation* was an entertaining account of how all groups in society struggle to lift the tax burden from their own shoulders and place it on someone else's. In autocracies, the government group simply imposes taxes on the rest. But democracy makes the whole process far more complicated, Eisenstein argued.

> Those who have less property have more votes. Since heads are to be counted, they must first be persuaded. Reasons have to be given for the burdens that are variously proposed or approved. In time the contending reasons are skilfully elaborated into systems of belief or ideologies which are designed to induce the required acquiescence. Of course, if an ideology is to be effective, it must convey a vital sense of some immutable principle that rises majestically above partisan preferences.

Eisenstein's skepticism about the motives of those arguing for tax concessions struck a responsive chord in Carter, who had just sat through the commission's interminable public hearings where businessmen and their lawyers repeatedly cloaked self-interest in the guise of public spiritedness. Carter was so taken by Eisenstein that he wrote Hartle from Bermuda telling him about this "champion debunker" he had discovered. Carter urged Hartle to read Eisenstein's book—Hartle already had—and to get copies for all the commissioners.

Once Eisenstein's irreverent approach to taxation was adopted, many of the most basic tenets of the tax system seemed to collapse. For instance, a major study of capital gains by the commission's research staff concluded that there was no rational basis for exempting capital gains—a conclusion that would have been heresy to the crowd at the tax foundation conferences. The exemption gave special advantages to those who earned their money through capital over those who earned it through labour, even though both sources of income had the same effect of enriching the individual receiving it. A taxpayer receiving a dollar of salaried income was no better off than someone receiving a dollar of capital gains, and yet one was subject to tax and the other was not. What's more, since capital was concentrated largely in the hands of high-income groups, the system was biased in their favour.

But the capital gains exemption was more than just unfair; it was illogical and ineffective, according to the study. It found no evidence that the exemption achieved its apparent goal—to increase savings and investment. Indeed, the study found little to back up the contention that tax reductions for investors increased the incentive to invest. The tax on dividends, for instance, had been lowered in 1949 and again in 1953, but there had been no significant change in investment levels. Besides, it was institutions, not individuals, which were the important investors in Canadian equity markets. The study concluded that sparing individuals tax on capital gains would make, at best, only a marginal difference to the economy.

In fact, the study set out an argument that was later to become the essence of the Carter philosophy: for tax purposes, it doesn't matter a damn how someone comes to receive a dollar. Whether it's in capital gains, salary, dividends, an inheritance or lottery winnings, it all ends up the same in the taxpayer's wallet. What matters is how much you receive and therefore how much richer you are. Or, as Carter himself was later to say: "A buck is a buck is a buck."

But the commissioners were by no means immediately won over to the concept that all income should be treated in the same way. Two of them—Walls and Beauvais—resisted strongly. And so, initially, did Carter, Perry and Stewart, the three kingpins of the commission. All three were keenly aware of the havoc they would create on Bay Street if they were to recommend an end to the capital gains exemptions. Besides, it was the only system the three men had ever known, and it was impossible to be sure what would happen if it were altered. Hartle, on the other hand, had by this point become a devout convert to the concept of removing the special tax treatment of capital gains. He kept putting the idea forward to the commissioners in various forms and, when he sensed resistance, withdrawing his proposals and redrafting them into a more acceptable form.

The deadlock continued for months. Carter and his two trusted allies, Perry and Stewart, became increasingly struck by the logic of the comprehensive income concept, but seemed unwilling to fully accept it and its consequences. Finally, on September 9, 1964, there was a breakthrough. Jack Stewart, the most conservative and business-oriented of the three, announced to the other commissioners that he had changed his mind. Capital gains, he said, should be taxed. Citing evidence from commission studies prepared by Geoffrey Conway, John G. Smith and Douglas Sherbaniuk, he argued that British judges, who had originated the tradition of exempting capital gains, had done so to protect their own rights as landholders. He pointed out that the United States, which had no similar tradition of landed aristocracy, made no legal distinction between capital gains and other income.

While Stewart's conclusion was revolutionary in terms of the tax system, he had not reached it from any commitment to social change. On the contrary, his dislike of anything smacking of radicalism had made it extremely difficult for him to reverse his position. But he was, above all else, a logical man, and he had been swayed when he came to fully appreciate the lack of logical consistency in the way the courts were treating capital gains.

Stewart's conversion was crucial to winning over Carter and Perry. Although it was a big jump for all of them, the stakes were highest for Carter, who, as chairman, would bear the ultimate responsibility for the commission's recommendations.

Carter wrestled with the decision. He certainly felt that the commissioners had a responsibility to rise above the narrow self-interest that dominated Bay Street and design a tax system that would be fairer and also better for the economy. Hartle encouraged this line of argument. In private conversations with Carter, Hartle repeatedly pointed out that the commission was in a position to make a unique and lasting contribution.

Although public finance economists in the United States had developed theories about the advantages of a tax system that treated all income in the same way, no one had actually devised such a system. It was a massive task, and it risked trampling on so many powerful private interests that it was unlikely any government would ever undertake it. The Carter commission, however, was in a position to do so, Hartle argued. With its large research staff and its isolation from political interference, the commission alone had the opportunity to make such a major contribution to public finance—to the country really. The thought of going down in history as the father of a brilliant new tax system was not without appeal for Carter.

But he was not oblivious to the personal risks. He knew how intense feelings were about the tax system among his business friends at the Toronto Club, not to mention his firm's corporate clients. After nearly thirty years, he had built up McDonald Currie's Toronto office from a one-room operation to a flourishing firm of seventy-five accountants, handling the affairs of some of the nation's major companies. And he had done so largely through hard work and a personal rapport with his clients. To place this in jeopardy was not something Carter would do lightly.

But then, his clients and colleagues were all rational men. They were men like himself, like Harvey Perry, like Jack Stewart. They just hadn't had the same opportunity for close study of the tax system. Once they saw the arguments laid out boldly and clearly in front of them—with the endorsement of people they respected—they would come to the same conclusions. If someone as conservative as Jack Stewart had so fundamentally changed his mind, then any intelligent person on Bay Street would too.

For all Carter's cautious conservatism, he was also a bit of a maverick. From the start, he had approached the commission's work with an almost zealous enthusiasm, firm in the belief that he had been given a free hand to design the best possible tax system. In the end, he decided to go with what he believed in his gut to be right, and let the chips fall where they may. Perry, the country's foremost authority on the tax system, was in agreement too. A huge hurdle had been cleared. All that was left now was to redesign the entire tax system from top to bottom.

For the next two and a half years, the commission and its staff worked at a frenzied pace. The Liberal government of Lester Pearson had replaced Diefenbaker's Tories, and the Liberals were anxious to have the secretive and long-deliberating commission deliver its report. With intense pressure to meet a continuing series of deadlines, the commission and its key staff members worked day and night. To get one particularly difficult chapter done, Harvey Perry locked himself in a room in Ottawa's Chateau Laurier Hotel and didn't emerge for a week, with instructions to room service to leave meals outside his door.

With the comprehensive income base as its guiding principle, the commission chopped away at the endless tangle of special privileges that permeated the tax system. All the special tax rates that had applied to different forms of income—from capital gains to dividends to inheritances—were to be eliminated, greatly streamlining and simplifying the system. All income received by an individual was to be collected into one big pool for tax purposes. This meant some dramatic changes. In addition to the sudden full taxation of capital gains, taxes would no longer be applied on the estates of the deceased. Instead, an inheritance would count as income in the hands of the person receiving it. (The recipient had the option of averaging any large amount over a period of five years.)

On the corporate side, the implications of the comprehensive tax base were equally staggering. The commission discovered just how massively the tax system had favoured certain industries, notably insurance, mining, and oil and gas. Through a few key deductions, including a three-year tax holiday for new mines and incredibly generous write-off and depletion provisions, the resource industries had been able to reduce their effective tax burden to 20 percent. Corporations outside the resource sector had an average effective tax rate of 42 percent, more than double. Furthermore, the advantages offered by the special tax provisions were highly skewed towards the bigger companies. The commission discovered that four large mining companies alone had saved $250 million under the three-year tax holiday.

The insurance industry had shown itself to be even more adept at avoiding tax. It had managed to convince successive governments that insurance was so vital to Canadians that it required special tax concessions more generous than those in any other industry. Despite assets of more than $11 billion, Canada's insurance firms paid only $1.9 million in tax in 1964.

Under the reforms advocated by the commission, these industries in particular faced much heavier tax loads. The insurance industry would immediately have had to pay an extra $73 million in taxes. The mining industry would have been forced to pay twice as much tax; the oil and gas industry, about 40 percent more. These higher taxes on the resource sector would have hit hardest against the largest companies which had been most able to take advantage of the special concessions. Eighty percent of the higher taxes, for instance, would have fallen on only fifteen large oil and mining companies.

The extra money collected from these and other industries, as well as additional funds collected through a tax on capital gains, meant the government would be collecting a great deal more money. The commission proposed the extra funds be used for a general lowering of the tax rates. The biggest reductions were to be at the upper end of the scale. For instance, the top tax rate (applicable only to incomes above $400,000) would drop from 80 percent to 50 percent—a considerable drop. Yet most high-income individuals would still see their tax bills increase because now all of their income would be taxed, instead of just a part of it—or none of it.

Under the system devised by the Carter commission, about 26,000 high-income taxpayers would see their taxes rise substantially. For the 10,790 high-income families with annual incomes ranging between $50,000 and $75,000—and this was definitely high-income in the 1960s—the average increase would be $2,829. The 3,113 families earning princely incomes of between $100,000 and $150,000, would face an average tax increase of $10,671. And for the chosen few, the 633 Canadians with incomes above $300,000, there would be an average extra tax bill of $67,549.

But almost half the population would benefit under Carter's scheme. For 3.1 million families, income taxes would decline by between $20 to $30. The amounts sound small by today's standards, but incomes then were much smaller. Close to 5 million Canadian households, by far the bulk of taxpayers, had incomes under $10,000, and many earned less than $2,000. A drop of $20 to $30 in taxes would reduce the tax bills of many low-income families substantially and provide enough of a saving to buy a new pair of boots or a bicycle for a child.

After four and a half years, the commission finally released its report in February 1967. Carter and Perry had failed to convince fellow commissioners Beauvais and Grant to accept the comprehensive income concept. (Grant, an avid hobby farmer, was apparently annoyed that the new system would eliminate special tax deductions enjoyed by hobby farmers.) Both Beauvais and Grant wrote dissenting minority reports. However, Walls, the farm representative, and Milne, who represented the interests of women, went along with Carter and Perry, giving them a majority.

The report's thirty-six chapters spanned six volumes. But the commissioners and staff had striven to write it in a

readable style. They knew it was crucial that it be under-
standable to the ordinary person, who stood to benefit. So
they decided to pull no punches. They stated their conclusion
bluntly at the outset: "The present system does not afford fair
treatment for all Canadians."

With his neck on the block, a tired but proud Kenneth
Carter waited for the country to react.

The initial response was mixed. Newspapers across the coun-
try reported the findings of the commission prominently,
picking up on the themes of fairness stressed in the report.
The Vancouver *Sun's* headline was typical: "Tax-the-Works
Report Would Aid Mr. Average—No More Dodges Under
New Plan." There was also a sub-heading, "While Lower
Wage Canadians Gain—U.S. Investors and Oil Industry to
Pay." In Montreal, *La Presse* spoke of Carter's plan to reduce
injustices and give the wage-earner a better deal. *The Toronto
Star* was enthusiastic, as were the *Peterborough Examiner* and
The Windsor Star, which praised the commission as "coura-
geous" and called on the government to show similar courage.
The St John's *Evening Telegram* said the proposals were so
revolutionary they would never make it over the political
obstacles.

There was plenty of negative coverage as well. *The Globe
and Mail* and *The Hamilton Spectator* emphasized the dissenting minority reports. The *Medicine Hat News* opposed the
taxation of capital gains, as did the Fredericton *Daily Gleaner*.
The *Winnipeg Free Press* called the resource industry taxes
"draconian," while the Winnipeg *Tribune* said the proposals
amounted to an attack on the sanctity of the home, property
rights and the rights of the individual. The Port Hope *Guide*
said the report was a threat to Canada as a "free society," and
the *Northern Miner* described Carter's "share the wealth philosophy" as an indication of how far Canada "had wandered
along the road to socialism."

Although the overall reaction of the business community was fairly moderate at first—there were proposals in the report that promised to help some firms and middle-income investors —the resource sector was quick off the mark in its attack and helped generate a sense of panic among businessmen. Day after day, newspapers ran "news" stories quoting mining and oil company officials predicting dire consequences if the report was enacted. Only two months after the report's release, the *Globe* ran a three-inch banner headline reporting Noranda's decision not to proceed with the $90 million development of two British Columbia copper mines—all because of the Carter report. Stelco warned that its $100 million investment program might be in jeopardy. W. O. Twaits, president of Imperial Oil, used the company's annual shareholders meeting in April 1967 to float similar vague threats and paint the commissioners as Moscow sympathizers: "The assumption of a fully mobile pool of capital committed to Canada, which could be shifted readily from one industry to another by tax policy, may be a perfectly practical assumption in the Soviet Union but certainly not where the investor has any choice of opportunity."

The resource industry and, increasingly, the business and investment community in general, was outraged by the egalitarian thrust of the report. "It is essentially a redistributionist, egalitarian argument and I am most surprised that Canadians are expected to swallow it," said A. G. Davies, executive director of Rio Tinto Zinc Corporation. Herbert Spindler, a chartered accountant from the Montreal office of Carter's own firm, perhaps expressed the feelings of many tax practitioners who saw the brilliance of the document but who somehow, in their guts, didn't like it. "It is probably fair, rational and even inevitable," said Spindler. "And yet—somehow it's rape."

Some of them certainly responded as if they'd been assaulted. "It wasn't so much the reaction [that surprised me]," recalls Harvey Perry. "It was the violence and virulence of it."

Perry, a courtly gentleman, was asked by one angry opponent at a meeting if he would like to step outside and settle things directly. Doug Hartle got a taste of the anger when he attended a two-day seminar for insurance executives at Queen's University and found himself under constant attack from the two hundred participants, who even yelled at him over the sound of the water as he took a shower. John Bossons, an economist on the commission's research staff, tried to defend the report to a meeting of western oil executives in Banff, only to find himself also hounded right into the washroom. Bossons, who felt he had striven in his research to be dispassionate and objective, was astounded by how the oil executives took it personally. "They seemed to be assuming the only reason you could have done this was because deep down you disliked them or you were anti-West or anti-horse," he said. "'What have you got against oil?' they'd ask. 'Don't you use it in your car?'"

The pressure wasn't just from hotheads looking for a scrap; some came from those at the highest levels. Jack Stewart returned to his law practice to encounter enormous hostility from major clients; he died of a heart attack soon after. And Harvey Perry was almost driven out of his job as executive director of the Canadian Bankers' Association by Neil McKinnon, chairman of the Canadian Imperial Bank of Commerce. McKinnon tried to get a meeting of the bankers' association council to fire Perry. In the end, the bankers decided not to.

For Carter, the growing hostility of the business and investment community was devastating. A cartoon in the *Globe* nicely captured the way Carter was rejected by his own friends and neighbours. The cartoon depicts a wealthy man, seated at breakfast, reading a newspaper account of the recommendations of the Carter commission. "I'm sure it's not the nice Kenneth Carter we know," the man says to his wife, seated at the far end of a long dining-room table. Carter even felt compelled to warn his son Tim, who was working in public relations for Dominion Stores, that Bud McDougald,

Dominion's ultimate owner and a personal friend of Carter's, was furious about the report.

Carter made only a few public comments about the report before largely disappearing from public view. Even if he'd had the inclination to defend it publicly against the burgeoning attacks, his health wouldn't allow it. He developed lung cancer shortly after the report's release. As he lay in his hospital bed, his close friend and colleague Harvey Perry lashed out at Carter's detractors in an emotional speech at a tax foundation conference in November 1967. Perry, who had been invited to speak for twenty minutes, spoke with animation for an hour and a half, chastising the audience for "an undertone of unwillingness to accept the need for any change at all. There are forces at work here—both economic and sociological—that I have personally found most disturbing." Perry went on to say that his experiences since the release of the report had led him to "be more concerned about the future of my country than about the future of the report."

In May 1969, Carter died of lung cancer. His son was surprised by the flood of telegrams of condolences from labour unions; his father had never had any connection with the labour movement. Carter had died a broken, bitterly disappointed man, clinging to the impeccable logic of what he had done, unable to fully comprehend why he had become a pariah to his own people.

He left the legacy of his report, which provided a far-reaching blueprint for a redistribution of wealth in Canada—and a nagging headache for a Liberal government faced with an increasingly hostile business community.

CHAPTER SIX
Running Scared: How Ottawa Handled Tax Reform

"Given the complexity and the political sensitivity of the task; the wonder about tax reform is, as Dr. Johnson said with respect to a dog dancing on its hind legs, that it can be done at all rather than whether it can be done well."
—**Robert D. Brown, vice-chairman, Price Waterhouse, Toronto**

Try as he might, Robert Bryce, the crafty deputy minister of finance, could not get Lester Pearson to budge. The cost was so small, in terms of Ottawa's multi-billion dollar spending, that it hardly seemed worthy of a conversation between the prime minister and his top Finance official. But Pearson was adamant. There was no way he would spend $50,000 to have the Carter report published. "I've got better things to do with $50,000," the prime minister told Bryce, who, as one of the most powerful of Ottawa's mandarins, was used to getting his way.

It seemed ridiculous to Bryce that the report, soon to be the subject of a graduate seminar at Harvard Law School, had only been released on typed, mimeographed pages, looking like the first draft of a thesis. That had been because of deadline pressures, and a notice on the report's cover had said that it would soon be published for general distribution. Now Pearson was saying that it would never be published. The damn thing had caused enough trouble already. Why fan the fury of the business community by making the annoying manifesto available to every university student in the country? Less than a year after the report's release, Harvard had to scramble to come up with one copy, to be shared among 25 students, of a government-financed document that had become an underground classic.

Indeed, as the business community hurled its salvos at the Carter report and the spectre of a fairer tax system, the Pearson government's basic response was to lie low. The issue was clearly a volatile one. The interests of the vast majority of voters appeared to be pitted against those of the powerful few —hardly the kind of situation where a government likes to wade in and take sides. Certainly there was no great incentive to rush ahead and implement the thing. With the business community dead against it, implementation would make governing the country difficult and raising funds for the Liberal party even more so.

On the other hand, it wasn't clear that tax reform could be quietly set aside. Although there was no popular cry to put the report's recommendations into effect, the message had more or less reached the public that Carter's reforms would help the little guy and hurt the big guy. Governments, particularly minority ones, don't shelve proposed reforms like that without pausing a little.

The government's quandary over what to do with the Carter report wasn't due to lack of preparation. In fact, it had long been gearing up for its response—or lack of response. Word had leaked out during the commission's long hibernation that the recommendations were going to be sweeping. To prepare itself for the anticipated shock, the Finance Department had set up its own team to investigate what the Carter team was up to. Headed by Jim Brown, an extremely bright young recruit from the Toronto accounting firm of Peat Marwick, the Finance team had already spent two years going over the commission's work in detail, on a strictly confidential basis.

Much as the government wanted to stay out of the tax reform fray, it found itself increasingly on the hot seat. Once the report was released, the government was quickly inundated with briefs and personal presentations from angered business leaders threatening to take their capital elsewhere.

The most vehement attacks continued to come from the mining and oil and gas companies. Carter had recommended an immediate end to depletion allowances—enormously generous tax breaks that permitted these companies, after all their other tax deductions, to further reduce their taxable incomes by 33 percent. These depletion allowances were particularly valued by the oil and mining giants, including Falconbridge, Denison Mines, Texaco, the British American Oil Company and Imperial Oil. Carter noted that roughly 85 percent of depletion allowances were enjoyed by only five mining companies and three oil companies in 1964. The U.S. multinational oil companies, led by Imperial Oil president W. O. Twaits, took a particular interest in fighting the removal of the depletion allowances. There were similar rumblings about clamping down on depletion allowances in the United States, and the last thing the U.S. oil companies wanted was a precedent for such action north of the border.

The western provincial governments joined in the chorus of objections, backing up the claims of the industries in their regions and portraying the Carter report as another federal assault on the West. Saskatchewan Premier Ross Thatcher claimed that uncertainty about tax reform was holding up two potash complexes in the province. And on top of the symphony of objections coming from outside the government, business had a key friend right at the cabinet table in Finance Minister Mitchell Sharp.

It took barely three months for the government to begin hammering the nails into the coffin of the Carter report. On May 11, 1967, Sharp told the mining industry that the three-year tax holiday for new mines, which Carter wanted to abolish, would be continued for at least the next seven years. The next day, Noranda responded to Sharp's generous concession by announcing it would proceed after all with plans for a $60 million copper mine at Penticton, British Columbia

—one of the two mines it had ceremoniously cancelled less than two weeks earlier.

How much of this was posturing is difficult to know. Many companies were threatening to withdraw investment. But were the threats real or were they just bargaining chips to force Ottawa to back down? Ottawa was clearly reluctant to risk calling their bluff. In one revealing episode, however, R.V. Markham, the vice-president of Anvil Mining Corporation, said that the Carter recommendations were not that bad and even echoed the commission's own suggestion that a more neutral tax system might eventually help business. "We made a study of the effects of the Carter commission recommendations on taxation. In the short term we found that if enacted they would reduce our profit," Markham was quoted in the *Globe*. "But in the long term we found they would not make any difference. In fact we would be better off over a period of ten years." Markham even pointed out that Anvil's decision to proceed with plans for a $56 million open-pit mine in the Yukon had nothing to do with Mitchell Sharp's assurances that the three-year tax holiday for mines would be extended.

If this suggested there was at least a chink in the wall of business opposition, that impression was quickly corrected. A week after Markham's comments were reported, he was forced to publicly disown them. His boss, Anvil president Kenneth Lieber, issued a statement from the company's head office in Los Angeles saying that his vice-president's comments were "totally erroneous and completely the reverse of the truth of the matter." Lieber insisted that Anvil had only decided to proceed with the Yukon mine development after assurances from the Canadian government that the three-year tax holiday for mines would continue. The chastened vice-president supported his boss.

Meanwhile, the barrage of opposition continued unabated. When Sharp invited industry to respond to the report, he was deluged with briefs. Some nine hundred briefs flooded into the Finance Department; more than a hundred from the oil industry alone. The three-volume attack prepared by Inco weighed about as much as a case of beer, one politician noted. Nine months after the release of the report, Sharp distanced the government further from the Carter reform package. While the report was a "monumental" document, Sharp said, the government would content itself with reforming the existing tax system, not opting for Carter's more radical solutions.

Almost five years in the making, the report was no longer to be a blueprint for reform. It had been relegated to the role of a background study, to be considered along with the hundreds of briefs from corporations and their associations. The business community had shown its muscle; the government had shown its willingness to retreat; the public had remained largely unaware of what was happening. The stage was set for tax reform, Ottawa-style.

The sweeping electoral victory of Pierre Trudeau in June 1968 brought a new Liberal team to power. Trudeau had the reputation of being somewhat left of centre, although he had little real interest in economic issues. The new prime minister did, however, replace Sharp with Edgar Benson, a chartered accountant from Kingston, Ontario, who was also considered left-leaning. As minister of national revenue, Benson had taken steps to clamp down on tax avoidance schemes. He had taught taxation in commerce courses at Queen's University and came into his new job with a healthy respect for the Carter report.

Despite the intensity of the emotions tax reform had generated in the business community, the rest of the new Liberal cabinet was neither particularly well-informed nor interested in the issue. A secret cabinet committee, which included Benson, Treasury Board chairman Bud Drury, Transport Minister Don Jamieson and Postmaster General Eric Kierans, met every Wednesday night from eight till midnight supposedly to oversee the tax reform process. But with little expertise among the ministers, the sessions often amounted to not much more than lessons in taxation conducted by the Finance Department staff, who simply informed the ministers about the department's plans. "I can't think of any contribution of that committee," recalls Kierans. "I didn't realize it at the time, but the government didn't want anything to come out of it." Kierans, an economist by training with a strong interest in the tax system, was particularly irked that cabinet ministers were handed Finance Department briefing papers at the beginning of each session but were required to hand them back before they went home, like school children who couldn't be trusted.

Kierans says that when tax reform issues came up in cabinet, there was little response around the table. Most ministers stuck to their own portfolios and rarely spoke about something outside their field. "That's the way the cabinet operated. It left everything up to the bureaucrats."

Indeed, the real direction of the new tax reform package was being decided inside Finance. Jim Brown, the Bay Street chartered accountant who had headed the Finance team investigating the Carter report, stayed on to direct the daunting task of finding some common ground between Carter's solutions and those of the business community. The result, a government white paper released by Benson in November 1969, pleased no one, enraged many and landed the government right in the centre of the storm over tax reform.

The white paper proposals partially adopted the central Carter concept of a comprehensive income base, under which special exemptions are eliminated and all income is taxed in the same way. But by only incorporating part of this approach and leaving some exemptions in place, the white paper was unable to offer the benefits of the comprehensive tax base—namely, the ability to raise more revenue and therefore lower the basic income tax rates. So while the Carter commission had offered lower taxes for the bulk of voters, the white paper could not; indeed, many middle-income earners would pay more under the new proposals. The white paper was a no-win compromise. It removed many exemptions that business and wealthy individuals had grown attached to over the years, but it left in place enough exemptions that there was insufficient revenue to permit a reduction in the tax burden on the ordinary citizen.

This kind of half-and-half approach permeated the white paper, making it an odd hodge-podge that one minute appeared to embrace the Carter philosophy and the next, to embrace the business community. It lacked the simplicity—even elegance—of the Carter report, whose ideas formed a logically coherent system that relentlessly removed the biases and favouritism of the existing tax system, creating a stunningly neutral system. Neutrality may seem like an odd concept to get excited about, but in a tax system, neutrality is important. It means the end to special concessions and advantages that certain groups are able to win from the government. Wherever the white paper deviated from the simple, neutral principles of the Carter philosophy, it usually ended up proposing solutions that were more complicated and often less fair.

Consider, for instance, its treatment of capital gains. While Carter wanted to tax them at full rates like other income, the white paper proposed a more complicated approach: tax some capital gains (such as profits made on the shares of small, privately held businesses) at full rates, and tax other capital gains (such as profits made on the shares of public companies) at only half-rates. This led to further complexities, as different sets of rules had to be developed for the two types of corporations. Although small business appeared to be the loser, it received other benefits that large public companies did not. But appearances are important, and the white paper appeared to discriminate against small business—a point that was noticed by small business.

In other areas too, the white paper compromised the simplicity of the Carter report, for no apparent advantage. Carter had devised an ingenious method of overcoming one of the basic grievances of investors—that corporate profits were taxed twice, once in the hands of the corporation and once in the hands of the investors receiving them as dividends. To get around this "double taxation," Carter advocated a system that would have effectively eliminated corporate tax and taxed only shareholders. Under Carter's scheme, a corporation would pay income tax on its profits, but when it paid these profits out in the form of dividends, shareholders would receive credits for their share of the tax already paid by the corporation. The corporation would essentially be paying tax on behalf of the shareholder.

This scheme of "integrating" the corporate and personal tax actually would have benefited many shareholders; but it aroused fierce opposition because it was seen as part of a package that included the taxation of capital gains. It was particularly opposed by industries, such as mining, which paid little corporate tax. Since the shareholder was only to receive a credit for corporate tax that was actually paid, shareholders of lowly-taxed industries would receive little or no tax credit. In fact, they would be better off with the existing system, under which all dividend income was taxed at a reduced rate, regardless of whether or not the company had even paid corporate tax.

In the face of persistent criticism from the mining industry, the government scrapped this straightforward solution to one of the most vexing problems of the tax system. In its place, the white paper proposed a more complicated dual system—the integration of corporate and personal tax would apply only to small privately owned firms, while a partial version of integration would apply to shareholders in public companies.

The extreme pressure from the mining industry was also responsible for the government's retreat on the taxation of the resource industries. The tough stand of the Carter commission would have virtually eliminated the special tax concessions these industries were enjoying. Yet the white paper proposed that some important tax breaks remain in place. And, in an interesting forerunner of the national energy program, the white paper recommended that concessions be made contingent on the amount of exploration companies carried out. Needless to say, these kinds of concessions were not nearly as popular with the industry as the no-strings-attached tax breaks already in place.

In only one area did the government fully adopt the Carter philosophy, taking it even farther than Carter and advocating a measure that would have significantly increased the tax burden on the wealthy. The measure was the brainchild of deputy minister Bryce. He had no ties to Bay Street and was, if anything, a little cynical about the way powerful interests were trying to bully the government. On the other hand, Jim Brown, who was from Bay Street and had every intention of returning to his accounting firm, was less enthusiastic about Bryce's exotic idea. In the end, a persistent Bryce was able to talk Benson into including his scheme in the white paper.

Bryce's idea was essentially a solution to one of the basic problems of taxing capital gains. That problem was how to prevent investors from avoiding the tax by simply holding on to shares indefinitely. Since investors only received capital gains when they cashed in their stocks and realized a profit, they could avoid paying tax on capital gains altogether as long as they didn't cash in their stocks. This problem cropped up particularly in attempts to tax the wealthy, who had no immediate need of cash and usually preferred to let their fortunes accumulate untaxed.

The guiding principle of Carter's philosophy was that an individual should be taxed on the annual increase in his or her wealth. Whether the individual keeps this wealth in the form of cash or stocks or jewellery should not be important. What should matter is how much the person's wealth increases from year to year. An increase in wealth increases the individual's purchasing power. So, by Carter's reckoning, if an individual simply holds on to stocks, and they rise in value, his or her wealth and potential buying power has still increased, whether the stocks are cashed in or not.

The Carter report argued that, in principle, increases in wealth should be taxed every year. But, perhaps out of fear of the reaction, the commissioners shied away from actually recommending such a plan, simply presenting the idea as something Canada might eventually want to adopt. The commission did, however, recommend that at least once a lifetime these increases in wealth be taxed. It therefore proposed that when an individual died his or her property would be treated *as if* it were sold, and any capital gain that would have resulted from such a sale would be taxed. This was called "deemed realization" at death.

But Bryce's idea went much farther. He suggested that rather than just a once-in-a-lifetime evaluation, shareholders should be taxed every five years on the increased value of their stock (in public companies), whether they sold the stock or not. This five-year-evaluation rule had dramatic implications. A rich person would no longer have the option of deferring all capital gains taxes until the end of his or her life. It also potentially threatened the concentration of ownership in the country. Major shareholders would face periodic tax bills for increases in the value of their shares and could conceivably be forced to sell some of these shares to pay the tax. While the proposal may have sounded extreme, in fact it was no more radical than laws that already existed in many European countries, where annual taxes are levied directly on wealth. But to Canadian investors, whose capital had long been carefully sheltered from the reach of the government, the idea was about as acceptable as highway robbery.

If the government thought it could wriggle off the hot seat with the compromises in the white paper, it soon discovered it was dead wrong. Although the white paper—with the exception of Bryce's five-year evaluation rule—was a substantial retreat from the Carter proposals, it still was not as favourable to many powerful interests as the existing system. What's more, this one had the stamp of government on it. It wasn't just the wild ideas of a few commissioners who had gotten out of control. This had come out of Ottawa's own Finance Department. What was to prevent the new Liberal government of Pierre Trudeau, who was, after all, a bit pink, from plowing ahead and introducing actual legislation?

With the stakes even higher this time, the business community swung into action. And this time there was a new protagonist on the scene—small business. In the past, small business had been represented by the large business umbrella organizations, such as Chambers of Commerce and Boards of Trade. But the white paper changed all that. It proposed ending the special low tax rate on the first $35,000 of corporate income. Small business had benefited from this low rate, but so had big business; and it was removed because it seemed a sloppy, indirect way of channelling aid to small business. Furthermore, the white paper created two different sets of rules—one for small, privately held firms and one for larger, public companies—and appeared to discriminate against small business.

Ironically, the authors of the white paper felt that small business ended up with a better deal overall than big business. Shares of small businesses would not, for instance, be subject to Bryce's five-year evaluation rule. However, the question of whether small business would have won or lost under the proposed reforms quickly became academic, when a business teacher at Toronto's Ryerson Polytechnical Institute, sitting in his bathtub one evening marking term papers, browsed through a copy of the white paper. There was a huge splash when the teacher, whose name was John Bulloch, got to the part about the lower tax rate being removed. Bulloch happened to be the son of a prominent men's clothing store owner, a fierce free enterpriser who liked to use his store's newspaper advertisements to expound on everything from the Soviet menace to the need to keep women at home. Before the bathwater turned cold, Bulloch came up with the bright idea of using his father's next ad to rally small business against the white paper.

Defending small business was something that came naturally to Bulloch. Under his father's keen tutelage, the young Bulloch had absorbed the values of the free enterprise system almost as early as he'd learned to sit up in his crib. His father's successful firm had been very much the centre of family life. Unfortunately, John was colour-blind, making a career in the family clothing business difficult. So, after a few years working for a fuel-oil company, he had ended up at Ryerson. It was a fine job, teaching about business, but it wasn't exactly like running your own business. Suddenly, almost overnight, Bulloch had his big chance.

The response to the ad was phenomenal. Bulloch's father gleefully phoned him at 10 A.M. the next morning and told him to come over and take the calls that were jamming the store's phone lines. From out of nowhere, people were offering him money. He quickly organized a rally at Toronto's Royal York Hotel, and the tall, lanky community college teacher found himself facing a crowd of 3,500 people, who offered up $50,000 for his crusade.

Bulloch had clearly tapped a huge pool of resentment. It was surfacing because of the white paper, but its sources were considerably deeper. Without any collective voice of their own, small businessmen felt angry and frustrated that government so often seemed to cater to the interests of big corporations and showed little concern for the special problems faced by small, struggling firms. It's unlikely that the individual dry cleaner or hardware store owner or electrical parts distributor even understood the full implications of the white paper, but they keenly responded to Bulloch's rallying cry that Ottawa was being insensitive to the needs of small business.

Bulloch took a leave from his Ryerson job and set up the Canadian Council for Fair Taxation. He went on tour, raising $150,000 in a cross-country sweep that kept up a constant, widely publicized attack on Ottawa and furthered the impression that the white paper was an assault on the little guy. Bulloch was fighting back, and his father could not have been prouder. Here was his son, directing a national campaign dedicated to keeping alive the entrepreneurial spirit. "He loved this kind of thing," Bulloch recalls of his father. So did the younger Bulloch. "It was a lot of fun," he says, leafing through his album of press clippings and reminiscing about the heady days of tax reform. Bulloch has good cause to look back fondly. When the tax reform debate ended, he diversified into other issues that angered small business, setting up the Canadian Federation of Independent Business, which claims 76,000 members and annual revenues of $9.3 million. In the front hall of the federation's new multi-million dollar complex in north Toronto hangs a picture of John Bulloch. Few entrepreneurs could ask for more.

Colin Brown also jumped into the tax reform brawl. Brown, a successful insurance salesman from London, Ontario, had come to public attention in the 60s with his Turn-In-A-Pusher ad campaign in the local newspaper and later with a similar campaign against a national medicare scheme. Like Bulloch, Brown saw the tax reform proposals as an attack on the entrepreneurial spirit in Canada. He took out full-page ads in several Canadian dailies and urged readers to send protest coupons to Ottawa—a campaign that showered tens of thousands of coupons on the already besieged Finance Department. Brown's philosophical objections were no doubt further exacerbated by the specific threats tax reform posed to the privileged status of the insurance industry. The Carter report had been unequivocal on the urgent need for higher taxes on insurance companies, and the government had already moved to implement some of these recommendations. The industry was putting up a tough fight, though, as the reforms wound their way through the senate. Brown, who had built a personal fortune in the insurance industry, was eagerly attempting to discredit the tax reform proposals, doing his best to preserve a system that had helped make him rich.

In Ottawa, the chorus of objections grew deafening. Pressure was building from the provincial governments, which were themselves under intense pressure from the mining and oil companies in their regions. One of the most beleaguered provincial premiers was Robert Bourassa, who had come to power on promises of creating 100,000 new jobs in Quebec. Now several major mining companies, including Quebec Cartier Mining and Iron Ore Company of Canada, were threatening to cancel plans for projects worth hundreds of millions of dollars, because of the white paper. Bourassa was desperate.

In case Bourassa wasn't getting the message across to his fellow Liberals in Ottawa, senior executives from Iron Ore's parent firm, Cleveland-based Hanna Mining, flew to Ottawa and voiced their objections directly to Benson. "Some tough guys came up from Ohio to call on Benson, Brown and myself," recalls Bryce. "They made it clear there were certain limits to what they, as investors, could stand in taxes." Another group of mining executives came by private plane to Benson's home in Kingston one weekend to make sure he was aware of their concerns. He assured them he was.

With no graceful exit in sight, the government was only too happy to refer the whole thing to the finance committee of the House of Commons. The business groups had a heyday at the committee, showing up in force and flaunting their objections noisily for the media. The MPs on the committee offered little real resistance as business representatives and their hired tax advisors tried to reduce the white paper to tatters. Still, compared to the committee in the Senate that was also sitting in judgment on the government's proposed tax changes, the Commons committee was a group of wild revolutionaries.

The smell of fine cigars hung heavily in the air, giving the stately old room the feeling of a men's club. Almost two dozen

Senators, a greying, balding lot of generally distinguished-looking gentlemen, sat on red velvet chairs and, for the most part, listened intently. For three months now, this august group that made up the Senate banking committee had heard witness after witness expound on the horrors of the government's white paper on tax reform. The Senators had turned out in force for the daily parade of angry business representatives; it was just what the members of Canada's unelected upper chamber wanted to hear.

As lawyers and executives and stockholders themselves, the Senators strongly objected to what they considered the anti-business thrust of the proposed reforms. Their ties with the financial and investment world were even closer than might appear on first glance. Almost all of the 33 members of the committee held at least one corporate directorship, and many of them sat on numerous corporate boards. Between them, they held an astonishing total of 211 directorships, including directorships in some of the biggest and most powerful companies in Canada: Consolidated Bathurst, Sun Life Assurance Company, Denison Mines, Atlantic Sugar Refineries, Canadian General Electric, Algoma Central Railway, the Royal Bank of Canada, the Bank of Montreal, the Bank of Nova Scotia. With virtually every major industry represented, the committee might as well have held its hearings in a corporate boardroom, the dining room of the Toronto Club or on the links of the Rosedale Golf Club. For businessmen making their presentations in the congenial, clubby atmosphere of the committee, it was as comfortable as taking a warm bath.

On this particular spring morning in May 1970, a number of the Senators were suppressing a chuckle as they shared an in-joke with one of the witnesses. The camaraderie was not surprising. Many of the witnesses knew the Senators personally or were representing firms on whose corporate boards the Senators sat. But on this morning, the intricate web of connections and interconnections was taking on the proportions of a seventeenth century French farce where one needed a program to remember who was in bed with whom.

With a mischievous air, Senator Keith Laird announced that he wanted to direct some questions to Neil Phillips, a lawyer representing Trizec Corporation, "to make him earn his counsel fee; and because I understand that he has had training in a good law office." A few Senators smiled. As the bright young Montreal lawyer fielded some soft questions on behalf of the prominent real estate development firm, one of the Senators weighing his words was not only a Trizec director, but also Phillip's law partner—and his father—Senator Lazarus Phillips.

In the cosy atmosphere of the committee room, the Senators and witnesses worked in harmony to build a coherent attack against the reform proposals. Despite the official position that they were operating as a "judicial" body in their investigation, the Senators made little secret of their biases. When an organization representing a group of small retailers wrote, expressing objections to the white paper, Senator Laird replied in a soothing letter: "Believe me, many of us [in the Senate] are deeply concerned with the problems created by these proposals." When the organization was invited to appear before the committee to voice its objections, it was asked to bring additional copies of its submission for distribution to the press. No opportunity was to be wasted in getting the anti-tax reform message out.

In fact the Senators seemed so keen at times to destroy the white paper that they heaped praise on strongly worded critiques and became impatient with witnesses who were mealy-mouthed in their outrage. On one occasion, Philip Vineberg, another law partner of Senator Phillips in the firm of Phillips and Vineberg, appeared before the committee as a representative of the Canadian Association of Real Estate Boards. Vineberg described one white paper proposal as a "tortuous, costly, intolerable, vexatious, round-about, slip-shod,

administratively deficit-inspired formula"—a description
which moved one senator to comment: "You've done a magnificent job on this."

Witnesses who were less sure of the white paper's faults or
less articulate in expressing them were given much cooler
receptions. Senator Hartland Molson, chairman of Molson
Breweries and head of the old-money Molson family of Montreal, was clearly disappointed when he found no criticism of
Bryce's five-year evaluation rule in the brief of the Canadian
Pulp and Paper Association. Yet when he asked association
president Robert Fowler for an opinion on the five-year rule,
Fowler simply offered that the association did not like it.
Committee chairman Senator Salter Hayden indicated that he
didn't find Fowler's reply quite up to scratch. "That is very
moderate language, Mr Fowler. We have had stronger in the
course of our hearings." Summoning up the requested bile,
Fowler quickly obliged: "Really this seems to be the ultimate
in complexity, difficulty, interference, all the things we ought
not to have in the tax system." The Senators noted his strong
objections.

In their attempt to mount a comprehensive broadside
against the white paper, however, the Senators were frustrated
by the inability to get adequate testimony from small business.
Despite the constant protestations of big business representatives that the proposed tax reforms would decimate the small
businessman, none of the endangered species themselves materialized to protest. Senator John Connolly asked the committee's senior advisor, Arthur Gilmour, where all the small
businessmen had gone. "We have been trying desperately to
get a submission from the small businessman, but to date we
have not succeeded," Gilmour replied, promising to deliver a
small businessman within six weeks.

No wonder Connolly was excited when he came into the
committee room one day soon after this and discovered a
whole delegation of small businessmen appearing on behalf of
the Retail Council of Canada. The Senator's enthusiasm was

tempered slightly, however, when it was pointed out that only one member of the delegation was actually a small business-man—the others were from Eaton's, Simpsons and Kresge's. "They are not small businesses," Connolly acknowledged; but, making the best of the situation, he added: "Still, the younger man, as you mentioned, the imaginative, creative man, is the reservoir of that kind of talent, and that is the age group of the people before us today." Besides, the committee was finally face to face with at least one "live, breathing, successful, small businessman," Connolly noted. And what a small businessman he was—an immigrant who had built up his own dry goods business from nothing. As the Senators sat back, he regaled them with a gratifying diatribe on the joys of free enterprise and the evils of a capital gains tax.

Big business was equally stirring in its tribute to the en-trepreneurial spirit. "Everybody in Canada is free to go and explore and prospect and live in the bush, but not everybody is willing to do so," said Stephen Roman, the bombastic presi-dent of Denison Mines who had made his fortune in uranium mining. One of the wealthiest men in the country, Roman was not keen on paying taxes. Despite more than $100 million in profits in Denison's first thirteen years of operation, Roman had concluded that his company owed not a penny in taxes. Ottawa disagreed but managed to collect some tax from Deni-son only after a long court battle.

Here, before the Senate banking committee, Roman, a self-made millionaire, was right at home urging the Senators to regard capital gains as distinct from other income. Roman argued that if people choose to spend their money, that was fine. "But if I deny myself something," he continued, "and put my capital into the economy and provide jobs and oppor-tunities for other people to get started, why should I be taxed on whatever that capital earns?" Roman's argument sounds almost compelling at first; why should the government tax such a worthwhile activity as saving and investing? But then, an employee could similarly argue that if he goes out and works hard all day at a difficult job, rather than lolling about, why should he be taxed on what he earns? Are his efforts any less worthy than the investor's?

Roman's agitation over the white paper paled in comparison to the dire predictions for the nation's future made by Canada's hockey establishment, however. Both Toronto's Maple Leaf Gardens Ltd. and the Canadian Arena Company, owner of the Montreal Canadiens and the Montreal Forum, argued in their submissions that the five-year evaluation rule would drive them out of business. But the most ominous scenario was extended even further. "In the event of the [enactment of the white paper] either NHL hockey and, to a very large degree, organized amateur hockey as well, would disappear from Canada," according to the Maple Leaf Gardens brief. "Hockey is not only Canada's national sport, it is a way of life of countless citizens, young and old, and beyond doubt, contributes in a multitude of ways to the building of young men, to the social structure and to the basic fibre of our people.... On balance it would seem to be questionable whether equity would really be served if hockey, in particular, and the sports industry in general, were destroyed." A vote for the white paper was a vote for the death of sports, a vote for skinny, spineless young men.

The Canadian Arena Company was owned by three Molson brothers, William, David and Peter, who are sons of a cousin of Senator Molson. (The Senator had sold his shares in the company to his three young relatives at a very low price two years earlier.) The Molson boys' argument was that the five-year evaluation rule would force them to sell some of their shares, possibly resulting in their loss of control over the company. This was actually a very far-fetched possibility. But even if it were likely, nobody ever explained why it would be such a terrible thing for one of the wealthiest families in the country to have less than full control over one of the nation's least risky ventures.

Not to be outdone by the apocalyptic vision of its competitor in Toronto, however, the Canadian Arena Company painted a picture of the bleak future that would be in store for the nation if the Molsons were to lose control of the company. "When we are sitting there with a franchise, and then it becomes worthless in Montreal because we are no longer able to operate there because the operation is no longer viable, I have to look to my American cousins, who make up ten-twelfths of the league and say 'What other cities in North America do you think would like to have the Montreal franchise?' This would not be a difficult thing to move. Of course, this would be a most distasteful thing to have to do, but inevitably if these things come into effect, this is what we will have to do." The brief did not explain why the franchise would be worthless in Montreal simply because the Molson brothers no longer had control. Also unexplained was why the Molsons would have to sell the franchise to another city rather than, say, selling some of their shares in the Montreal operation to other investors.*

But more disturbing still was the portrait painted by Harry Jackman, the outspoken Toronto businessman, president of Dominion and Anglo Investment Corporation. Jackman told the Senators that, with severe tax laws, young men were not going to "want to play this game" and would leave the country. He suggested that the white paper proposals were really the beginning of a trend towards socialism and that Canadians seemed dangerously unaware of the revolutionary changes ahead. "It was that way with Hitler. It has been that way many times in our history," he warned.

Jackman's central argument was that Canada's tax laws discouraged the accumulation of capital. (In a digression, he also noted that "because of the general affluence, domestic

---

*None of the Molson's dire predictions materialized. Even though the five-year evaluation rule was scrapped, the brothers decided to give up their control of the hockey team anyway. They sold it to Peter and Edward Bronfman for $13 million in 1972, collecting a $10 million profit in just four years.

servants are almost impossible to get.") Jackman didn't confine himself to the proposed tax changes. He also attacked the
existing estate tax, which he said made it "impossible to
accumulate capital from one generation to another." In fact,
Jackman was so concerned about the estate tax that he was
willing to accept a moderate tax on capital gains if the estate
tax were removed in exchange: "it might be considered a not
too injurious set-off if the estate tax were abolished and the
capital gains tax introduced."

The Senators apparently found merit in Jackman's proposed trade-off; it found its way into their final report on the
white paper. They suggested that capital gains be taxed at half-
rates, as they were in the U.S., with no "deemed realization"
at death—the one rule that would give a capital gains tax some
teeth. At the same time they suggested the removal of the
estate tax. This was an odd suggestion. Neither the Carter
commission nor the white paper had called for an end to the
estate tax. But, on this point at least, the Senators and Jackman
were soon to get their way.

The tax reform legislation finally introduced by the government in June 1971 was a pale version of the white paper, itself
a pale version of the Carter report. Business had won.

With the exception of Kierans, who expressed bitter disappointment over the abandonment of the Carter principles, the
Trudeau cabinet had had enough of the fury of the business
community and was satisfied with a compromised version of
tax reform. Under the relentless pressure of the resource
industries, the government had already largely retreated from
its plan for significantly heavier taxes on mining and oil companies. Under revisions announced in August 1970, depletion
allowances were extended and a more generous credit for
provincial mining taxes was created. The net effect was to
remove almost two-thirds of the tax increase the resource
industries would have faced under the white paper proposals,
while still raising their taxes above existing levels. Within a few

weeks of Ottawa's capitulation, Iron Ore announced it would proceed after all with its new pelletizing plant in Sept Iles, Quebec—a move that Kierans is convinced the company would have made anyway to meet competition from foreign producers.

Another victory for the resource industry, and for other industries paying low rates of tax, was the defeat of Carter's scheme for integrating the personal and corporate tax. Carter's idea of giving shareholders credit only for corporate taxes that were actually paid was simply not acceptable to industries that paid little corporate tax. Instead, they argued for and won a more generous version of the existing system—a tax break for the shareholders on dividend income whether or not the corporation had paid any tax.

Small business, the new kid on the block, got an early, delicious taste of its power, forcing Ottawa to retain the special low rate of tax for the first chunk of corporate income. In an attempt to restrict the benefits to small, private Canadian businesses, the new legislation stipulated that the special low rate ceased to apply once the business had accumulated $400,000 of taxable income over the years—an amount which most large firms would quickly surpass.

Ottawa also introduced a new tax break for companies taking over other companies. From now on, the acquisitors would be allowed to deduct the costs of borrowing money to finance a takeover bid. This change helped unleash a take-over mania in Canadian businessmen.

In the controversial area of capital gains, Ottawa settled for a partial victory: capital gains would be taxed at half-rates. This was what the white paper had proposed for shares of public companies. But the white paper had coupled this generous provision with the not-so-generous five-year evaluation rule. Essentially, the white paper had stipulated that if gains were only going to be taxed at half-rates, they should at least be taxed every five years, whether or not the gain was actually realized. In the final legislation, however, the government retained the generous provision and withdrew the not-so-generous one. Instead of taxing the increase in the value of capital every five years, Ottawa would only tax it at death. (Carter had recommended this once-in-a-lifetime system, but then he had urged that capital gains be taxed at full rates.)

But what was most striking about the final package was something that received relatively little attention—suddenly, the estate tax was gone. Clearly this was out of line with what Carter and the white paper had advocated. Nor had the Commons committee called for such a move. The Senate banking committee, hardly a group representative of Canadian society, had been alone in urging such a dramatic course of action. Only one percent of Canadians left estates large enough to be affected by the tax. Suddenly this privileged group was to receive a huge windfall, which economist John Bossons estimates was worth $12 billion.

Here's how that windfall came about. As of January 1, 1972, when the new legislation came into effect, all capital would be considered for tax purposes to have, in effect, zero value. From that day on, any increases in the value of that property would be taxed as a capital gain when the property was sold, or at death, when it was deemed to be sold. But—and this is the key part—all increases in the value of property that took place *before* January 1, 1972, disappeared for tax purposes. If in 1971 an investor held $5 million in shares that had been worth $1 million a decade earlier, that increase in value represented an unrealized capital gain of $4 million. Any future increase would be subject to tax as a capital gain, but the $4 million escaped taxation entirely.

Under the old legislation, this $4 million would have been taxed by the estate tax when the investor died. The net result of the new legislation was that these pre-1972 accumulations of wealth entered into a special tax-free zone where they would be subject neither to the new tax on capital gains nor to the old estate tax. Therefore, the combined removal of the estate tax and the lack of retroactivity in the new capital gains tax had the effect of giving an enormous one-time break—the above mentioned $12 billion—to Canada's least needy families.

Certainly there seemed to be little to substantiate Harry Jackman's fear that capital accumulations couldn't be passed on to the next generation. Jackman left a massive investment empire which his son Hal has built on. With a personal fortune estimated at $390 million, Hal Jackman stands twelve miles high in the current wealth parade.

Although the amount involved was staggering—enough to reduce tax rates a full 10 percent for all Canadians earning $15,000 or more—the inheritance tax disappeared almost without public comment. After a period of several years, during which nearly every aspect of the tax system had been trotted out on the public stage in a daily show, here was a huge development on the tax front, a concession greater than any other that had been talked about in the endless debate, and yet it was handled almost as a private matter. It wasn't that the rich didn't notice. It would be hard not to notice a few extra million dollars, as the windfall was in some cases. It was just that this time they were happy with the change.

The reasons for the abrupt move were revealing. Foremost was simply the fact that, due to the complex way the estate tax had evolved, most of the revenues from it went to the provinces. Benson, who had previously defended the estate tax on the grounds of fairness, says he made the decision to abolish it suddenly one day in his office, out of frustration over the fact that the federal government took all the heat for the tax, while the provinces got the bulk of the money.

But Benson also argued at the time that the estate tax was being eliminated because, with the new tax on capital gains, some taxpayers would have faced both taxes at death. This complaint about "double taxation," which was frequently advanced by well-to-do investors, ignores the fact that the two taxes are completely separate.

Capital gains are taxed, along with other forms of income, because they represent an increase in the individual's buying power that year. But the estate tax was meant as a once-a-generation tax on the holdings of very wealthy families. The two taxes only coincided at death because holders of capital were allowed to defer paying taxes on their capital gains until then. But this in itself was really a special concession. The fact that a shareholder had not been taxed on the increased value of his shares and other assets all his life amounted to a huge tax deferral and, consequently, a huge saving for him. The equivalent would be if salary-earners were allowed to put off paying all their income taxes until the end of their lives, permitting them to use that money to invest over the years.

In winning the removal of the estate tax, the powerful interests had managed to parlay one tax break into another. They had won the fight to scrap the hated five-year evaluation rule for capital gains, rolling it back to the much more acceptable rule of deemed realization at death. But rather than appreciate this for the tax deferral that it was, they treated it as an opportunity to protest about what was now a heavy tax burden at death. Their complaints were heeded, and yet another tax burden was lifted from their shoulders.

An interesting post-script: in Canada, heavy tax burdens at death have gone the way of the hoola-hoop. With the lifetime capital gains exemption introduced by the Mulroney government (up to $500,000 for small business owners), there is now no capital gains tax at death for many well-to-do people, and there is also no estate tax. For the rich at least, it seems that one good tax break deserves another . . . and another . . . and another. . . .

Ten years after the Carter commission embarked on its odyssey into uncharted waters, Canada had a new tax system. But the decade of effort to make the system more logical, simpler and fairer had resulted in astonishingly little change. Despite the magnificent blueprint laid out in the Carter report, Canada had ended up with a highly flawed system not unlike the loophole-ridden American system. Economists Meyer

Bucovetsky and Richard Bird described the Canadian tax reform process as "reaching for the moon and landing, more or less, in the United States."

The biggest change was the addition of a partial tax on capital gains—for which the estate tax was sacrificed. It was a dubious victory, to say the least, particularly in light of the subsequent reduction in the taxation of capital gains. All in all, the new legislation had the effect of reducing taxes slightly for corporations. For individuals, there were overall tax reductions for those in the very lowest and highest income brackets. The losers were that vast bulk of taxpayers known as the middle class. They ended up with higher taxes as a result of the reform.

Since taxpayers generally don't like paying higher tax, it's fair to question whether democracy worked in the case of the great tax reform exercise. All the proper institutions were functioning—parliamentary committees, debates in the House of Commons, public hearings, close press attention—yet somehow the majority of voters, who are supposed to run things in a democracy, ended up worse off.

The reason for this apparent contradiction is clear: the business and financial interests, who had a great deal at stake, were far more adept at using the political system to their own advantage. Some of their pressure, arm-twisting and sweet-talking took place behind the proverbial closed doors, at cocktail parties and in the offices of cabinet ministers and government officials. But much of it also took place right out in the public arena, in the halls of Parliament and the Senate and on the pages of the press. With their vast resources, they simply dominated the debate. Their objections reverberated with such force that they came back on the echo sounding like irrefutable facts.

They used every avenue available to them. When Mitchell Sharp asked disgruntled members of the business community to make submissions explaining their objections to the Carter report, they did so *en masse*. They could afford to hire high-priced legal talent to attack the proposed reforms. Those attacks were cleverly constructed. They rarely came right out and opposed the idea of redistributing wealth from the rich to the rest. Rather they simply tried to show that the solutions suggested were impractical or unwise, usually because they would result in a decline in investment and consequent greater suffering for society as a whole. Since the business community largely controlled investment in the country, its threats had a degree of credibility; the seriousness of the threats was hard— and frightening—to assess. This power to intimidate was the real power of business.

The press, which is largely owned by wealthy investors, was generally sympathetic to the concerns of the business community. As a result, newspapers were full of stories of business executives recounting the dangers of the various reform proposals in public speeches, at annual meetings, in appearances before the Parliamentary committees. All this left the impression that there must be a great deal wrong with the proposals to provoke so much agitation in so many people.

As Leslie MacDonald has noted, it is one of the great ironies of the tax reform exercise that the most progressive solutions were developed by the body that was farthest removed from the public arena—the royal commission. In its four and a half years of secret deliberations, the commission was able to extricate itself somewhat from the world where powerful interests dominate. The Carter commission, for instance, showed a delightful indifference to the maintenance of family dynasties, one of the basic real-world facts of Canadian society. The investment community had traditionally argued against estate taxes on the grounds that they could cause wealthy families to lose control of family-owned businesses—the same argument later advanced by the Molson brothers to fight the five-year evaluation rule. The Carter commission reported that it had found no evidence such situations had occurred. And then, with that relentless neutrality so characteristic of the Carter report, the commissioners added that, even if this were to happen, it was nothing to be concerned about anyway, since there was no evidence that family-controlled businesses were more productive than others. Such a straightforward, logical approach ignores completely—and rightly—the power and influence wielded by the Molson family and the other ultra-rich dynasties in Canada.

Governments generally feel the need to act with more political caution than do royal commissions. In this case, the Liberals inherited a set of solutions they had not asked for and would have preferred to avoid altogether. Having had the Carter report thrust upon them, however, they showed a degree of interest in enacting at least some of the progressive reforms recommended. But, in the face of fierce and continuing opposition from the business and investment community, as well as the apparent indifference of much of the wage-earning population, the Liberals wavered and eventually retreated.

The final scenes in that retreat seem to have been stage-managed. Benson points out that the Liberals had a majority on the Commons committee. This allowed the government to control the committee's agenda and its recommendations. One of the key decisions made by the committee was not to hear testimony by public finance specialists—that is, academic tax experts without ties to the investment community. This group of experts, who had widely supported the Carter report, would have made the case for a more neutral, Carter-style reform. They could have been counted on to prick holes in the arguments of the business community and, more generally, just to speak out in the public interest. With considerable media attention focussed on the hearings, this could have helped redress the balance of influence and redefine some of the issues for the public. It also could have stirred up strong feelings on the other side at a time when the government really just wanted to put the whole subject to rest. In any event, the Liberal-controlled committee decided that, with so many business groups wanting to make presentations, there simply wasn't time for academics defending the rest of the public. (The two NDP members of the committee, Max Saltsman and John Burton, produced a dissenting report attacking the committee for its willingness to preserve the distinction between income earned from capital and income earned from labour.)

By adopting much of the majority report of the Commons committee, the government was able to retreat gracefully from its own white paper. After all, it was taking the advice of an elected Parliamentary committee, which had listened patiently to the concerns of Canada's citizens. It certainly looked like democracy.

The raucous spectacle of tax reform had been an odd experience for Canadians. Not since the First World War had the country been exposed to such a public debate over what kind of tax system Canada was to have. Although the vast bulk of the population wasn't really taking part, the public nature of the exercise was highly unusual. None of this would have happened if the Carter commission hadn't rocked the boat so violently, stirring up a once-peaceful sea.

But now, with the threat of serious reform gone, tax matters returned to their traditional home behind the closed doors of law firms, corporate head offices and government bureaucracies. And although much less was said on the public stage, a great deal was done offstage. As tax practitioners pressed quietly for "technical" changes to the new legislation, they were able to win concessions that left the modest reform package full of gaping holes. A new era began: tax reform for the rich.

CHAPTER SEVEN
Revenge Of The Lobbyists

"To tax and to please, no more than to love and be wise,
is not given to men."
—**Edmund Burke**

If business had won the battle against tax reform, the victory had only come after a long and bitter fight. Corporations had had to flex their muscles hard to defend their privileges. In the end, their big-stick approach largely succeeded, but success had a price. One of the casualties was the public image of business.

Opinion polls at the time showed that Canadians had little trust in business; in fact, business was ranked below government and labour in trustworthiness. This was attributable to a number of factors, of course. Throughout North America, it was a time of growing public consciousness and of politicization over the environment, workplace safety and the Vietnam war—all issues on which business appeared to be on the wrong side, while profiting handsomely. But, in Canada at least, one of the issues on which business had been most belligerent and heavy-handed was taxation.

Sensitive about their bad press, corporations pumped money into campaigns to shake the tough-guy image. Companies that had never worried much about the public's perception of them started setting up public relations departments and hiring media consultants. Mining and oil companies, the most vociferous critics of the tax reform legislation, tried to counter any bad impression they might be making with advertising campaigns designed to put a better gloss on their intentions. Inco spent $750,000 in print advertisements after the furor over the Carter report, to "broaden knowledge of its activities." Other mining and steel companies, such as Dominion Foundries and Cominco, as well as the Mining Association of Canada, launched radio ad campaigns across the country to sell the public on the importance of mining.

But the image of business as self-serving and insensitive was hard to shake. In April 1972, *Toronto Star* columnist Alexander Ross wrote a dramatic column detailing how several large companies were virtually untaxed, and suggesting that someone should make this an election issue. NDP leader David Lewis seized the initiative and was able to ride a groundswell of support when he fought the 1972 federal election largely on a platform of reducing tax advantages to business. In city after city across the country, Lewis made rousing populist speeches that turned upside down the frequent criticism of "welfare bums." He zeroed in on those he considered to be the real welfare bums—the *corporate* welfare bums who were getting mammoth government hand-outs in the form of tax breaks. Borrowing material dug up by the Carter commission, Lewis trotted out case after case where major corporations—Imperial Oil, Aluminium Company of Canada, Canadian Westinghouse, Michelin Tire—had been spared millions of dollars in taxes. Shell Oil, Lewis noted, had managed to avoid taxes completely from 1964 to 1969, despite net earnings of $516 million. Editorial cartoons depicted big business as greedy and overfed. The NDP campaign even got an endorsement from Eric Kierans, the former Liberal cabinet minister who had resigned in part over his dissatisfaction with the Trudeau government's tax reform package. Lewis's charges apparently struck a responsive chord. In the October 1972 election, in which the Liberals lost their majority and ended up with a mere two-seat margin over the Tories, the NDP picked up nine seats, bringing its total to thirty-one—the party's best showing to that point.

The apparent popularity of the NDP's corporate welfare bums campaign was a sobering blow to business. Inside the Canadian Manufacturers' Association and the Chamber of Commerce there was talk of setting up a new research organization to counter the kinds of charges Lewis was making and to come up with statistics that would reflect favourably on business.

But in the big corporations themselves, there was a feeling these old-fashioned business organizations, with their somewhat clumsy, unsophisticated leadership and their unwieldy array of big and small firms, were part of the problem. This idea gained momentum after about a dozen senior executives, including Noranda president Alfred Powis and Imperial Oil president W. O. Twaits, wrote a letter to Prime Minister Trudeau in 1972, laying out their grievances on several important issues. Among their concerns were tax reform and competition policy. Trudeau, who was never trusted much by the business community, decided to invite the group to Ottawa to meet with him directly.

The meeting went well and the group was invited back for several more encounters with the prime minister, leaving the senior executives feeling flattered and impressed with their access to power and their ability to get things done. Says Powis: "We decided that what we needed, in effect, was a group of CEOs to put a determined effort behind ensuring the voice of business was effectively heard." The idea seemed to work. Powis notes that Ottawa dallied endlessly over bringing in a new competition bill, much to the satisfaction of business, which was opposed to any tougher competition rules. "They [the changes] got hung up from 72 to 86," says Powis. "So I guess we were modestly effective." He might have added that they didn't do badly on the tax front either.

The success of the CEOs' meetings with Trudeau led Powis and Twaits to develop the idea of a formal organization. Thus was born the Business Council on National Issues in 1976. The BCNI quickly became a sophisticated operation that changed the face of business lobbying in Canada. Whereas

the Chamber of Commerce and the Manufacturers' Association were largely run by career lobbyists—men with little real
clout on their own—the BCNI was a council composed of the
most powerful executives in the country.

So, the BCNI's policy committee, for instance, includes the
CEOs of Alcan, Inco, the Bank of Nova Scotia, Ford Motor
Company of Canada and Texaco. When the BCNI makes a
presentation to the minister of finance, some of the country's
top business leaders are there doing the talking. When the
BCNI takes a stand on something, it isn't just speaking as a
general voice of business, it is speaking as the voice of 150 of
the most important businessmen in the country. Their personal prestige and influence back what the organization is
saying. Or, as the BCNI itself says, with perhaps a touch of
condescension towards the rest of the business community,
the council is the "senior voice of business in Canada."

Indeed, while most organizations operating in the political
arena at least pretend to be open to all comers, the BCNI
prides itself on its exclusivity. That exclusivity has no doubt
contributed to its aura of importance. It isn't just another
umbrella business organization that accepts any corporation,
regardless of its assets or revenues. A company not only has to
be big and important to get in, it has to be *invited*. Nothing
enhances the prestige of an activity more than the old childhood trick of telling some kids they can't play.

But if the BCNI wants to impress government with the
personal clout of its members, it doesn't want the public to
see it as just a bunch of powerful fat cats. "We've tried very
hard to get away from the idea of a group of power brokers
working behind closed doors," says Tom d'Aquino, the president and CEO of the BCNI. Since the BCNI *is* essentially a
group of power brokers working behind closed doors, d'Aquino has had his work cut out for him. His main tactic has
been to present the BCNI as being above the fray, so far above
the ordinary petty concerns of most businessmen that it can
see the interests of the country as a whole.

So, for instance, the council has steered clear of the traditional bullying tactics of business, with its threats of taking its capital elsewhere if it can't get its way. Instead, d'Aquino has cultivated a statesmanlike image for the BCNI, stressing commitment to social responsibility and the national good. To hear d'Aquino describe it, this ultimate big business lobby group sounds almost like a charitable trust, a kind of corporate CUSO.

Indeed, the BCNI is an odd mixture. It has an air of refinement and affluence about it, from d'Aquino's dark pinstriped suits to the organization's fashionable location in Ottawa's Royal Bank Centre to its extravagant brochures. (It is hard to imagine a brochure more lavish than the one the BCNI produced for its tenth anniversary.) But the BCNI also goes to considerable effort to foster the image of a group of progressive reformers. Even the organization's office has a kind of low-key feel to it, with its early Canadian pine furniture. And the friendly, personable d'Aquino doesn't really seem like a businessman at all. (He's not; he's a lawyer who did a stint in the prime minister's office under Trudeau.) With his relaxed manner and his talk about social problems, he comes across more like an environmental lawyer or maybe a hip advertising executive. When he really gets going, he has an almost Kennedyesque aura.

He speaks of the BCNI as a creator of "new frontiers," a "harbinger of what is to come," an organization whose standards "are motivated by genuinely lofty ideas." He talks about its "missionary activity" and sounds indistinguishable from a card-carrying, whale-loving member of the environmental group Greenpeace: "Business just can't drop nitric acid into the environment; there's a responsibility to society as a whole." As for the less privileged members of society, d'Aquino says, "The poor and the disadvantaged must not in any way be victimized as we return collectively to a position of fiscal responsibility." From the old days of narrow self-interest, d'Aquino suggests in his soft, soothing voice, "business must cross the Rubicon to broader issues."

This statesmanlike approach permeates the BCNI. The

organization takes up issues that seem beyond the ken of traditional business interests. It has prepared detailed studies on
subjects of public concern such as Senate reform and federal-
provincial relations. All this underlines the notion that, far
from being a special-interest lobby, the BCNI is more like a
senior advisory council to government, a round table of wise
and selfless men. D'Aquino describes the selection of the
council's policy committee as "almost like putting together a
cabinet." And when the BCNI calls on government to cut
spending, d'Aquino insists that it shuns the traditional business approach of suggesting that others do with less while
business gets more. "That's not good enough. What we've got
to do is put ourselves through the wringer," he says. "We had
to ask ourselves: 'Are we prepared to gore our own ox?' We
said yes."

But the goring d'Aquino has in mind for the business ox is
mild indeed. In fact, the new lobbyists are really pushing for
the same things as the old lobbyists, but with more style,
more flair for public relations. They have learned to say
"Gimme, gimme, gimme" and make it sound like a hymn to
the downtrodden. They have cloaked self-interest in the guise
of Robin Hood.

Indeed, once the language of caring and sharing is stripped
from the BCNI's proposals, its members seem to be seeking
what any group of lobbyists seeks—more for themselves. One
of the BCNI's top priorities has been to cut back the scale of
Canada's social security net, which it considers heavily responsible for the country's deficit. But while the BCNI calls
for sacrifice from all groups to reduce the deficit, the bulk of
its suggested cuts would have little impact on business.

In a 1984 brief, the BCNI argued that business should make
sacrifices in the area of economic development and energy.
But closer examination of its proposals in these areas reveals
that the cuts the council had in mind for business would
actually inflict most of the pain on others. For instance, when
the BCNI advocated slashing direct grants to industry—such

as the $1 billion given out under the Industrial and Regional Development Program—the cutbacks turned out to be not much of a sacrifice for business. The grants, which were contingent on companies locating in remote or depressed regions, had been put in place largely to promote local employment, and the business community had long sought to replace them with more open-ended tax breaks. Similarly, in the energy field, the BCNI raised the possibility of cutting back the Petroleum Incentives Program, which channelled $1.6 billion a year to oil companies. The program, which emphasized Canadian ownership and Arctic exploration, had long been disliked by the oil industry. The BCNI took up the industry call that the program be replaced by tax breaks. (It was due to expire in 1986 anyway.)

When it came to social programs, however, the BCNI was tougher. While insisting that the poor should be protected, it called for an end to universality in family allowance payments and possibly cutbacks in old age pensions for the non-poor. It also wanted cuts in federal financing of post-secondary education and reductions in federal housing subsidies. (It did not, however, recommend cutting back *tax breaks* for housing, which, as we've seen, are far more beneficial to the rich than the direct housing subsidies the BCNI wanted removed.) And, in a 1986 brief on social policy reform, the BCNI also indicated it was willing to do without pensions for homemakers. One can imagine how easily such a recommendation won the endorsement of the council, which included not a single woman.

Similarly, in its 1986 brief on tax reform, the BCNI sounded committed to fairness and progressive change. It urged the elimination of special exemptions, which it said favoured high-income people! It even raised the idea of taxing capital gains at full rates, an idea business fought ferociously in the days of the Carter reform! Were these really the thoughts of the big business lobby group par excellence, or was this in fact some left-wing pamphlet picked up by mistake?

But there was a snag. The BCNI, it turned out, intended to barter one exemption for another. While willing to consider giving up the valuable capital gains exemption, it wanted a new tax break in return, modelled on the exemption for RRSPs. The BCNI was very keen on the RRSP deduction—a deduction that definitely favours high-income individuals who have the extra cash to set aside money for their retirement. The BCNI wanted to retain the RRSP deduction and to create a whole new similar tax break for other savings and investments. The new measure would be modelled on the RRSP but would include a broader range of investment options and would not be confined to retirement savings. "So people could take savings up to a certain amount, put them into a registered program, not pay taxes on them in the year in which [they are] put in, use that income to invest and invest in a more flexible fashion," explained John Benesh, a lawyer on the BCNI staff. Benesh would not specify how much an individual would be allowed to exempt from tax each year under the program. But, by allowing investors to defer paying tax on whatever amount was allowed, the scheme would be providing considerable tax savings for those able to invest—primarily those with large incomes.

Indeed, the BCNI's proposed scheme could well be more favourable to the rich than even the capital gains exemption. Whereas the capital gains exemption spares individuals from paying tax on the profits of their investments, the BCNI scheme would allow them to shelter other types of income as well—such as salary and dividends—by investing it. As long as they kept reinvesting it, as many wealthy people do with the bulk of their money, the scheme would allow them to defer tax. They would only pay tax on the portion they chose to withdraw from their registered plan.

Such a system would offer few tax advantages for low- and middle-income individuals, who tend to spend most of their incomes just to get by. The bottom line is that, if you don't have money to invest—and most low- and middle-income people don't—you can't benefit from special tax breaks for investors.

The BCNI went on to argue in its tax reform proposal that personal income tax rates should be reduced, with the top rate dropping down to 35 percent (combined federal and provincial)—about 15 points below the current 50 percent level and even well below the 44 percent level proposed in the June 1987 reform package. Taken together, these two measures advocated by the BCNI would more than compensate for the loss of a capital gains exemption, leaving high-income individuals significantly better off. They would have a new investment tax break, probably even more generous than the capital gains exemption, plus they would have a much lower tax rate. Not bad for people whose ox is being gored.

And how would the less well-to-do fare in the BCNI's world? The BCNI doesn't come right out and recommend higher taxes for the rest of society. That would destroy its image as being socially caring, and it might attract public scrutiny of some of its proposals. But what the BCNI called for would have the *effect* of raising taxes on the middle- and lower-income groups. It recommended that any revenue lost due to the changes it proposed should be made up by a new "transaction" tax, which is just another word for a sales tax. The tax would apply on virtually all transactions, thus penalizing the people who have to spend most of their income on basic living expenses. (The poor would be entitled to tax credits to compensate for this expanded sales tax, although the BCNI does not specify how generous these credits would be or who would qualify for them.) So what it comes down to is that with its heavy emphasis on tax breaks for investors the BCNI seems willing to impose a virtually limitless new tax burden on those who don't have the money to invest.

These ideas are actually variations on old ideas that have long been nurtured by BCNI members. The council's co-founders—Powis and Twaits—were two of the harshest critics of the earlier attempts at progressive tax reform and vehemently defended the rights of investors to special tax treatment. As executive vice-president of Noranda, Powis was one of the key players who forced Ottawa to back off from Carter's plans to raise taxes on the mining industry. And Twaits, as president of Imperial Oil, revealed his strong biases against Canadians who spend rather than invest their income. "Is it consistent with equity to tax the man who works and saves as hard as the non-saver?" Twaits asked a 1967 tax conference. "Is it equity to tax the innovator, the entrepreneur, at the same rate as the drones in society?" Twaits' apparent contempt for those who don't or can't invest— roughly 90 percent of the population—is still evident today in the BCNI's willingness to stick it to the hapless non-investor. All the BCNI has really done is smooth over the rough edges. From the days of blatant self-interest, business now stands for tax injustice with a human face.

But apart from its harsh specific agenda, the BCNI sets a general agenda. It poises the country's top corporations to play a powerful, ongoing role in setting Ottawa's course, especially in the crucial area of tax policy. Abandoning the sabre-rattling posture of the tax reform years, business is now cultivating a co-operative, nice-guy image. But the very existence of the BCNI is a reminder to Ottawa of just how organized and strong big business is. The 150 CEOs who make up the council oversee 1.5 million employees and $700 billion in assets, as the BCNI constantly points out. Business may now be walking softly, but it still carries a big stick.

The old lobby groups have tried to adopt the BCNI's style as well, although they haven't always succeeded. The Canadian Manufacturers' Association, for instance, has greatly improved the packaging of its submissions in recent years, but an old-style mentality occasionally shows through its newly acquired savvy. At a 1984 press conference in Ottawa the CMA presented a glossy brief calling on the newly elected Tory government to review all labour legislation. When a reporter asked if this would include a review of child labour laws—forgotten nineteenth century laws designed to keep youngsters out of factories and coal mines—a CMA spokesman answered yes, even though the brief hadn't mentioned child labour laws. The otherwise dull news event was promptly turned into a story on the Neanderthal designs of big business.

Perhaps the most successful group on the lobbying scene in recent years has been small business. Unlike its big business counterparts, who must always fight off their power-monger image, small business evokes nostalgic images of a utopian free-enterprise society where entrepreneurs each have a small stake in the community and no one wields enormous economic power. Since its dramatic entrance into the tax reform debate under John Bulloch in 1969, small business has come to exercise surprising clout over the tax system. This was evident in Michael Wilson's June 1987 tax reform, which preserved the generous $500,000 lifetime capital gains exemption for small business owners.

As Bulloch built up his massive empire over the years, signing up small businessmen around the country in a highly organized, ongoing campaign, his success did not go unnoticed. Other enterprising types were also keen to get in on the small business action. The Canadian Organization of Small Business appeared in the late 70s, and its energetic vice-president, Geoffrey Hale, emerged as another prominent lobbyist.

Hale, a former young Tory, is an odd throwback to the old-style lobbyist. An intense young man who dresses in dark suits and colourless shirts, Hale has the air of a 50s high school student who spent his time preparing for the school debating tournament, while his classmates spent their time greasing down their hair and fixing up their cars. Lacking the easy touch of d'Aquino, Hale is given to haranguing. One reporter recalls a visit from Hale in which the intense young lobbyist launched into a heated critique of the way the government was handling small business. The reporter became increasingly unable to concentrate after he noticed a spider crawling up Hale's pallid neck. Hale apparently felt something and, still talking, brushed the spider away. A few seconds later the spider reappeared from beneath Hale's collar. As the spider moved relentlessly up his neck, Hale continued his animated critique.

Hale seems oblivious to public relations. When he received national exposure as a participant in a televised 1984 panel on pay equity for women, Hale put forward the anti-pay-equity position with an anger not normally seen on television. He became so agitated about the rights of small business to be free of government interference that he was shaking visibly in front of the cameras, leaving the other panelists looking like a study in reason and rationality.

Yet such is the power of the small business lobby that these apparent shortcomings have not prevented Hale from establishing himself as a force to be reckoned with in Ottawa. In a move that surprised many observers, the Mulroney government appointed Hale in 1984 to a key committee of the prestigious task force reviewing government spending, headed by former deputy prime minister Erik Nielsen.

Meanwhile, at the headquarters of the National Anti-Poverty Organization (NAPO), Havi Echenberg tries to do for the poor what Bulloch and Hale do for small business and d'Aquino does for big business. Here there are no glossy brochures or early Canadian pine furniture; just plastic chairs, arborite tables and brown indoor-outdoor carpeting. NAPO, which receives an annual $250,000 federal grant, attempts to be an advocate for the interests of poor people to both the federal and provincial governments. Like d'Aquino, Bulloch and Hale, Echenberg wants to influence the shape of the tax system. She ranks as one of NAPO's top priorities making sure the current tax reform exercise leads to fewer tax breaks for the rich.

But Echenberg finds her organization lacks the resources to put together the kind of well-argued brief about the tax system that the BCNI presented. "I often go into policy discussions without the background I'd like to have," Echenberg says. "The BCNI wouldn't do that."

Echenberg argues that NAPO is always fighting an uphill battle to try to make people like Michael Wilson understand poverty. "I don't think he can imagine what it's like to be cold, not to mention hungry. When you're so far removed from it, I don't know how you understand that poverty doesn't go away. It stays with you like a skunk." Echenberg has had some direct experience. Although her mother's family was middle class, her father was an unemployed truck driver. Through much of her childhood, the family had little money. "We had middle class values and a working class income."

The difference in the resources of NAPO and the BCNI is, of course, enormous. NAPO struggles to get by on limited sums, which Ottawa could cut off at any time. Indeed, Ottawa has already told NAPO there will be no growth in its future funding. The BCNI, on the other hand, can draw on the virtually unlimited resources of Canadian business. Echenberg is struck by the impressiveness of the BCNI's heavily researched studies. "Their reports look so pretty," she says. "The language is so reasonable, but the ideas so regressive."

This vast discrepancy in resources is typical in the field of lobbying. According to a 1981 study by the Economic Council of Canada, an estimated three hundred business, professional and trade associations on the national scene spend more than $122 million a year on lobbying. This does not even include the significant resources allocated to lobbying by individual companies. The handful of public interest groups, including NAPO and two others involved in representing the rights of the poor—the Public Interest Advocacy Centre and the National Council of Welfare—have collective resources of only about $2 million, less than one percent of what's available for business lobbyists.

Ironically, the tax system is partly responsible for this discrepancy. Corporations are allowed to deduct both their lobbying costs and the costs of membership in lobbying groups like the BCNI. So the money business spends lobbying Ottawa for more tax breaks is itself subject to a tax break. All taxpayers are, in effect, subsidizing the business community in its efforts to wangle more money out of the national treasury.

Of course, the real clout business enjoys with government comes not from its access to ample lobbying funds, but from much more basic factors. Many cabinet ministers rely on business for campaign donations. And, of course, business can easily intimidate a government with threats that it will withdraw investment. Furthermore, on a human level, cabinet ministers are more likely to understand and identify with members of the BCNI—who in many cases went to their schools and live in their neighbourhoods—than with Havi Echenberg or people who have known hunger and cold.

It is interesting to compare the relative ease with which the business community has gotten its way on the tax front with the difficulties corporations face in other areas. In the environmental field, for instance, a highly sensitized public and press place considerable pressure on governments to clamp down on corporate polluters. But when a business group comes asking for tax breaks, it encounters little opposition or even attention. As a result, governments can distribute tax favours to appreciative corporations while risking little political fallout. Tax breaks for the business and investment community can be handled almost like a private matter.

Indeed, as the 1971 tax reform package was dismantled over the decade that followed, almost no one outside the tax community even realized what was going on.

When Jim Brown headed back to his Toronto accounting firm after shepherding the tax reform package into law in 1971, he left behind a reasonably tight piece of legislation. Despite its retreat from the purer positions of the Carter report, the new tax put an end to some important methods by which companies and individuals had managed to avoid tax over the years.

But with the departure of Benson, Bryce and Brown, a new team took over at Finance, and the tax reform package soon began unravelling.

Ironically, while tax disappeared from the public stage after 1971, corporations and investors were aware of tax issues as never before. The constant lobbying of the previous years had, in effect, raised the profile of tax in the business community. Furthermore, there was a huge new tax act to digest and understand.

As more and more companies and investors sought professional advice on tax matters, a new tax industry sprang up and flourished. Ambitious young law and accounting students started thinking of careers in tax. All the major law and accounting firms started hiring professionals specializing in tax, and large companies developed significant tax departments. Many tax experts left Finance and found lucrative new careers in private firms, bringing both expertise in the new laws and familiarity with the workings of the Finance Department. Suddenly thousands of young, aggressive, highly trained experts were poring over the laws looking for one thing: holes. "No other statute is so carefully scrutinized," said one former Finance official. "If there's a misplaced comma, and it can be exploited, it will be."

Of course there had always been bright tax practitioners looking for ways to save their clients money. But in the pre-tax-reform days, there were fewer of them and they had adopted the new schemes more cautiously. In those days, it typically took several years from the time a new scheme was devised and gained popularity until the Finance Department clamped down and blocked it with an amendment. In the post-tax-reform era, however, the whole process happened in a matter of months. Now that tax had become so important in the eyes of the corporate mangers, tax lawyers feared missing out on the latest tricks and started getting together regularly in informal meetings to share ideas. With such rapid dissemination of knowledge and such keen interest, Ottawa found itself having to introduce literally hundreds of pages of amendments each year just to stop flagrant abuses.

The tax reform exercise had also had a major impact on the Liberal government. After years of acrimonious relations with business over tax reform, the government mostly wanted peace. The choice of John Turner for finance minister was apparently an olive branch proffered to the business community. A corporate lawyer who had worked for Stikeman Elliott in Montreal, Turner was fairly knowledgeable about tax and had actually done some tax work. He ushered in the new era of friendly government-business relations with broad new tax breaks for business. In his first budget as finance minister, Turner brought in a generous new measure that allowed firms to write off new investments in manufacturing and processing equipment in only two years, much faster than these assets depreciated on their own books. Turner also singled out the country's manufacturing and processing companies for an additional bonus, giving them a 9 percent reduction in their corporate tax rate.

And, in a major political initiative stolen from the election campaign of Conservative Leader Robert Stanfield, Turner indexed the entire personal income tax system to the cost of living. This meant that individuals would not automatically be bumped into higher tax brackets when their incomes rose in pace with inflation.

The government's new generosity to individuals and corporations kept the Canadian economy relatively buoyant while others around the world faltered badly under the weight of massive oil price increases. But it also greatly diminished Ottawa's power to raise revenues, thereby planting the seeds of the huge national deficit that would grow in future years.

Inside the Finance Department, the approach to the nation's finances was changing as well. The new assistant deputy minister for tax policy, Mickey Cohen, was a bright young Bay Street tax lawyer who had come to Ottawa to provide technical advice to the Commons committee reviewing the white paper. Cohen felt that the tax legislation as it stood was too tight and needed loosening—a view that was in sync with the new approach John Turner had brought to the Finance portfolio. Arthur Drache, a tax lawyer who joined Finance in November 1972, not long after the new team took over the department, recalls that unravelling the tight tax reform package was very much on the agenda. "By the time I came in, the name of the game was to unwind tax reform without saying that, and that process took almost a dozen years," comments Drache. "Nobody would admit it in so many words, but in the tax community it became very apparent."

With its unstated plan to undo the work of the past decade, the department introduced changes that greatly helped business and well-to-do taxpayers while offering little benefit to the wider public. Most of these measures provided increased opportunities for high-income people to avoid tax in two ways: by deferring tax or by converting income into a form where it would be taxed more lightly.

Here's how the situation looked to the high-income person in 1972. There were basically three different types of income and each was subject to a different rate of tax, some more punitive than others. The most desirable type of income to receive was capital gains, which were taxed at the low rate of 25 percent. Next was dividend income, which, thanks to the dividend tax credit, was taxed at 33 percent. All other income, which principally meant employment income, was subject to the regular income tax rates, which rose at the top end to 65 percent. The first two categories of income involved investments and were therefore confined to investors. The salary-earner was really the only one stuck with the high rates of the regular income tax system.

There was another tax rate to consider too—the corporate tax rate. It was roughly 50 percent, but with the small business tax credit, the corporate rate could be reduced to 25 percent. If high-income taxpayers could have their salaries paid into a corporation they controlled, they could take advantage of this generous tax break for small business.

Here's how it worked. An investor could set up a personal

corporation to receive his income. This way, he would be faced with two taxes—the corporate tax, which was only 25 percent thanks to the small business tax credit, and the tax on dividends when he took money out of the company in the form of dividends. But he could avoid paying himself a dividend as long as he wanted. If he chose to leave his money in the corporation for many years, he could defer a substantial amount of tax, allowing him to hold onto that money and invest it to earn more money. He could also leave that additional investment income in the corporation, building up a nice little fortune in his personal corporation that was only subject to a 25 percent rate of tax. For this reason, high-income taxpayers frequently used personal corporations to hold their investment income. In one celebrated case, the courts upheld the right of Hamilton Tigercat coach Ralph Sazio to have the football club pay his salary into a personal corporation, allowing Sazio to do an end-run around the high rates of the personal income tax system.

But the 1971 legislation rained on this parade. It stipulated that a corporation would be denied the benefits of the small business tax credit unless it used the money saved through the credit to re-invest in the growth of the business. For instance, a small widget manufacturer would be entitled to receive the credit if it re-invested the savings in new equipment for its widget manufacturing operation.

But a corporation would be cut off from the benefits of the small business tax credit if it used the savings to simply invest in stocks for the purpose of accumulating investment income in the corporation. So under the new laws, a personal corporation owned by an investor, a hockey player or a rock star would lose the credit unless it re-invested in plant or equipment—in other words, re-invested in some kind of real business operation—which was usually not what the investor, hockey player or rock star had in mind. This was a blow to many a high-income taxpayer who hadn't the slightest desire to operate a bona fide small business but who still wanted to enjoy the tax benefits available to small business.

The personal corporation was near death as a result of the

1971 legislation. But, in a generous concession, Ottawa revived it in 1973 by withdrawing the strict rules on re-investment. Investors and others could once again use personal corporations to hold investment income, thereby deferring substantial amounts of tax. In a flash, personal corporations made a comeback.

But the small business honey pot was to get sweeter yet. One measure, introduced in the April 1977 budget, surprised even the tax community. It called for an enrichment of the dividend tax credit so that a taxpayer in the top income bracket would now face a tax of only 25 percent on dividend income, instead of 33 percent—a substantial benefit.

The reasoning behind this measure was that by taxing dividend income at the same rate as capital gains income, the incentive to convert dividends into capital gains would be removed. This much was achieved. But in correcting this problem, the government created a major new one. With a richer dividend tax credit, it now became possible once again to receive income through a corporation, pay both a corporate and dividend tax, and still end up paying less tax than if the money had simply been received directly as regular income. In fact, on $150,000 of income, the saving could be as high as $9,000 just for funnelling the money through a corporation that existed only on paper. The floodgates were open.

Personal corporations returned with a vengeance now. Corporate executives, insurance agents, athletes, performers—anyone with a high income and access to an accountant—set up personal corporations in record numbers. Professionals, such as doctors, lawyers, accountants and dentists, who are generally barred from incorporating under provincial legislation, began clamouring for the right to incorporate so they could reap the rich tax benefits too. Lawyers and accountants got around the restrictions in some cases by setting up management service corporations, which would provide their financial and administrative services for a fee. The tight little package of rules designed to carefully target the small business credit had been rendered as leaky as a sieve.

The business and investment community had also longed

for more leniency on the new capital gains rules. In 1974, many of their pleas were answered. While capital gains were still to be taxed at half rates as specified in the 1971 legislation, the new rules opened up some new possibilities for deferring the tax. Under the dull heading of "corporate reorganizations," the government introduced changes that were anything but dull to the investment community. They were manna from heaven, worth millions of dollars. Basically, they allowed individuals and companies in certain situations to receive the benefits of a capital gain and defer paying tax on it indefinitely. Again, all that was involved was a little extra paperwork.

Consider the following scenario. An individual owns an office building which he bought for $1 million. A few years later, it has risen in value to $10 million. If he simply sells it, he will receive a $9 million capital gain. With a 25 percent tax rate on capital gains, he will owe the government at least $2 million in tax.

But under the 1974 "corporate reorganization" rules, he could pay considerably less tax. Now, the company purchasing the building could pay him his $10 million in a slightly different way. It could give him $1 million in cash and $9 million worth of company shares. Under the 1971 rules, his $9 million capital gain would have been taxable whether he received it in cash or shares. But under the 1974 rules, the capital gain would only be taxed when he cashed in the shares, which he might not choose to do for many years.

There were many variations on this basic theme in the 1974 changes. One interesting one had the effect of making it easier for companies trying to buy up other companies. Consider a case in which the shares of a target company are worth $50 at the time of the takeover bid. Under the old rules, a stockholder who had purchased those shares years earlier for, say, $20 would have realized a capital gain of $30 if he had sold his shares to the takeover company. Since the shareholder would have had to pay tax on this capital gain, he would have asked a higher price from the takeover company trying to buy his shares. But under the new corporate reorganization rules, the shareholder could trade his shares in the target company for an equivalent value of shares in the takeover company—without triggering a capital gain. Since he would not be faced with any tax as a result of the transaction, he would be willing to trade his stock at a lower price, making the deal less expensive for the takeover company.

The April 1977 budget also included a host of new tax deferral opportunities. From now on, executives could receive part of their salaries in corporate stock, rather than in cash. Until the stock was sold, they would pay no tax on it, providing them with a substantial tax deferral. Furthermore, when it was sold, it would be treated as a capital gain and only taxed at half rates. Had they received the money directly as part of their salaries, it would have been taxed on the day they received it—and at full personal income tax rates.

In a similar move, the 1977 budget created some tax savings for shareholders who received dividends in the form of stocks, rather than in the usual form of cash. By receiving payment in stocks, shareholders could avoid paying tax indefinitely, until they cashed in the stock and realized a capital gain.

The 1977 budget also offered a new concession that calmed the fears of speculators. Investors had sometimes worried that certain types of investments could be regarded by the courts as speculative business ventures, whose profits, therefore, could be disqualified from the lower capital gains rate. But the budget gave shareholders the right to simply choose to have their shares treated as capital gains rather than income, no matter what the circumstances.

Although the budget made far more concessions to high-income investors than it did to ordinary salary earners, there was barely a murmur of protest from a largely unsuspecting public. The architect of the budget, Mickey Cohen, escaped criticism entirely. Indeed, he won kudos from his political masters for the peace that reigned between government and business in the years during which he steered Ottawa's tax policy.

But Cohen had bought this peace largely through concessions. While his predecessors had enraged investors with tax reform proposals that threatened to remove their privileges, Cohen soothed and delighted them as he gradually restored their favoured position. After years of enriching the rich, Cohen emerged unscathed—even uncriticized—from his key job at Finance and went on to a higher job as deputy minister of industry and trade. In his years at Finance, Cohen had managed to unravel much of the tax reform package. Five years later, he would return to finish the job.

In the meantime, however, the tax community continued to pick holes in what was left of the tax reform package, coming up with ever more inventive methods of tax avoidance for the rich. "There was such a bag of stuff, it was pure gimmicksville," said one former Finance official.

For the vast majority of taxpayers, however, there were no gimmicks and no bright spots on the tax horizon. Ironically, the controversial 1979 budget of Conservative Finance Minister John Crosbie would have provided some tax benefits for those at the lower end, through his proposed energy tax credit. But with the defeat of that budget and the end of the brief Tory reign of Joe Clark, those hopes were dashed. By the time Allan MacEachen took over as Liberal finance minister in 1980, the tax avoidance gimmickery called out for action. MacEachen decided to tackle the problem, apparently unaware of the fierce opposition that awaited him.

CHAPTER EIGHT

The Cosy World Of Tax Meets The Kilted Priest: Allan MacEachen's November 1981 Budget

"The big boys of business and finance are the real source of trouble."
—Rev. Moses Coady, leader of the Antigonish Movement and mentor of Allan MacEachen

"Immense power and despotic economic domination is concentrated in the hands of a few. . . . The whole economic life has become hard, cruel and relentless in a ghastly measure."
—Pope Pius XI, in a 1931 Papal encyclical

"Tax reform is the hobby horse of every radical bourgeois."
—Karl Marx

When Allan MacEachen stood up in the House of Commons to make his budget speech on the evening of November 12, 1981, he was at the height of his career. He not only held the prestigious and powerful position of finance minister, but he had been officially elevated to the number two rank in the Canadian government: deputy prime minister. It was a mark of Pierre Trudeau's respect for the veteran politician from Cape Breton, one of the few anglophone ministers ever to gain his trust.

After twenty-four years in Parliament, a number of demanding cabinet posts and a long, successful stint as government house leader, MacEachen had developed an uncanny grasp of politics. Through his shrewd understanding of the workings of Parliament, he had often steered the Liberal party safely through difficult waters. And, unlike so many other powerful ministers, he never seemed to get into any political scrapes. Indeed, he was always saving the skins of other ministers, using his skill and strategy in the House to turn treacherous situations to the government's advantage. For that he had earned a reputation as a wily and crafty political animal. He had played a key role in returning the Liberals to power after their 1979 defeat, chairing the party's policy committee during the difficult 1980 campaign. All this gave him, if not popularity in the Liberal caucus, at least considerable clout. It was not vain ambition which led him to believe that, after Trudeau resigned, he might finally have a shot at the top job himself—something he keenly wanted after almost half a lifetime in politics.

In many ways, the budget he delivered on that cool November night was perfectly in line with his past achievements and his future goals. MacEachen had always been considered on the left wing of the Liberal party. In the 60s, he had played a crucial role in the implementation of two key social welfare programs—the national medical insurance scheme and the federal pension plan. In his first budget as finance minister in October 1980, he had introduced the national energy program in a bold and generally popular attempt to gain Canadian control over the nation's oil and gas resources.

Now in this 1981 budget he was proposing a dramatic assault on a tax system that he said favoured the rich. It was brave talk for a minister of finance, who must rely to some extent on the co-operation of the business community. But MacEachen stated his intentions clearly that night: "Some higher-income individuals are able to reduce their tax rate to well below that paid by lower-income Canadians. Some can escape paying tax entirely. This is unacceptable." The budget amounted to a declaration of war on tax breaks for the rich. About 25,000 of those with incomes over $100,000 would face average tax increases of $23,000 the following year. Not since the Carter report and Edgar Benson's white paper had there been such far-reaching recommendations aimed at limiting the tax breaks enjoyed by the well-to-do.

When MacEachen sat down after his speech, in his seat next to the prime minister, he was given a rousing round of applause by the large Liberal majority in the House. It was a moment to be savoured, a moment of approval and satisfying political power the likes of which he would never fully experience again. Even as he sat there basking in the praise of his colleagues, the measures he announced were being soundly denounced on national television. They were soon to unleash a torrent of abuse beyond anything he had experienced in his many years in the political limelight. Nobody, not even the wily finance minister himself, had realized the enormous gamble he was taking. Within weeks, his reputation as the shrewd, invincible politician was gone, and with it, his long-cherished dream of someday leading the country.

Inverness, Nova Scotia was a bleak coal mining town in the 1920s, and Allan MacEachen grew up on the wrong side of the tracks. His father was a coal miner and the family lived in a humble company-built house on River Street, known locally as Shithouse Street because the outhouses had been built along the street instead of behind the houses. The MacEachen family—there were two sons in addition to Allan —was closely knit and traditional, and they struggled to get by in the difficult lean years of the depression. Catholicism and Scottish tradition played a key role in the life of the town, and they shaped much of the early life of Allan MacEachen. He learned to speak fluent Gaelic as a child and developed a love of Scottish culture, an interest he was to maintain all his life.

The Nova Scotia MacEachen grew up in was more Scottish than Scotland. Many in Inverness county spoke English with a lilting accent, an indication that they'd learned Gaelic before English. The annual Highland Games, when the rural communities congregated each summer in Antigonish, Nova Scotia, were more avidly anticipated than Christmas. For almost a week, the town was awash in tartans. There was a huge parade, led by the bishop, caber-tossing events and days of bagpipes and highland dancing. Virtually everyone claimed some kind of Scottish ancestry and did so with great pride. When a prominent clan chieftan arrived from Scotland for a visit one summer, he was greeted with great fanfare by Angus L. Macdonald, the Nova Scotia premier. Macdonald delivered his welcoming remarks in fluent Gaelic—which then had to be translated into English for the clan chieftan.

The other profound influence on MacEachen's early life was Catholicism. He was educated by nuns in the local Catholic school, where his intelligence was noticed from an early age. The nuns were always looking for bright young recruits for the priesthood and would tell the local priest when a student showed particular promise. The Church could then provide whatever financial help was needed to ensure the boy got a proper education at St Francis Xavier University in Antigonish, about a hundred miles from Inverness. And so MacEachen, the poor son of a miner, was sent off to university, carrying his belongings in a cardboard box.

At St Francis Xavier, or St FX as it is locally known, MacEachen encountered a tight little world of traditional Catholicism, a world for which he was well prepared. The university provided a very traditional education, with emphasis on the classics. Latin was virtually compulsory; philosophy courses were even taught in Latin. There was also, of course, a heavy emphasis on religion, with daily mass and religious instruction. It was a close, intense, patriarchal environment, presided over by priests, who lived in residence at the university. Nuns played a humble back-up role, making the beds and darning the priests' socks at night.

The aim was to take the best and the brightest young Catholic men, give them basic classical and religious training and turn them out as priests, able to assume a senior role in the lives of their communities. Indeed, this was the expected route for bright, ambitious boys. Dr Pat Nicholson, the rector of the university, assumed that young men at St Francis were in training for the priesthood, until confronted with evidence to the contrary. It was not uncommon for young men to sign up for science courses, even if they hadn't the slightest interest in science, as a way of indicating that they were inclined towards more worldly pursuits.

But if the life at St Francis Xavier was still cloistered in the 40s and 50s, it was by no means sedate. Throughout Nova Scotia, established society was facing a challenge from a religious and social movement pushing for radical change. And that movement was centred at St FX. Its leader, a rough-hewn priest at the university by the name of Moses Coady, was a towering figure—both physically and intellectually—who had a strong humanitarian bent and a flair for dramatic oratory. Coady and a group of priests around him were raising fundamental social and political questions that were causing waves well beyond the university.

In many ways, their movement had overtones of the liberation theology that was later to emerge among elements of the Catholic clergy in Latin America. The Antigonish movement, as it came to be known, was steeped in religion and drew inspiration from the papal encyclicals of 1891 and 1931, which had attacked the growing concentration of economic power. The movement emphasized the role of the Church in improving the lives of its parishioners materially as well as spiritually. While many religious leaders still accepted poverty as part of the divine plan, Coady denounced poverty as the product of an evil economic system. In its place, he wanted a system of worker-run co-operatives that would free the individual farmer, miner and fisherman from the domination of a small economic élite.

Coady and his followers therefore championed the cause of

Nova Scotia fishermen in their struggle to gain independence from the powerful local fish merchants, who both bought their fish and sold them their fishing gear. The fish merchants were a key force in the business community of the province, and a very comfortable relationship had developed between the business élite and the Church élite. Coady and the Antigonish movement sought to shake this up, to push the Church out of its cosy corner in the establishment and into the frontlines of social reform.

With all this intense intellectual ferment, the university was a very exciting place for Allan MacEachen. He became deeply involved in the continuous political and theological debates that raged around him. Coady and Dr Dan McCormack, another priest-activist on campus, became powerful figures in MacEachen's life. Their intellectual vigour and deep concern for the province's poor—the ranks from which MacEachen came—was an endless source of inspiration to him.

When MacEachen later joined the university teaching staff as a professor of political science, he became even more intensely involved in the intellectual and spiritual life of the priest-reformers. He lived in a suite on campus, as the priests did, went to mass with them each day and ate his meals with them in the priests' dining-room. "They looked on him as one of them," said a close observer. "They accepted him as one of them, someone who for some inexplicable reason didn't become a priest. They talked to one another as equals."

But the reformers in the Antigonish movement didn't just confine themselves to debating the great political and theological questions. They wanted to *change* things. They believed they could change things. And they didn't want to impose these changes from above. They wanted to involve the impoverished people of Nova Scotia—the fishermen, farmers and miners—in working out their own solutions, in fighting to gain control of their own economic futures. An important thrust of the movement, therefore, was aimed at educating the simple people of the province about the world and about their own situations. Education was seen as the key to a better life—just as it had been for Allan MacEachen.

With parts of the province still inaccessible by road in the winter, radio seemed like the ideal way to bring education and new ideas to the isolated fishing communities along the coast. Coady's followers set up a co-op educational radio station, CJFX, and the reform movement took on an exciting new dimension. The power of radio seemed immense. Suddenly the reformers could bring their intellectual world to people beyond the university. Every Sunday afternoon, the radio station had a special program called "The People's School," which would focus on a broad range of national and international issues. The aim was to educate the people through radio debates about everything from unemployment and inflation to such remote and esoteric subjects as, Should Red China be admitted to the United Nations? On Monday nights, a program called "Life In These Maritimes" used the same format to address local topics and to encourage people towards greater self-sufficiency. So instead of pondering the fate of Red China, Monday night listeners were treated to discussions on the need for more local libraries or the merits of planting one's own blueberries or Christmas trees. Nova Scotia's renaissance man, as envisioned by the reformers, would be an expert in blueberry cultivation as well as world politics.

To further enhance the impact of the radio programs, the reformers arranged local clubs, which held study sessions just before the broadcasts came on the air. A group would gather in someone's kitchen or in a local parish hall and spend an hour discussing the day's topic and then stay on and listen to the broadcast together. The priests conducting the study sessions relied on special explanatory bulletins sent out from the university—bulletins that were often written by Allan MacEachen. He and the other reformers would also participate in the radio debates and drop in on the various study clubs, providing direct input into the debates.

All this was really quite subversive, and the implications were not lost on the conservative forces within the province. Both inside and outside the Church some regarded Coady as a communist. Certainly his ideas had dramatic implications for the highly conservative, Church-dominated society of Nova Scotia in the 30s, 40s and 50s. A big issue for the reformers, for instance, was the creation of regional libraries. The lack of libraries was considered an impediment to the process of educating—and thereby politicizing—the people. The reformers had tried to compensate by establishing a public library system through the university extension department, which had been set up by Coady in the 1920s. The librarian, Sister Marie Michael, had a weekly radio program on CJFX called "This is Your Library." Listeners would write to her, requesting books she had described on the air, and she would parcel them up and send them out through the mail. But this was clearly a slow and cumbersome way of preparing the population for radical social change.

But regional libraries did not sit well with some members of the Church who saw no particular need to further educate their parishioners, to fill their heads with ideas about changing society. Many churches already had libraries, and they offered all the books that any sensible Catholic needed to read. Public libraries would reduce the Church's control over the dissemination of ideas among the simple townspeople of the province. Just like the radio broadcasts, which threatened to politicize people on some key issues, the libraries were sure to bring new ideas into a world where the Church had traditionally provided all the ideas.

MacEachen was deeply affected by the intense world of the Antigonish movement. It was a world of constant debate, and MacEachen's intelligence and philosophical orientation drew him into the thick of it. Almost every day at 3:30 P.M., MacEachen, Coady and McCormack, known affectionately on campus as "Dr Dan," would set out on a long walk from the university, strolling into the town, sometimes stopping for tea at the Golden Glow restaurant. And through those long daily walks, the talk and debate would continue. Some days the reformers would take a car trip to a nearby town to meet labour leaders or to visit with an activist priest over cheese and biscuits. As the group headed off in the car, everyone would join in a rosary and a litany, and then plunge into more talk, more animated debate: Should civil servants be allowed to organize politically? Was an unemployment rate above 5 percent morally acceptable? What should be done with Red China?

The talk never stopped. Behind it all was a deep and exhilarating conviction on the part of the reformers that they could actually bring about social change. "Everybody was talking and discussing as if we had power," recalls one reformer. "There was a sense we could change the world." Nobody felt this spirit of the Antigonish movement more deeply than MacEachen. "It was the bone of his bones, flesh of his flesh." MacEachen was often compared on campus with two other political science professors at the university, Hugh Gillis and John Stewart. Of the three, Hugh Gillis was considered the most intelligent, Stewart, the most political, and MacEachen, the one with the greatest social conscience.

That social conscience apparently stayed with MacEachen throughout his long years in politics. It is evident in many of the causes he championed in the Trudeau cabinet and the social welfare legislation he helped put in place. He played a crucial role in championing Judy LaMarsh's medicare scheme against right-wing elements within the Liberal cabinet who opposed the plan. Interestingly, MacEachen had once written a bulletin for a "People's School" radio broadcast on the need for a national medicare scheme. Twenty years later, he was able to turn the idea into the law of the land. As one observer noted: "The Antigonish movement taught him that things could be changed. When he went into politics, he saw national politics could be used to change things as the Antigonish movement had been used."

First elected as an MP from Cape Breton in 1953 and defeated in the Diefenbaker sweep of 1958, MacEachen was spotted by Lester Pearson as a promising talent. While many defeated Liberals simply headed home after the 1958 Liberal rout, MacEachen landed one of the few Liberal jobs in Ottawa in the Opposition leader's office, where he became a key Pearson aide and strategist. In the 1963 election, when the Liberals regained power and MacEachen regained his seat, Pearson brought his trusted aide into the cabinet as labour minister. MacEachen was to remain an important cabinet figure, holding a number of portfolios and commanding respect in the Liberal inner circle.

But it was as government House leader that MacEachen made perhaps his strongest mark within the party. After the Liberals were reduced to a two-seat margin over the Tories in the 1972 election, MacEachen's role became particularly crucial, as he manoeuvred and negotiated over legislation in the House to keep the NDP satisfied and the Tories at bay. Trudeau had little interest in the goings-on of Parliament, which he regarded somewhat contemptuously. He was happy to leave the intricate business of the House to MacEachen, who handled it with skill. Tory House leader Ged Baldwin, who had to deal regularly with MacEachen over House business, recalls him as a straight shooter. "When MacEachen gave his word, he always kept it."

MacEachen also played a key role in whipping the party back into shape during the chaotic 1980 election. When the Liberals returned triumphant after the brief reign of Joe Clark's Tories, MacEachen was entrusted with the sensitive post of finance minister. It was in some ways an odd portfolio for MacEachen. Although he had a background in economics, he had little experience with the businessmen who beat a regular path to the finance minister's door and expect to receive a warm welcome there.

In MacEachen, businessmen discovered a remote man with few of the social graces they were used to. At least that's what they discovered when they could find him. He could be highly evasive, to the point of retreating to the more familiar world of Cape Breton, when he felt like not seeing anyone.

If MacEachen was something of an odd choice for Finance, he had stepped into the job at an extremely difficult time. The improvement of social programs over the previous twenty years had led Canadians to expect a wide safety net beneath them—a net that became all the more important with the ravages of inflation and unemployment during the 70s. But the business community increasingly came to see these social programs as the source of the country's growing deficit. What business wanted was a firm indication that the government was prepared to abandon its social spending, shrink the public sector and curb the growing expectations of the population for ever-improved facilities and services.

The business community was right in believing that the deficit had its roots in the expansion of the country's social programs. But this was only part of the story. As we have seen, while Ottawa had been extending the welfare net in the 60s, it had spent much of the 70s undermining its method of paying for the programs. By opening up more and more corporate tax breaks throughout the 70s, the government had lost millions of dollars in revenue. "The persistent efforts to buy the corporations' affections with their own tax dollars created gaping holes in both the tax structure and the fiscal position of the federal government," notes U of T political scientist David Wolfe.

At the same time, Ottawa had indexed the personal income tax system and introduced a number of tax breaks for individuals. So, with an eroding tax base and growing expenditures, the country was sinking ever deeper into debt. The solution of business leaders was to keep the tax breaks and stop the spending.

The Liberals, however, had had little corporate support in either the 1979 or 1980 election and were not inclined to start

slashing programs they had painstakingly developed just to
please a disloyal business community. If anything, there was a
sense in the new government that business had unfairly abandoned the Liberals, despite the generous tax concessions Liberal governments had dolloped out to the corporate sector in
the 70s. With a comfortable majority and a renewed excitement about traditional liberal goals, the Liberal cabinet of
1980 keenly set to work mapping out grandiose plans for
expensive new megaprojects and regional development
schemes. "There's no question it was a more leftist, interventionist cabinet than the [Liberal] one in 1979," said a high-
ranking civil servant. Restraint and deficit reduction were
certainly not tops on the agenda.

To the extent that deficit reduction was an issue, some
Liberals were focussing their attention on the side of the
equation that business was happy to ignore: the revenue lost
through tax breaks. In 1979, Joe Clark's Conservative government had produced a telling little document called the "Tax
Expenditure Account," which detailed how much revenue the
government was losing through various tax breaks. Although
ostensibly a dry set of figures, the Clark government's document contained some shocking information: Ottawa had given
up more than $7 billion in 1977 through tax breaks to corpora-
tions alone, and another $25 billion to individuals. No wonder
the country was in debt.

Having made this tantalizing information available for the
first time—perhaps to show how irresponsible the Liberals
had been with the federal treasury—the Tories seemed reluctant to do anything about it. They still clung to the notion that
the only way to cut the deficit was to cut spending. Eliminating tax breaks seemed out of the question.

But the dramatic numbers in the "Tax Expenditure Account" had aroused interest among Liberals. MacEachen recalls the subject surfacing a number of times in the party
policy committee he chaired during the 1980 election campaign. It never became an election issue, but it was a concern
among Liberals who feared reduced corporate revenues would

mean less money to finance spending programs. "Within the Liberal caucus, there was a demand . . . [that we] tackle the question of tax expenditures," said MacEachen. "They were so enormous that they distorted the system and impeded the ability of the government to undertake expenditures."

MacEachen got a taste of just how much spending his colleagues had in mind. At a pre-budget cabinet meeting in Cape Breton in September 1981, they asked for a total of $10 billion to finance new projects and development schemes. But MacEachen, despite his own sponsorship of some costly programs in the past, was anxious in his new role as finance minister to hold the line somewhat on the deficit. In the end, he agreed to a spending increase of $4 billion, on the understanding that $2 billion of that would be financed by a drop in federal transfer payments to the provinces and $2 billion would come from increased tax revenues. Cutting the provinces' payments was bound to be dicey politically; raising taxes by $2 billion was sure to be even more so.

An assault on tax expenditures seemed like an attractive option. The idea had been wafting around in the Liberal caucus since the election campaign. It appeared to be one of the few alternatives to cutting back spending plans, which the Liberals were loathe to do. At the time, risking the wrath of business seemed like the lesser evil. "I don't think there was any strong reluctance," recalls one who attended the meeting. "The cabinet ministers around that particular table were more interested in getting a licence to spend." Furthermore, they had reason to believe the reaction from business might not be that intense. They were told that some prominent businessmen had recently communicated to Ottawa their concerns about the proliferation of tax breaks popular with executives. So great was the demand among senior executives for tax-free perks that a few major companies were balking at the costs and were privately urging the government to impose limits. This hint that maybe even business would welcome reforms surely meant it was time to act. MacEachen was given the go-ahead.

If concern had been growing about tax breaks among Liberal politicians, those feelings were even stronger within the Finance Department. The 1971 tax reform package had been almost completely unravelled by 1981. Tax avoidance schemes had become the rage among high-income investors and professionals. The high inflation rates of the late 70s and early 80s only made these schemes all the more popular, as investors faced high rates of tax on what were often inflationary gains. On the other hand, the tax system also allowed inflation to work to the advantage of investors. If they borrowed money to make investments, the interest costs on the loan were deductible. Part of the interest cost was purely inflationary, yet they were able to deduct the full amount against other income.

Attention inside the department centred on how more and more high-income executives were arranging to be paid in ways that would spare them tax, principally through stock options and interest-free loans from their companies. In fact, the tax avoidance schemes were far more popular among Canadian executives than Finance officials realized—a fact that only became clear later, when the protests started rolling in over the government's moves to shut them down. At the time, however, it was difficult for Finance to assess the extent of the tax avoidance, since executives were not required to report the full details of their compensation package on their tax returns.

Ironically, some of the information Finance was seeking about Canadian executives was available in Washington, since firms whose stock was traded on the U.S. stock markets were required to divulge detailed information about the compensation of their top five executives. (Conrad Black often spared himself the embarrassment of public disclosure of his handsome income by having his companies pay him slightly less than the firm's fifth most highly paid official.)

Using data filed in Washington, *The Financial Post* calculated the compensation packages of Canada's top-earning executives. In a front page story in May 1981, Allan Robinson showed that some of Canada's best-paid executives were receiving large chunks of their income in stock options. Indeed, Jack Gallagher, chairman of Dome Petroleum Ltd., received a compensation package worth $682,000, all in the form of interest-free loans that allowed him to buy company stock. There were other interesting cases too. A. A. MacNaughton, vice-chairman of Genstar Ltd., and R. J. Turner, Genstar's president, each had low-interest loans for $2.5 million for the purchase of stock options. William Wilder and A. M. McIntosh, two senior executives at Hiram Walker-Consumers Home Ltd., had interest free loans worth more than half a million dollars each.

The revelations raised eyebrows inside the Finance Department, and an official was dispatched to Washington for more details. What interested Finance was the extent to which such corporate benefits were allowing these high-income executives to legally avoid tax. Gallagher, for instance, had received no basic salary from Dome. So, despite his generous package of interest-free loans, which made him the most highly compensated executive in Canada, he had managed to almost completely avoid tax.

U.S. records showed the practice of paying senior executives in tax-free perks was widespread throughout the Canadian corporate world, and was particularly rampant in the oil patch. The data only furthered the conviction inside the department that the Canadian tax system had become an unsupervised playground for the rich.

It was a view that found some favour with the new deputy minister, Ian Stewart. He encouraged his officials to delve deeper, allowing the department to carry out a significant investigation of just how little tax many high-income Canadians were paying. They even went over to Revenue Canada and got access to the tax records of some high-income individuals. By allowing his officials to pursue this course, Stewart played a key role in shaping the November 1981 budget.

Born and raised in Toronto, Stewart had studied economics

at Queen's, Oxford and Cornell universities before returning in the mid-60s to work for the Bank of Canada and later for the Treasury Department and for Energy, Mines and Resources. He quickly rose to the top ranks of the civil service, joining the Privy Council in 1975, where he served as Trudeau's senior economic advisor. In that capacity, he wrote a controversial document called "The Way Ahead"—a futuristic look at the problems to be tackled after the removal of wage and price controls. In 1978, Trudeau sent Stewart back to Energy Mines and Resources as deputy minister, where he developed the blueprint for the national energy program. When the newly elected Liberals returned in the spring of 1980, Stewart was awarded the top deputy minister slot at Finance. The carefree days of Mickey Cohen's tax reign were definitely at an end.

And yet, despite the reformist inclinations of both Mac-Eachen and Stewart, the November 1981 budget, with its vision of a fairer tax system, can almost be seen as the result of a series of accidents. As late as the summer of 1981, with less than three months to go before the budget, Finance officials were still toying with a whole different set of tax changes whose central purpose was to curb inflation. Called a "tax-based incomes policy," the idea of these measures was to give tax breaks to companies which kept their wage increases below a certain point, providing a kind of tax version of the anti-inflation board. The scheme would have no doubt been as unpopular with labour as direct controls had been.

With Finance unsure of exactly where it was heading, Glenn Jenkins arrived in the department in August to take up the job of assistant deputy minister for tax policy. An economist and strong believer in the free market, Jenkins had little interest in intervening against inflation with the kinds of tax measures under consideration. But he was concerned about the way inflation was luring high-income investors into ever more exotic tax avoidance schemes. He had just returned from teaching in the United States, where he had been influenced by Reagan's dramatic lowering of taxes for high-income Americans. Jenkins wanted to see the top Canadian tax rate reduced from 65 percent to 50 percent, bringing it into line with the new top U.S. rate. But Jenkins was also well aware that Ottawa couldn't afford to simply lower the top tax rate and lose a huge chunk of revenue. The government would have to make up the loss somewhere else.

Essentially, Jenkins was coming backwards at an idea that had already become popular with Finance: cutting off tax breaks. And while many of his officials were less than thrilled about the idea of dropping the tax rate on high-income individuals, they eagerly provided Jenkins with a list of tax breaks they felt should go.

What was emerging, almost by coincidence, was a consensus that something should be done about tax breaks. For the Liberal cabinet ministers, it was the only real alternative to reducing their spending plans; for Glenn Jenkins it was the way to lower the top tax rate; for experts in the Finance department, it was a long-overdue attempt to replug the gaping holes and restore a more neutral tax system.

The result was a package that captivated the finance minister. When MacEachen saw statistics showing the extent to which tax breaks benefited the rich at the expense of others, he became convinced of the rightness of the reform. "I thought it was a super series of proposals," recalls MacEachen, "which related very directly to social justice and equity in our society." The tax system "cried out for correction," he says.

The budget's theme of fairness and social justice were central in the minds of MacEachen and Ian Stewart. These themes were expressed rather eloquently in a budget document which both MacEachen and Stewart considered essential to the budget. Called "Analysis of Federal Tax Expenditures for Individuals," it outlined, in simple laymen's language, how the wide assortment of tax breaks had resulted in a serious erosion of the federal tax base. In the case of personal income tax alone, an astonishing $47 billion of income managed to escape taxation in 1979. The paper went on to show how unevenly distributed the benefits of these tax breaks were. For the millions of taxpayers who earned between $10,000 and $15,000, tax breaks resulted in an average saving of only $771. But for the small group with incomes over $100,000, the average saving from tax breaks amounted to a staggering $46,000. "Some high-income individuals are extraordinarily successful in reducing their taxes," the paper noted wryly. Indeed, 3,400 tax filers with incomes over $50,000 had managed to reduce their tax burden to zero.

And then came the clincher: if all these tax breaks were to be eliminated tomorrow, there would be enough revenue for everybody's tax rate to be dropped 45 percent! Clearly this would benefit the ordinary person. The paper gave the November 81 budget a philosophical framework and potentially wide appeal. "We thought it would blow people away," says Stewart. "But nobody paid any attention to it." The information in the paper, which amounted to a stinging indictment of the tax system created by successive Liberal governments, remains one of the best-kept secrets in Ottawa.

The budget also went after a number of important tax breaks enjoyed by corporations, particularly the loose rules which allowed extraordinarily fast write-offs for plant and equipment. Finance had considered preparing a document, similar to the one showing how individuals avoided tax, exposing how corporations did so and how the bigger corporations got the bulk of the benefit. But in the end, the idea of focussing negatively on corporations was considered too politically risky. Although the budget raised corporate taxes, it did so without much fanfare.

Presumably, the point of getting more tax out of rich individuals and corporations was to ease the tax burden on the rest of society. The tax policy branch had been working throughout the summer of 1981 on a special low-income credit, possibly to take the form of an energy credit. The credit was expected to cost Ottawa about $200 to $300 million, but would have meant that a lot of low-income people would have benefited from the budget. By September, however, the idea of a low-income credit had been killed on the grounds that the government simply couldn't afford to give up the revenue. Finance also toyed with plans—right up to the last weeks before the budget—to reduce tax rates at the lower end of the income scale, only to finally abandon such ideas because they were too costly. (Since there are so many low income people, any reduction in their tax rates results in a massive revenue drain.)

So, as the department prepared to deliver its dramatic budget, one key factor was missing. The rich were to pay more, but no one was to pay less, or at least not very much less. MacEachen was going to be selling a budget for which there were no clear winners, just a lot of well-to-do losers, who—on the tax front at least—had already exhibited extremely poor sportsmanship when it came to losing.

Strangely enough, nobody in the government was really ready for the assault that followed. It began almost immediately. The press ignored the fascinating information Finance had compiled about how the rich avoid paying their share of tax. Instead, it followed religiously the outcries of business groups, tax practitioners and vested interests across the country.

Within days, the budget had acquired the image of being a disastrous mistake. The government, which had not really mapped out a strategy for selling the new measures, was thrown on the defensive, beaten back by a furious business community, an aggressive press and a reinvigorated Tory opposition. So massive was the attack, that a counter-attack seemed foolhardy. Better to look reasonable and willing to listen to the chorus of objections, many of which were coming right from within the ranks of the Liberal party. Finance had underestimated the number of local party officials and fundraisers—not to mention donors—who had been comfortably sheltering their incomes from taxation.

The vehemence of the attack doesn't lend it credibility. There is no question that by 1981, many corporations and high-income individuals were managing either to avoid paying income tax completely or to reduce their tax burden to a negligible amount. When Finance officials examined how this was being done, they noticed that certain tax breaks kept cropping up in the cases of these high-income tax filers. (Finance took to using the expression "tax filer" rather than "taxpayer," since, strictly speaking, many of these people were not actually tax*payers*.) Not surprisingly, much of the controversy over the November 81 budget centred on the removal of those very breaks.

One of the most controversial measures was the proposal to eliminate the income averaging annuity contract, better known as the IAAC, a popular device offered by insurance companies. When an individual received a large chunk of income in one year—from capital gains, stock options, entertainment or athletic contracts, for instance—he could find himself bumped into the top tax bracket, facing a large tax bill. By putting his money into an IAAC, he could arrange to pay it out to himself gradually over a period of years. This way he could avoid being caught in any one year with an unduly large amount of income. He could remain in a lower tax bracket and defer paying tax on the income for a number of years. The government was losing hundreds of millions of dollars a year through IAACs.

For example, finance officials came across one case in Revenue Canada files where an individual had received a total income, largely from investments, of $1.5 million. He put $1 million of this into an IAAC and, along with real estate and other deductions, was able to reduce his tax liability that year to zero.

This case was particularly dramatic, but there were 12,500 Canadians with incomes above $50,000 who claimed IAAC tax deductions averaging $55,300 in 1979. Indeed, IAACs were one of the main reasons some 3,400 Canadians with incomes over

$50,000 were able to avoid paying income tax entirely that year. But these were 1979 figures; by the summer of 1981, IAACs had become even more popular. Hockey players, with average incomes of $120,000, were addicted to them. Superstar Wayne Gretzky had a number of IAACs, as did singer Anne Murray, who had accumulated so many that the small annual pay-outs of all of them together kept her in the top tax bracket anyway.

The insurance industry, which was doing a thriving business selling IAACs, had also grown attached to them. Insurance agents, who had profited handsomely from commissions on sales of IAACs, were among the staunchest defenders of the tax deferral scheme. When the government eliminated IAACs in the November budget, it found itself facing the wrath of not only high-profile hockey stars but also 20,000 aroused insurance agents, who were furious to see their lucrative money machine disappear. "We didn't realize we were striking such a large community," says Stewart.

Hockey officials descended on Ottawa too. NHL president John Ziegler and a host of NHL executives harangued Finance officials about how devastated hockey players would be by the elimination of IAACs. Ziegler claimed that the change would cost the average hockey player $500,000 over his career—a grossly exaggerated estimate. (Later estimates prepared by accounting firms on behalf of hockey teams put the estimated loss at somewhere between $60,000 and $120,000; Finance estimated it to be more in the range of $20,000.) Hockey team owners and managers tried to explain to Finance officials that a team needed a few superstars to win the Stanley Cup and, without IAACs, Canadian teams just wouldn't be able to hold on to superstars. No IAACs, no cup. It was as simple as that.

The hockey establishment also took its grievances to the press, where they were prominently reported. "It doesn't pay a kid to play sport," Montreal player representative Billy Mauer was quoted as saying. "He's better off not risking his life and limb. He's better off driving a beer truck, making

$30,000 a year and getting a pension." Alan Eagleson, the outspoken Toronto hockey lawyer and agent, told the press he was advising a mass exodus of hockey players from Canada. "I'm telling them to get the hell out of the country and play for a U.S. team." And Gretzky's chartered accountant Ed Ross predicted that, without IAACs to look forward to, aspiring young Canadian hockey players would start looking to Europe. "Kids on the way up won't want to be drafted by Canadian clubs."

Hockey players, it was argued, had a short career and so should be able to average their high incomes over later years when their earnings, and, consequently, their tax rates, were lower. But the budget proposed a new measure which would allow them some forward averaging, although not as much as IAACs had offered. The more significant loss was the end of the enormous tax deferral advantages of IAACs. Still, with average incomes of $120,000 a year, were hockey players really such hard-luck cases?

Whether or not the players themselves were particularly agitated isn't clear. Guy Lafleur of the Montreal Canadiens was portrayed in one sports article as being sufficiently upset about the tax changes to desire a trade south. But the same article quoted Lafleur as saying: "The tax structure isn't that bad, but it could be better." Devastating blows like that Finance could probably survive.

In fact, a good part of the hype seemed to be coming from accountants and lawyers trying to drag high-profile stars into their slugging match with Ottawa. Mike Levine, bass player and keyboardist for the Canadian rock group Triumph, said he was surprised to read a newspaper report that his band, and others like it, would probably soon be leaving the country because of the demise of IAACs. Not so, said Levine. "We grew up in Toronto, and a lifetime of friends are here." Although IAACs were eliminated, Triumph is still here belting out its hard-rock rhythms without the benefit of IAACs, and Canadian hockey teams still seem able to win the cup.

Despite ferocious opposition, many controversial items in the budget were passed into law. The low-interest corporate loans that had been such a boon to Jack Gallagher were to be taxed from now on. The exemption that spared individuals from paying tax when they sold their homes was to be limited to one home per couple, ending the practice of one spouse claiming the exemption for the family house and the other claiming it for the family cottage. A highly lucrative tax break that allowed investors in real estate developments to write off immediately all the upfront legal and promotion costs of the development was ended; in its place, investors were able to write off such costs over time, along with the rest of the building costs. (The pre-budget write-off rules for real estate developments had allowed one taxpayer investigated by Finance to pay income tax of $250 on an income of more than $160,000.)

And, in an effort to remove the tax-avoidance opportunities offered by personal corporations, the budget imposed a special tax on dividends paid out by companies benefiting from the small business tax credit. The move restored the "integration" of corporate and personal tax that had been destroyed by the 1977 budget; once again, high-income people would pay the same tax whether they funnelled their income through a corporation or received it directly.

Another tightening of the rules prevented top executives from receiving million-dollar tax-free retirement bonuses from their companies. Under the pre-budget rules, there were limits on the amount that could be contributed tax-free each year to an employee's RRSP. These limits were extremely generous, allowing some senior executives to accumulate pensions worth hundreds of thousands of dollars, enough to pay them a comfortable $60,000 a year stipend throughout their retirement. Even so, the rules were being increasingly circumvented by executives negotiating additional "retirement allowances" from their companies, often worth more than $1 million. These allowances really amounted to income for the executive, and should have been subject to tax. But the executives were tucking the money tax-free into their RRSPs, allowing them to draw retirement incomes well in excess of $100,000 a year. The executives were therefore getting a huge tax subsidy for their retirement—a subsidy far bigger, for instance, than the subsidies in civil servants' pensions, which were regularly criticized as too generous.

The budget stipulated that these additional retirement allowances were to be taxed—a move protested by, among others, the irate president of Iron Ore Company of Canada, who was later to be the country's prime minister. In private correspondence, Brian Mulroney made strong objections to senior Finance officials about the change—which would affect only a small group of highly paid corporate executives—as well as another change which would affect iron ore company workers.*

It should be noted that the budget's attempt to restrict the tax advantages of retirement allowances in no way prevented companies from giving out such allowances, nor did it place limits on how generous the allowances could be. It just required that these bonuses be taxed. Some companies continued to give them out even after they were subject to tax.

---

*Several years later, Liberal Finance Minister Marc Lalonde raised the issue during a verbal exchange in the House of Commons with Opposition leader Mulroney. Lalonde accused Mulroney of having lobbied the department to preserve tax breaks for high-income executives—a charge Mulroney vehemently denied. Lalonde was referring to Mulroney's attempts to convince the department to preserve the retirement allowances that the 1981 budget sought to eliminate. In 1982, when the fate of retirement allowances were still up in the air, Mulroney had allegedly written a letter to deputy minister Mickey Cohen, asking Finance to reconsider the removal of the tax break. But when Mulroney challenged Lalonde to produce evidence of his alleged lobbying, Lalonde discovered to his chagrin that his department had lost the letter! "They turned the place upside down," said one source. "But they couldn't find the god-damn letter." Without evidence to back up his charge, a red-faced Lalonde publicly retreated.

When Ian Sinclair retired from Canadian Pacific Enterprises Limited in 1984, the company gave its former chief executive officer an allowance large enough to provide an annual stipend of $285,501.

But if some key budget measures managed to survive the onslaught of opposition, others fell in the face of the gathering storm, leaving some highly prized tax avoidance mechanisms intact.

One of the most important ways that high-income people avoided tax, as Finance discovered in its investigation, was through "interest deductibility." The 1981 budget proposed changes that would have greatly limited the tax avoidance opportunities of this deduction; but the changes were defeated in the face of massive opposition from investors and investment dealers.

Under the pre-1981 rules, an individual borrowing money to make investments was entitled to deduct the full cost of his interest payments from his income before calculating his tax. The rationale for this was that an investor needed to borrow money to earn income, just as a farmer needed to buy livestock feed or a carpenter needed to buy nails to earn income. If something is needed to earn income, then it is considered a necessary cost of doing business or making a living, and it is allowed to be deducted from an individual's income before tax is calculated.

But when farmers buy feed or carpenters buy nails, they do so to earn income right away—income which will be taxed at full rates that year. When investors borrow money and invest it in stock, however, any income they receive from that stock, whether in the form of dividends or capital gains, will be taxed at favourable rates. (Indeed since the introduction of the capital gains exemption in May 1985, there may be no tax owing at all on the capital gain.) Furthermore, investors can delay receiving capital gains for decades if they choose to. Thus, they are receiving an immediate deduction for their interest costs on the loan, even though the money they are borrowing may not produce any taxable income for years.

The 1981 budget said that such interest costs should only be deductible against income earned from investments. If no investment income was earned that year, the interest costs could be used in the future. The change was reasonable, yet it sparked enormous anger among investors. MacEachen recalls that there was probably more hostility to the interest deductibility change than to any other measure in the budget. "People thought they should be able to finance their stock purchases with public funds," says MacEachen. "I remember one man I met in Halifax who was enraged that anyone would touch his ability to expense all his purchases on the stock market."

For the 3,400 people with incomes over $50,000 who paid no tax, the average amount claimed in interest deductions—beyond what was deducted against their investment incomes—amounted to $43,000. The deduction had become particularly popular as interest rates had climbed relentlessly in 80 and 81, providing investors with huge interest payments to be written off against their other income.

The budget also proposed to eliminate some of the important "corporate reorganization" tax breaks, opened up in 1974. As noted earlier, these assorted measures had had the effect of allowing individuals and companies to receive capital gains in forms that were not immediately taxable. Typically, someone selling a piece of property would accept payment from a company in the form of that company's shares, rather than in cash. While the cash payment would have been treated as a taxable capital gain, the share payment was not—at least, not until the shares were cashed in.

The proposal to eliminate these special provisions threw corporations into a rage. The top executives of Dome Petroleum flew in for a special weekend meeting with senior Finance officials just days after the budget. "This god-damn thing is going to kill our take-over of Hudson's Bay," snorted Dome president Bill Richards. He and chairman Jack Gallagher were completely unmoved by the arguments of the officials they confronted. Gallagher probably would have been even less sympathetic had he known that Finance had been carefully studying his personal compensation package for clues about how the rich avoid tax. Intense pressure from Dome and other major corporations forced Ottawa to back down, restoring the full range of "corporate reorganization" tax breaks.

Attempts to tighten the restrictions on charitable foundations also ran into massive opposition. Members of the wealthy Molson family, which had its own private foundation, made several trips to Ottawa to personally protest to MacEachen and his officials. The measure was soon withdrawn.

With so many angry people trekking to Ottawa to oppose various aspects of the budget, Finance officials were beginning to develop a bunker mentality. When delegations of angry real estate moguls or insurance company executives came barrelling down the corridors of the Finance Department offices in Place Bell Canada, officials increasingly closed their doors and hoped, by lying low, they might not be called in for the "consultation" meetings.

The pressure only intensified as a recession set in. With raging inflation and the economy sinking into a deep slump, companies slowed down operations and laid off workers in scary numbers. Unemployment rose dramatically. Middle class people lost their homes, unable to afford the catastrophic new interest rates when their mortgages came up for renewal.

Business insisted that the tax changes of the November 81 budget had been instrumental in destroying their confidence and creating the dreary economic picture. It is true that the $2 billion tax increase undoubtedly contributed to the malaise by taking money out of the slumping economy. But there were many other factors involved in the downturn—most notably the high interest rates set by the U.S. Treasury Department and the Canadian government's insistence on topping them to prevent a slide in the value of the Canadian dollar.

Still, for the powerful interests fighting off the budget's

assault on their privileges, the worsening economic climate proved a lethal weapon. The tax changes and the economic collapse happened around the same time and somehow appeared to be linked. It was all part of Ottawa's failure to deal with the economy. The Canadian Labour Congress organized a mass rally on Parliament Hill that was really against unemployment but got lumped in with general protest over tax changes.

Moving at full speed, the anti-budget bandwagon quickly attracted a crowd. Just about anybody could make headlines simply by linking a grievance to the budget. "Higher food bills blamed on budget" blared a front page headline in *The Toronto Star*. The article explained that the president of the Ontario Federation of Agriculture was predicting higher food costs and eventual food shortages because the budget failed to give farmers the $1 billion in low-interest loans that they'd asked for.

The budget pumped new life into John Bulloch, who had been wafting around somewhat lost since his anti-government heyday in the early 70s. After cutting his teeth on the white paper tax reform exercise, Bulloch had settled into a comfortable life of high-profile small business lobbying through his Canadian Federation of Independent Business. He met frequently with cabinet ministers, usually managing to have his picture taken with them. The photographs inevitably found their way into the CFIB's regular newsletter, just in case members were wondering what Bulloch had been doing for them lately.

Still, it hadn't been the same for Bulloch without a big tax fight. The other issues hadn't worked out as well; the government hadn't retreated nearly so easily. There were grumblings within his small business domain about just how effective Bulloch was. And with competition now looming in the form of Geoffrey Hale's aggressive new small business organization, Bulloch's empire was all the more fragile. The November 81 budget couldn't have come at a better time. At last, Bulloch could breathe some of his old fire.

Ignoring some of the measures that clearly aided small business, Bulloch swung into full protest gear. He took out full-page newspaper ads announcing the CFIB's opposition to the budget and raged angrily against it into every available microphone. "I'm front and centre on the budget and this is a four-year war," Bulloch told *The Globe and Mail*, vowing not to call off the troops until Canada was once again a safe place for entrepreneurs. He arranged for a highly publicized meeting with MacEachen within weeks of the budget. When Bulloch emerged from the session to meet the waiting press, he portrayed the encounter as a stormy shouting match, a confrontation of wilful titans. Finance officials who attended the meeting were taken aback by Bulloch's account. They quietly let out the story that the session was actually quite polite, with Bulloch urging MacEachen to stimulate the economy.

Indeed, meetings with MacEachen were rarely shouting matches. In sessions with countless lobbyists over the 1981 budget, MacEachen would do something far more infuriating than shouting. He would be distant, impassive, impenetrable. Indeed, he was often this way with his own colleagues, failing to return phone calls from fellow cabinet ministers, who would simply shake their heads and mutter: "That's Allan." At meetings MacEachen often said little. One former official recalls him saying almost nothing during a three-hour briefing. Another recalls him reading a controversial speech written for him and making only one comment to the writer: "Why do you split your infinitives?"

With visiting delegations of protestors, MacEachen was at his most infuriatingly opaque. He would listen patiently as they made their pitch, then remain silent, sometimes for minutes on end. So the delegation would make the pitch again, this time in a more frenzied fashion. Still MacEachen would be silent. This process could go on until the visitors eventually left, frustrated and unsatisfied. "I've never known any person who could use silence like he did," said one close observer. "He had enormous self-control."

Indeed, the long silences were deliberate, a way of disarming his opponents. "He understood the psychology of two people in a conversation: if one person doesn't talk, the other feels the need to fill the air," said a former aide. "He was a tremendous negotiator. When he wanted to, he would just take it. They would be badgering, and he would just sit there like a sphinx. If he doesn't want to give you a message, he can do that." This self-imposed silence may seem surprising coming from a man so enormously fond of talk and debate. But MacEachen was selective. With people he liked or respected, he could be highly animated, a deeply engaging conversationalist. But with angry businessmen, whose self-serving motivation didn't impress him, he was inclined to reveal little of himself or his thoughts.

As the budget protest gathered steam, MacEachen's colleagues were quick to desert him. After years of commanding respect within caucus, he was left virtually alone defending his budget, as Liberal backbenchers and cabinet ministers alike sought to distance themselves. "It was remarkable how they ran for cover," says MacEachen. "It was not a marked example of political courage."

MacEachen's sense of betrayal is fuelled by the fact that he feels his colleagues had, in a broad sense, approved the budget. Although no other cabinet ministers knew its contents—including Treasury Board president Don Johnston, who was a tax lawyer—MacEachen insists that they all knew and approved the budget's general thrust against tax expenditures. "The fact of the matter is that the question of tax expenditures had been constantly raised prior to that," MacEachen says. "I didn't hear anybody say 'Shut up, this is dangerous.'" Furthermore, according to MacEachen, the prime minister, his principal secretary, Jim Coutts, and the clerk of the Privy Council, Michael Pitfield, had been made aware of the budget's contents "in detail."

Perhaps the most bitter disappointment for MacEachen—and one that he shuns talking about—was the lack of strong support from the prime minister. MacEachen and Trudeau were in some ways close, although both were intensely private men. "They were both enigmas to each other," said one high-ranking official. MacEachen's impassivity would leave even Trudeau frustrated at times. On one occasion when Mac-Eachen was being more silent than usual, Trudeau finally snapped: "For Christ's sake, Allan, speak up." Yet the prime minister continued to rely on MacEachen's judgment, even after the November 81 budget. Years later, when Finance Minister Marc Lalonde held up secret budget papers at a photo session in such a way that they were visible to TV cameras, Trudeau advised Lalonde to seek MacEachen's advice on how to handle the embarrassing gaffe.

Indeed, Trudeau remained basically loyal to MacEachen. He never pressured him to retreat from the controversial measures in the budget, MacEachen says. Furthermore, the prime minister told him he could stay on at Finance as long as he wanted. When MacEachen decided he'd had enough in September 82, Trudeau handed him the prestigious, but sedate, external affairs portfolio. When MacEachen retired in May 1985, Trudeau appointed him to the Senate.

Still, the prime minister never came out and really stood four-square behind his embattled minister when MacEachen needed it most, when day after day in the House the hungry Tory Opposition, backed up by a host of allies in business and the media, relentlessly ate him alive.

In the hubbub and commotion over MacEachen's attempt to eliminate an array of tax breaks, a crucial aspect of the budget went largely ignored. While it sought to cut off a number of key tax breaks benefiting the rich, it also proposed a dramatic reduction in the top personal tax rate from 65 to 50 percent. Some Finance officials had had misgivings about this rate reduction, but it also seemed like a good way to reduce the inevitable opposition that would come from those in the top income bracket. Although they would still pay more as a result of the budget, the rate reduction would cushion the blow. Some high-income taxpayers would even end up better off.

But while they fought tooth and nail to hold onto their tax breaks, they had little to say about this new benefit. In the end, many of the crucial tax breaks were retained in response to the massive protest. But the top tax rate was lowered anyway. The rich still had most of their tax breaks—and a whole new rate reduction to boot. All in all, it hadn't been such a bad budget for them.

The November 1981 budget and its political aftermath were, in many ways, a clash of different worlds—MacEachen's and the world of tax.

Some observers have argued that MacEachen didn't understand his own budget. This isn't true. While he was not a tax expert and therefore had less than a full grasp of the technicalities, he understood—and enthusiastically endorsed—the general thrust of the budget. The notion that the tax system was biased towards the rich was not one that sat well with MacEachen, particularly when so many of those rich beneficiaries were the wealthy investors and high-income professionals from central Canada and the West. All his life he had sought to improve the lot of the poor in rural Cape Breton. When his officials confronted him with dramatic information that the tax system favoured those who least needed help, MacEachen was motivated to act.

Even after thirty years in politics, MacEachen remained tied to his Cape Breton roots. For him, recreation still meant going to the Highland Games in Antigonish, where he would dress up in kilt, sporran and dancing slippers laced to the knees. One of the biggest events in his life, in fact, had been a special gathering of Cape Breton dancers and fiddlers in Scotland in 1975 to mark the opening of a school of Canadian studies at Edinburgh University. MacEachen had used his influence to get permission for the group to hold the celebration in the imposing great hall of Edinburgh Castle. This was an amazing coup. One participant described it as roughly equivalent to a group of foreigners coming to Canada and "getting the chamber of the House of Commons for a high school debate." The great hall of the medieval castle was one of the grandest and most historic spots in Britain, the participant noted. "The Royal Family would have trouble getting it!" The evening was a moving, almost magical celebration of the survival of Celtic culture in Canada, as some of Scotland's dignitaries mingled with humble Cape Bretoners, singing and dancing to old Nova Scotia fishing songs. MacEachen watched over the whole event with the satisfaction of a proud laird.

Throughout his years in government, MacEachen came back often to Cape Breton. There, he would spend evenings with priests who had remained his lifelong friends. He would sometimes have Scottish gatherings, or ceilidhs, at his cottage on Lake Ainslie, not far from his boyhood home of Inverness. At these gatherings, still a popular tradition in Cape Breton, there would be fiddlers and pipers and highland dancing. Despite the power he came to wield in Ottawa, MacEachen remained tied to the forces that had shaped him. In many ways, he was still the poor Scottish boy from Inverness who arrived at St Francis Xavier with his possessions in a cardboard box.

Although he had lifted himself out of poverty, MacEachen had little in common with the successful businessmen and tax practitioners who came in convoys to lobby him. They had grown up in Westmount or Rosedale or West Vancouver, ate lunch in their private clubs and spent their weekends yachting or golfing. Yet here was a finance minister who was known to wear a kilt and to enjoy nothing more than a theological debate with a room full of priests! And business— the religion of those coming to lobby—was not something that inspired MacEachen. If these businessmen and tax practitioners resembled any group from MacEachen's past, it was the Cape Breton fish merchants, whose stranglehold over the economy MacEachen had fought to overturn. Their self-interested pleading was a far cry from the world MacEachen respected—the world of Moses Coady and the dedicated priests who sought to improve the lives of the poor. The cosy world of tax was as foreign to MacEachen as a gathering of Scottish dancers and fiddlers would be to a Bay Street tax lawyer.

Years later, MacEachen's November 1981 budget remains inextricably linked in the public mind with failure. Any reference to it is inevitably accompanied by adjectives such as "disastrous," "ill-conceived" or "bumbling." *The Financial Post* has referred to it as "The Tax Debacle."

As in the earlier tax reform effort, the November 81 budget threatened to dismantle a system that favoured a small but powerful segment of society. That this segment reacted angrily was no surprise. Strangely enough, however, the reaction did come as a surprise to MacEachen, who should have been prepared for it, having served as House leader when the Benson tax reform made its perilous way through the House. But MacEachen does appear to have been caught off-guard by the harsh criticism of his budget. "It was absolutely explosive and intemperate," he says. "It was extraordinary the number of persons who came forward to defend their privileges."

Perhaps what is most extraordinary was that these protests were not seen as the cries of vested interests fighting to defend their privileges. Rather they were portrayed as an expression of a popular despair over the budget. The media played a key role in fostering this image. Not only did newspapers regurgitate much of the criticism on their editorial pages, but, perhaps more important, they kept up a constant patter of "news" stories reporting the objections of businessmen, professional associations and tax practitioners, making the objections appear relentless and pervasive. By contrast, there was little reporting of the views of a substantial number of academic economists who approved of the thrust of the budget.

Many people—MacEachen among them—have argued that the budget's fatal flaw was its failure to provide an adequate transition period for many of the proposed measures. By changing the financing rules for real estate deals already underway, for instance, the budget caused considerable disruption. It could have provided "grandfather clauses" for deals already underway before November 12.

While this is true, it is simplistic to suggest that this would have been an easy, harmless solution. Offering grandfather clauses to tax practitioners is like waving a bright red flag in front of a raging bull—as the Conservative government found out when it imposed a moratorium on the Scientific Research Tax Credit in October 1984 and added a grandfather clause for deals already underway. Inventive tax lawyers came up with no end of ways of indicating a deal had begun before October 1984, and for the next fourteen months the offices of tax lawyers and accountants buzzed with deals exploiting the lucrative tax break, despite the moratorium. By the time the Tories finally bolted the barn door shut in December 1985, grandfathered deals worth more than $1.5 billion had been made.

A more basic and ultimately crucial flaw of the November 81 budget was its failure to redistribute to poorer Canadians some of the extra revenue raised from the rich. Nobody appeared to gain from the budget. In fact, in their zeal to close off tax breaks, the architects of the budget had gone after a few measures that had also benefited low- and middle-income people. They had proposed to tax employer contributions to an employee's private health and dental plans and to tax free travel passes enjoyed by employees of transportation companies.

These measure provoked criticism from unions, which otherwise would likely have supported an assault on the tax privileges of the rich. In the long run, the elimination of major tax breaks would have benefited ordinary Canadians, by allowing the government to raise more of its revenue from corporations and investors. But it is perhaps unrealistic to expect people to have this kind of long range view in the midst of a full-blown political crisis and a desperate economic situation. In the fall of 1981, the government appeared to be robbing from the rich and giving to itself. This mangled version of Robin Hood just wouldn't fly.

Those responsible for the budget paid a heavy price for its flaws. As finance minister, MacEachen bore the brunt of the abuse. Sitting on the red leather sofa in his spacious corner office in the Senate Block, MacEachen talks with animation about the experience. There are no brooding silences now. "It was a damn good budget. No question about it," he says defiantly, showing some of the spark that made him at times a powerful orator in the House of Commons. At one point he paces around the room recounting with distaste how special interest groups pretend they are acting out of anything but self-interest.

There is clearly resentment too. After he left Finance, MacEachen had to sit by and watch his successor, Marc Lalonde, win kudos from the business community for giving them back their tax breaks. "It was a sad thing that [the budget changes] didn't stand up, that they were eroded so greatly by Mr Lalonde. It's easy to give in to pressure. I'm quite disillusioned by the brutality of the revisionism." MacEachen candidly admits that the furor over the budget brought his political ambitions to an end. "It removed for me any prospect of ever being leader of the Liberal party," he says, staring out the window. "It certainly closed that door totally."

For Ian Stewart, the budget spelled the end to what had been a meteoric rise to the top of the civil service. After MacEachen's departure from Finance, Stewart realized the government intended to undo the reforms—something he had little desire to supervise. He left the department in October 82, within weeks of MacEachen's departure. The Trudeau administration found a face-saving spot for Stewart as head of the Central Mortgage and Housing Corporation. But when the Tories came to power, the writing on the wall was clear. In August 1986, a disillusioned Stewart, once hailed by Marc Lalonde as one of the country's finest civil servants, left the government entirely and returned to academic life at Queen's

University. The whole episode may have been hardest on Stewart. Intense and intellectual, he was interested in the big picture and was given to soulful reflections. He worried about social responsibility, the plight of the Third World and the ethical basis of public policy. "Ian felt the weight of the world on his shoulders. He was always walking around like he was Atlas," said one former official. "Wilson, Lalonde and Cohen went home and slept at night. MacEachen brooded for a while and then slept. Ian never slept."

Stewart was replaced by Mickey Cohen, who returned to Finance as deputy minister in the fall of 82. In a sense, Cohen's return meant that the process had moved full-circle. His loose approach to the tax system in the 70s had been followed by the tightening up efforts of Stewart. But now, as Ottawa tried to woo business, Stewart's attempts to reform the tax system were as out of date as yesterday's lapels.

The new looser approach showed up first in the government's decision to satisfy business demands for enriched tax breaks for research and development. Such demands had been around for a long time, but had been spurned by Stewart, who considered them unnecessary and excessive. With Cohen now in charge, however, the business community was soon to have a brand-new tax break for R & D more generous than anything it had had before. The stage was set for the worst fiasco in Canadian tax history.

CHAPTER NINE
Tax Credits For Sale: No Experience Necessary

*"What Finance officials did not know was that there were
so many dishonest Canadians. . . ."*
—**deputy finance minister Stanley Hartt, May
1986, commenting on the extent of the abuse of
the Scientific Research Tax Credit**

In his comfortable Toronto office, Ken Mathieson was toying
with an idea. The affable, energetic vice-president and director of the prominent Toronto investment firm McLeod
Young Weir was thinking about the possibilities of buying
and selling tax credits.

On the surface, the idea may have seemed bizarre. Tax
credits were incentives that allowed companies to reduce their
tax bills if they carried out some activity the government
wanted to encourage, such as research and development. But
if a company wasn't paying any taxes, it wasn't able to take
advantage of available tax credits. And with the recession of
the early 80s, many corporations were not paying taxes, leaving hundreds of millions of dollars worth of tax credits
unused.

Now, thought Mathieson, if those unused credits could be
sold to companies or individuals who were paying taxes and
who could use them to reduce their tax bills, everyone would
benefit. The seller could get some cash for an unusable tax
credit, the buyer could reduce his taxes, and investment firms
like McLeod Young Weir could charge fees for setting up the
transactions. The possibilities were intriguing.

In July 1981, McLeod Young Weir experimented with the concept. The firm privately arranged the sale of some $20 million worth of tax credits for Northern Telecom Limited. The following January, the firm sold another $70 million of Northern Telecom's tax benefits. This was a somewhat creative use of the tax law. The financial community watched with interest and began approaching Revenue Canada with requests for advance approvals of similar deals. By mid-1982 Revenue Canada was so flooded with requests that it declared a moratorium while the Government reviewed its R & D financing policies.

Officials in the departments of both Revenue and Finance were wary about these new schemes. Allowing an open market in tax credits seemed to be drifting from the original purpose of the tax incentives—to encourage more investment in R & D. By selling its unused tax credits, a research company was often just collecting money for research it had already done. There was no guarantee of new research being generated. Indeed, the companies buying the tax credits had no real interest in the research projects and were just seeking a means of reducing their own tax bills. The benefits to Canada seemed questionable, and, if the requests pouring into Revenue Canada were any indication of the popularity of such deals, the revenue losses seemed potentially enormous.

Ottawa's tax breaks for R & D were already considerable. In fact, Canada already had virtually the most generous incentives for R & D in the industrial world. A study by Carleton University economist Donald McFetridge in February 1983 showed that, with the exception of Singapore, Canada provided more lucrative tax breaks for R & D than any other country. The Canadian incentives were so generous that the investor was only putting up forty cents of every dollar he invested in R & D; the government picked up the remaining sixty cents.

Still, the business community wanted more. In October 1980, the Canadian Chamber of Commerce had levelled the outlandish accusation that Canada was way behind other countries in its subsidies for R & D. The chamber urged additional tax incentives that would reduce the Canadian investor's costs to ten or fifteen cents on the dollar, leaving the government to pick up the remaining eighty-five to ninety cents. A task force appointed by the Nova Scotia government wanted Ottawa to go further still. In 1981, the task force proposed a mix of benefits that would reduce the investor's share of the costs to a mere one cent on the dollar. Although this suggestion was rejected at the time, Ottawa was later to go farther and, in the SRTC program, reduce the investor's cost to zero.

In December 1982, Revenue Canada announced new restrictions on the McLeod Young Weir-style schemes, leaving the business and financial community frustrated. But their gripes found sympathetic ears over at the Finance Department. Allan MacEachen and Ian Stewart were now gone and the new minister, Marc Lalonde, and his deputy, Mickey Cohen, seemed bent on placating the business community in the aftermath of the November 1981 budget. A more flexible approach to R & D financing seemed like an excellent way to signal friendly intentions, without causing a stir among the electorate. After all, next to "small business," few notions were more sacrosanct with the Canadian public than R & D.

Indeed, R & D had always had a certain mystique. It was what led to new discoveries and pathfinding advances. The goal of breaking new ground—whether finding a cure for cancer, a way to reach the planets or a better method of building bridges—had always had a certain nobility. It was all part of the advance of the human race.

In Canada this took on a special meaning. As a small, underpopulated country next to an industrial giant, the theory went, we had to rely on our ingenuity to make our place in the modern world. The desire to rise above our traditional role as hewers of wood and drawers of water was as Canadian as Robert Goulet and Jeanette MacDonald. And, as competition from Pacific Rim nations posed a growing threat to Canadian industry and employment in the early 1980s, there was a tendency to look for the answer in R & D.

Few industrial developments were more prized in the country than the little group of high-tech companies nestled in Canada's own Silicon Valley, right in the shadow of the nation's capital. The shipbuilding industries of the Maritimes might be floundering, once-thriving mining centres might be turning into ghost towns across the country, Cape Breton coal plants might be nothing more than a costly drain on the nation's resources. But there, in the bosom of the country, was Canada's future: high tech.

Lalonde's first budget in April 1983 was peppered with generous tax concessions for business and investors and it included a discussion paper promising enriched R & D incentives. For several months prior to the budget, the Finance Department had been consulting with companies involved in R & D, and that process intensified over the next few months. In October of that year, Lalonde introduced draft legislation for a new measure called the Scientific Research Tax Credit.

The new measure caused a stir of excitement on Bay Street. Smart tax lawyers and brokers, some of whom had been pushing Ottawa to design a "flexible" measure, were thrilled to see the government had gone so far in heeding their advice. In fact, Ottawa had almost gone *too* far. There was a sense of incredulity in the finance community that Ottawa would design a measure so wide-open and so potentially costly to the national treasury. "The day it was released, everyone [in the financial community] was saying: 'Good Lord, what are they doing?' Nobody could understand what the government was doing," says David West, vice-president (tax) of Imperial Oil—a company which wasted no time buying up $500 million worth of the R & D tax credits within the first two months of the program.

Within Revenue Canada there was similar consternation about what the new team over at Finance was doing. Revenue officials were aware of the excitement that the new measure was generating in financial circles and worried about how seriously the program might erode the tax base. The SRTC was certainly much more flexible than what had been proposed in Revenue Canada's 1982 guidelines. Whereas Revenue had frowned on the notion of companies selling their R & D tax breaks, except in limited circumstances, the new legislation seemed to be giving this idea the green light. In meetings between the two departments, Revenue officials voiced their concern to their counterparts at Finance that the new credit was ripe for abuse.

Even elements in the business community worried that the new measure was not properly targeted. For instance, the forest products giant MacMillan Bloedel Limited, which did a great deal of R & D, was concerned about the fact that the new mechanism included an unnecessary role for investment firms like McLeod Young Weir. Back in June 1982, when the idea of selling tax credits was floating around the investment community, MacMillan Bloedel had specifically urged that Ottawa design a measure that did not require such middlemen, since their fees would inevitably come out of the money earmarked for research.

Basically, the Finance Department had tried to design a tax break that was so generous and so flexible that it would lure investors to R & D—something they were not generally keen on. Despite the cachet attached to R & D, the truth of the matter was that investors didn't much like putting their money into research. It was just too risky. The chances of a research project leading to a discovery or the development of a new product were so small that the risks almost always outweighed the rewards. Even the rich tax breaks already available were not enough to entice most investors into the high-risk game. For all the rhetoric about risk-taking, most investors, when confronted with the genuine riskiness of R & D, headed for the hills.

How could the government overcome the aversion of investors to taking such risks? Under Marc Lalonde and Mickey Cohen, the Finance Department came up with an answer: *let the government take all the risks, but let the private sector take all the profits.*

Cohen later explained that the government figured that only by removing from the investor any responsibility for the performance of the research project would the investor be willing to invest. "The view both internally and externally from those we talked to was that, if you put that obligation on . . . the investor, he would not invest. He would not take the responsibility of policing the unreliable performance," Cohen told the House of Commons public accounts committee.

But policing the performance of an investment was a crucial role traditionally played by the investor. Unless the investor had reason to believe that the investment was going to perform well, he would not put his money at risk. If it performed badly, he would cease to invest in the future. The investor's insistence on good performance was what kept the free enterprise system functioning. The investor's concern about his own money acted as a screening system for bad investments. Any company that looked like it would squander the money foolishly would never attract investors. But here was the deputy finance minister saying his department had looked for a mechanism that would remove the investor's risk element from an R & D investment. What Cohen was talking about wasn't an investment at all. It was what became known as the "quick flip."

The quick flip was really just a variation of what Mathieson and McLeod Young Weir had pioneered in the 1981 Northern Telecom deal. The essential ingredient was that a company could sell its unused R & D tax credits to someone who could use them. There were several serious problems with this, springing largely from the fact that the so-called investor wasn't really an investor at all. The whole transaction was a sham investment designed with one purpose in mind: to milk the tax benefits.

This is roughly how it worked. A company came up with a plan to carry out, let's say, $10 million worth of research. Under the SRTC program, that would entitle the company to a tax credit equal to 50 percent of the amount to be spent on research; in this case, $5 million.

Under normal circumstances, a tax credit of $5 million would be used to reduce the company's taxes by $5 million. But the whole purpose of the SRTC was to allow companies that paid no taxes to be able to take advantage of this tax break. Therefore, the R & D company was allowed to sell its tax credit to an investor who could use it to reduce his own taxes.

This is typically what happened. In a meeting in the boardroom of a law firm, an investor or groups of investors would hand over a cheque to the research company for $10 million. This, in theory, represented an investment of $10 million in the research company. But what followed immediately after the $10 million was "invested" bore little resemblance to any other kind of investment.

Right then and there, the investor would get in return papers entitling him to a tax credit worth $5 million and a refund cheque for $5 million, *plus a bonus*. These bonuses varied from 1 percent to 10 percent, or more. Typically, in this case, the investor would get a bonus of about $500,000. The bonus was the sweetener that attracted him to the deal. That way, he put down $10 million and received, in essence, $10.5 million back—the $5 million tax credit, the $5 million refund cheque, plus the bonus of $500,000. The investor wasn't an investor at all. He was simply a purchaser of tax credits.

He didn't, for instance, care whether his "investment" turned out to be a good one. He received his profit upfront, before he left the boardroom. Indeed, the entire transaction was completed in the boardroom meeting. "The money never leaves the table," said one Toronto lawyer who participated in a number of such transactions. The "investor" walked away that same day with his instant profit—and washed his hands of any responsibility for the future performance of the research company.

Since the "investor's" responsibility essentially ended there, it's not surprising that he paid only passing attention to the research proposal. When Esso Resources "invested" $68 million in Frank Hertel's International Electronics Corporation, Esso officials didn't even bother to check out Hertel's credentials or the merits of his project. "These weren't investments," said West from Imperial Oil, Esso's parent company, describing the $500 million Esso put into such transactions. "We were just acting as bankers." Indeed, Esso had paid so little attention to the research project involved that company officials were surprised when Hertel announced at a press conference that he had the backing of Esso. They denied any connection to Hertel when contacted by reporters, and only later recalled that in fact they had "invested" $68 million in IEC—through the quick flip.

But all this raises the question, Why were these "investors" needed at all? They were not performing the crucial role of investors in screening out bad projects that didn't deserve to be funded. They certainly weren't putting any of their money into the projects. The money that they handed over to the research companies—in exchange for the tax credits—was money that they would otherwise have had to pay in taxes. So the money was really government money. But Ottawa had chosen to hand it over to the research company via this convoluted route which, in the process, provided a nice bonus for the "investor."

But who paid for the bonus? To see this, it's necessary to look at the deal from the vantage point of the research company. Assuming that the owner of the research company had honest intentions of carrying out bona fide research—and many of them did, initially at least—the SRTC was a mixed blessing. It provided him with cash up front that would otherwise have been extremely difficult or impossible to obtain. Since investors and bank managers have traditionally been reluctant to put money into new research projects, the SRTC program provided an unusual opportunity for all those scientists and would-be inventors who had dreamed all their lives of developing a product. Receiving millions of dollars to carry out their plans was beyond the wildest imaginings of many of these individuals.

But there was another side. Back there in the law firm's boardroom, where the "investor's" only worry was how big his bonus would be, the owner of the research company was taking on an awesome responsibility. Although the scheme was supposedly designed to benefit him, he was generally the most nervous individual in the room. Indeed, he was the only one taking a risk.

Those tax credits he had just sold had come with strings attached. His company could qualify for the $5 million tax credit only if it did $10 million worth of research. And even though it had sold the tax credits to someone else, it remained responsible for the research. With $5 million in his pocket, in effect, the owner of the research company now had to figure out how to find another $5 million, so he could carry out $10 million worth of research. If his company didn't do $10 million in research, he would personally owe the government $5 million. (The company could not shed its tax obligation by declaring bankruptcy. Under the SRTC legislation, directors of the research company were to be held personally liable for the tax owing.)

In fact, his situation was worse than this, because by the end of the boardroom meeting, the research company owner wouldn't even have the full $5 million the "investor" had given him. Out of that $5 million, he had to pay the "investor's" bonus of about $500,000, plus fees for the others involved in the transaction. There might be as many as a

dozen other people in the room, including a stockbroker who
had arranged the deal, a lawyer who had done the legal work,
an accountant who would supervise the handling of the SRTC
money and a banker who provided a draft for the money. Fees
for these individuals were often exorbitant and were usually
demanded immediately, right there in the boardroom. The
research company owner left the meeting with, if he were
lucky, $4 million, frequently less. That meant he had to raise
$6 million or else he would owe Revenue Canada $5 million—
$1 million more than he had.

It is not hard to imagine how the situation got out of
control. To begin with, the lack of effective restrictions attracted the unscrupulous. The research money was usually
held by a trustee, such as a bank or trust company, and only
released on the authorization of an accountant. But, as many
con artists quickly discovered, the rules of the program were
so loose that it wasn't difficult to gain access to the money. If
the research company purchased a $1 million piece of equip-
ment, for instance, the accountant could authorize the release
of $500,000 from the account (half the value of the purchase,
since the tax credit was supposed to cover 50 percent of the
research costs.) But if the research company had only put
down, say $100,000 towards the price of the equipment, it
would have $400,000 left over after the down payment.

Toronto businessman-playboy Harold Arviv used this
method. Arviv, best known for blowing up his fashionable
Bloor Street discotheque in order to claim the insurance, set
up two research companies and sold tax credits worth $10
million, while charges against him in connection with the
bombing were still pending. Arviv then turned around and
purchased an $8 million building at the prime St Clair and
Yonge location. Although he only put down $3 million, Arviv
was able to put the full cost of the building through as an
expense and get an immediate release of about $4 million (half
the cost of the building).

Some of the legal work on Arviv's SRTC deal was handled

by Dan Cooper, a partner in McCarthy and McCarthy, one of the oldest and most prestigious firms in the country. "I don't think professional advisers are guarantors of their clients' business successes," Cooper told *The Globe and Mail*'s Jock Ferguson. "We carried out our professional responsibility."

Once the money was released to the research company owner, there was really no one supervising how it was spent. In a number of cases, owners spent their new-found wealth on expensive cars, foreign travel or luxury goods. These kinds of expenses would undoubtedly be questioned when Revenue Canada started auditing the company's books. But by that time the owners might be out of the country. (In Arviv's case, he was on his way to jail for the disco bombing.)

For the unscrupulous who didn't want to leave the country or go to jail, there were other popular methods of avoiding Revenue Canada's grasp. The full responsibility for the research lay with the directors of the research company, who, as we've seen, were to be held personally liable for the taxes in cases where the company failed to carry out the full amount of the research. But if the directors had no assets, there would be nothing for Revenue Canada to collect. "You literally found people with no assets," said one tax lawyer with a small Toronto firm that handled SRTC deals. "For $5,000 to $10,000 they would sign their names [as directors of the company]." The lawyer referred to these individuals as "professional SRTC directors" who, "once on the hook" for one deal, didn't mind signing up for many more. Some of these "directors" were fairly down-and-out individuals who had to be primed to be presentable when they met the "investors" for the signing of the deal in the elegant atmosphere of the law firm's boardroom. Recalls the lawyer: "Some of those deals were hilarious."

Another lawyer at a large, prominent Toronto firm recalls a case where an individual presented himself to the law firm as the sole director in a research company involved in an SRTC transaction. The man seemed basically presentable at the brief signing ceremony for the $2 million deal, although he said little. However, when the lawyer had to contact him subsequently on a number of occasions, the director seemed "mentally clouded." The lawyer would phone him at home in the middle of the afternoon and find him drunk, "barely coherent at times." "Six months after the deal closed, the director wouldn't know what time of day it was, let alone anything about the research project." The lawyer said it was clear the director had no control over the SRTC money, which had undoubtedly been passed along to someone else. "This guy was just a straw man to take the tax hit."

But the abuses weren't limited to the unscrupulous. Even those who began with every intention of carrying out the research often found themselves unable to do so because they couldn't raise further financing. Without additional financing, a research company would have less than half the money it needed to carry out all the research it was required to do. This was the situation that the vast majority of research companies soon found themselves in. Of the 1,204 research companies receiving money through quick flip transactions, only 442 were able to find any additional financing at all.

Many became desperate. Facing a huge potential tax liability if they didn't spend the full amount they were supposed to spend on research, they started spending foolishly to push up their research expenses. One lawyer said he recalled the owner of a research company paying $1.2 million for a building that wasn't worth more than $700,000. When the lawyer tried to talk his client out of the purchase, the client explained that he needed to spend the extra money to inflate his research costs. (Although he only put $90,000 down on the building, he could claim the full cost of the building—minus the cost of the land —as a research expense. That way he could appear to be spending more money on research than he actually had spent.)

In the mad scramble to spend as much as possible before the end of the tax year, companies made purchases that were illogical and wasteful. In fact, there was little to ensure that they spent their money wisely. A research company could, for instance, spend all its money on research buildings and consulting fees and then discover it didn't have enough left over to actually carry out any research. All that mattered was spending the dollar amount required—twice the value of the tax credits sold.

Some companies didn't even try to hide their overpayments. Harry Rogers, then deputy revenue minister, said that in some cases research company owners would openly admit to his officials that they were inflating their costs. "They were so bald-faced as to almost be an insult to your intelligence in some instances," said Rogers. He recalled a case where he had personally questioned a couple of young hotshots about the fact that they had marked up research equipment by 4,000 percent, only to be told that they had done so because it was necessary to eliminate their tax liability. "I've had them sit in my office, stare at me with confident-looking eyes, stare at me and say these things."

With so much money floating around, it was inevitable that the financial middlemen—the lawyers, brokers and accountants—were going to end up with a significant chunk. The same lawyer who had had the dealings with the drunken "director" explained that his firm originally charged their normal hourly rate for quick flip deals. But the firm began to question its restraint when it noticed the exorbitant fees being charged by stockbrokers. The brokers, who basically put the deals together by matching up a research company with a group of "investors," were charging anywhere from $500,000 to $750,000 on a sale of $10 million worth of tax credits. "Everybody got pissed off seeing what the brokers were making," said the lawyer. Increasingly, the lawyers abandoned their hourly billing rates and started taking a percentage of the action, so that they were earning, in some cases, more than $100,000 on a fairly straightforward transaction. The accountants would take a hefty cut as well.

Then there were the bankers, representatives of any one of the five chartered banks, who made only brief appearances at the actual signing ceremonies in the boardrooms. The bankers would bring to such meetings a draft for part of the money involved in the deal. If the deal was for $5 million worth of tax credits—and therefore $10 million worth of research—there had to be a total of $10 million in cheques or bank drafts at the meeting. This was technically the amount the "investors" were putting into the project, and it was necessary that the actual amount be there in the room to satisfy the legal requirement that the full amount of the research costs be involved in the transaction, not just the amount of the tax credits.

It was actually just a bit of dramatic fiction. In fact, the "investors" weren't putting $10 million into the company at all. They were putting in less than $5 million—and only in exchange for $5 million in tax credits. As we have seen, what was going on was strictly the sale of tax credits. The $10 million worth of research was something the research company alone had to worry about. Everyone else around the table was concerned solely with what he could make from the tax credit sale.

But, to make everything comply with the rules, the $10 million in drafts and cheques would be presented so that everyone in the room could see them. They might even be passed to the research company owner. For a precious few moments, the owner would have in his hands the full amount that he needed to carry out the research he was committing himself to doing. Alas, when the few seconds were up, he was obliged to pass the drafts back to the banker and keep only the cheques from the "investors" for less than half the total amount. For providing the bank draft, which involved nothing more than drawing up the papers for a draft that would never be cashed, the bank was paid about $15,000.

The sums of money paid out to the financial middlemen were substantial. The relatively small group of lawyers, accountants and brokers involved in such transactions—perhaps two thousand individuals across the country—collected fees of more than $200 million. All of that money came out of the public funds supposedly going to subsidize research. McLeod Young Weir, which pioneered the quick flip concept, boasted that the firm handled $165 million of the R & D transactions in the first three months of the program alone. Asked how much McLeod Young Weir made from the transactions, Ken Mathieson's lips were sealed. He just smiled broadly at the question.

In no time at all, the most unlikely people were buying or selling SRTCs.

Ed Fitch, for instance, a twenty-eight-year-old stock promoter in Victoria, was quick to spot the lucrative advantages of the new program. All he had to do was come up with an idea. Why not something high-tech, like computers? Perhaps he could design an advanced computer system that would revolutionize the computer business. The only problem was that Fitch knew next to nothing about computers. Undaunted, he signed up for a beginner's course in computers at the University of Victoria. The course proved a little trying, however, and after a few months he dropped out. Still, Fitch decided to pursue his plan to set up a company that would carry out research into robotics, artificial intelligence and integrated microcircuit chips.

Under normal circumstances, Fitch wouldn't have made it past square one. He would have had to raise money from investors or borrow funds from a bank, and it would be unlikely that any bank manager or half-shrewd investor would hand over cash to a rather unimpressive young man who wanted to research a subject he knew nothing about.

But Fitch knew the requirements of the SRTCs were not nearly so rigorous. He knew that through the SRTC program he could get access to government funding without having to go through a lot of red tape. All he had to do was set up a company and put together an idea for a research project, and then he would be entitled to claim tax credits on the promise that he would do research. Although these tax credits would be useless to his company, he could sell them—for cash. Better still, he could get the money up front, before he'd so much as bought a microchip, or even figured out what it was. And, astonishingly, no government bureaucrat would come nosing around, checking out his project idea or his credentials. The government had decided to let the private sector make the decisions. In this case, Fitch was the private sector, and he alone would decide whether his project was worth a government subsidy.

In April 1984, Fitch set up Fitch Research Corporation and, through the SRTC program, quickly sold tax credits worth $5 million. Once commissions and bonuses were paid, Fitch was left with $3.4 million of this $5 million. But to qualify for the $5 million worth of tax credits he had just sold, Fitch was going to have to do twice that amount of research. That meant his firm would have to carry out $10 million worth of research within a year—no small task for someone who had just dropped out of a beginner's computer course. Obviously what he needed were some experts to carry out his research. So he set off to find some. One of those he approached was Andreas Antoniou, chairman of the University of Victoria's department of electrical engineering. Antoniou looked at Fitch's plans and gave him a quick no. Other professors were similarly unimpressed.

Indeed, as Fitch made his rounds, a shock went through the scientific community at the university. What in the world was this immature, not particularly bright young man doing with all this money—money that, in effect, came from the government. "What we're seeing is the phenomenon of people running around with bags full of money that they've got to get rid of within a year," said Len Bruton, dean of engineering at the University of Victoria. "There should be some mechanism to prevent money from going to a project based on an idea I had whilst I was brushing my teeth this morning."

The alarm went right to the top of the university. Howard Petch, president of the university and a physicist, expressed concerns about whether Fitch and others like him would know how to spend $10 million usefully on research. Petch said that despite his own thirty years experience as a scientist, he would have trouble usefully spending such a vast sum of money so quickly. It takes considerable time to assemble staff and line up equipment, not to mention develop a project plan, he noted. This view was shared by Bruton, the engineering dean, who also ran his own engineering consulting business. "If you gave me $10 million tomorrow, I'd have trouble getting the people I'd need," Bruton said.

None of these concerns fazed Fitch, who assembled a small staff, some pricey computer equipment and luxurious office furnishings, and then set up shop in Victoria. One of the key problems he faced, in addition to developing a viable scientific project, was how to come up with the rest of the money he would need in order to carry out $10 million worth of research. With only $3.4 million, he was $6.6 million short. If he failed to spend $10 million on research, he would end up having to repay Revenue Canada for the $5 million worth of tax credits he'd sold. In other words, he would face a personal tax bill of $5 million. Fitch said that he had other investors willing to put up the rest of the money. But as the year wore on, that seemed less and less likely.

Finally, in April 1985, a year after Fitch Research Corp. had sprung up from nowhere, the company collapsed. It had utterly failed to carry out the required amount of research, and Revenue Canada officials came calling, demanding $5 million. But of the company's original three directors, two had left their positions months earlier. Only Fitch remained a director —and he was nowhere in sight. As the sheriff's office seized some $200,000 worth of furniture and computer equipment from the company's posh third floor office on Broughton Street, Fitch himself was rumoured to be in Hong Kong on other business. (The other business, it appeared, was his plan to market decks of cards that, when snapped quickly, showed moving pictures of people break-dancing.) Fitch has yet to return to pay the $5 million in Canadian taxes he owes. And, as for the "research," there appears to be nothing to show for it.

Interestingly, the company that bought Fitch's tax credit, International Electronics Corporation (IEC) was itself making money selling its own tax credits. In fact, Fitch was just a small fry in the tax credit business, compared to IEC.

IEC was run by Frank Hertel, a pudgy, balding West German immigrant with a varied background that included an audio-visual systems company, a regional airline and a used car business. The first two businesses, located in West Germany, went bankrupt in the late 1970s. After he came to Canada, Hertel supported himself importing and selling used Mercedes.

Hertel, 47, noticed the potential benefits in the SRTC program early on in 1983, when the Government had floated the idea before putting the legislation in place. A sharp talker with a quasi-scientific background, Hertel came up with a stream of research projects that he claimed would do everything from creating desert oases to tripling the output of oil wells. Unlike Fitch, Hertel could talk endlessly about his projects, using appropriate scientific jargon.

Hertel identified himself as a registered professional engineer. He claimed to have an engineering diploma from the State Polytech in Geissen, West Germany—a degree that does not qualify him to put P.Eng. after his name in British Columbia, as he did on his business cards. He also said that he completed a doctorate in engineering at Columbia Pacific College, a California institution whose academic standards are not recognized by, for instance, the University of Victoria.

Despite his dubious credentials, Hertel managed to sell tax credits worth $34 million to Esso Resources Limited, a subsidiary of Imperial Oil. Esso paid Hertel $32 million for his tax credits, leaving Esso with a $2 million investor's bonus. Overnight, the twice-failed entrepreneur with less than impressive scientific credentials had landed himself a huge fortune in Canadian taxpayers' money to carry out projects that no independent authority had examined. Hertel was now faced with the huge task of performing $68 million worth of research that year. Otherwise, he would owe Revenue Canada the full value of the tax credits he'd sold—$34 million.

But Hertel had another scheme up his sleeve. He could take the $32 million he'd received from Esso and spend part of it buying up tax credits from other research companies, becoming in effect an "investor" in other quick flip transactions. With the tax credits he purchased, he could effectively wipe out his own $34 million tax bill and make a handsome profit in investor's bonuses as well. He could work both ends of the quick flip game. With this in mind, Hertel bought tax credits from Fitch and five other companies.

Hertel set about spending money in earnest, buying properties around Victoria and setting up a headquarters for his empire in a lavish $3.3 million building on Fort Street. He travelled widely through Europe and the Middle East in search of markets and investors. He diversified into heavy equipment manufacturing and mining stock speculation. Within a year, he had acquired assets, many of them in real estate, of $40 million.

He spoke glowingly of the progress of his research projects, claiming that Saudi Arabian investors were interested in getting into a $160 million joint venture on one of his ideas, an "optical media storage system." Hertel always made it sound as if the fruition of his plans was just around the corner, even though the products—or the Saudi Arabian investors—never seemed to appear. In one case, he boasted to a reporter touring his building that his company was developing a new power carrier line that would enable the user to plug a computer into any electrical outlet in British Columbia and send a message all the way to St John's without using telephone wires. At that point, one of his scientists pointed out that, in fact, the company hadn't yet figured out how to get the system working *within the building*. Hertel dismissed this cautionary note with his customary bravado and the assurance that the technical problems wouldn't be difficult to figure out.

One thing Hertel had little difficulty figuring out was that it was best to be elsewhere when Revenue Canada came visiting at the end of the year. Hertel, who owes the Canadian government $30 million according to court documents filed by Revenue Canada, is believed to be in Brazil.

News of the lucrative new tax break spread like wildfire in business and financial circles. In Walton, New York, Canada's generous new scheme caught the attention of Frank Wood, president of Dreamstreet Holsteins, a prosperous firm that bought and sold high-priced livestock for cattle breeding. The company had some 10,000 Holsteins at farms in New York, Pennsylvania and California and had been known to pay more than $1 million for exceptionally fine breeders.

Although Dreamstreet was not in the research business, Walton was excited by the possibilities offered by the Canadian tax credit scheme and began looking for ideas for research projects. Within a few months, his firm had done a deal that delivered $22 million in Canadian taxpayer's money to a new Canadian subsidiary established by Dreamstreet. And what was Dreamstreet going to research? The company had decided to investigate the differences between black-and-white cows and red-and-white cows.

The question of how the two colour types differ is one that agricultural experts dismiss as trivial. "There's no evidence to suggest that it is more worthwhile than [studying] eye colour and hair colour in people as a way of determining intelligence," says Larry Milligan, dean of research at the University of Guelph in southern Ontario. Milligan and others suspect that the real appeal of the coloured cow project for Dreamstreet was that it would involve the amassing of a very large herd. The cost of purchasing the herd could be treated as a research expense and would be counted as part of the company's research costs. Yet when the research was completed, Dreamstreet would own the cattle it had assembled. It could then sell them, or their embryos or offspring, at great profit. The Canadian taxpayer would be subsidizing Dreamstreet as it amassed a huge, highly valuable herd. This might explain why Dreamstreet had settled on a research project that involved large numbers of cattle.

Two Dreamstreet staff members from New York came north and set up temporary headquarters in a hotel in Woodstock, Ontario. From there, they began buying up heifers and calves and putting in offers on local farm land. As news of their project spread in the farm community, Canadian farmers were confused and angry that Ottawa appeared to be bankrolling an American firm to carry out a massive project that seemed so silly. There were protests against allowing Dreamstreet to scoop up valuable milk quotas. Meanwhile, agriculture experts in government and universities got wind of the project and reacted with shock. Rejean Bouchard, animal research co-ordinator for the federal Agricultural Department, said there was "no scientific value" to Dreamstreet's project.

Milligan, the research dean from Guelph, was horrified. There was simply no justification for the project, he argued. The colour question had been studied before and yielded little of substance; there was no need to launch a massive new study into it. On the other hand, Milligan argued, there were lots of pressing dairy questions that did merit research, such as perfecting embryo transfers, developing multiple ovulation embryos and improving the reproduction of high-performance dairy cattle.

Agriculture experts in Canada were trying to investigate some of these areas, but the funding was woefully inadequate. At the University of Guelph, one of the top agricultural schools in the country, the entire budget for dairy research was a pitiful $1 million a year. Indeed, the total federal spending on university research *in all fields*—agriculture, engineering, medicine, etc.—was $540 million a year. And yet here were Dreamstreet officials blithely spending $22 million of taxpayers' money on a project that no one thought was even worth the effort.

Stung by public attention and criticism, Dreamstreet revised its project. It is now studying the question of how to separate semen likely to produce male offspring from semen likely to produce female offspring. Milligan notes that while this new question is "more worthy," the project still allows Dreamstreet to build up a valuable herd partly at the expense of Canadian taxpayers. Furthermore, there is little reason to believe the Dreamstreet technique is any more promising than other methods of semen separation that have been tried. Besides, even if it proves successful, the benefits to Canada are dubious. The licence for the method is owned in the United States, so future profits would accumulate there. "We pay for the testing now," scoffs Milligan. "We'll buy the product later."

But perhaps the wildest SRTC story of all is that of DWS Naval Research. It has all the ingredients of an exciting espionage tale: fast cars, easy sex, exotic travel, international arms trading, a cocaine-smuggling ring and even a company official who appears to have faked his own death.

In March 1985, DWS Naval Research and Design Inc. appeared on the scene in the quiet Ontario city of Kitchener and announced a plan to build a $20 million facility to research and manufacture miniature submarines. Claims by company officials that the new facility would eventually create five hundred jobs made the new project seem like manna from heaven.

The owner of the company was Paul Hera, a middle-aged German citizen who described himself as a former employee of the U.S. State Department and the United Nations, as well as boasting a doctorate in political economics. Hera had collected $1.7 million through selling research tax credits, and claimed that this money would be added to more than $13 million that the company planned to spend on research.

Hera and a few others, including his twenty-two-year-old son Stefan, booked a block of suites at Kitchener's Valhalla Inn and began drafting plans for their submarine project. The plans called for a custom-made factory complete with helicopter pad and a pool of water big enough to accommodate a miniature submarine. But while the factory and the submarine remained on the drawing boards, Hera and his associates started working their way through the $1.7 million they'd received selling the company's tax credits. They spent about $150,000 leasing luxury cars and ran up unusually high bar and restaurant bills. They quickly developed a reputation for high-living among the Valhalla's staff, who were delighted to receive as much as $50 in tips for late-night champagne deliveries to their rooms, where attractive women unconnected to the submarine business were frequently found.

The DWS situation was so suspicious that Revenue Canada moved in early. Six months after the arrival of DWS in Kitchener, government officials seized the remaining $1 million in the company's treasury. Investigations by *The Kitchener Waterloo Record* revealed that vice-president Alan Jurdi had been involved in international weapons sales. While he was on a DWS "sales" trip to Tokyo and Korea, Jurdi had tried to sell fighter jets equipped with rocket launchers.

The $700,000 the company spent in its brief existence proved difficult to recover. Hera, it turned out, had been wanted in connection with fraud charges in Cologne, West Germany. But he had died unexpectedly in June, only months after the company got its tax credit money. One of the few mourners at the funeral later told Waterloo Regional Police that the corpse did not resemble Hera.

A few months later, his son Stefan was arrested in Pennsylvania in connection with a multi-million dollar cocaine-smuggling ring, and was convicted the following January. Meanwhile, Alan Jurdi had left for Miami.

The SRTC program involved some of the most blatant abuses of the tax system in Canadian history. So badly designed was the scheme that it allowed common hucksters and con artists to abscond with about half a billion dollars in taxpayers' money, according to the government's own figures.

But apart from the obvious fraud artists—the ones languishing on foreign beaches or substituting corpses at their own funerals—there is much more that was deeply, seriously wrong with the program. In designing it, the Finance Department had devised a scheme that provided a rich bonanza for the investment and financial community with virtually no mechanism for ensuring that Canadian taxpayers were getting anything in return.

The costs of the program were phenomenal. In the less than ten months that it was officially in place in 1984, it drained more than $2.8 billion from the federal treasury. About a third of that amount—$925 million—was wasted, half a billion of it in fraudulent deals and the remaining $400 million in ill-conceived research projects that either fell apart for lack of other financing or simply failed to qualify as legitimate research. This $925 million is theoretically owed Revenue Canada by hundreds of research companies across the country, many of which no longer exist. But while Revenue Canada is still pursuing this money, it considers the $925 million will probably end up being "uncollectable."

But focussing on the lost $925 million can be misleading. The problem by no means ends there. The $925 million was only part of the $2.8 *billion* that the program drained from the federal treasury. That leaves almost $2 billion of research that apparently was not fraudulent nor part of a project that fell apart. This could lead one to take comfort in the thought that perhaps the SRTC program spawned $2 billion of valuable research.

In fact, there is no guarantee that the $2 billion was spent on projects of any value. Undoubtedly some of it must have been; but there is no information on how much of the money went into useful projects. Since no department or agency or council was in a position to approve or disapprove of the research projects, companies were not obliged to come up with projects that might benefit society either by developing socially useful new products or by creating new technology that might make Canadian industry more competitive. As long as a project met a very limited technical definition of research, it could qualify and receive millions of dollars up front. So, an experiment comparing coloured cows could claim the benefits of the scheme just as readily as an experiment of real value. Even though the SRTC program was doling out public funds, a company researching a cure for cancer would be no more qualified for funding that one researching a cure for hiccups.

And beyond this gaping omission, there was yet another key problem. The measure was so designed that it involved members of the financial community in an entirely superfluous but highly lucrative manner. Thus, as we have seen, some $200 million of taxpayers' money from the program went into the pockets of stockbrokers, lawyers and accountants. Often hundreds of thousands of dollars on a multi-million-dollar deal would end up spent on the services of these financial middlemen. A number of them, now legends in the financial community, made personal fortunes.

The program ended up being a cruel joke on Canadians. Created in the name of stimulating research and development, it was meant to usher Canada into a high-tech Shangri-la where Canadian firms could compete with the world's best. Armed with homegrown technology, Canadians were going to be able to wrestle the Japanese to the ground. Instead, we wrestled ourselves far more deeply into debt, squandering an immense fortune on those who needed it least.

How could all this have happened without anyone blowing the whistle? Revenue Canada officials made a few early attempts to draw attention to the potential dangers, but those warnings went unheeded. Since the Finance Department sets tax policy, while Revenue only enacts Finance's laws, Revenue's concerns had little impact.

Almost immediately after the draft legislation was introduced, Revenue was flooded with requests from the investment community asking the department to confirm that quick-flip-type transactions would be allowed. Revenue asked Finance if the new legislation was meant to permit these kind of deals. The answer came back: yes. So Revenue issued a press release at the end of January 1984, less than a fortnight after the law was passed, confirming that the quick flip was acceptable. "The Department of Finance has indicated that this type of transaction is within the intent of the legislation," noted the Revenue Canada press release drily. The Revenue Department was washing its hands of responsibility for the disaster it expected to follow.

At first, Ottawa's knowledge of what was happening was largely anecdotal. Since the SRTC deals were done privately, without any advance government approval required, the magnitude of the problem was difficult to see in the first few months. From the beginning, however, there were stories floating around the financial community about how popular the new measure was. Indeed, smart tax lawyers had immediately spotted an unintentional flaw in the program that allowed companies to save millions of dollars by reducing their quarterly tax instalments.* The loophole was plugged five weeks after the program was introduced, but corporations had already saved hundreds of millions of dollars in taxes due to a wrinkle that had absolutely nothing to do with research. Indeed, this loophole was the main reason Esso purchased $500 million worth of tax credits.

By April, Ottawa started to get a picture of just how much money the national treasury was losing. Research companies

*Since these instalments were based on the amount of tax paid in the previous year, tax credits used in the previous year had the effect of reducing the next year's instalments. This allowed companies to defer large portions of tax until the end of that year.

were required to notify Revenue Canada within three months of the sale of their tax credits. In late April 1984, the first batch of these notices arrived in Revenue offices across the country. The sheer volume of the quick flip transactions was ominous.

Around the same time, Harry Rogers had arrived as the new deputy minister of revenue. The department was up to its neck in controversy, none of which revolved around the SRTC program. The Conservative Opposition had been besieging Revenue Minister Pierre Bussières with charges that his department had been harassing innocent taxpayers. Day after day, Bussières was taking a beating in the House of Commons over the alleged abuses. Although the SRTC program was hardly the most pressing item on the new deputy minister's agenda, the reports he heard in his initial briefing were sufficiently alarming that he ordered a review of the new program.

By May 23, Rogers had a chilling report from his director of corporate rulings, Robert Beith. Already, 804 research companies had sold tax credits worth $914 million—a phenomenal increase over the $110 million worth of tax credits sales the Finance Department had predicted for the whole of 1984. Beith's internal report spoke of the need to "alert" the new deputy to some of the problems. It pointed out that quick flip transactions often left the research firms with only forty cents when they had to do one dollar's worth of research. Beith noted that in such cases "the investor realizes a quick-no-risk profit equal to ten cents on each dollar."

The first week of June, Beith's report was forwarded to Finance, and some of the numbers leaked out in the press, causing a minor stir in Parliament. Lalonde's response, however, was to treat the dramatic surge in quick flip transactions as evidence of the success of the program. "While the cost of the program is somewhat higher than estimated, I am pleased with its success in providing assistance to R & D in Canada," he said. "This program has generated substantial private investment in new Canadian R & D which is essential to our long-term competitiveness in world markets."

All summer, with the country in the throes of a federal election campaign, the Liberals left the SRTC program in place, despite the increasingly well-known abuses. Lalonde, who had gone out of his way to win friends in the investment community, was in no mood to take away a favourite new toy, especially one he had just given them months earlier.

With the election of the Conservatives in September, Revenue renewed its attempts to prod Finance into doing something about the massive drain of tax dollars. In a letter to Mickey Cohen, Rogers expressed his concerns about the program. "There are also indications," Rogers wrote, "that many small companies may have been oversold by promoters who are mainly interested in the fees they can earn.... For the unscrupulous, the program is an open invitation to misuse or appropriate government funds either as a promoter exploiting the unwary or as an issuer with little or no intention to carry out the qualified research." On October 10, only a month after taking office, the new Conservative finance minister, Michael Wilson, declared a moratorium on the quick flip. In its brief ten-month existence, it had drained about $1.2 billion from the federal treasury.

But, as we have seen in Chapter Four, the moratorium only quickened the pace of the transactions. In imposing his moratorium, Wilson had included a grandfather clause that was meant to allow deals already substantially underway to be completed. But an amazing number of companies produced apparent evidence that their deals had been substantially underway and just continued selling their tax credits. Six weeks after Wilson's announcement, Revenue Minister Perrin Beatty expressed shock at the number of companies claiming grandfather status. "It's phenomenal the number trying to get in through the grandfathering provision," Beatty said. "In some cases, it's pretty tenuous how grandfathered they are. You know it's amazing. The grandfathers are still having children."

For months afterward, the grandfather deals continued unabated. Indeed, the moratorium's only real impact seemed to be to drive up the fees of the middlemen. Since lawyers were now called upon to give opinions on whether deals would qualify under the grandfather rules, many of them wanted a bigger cut.

By March 1985, the total value of tax credits sold reached an astonishing $2.8 billion, with almost $1.6 billion worth of deals happening *after* the moratorium. The deals had taken place right across the country. In Halifax, $4.7 million in tax credits had changed hands; in Montreal, $186 million; in Toronto, $874 million; in Winnipeg, $77 million; in Regina, $6.7 million; in Calgary, $251 million; in Vancouver, $586 million; in Victoria, $235 million, according to internal government documents. Even the smaller centres had seen a flurry of activity. Deals involving some $1.7 million of tax credits took place in Charlottetown, $117 million in St Hubert, Quebec, $19 million in Sudbury, Ontario and $6 million in Penticton, British Columbia.

For nine more months, deals were still sneaking through under the grandfather provisions. With the final deadline of December 31, 1985, a last frenzy of deals went through right after Christmas. When the program finally died on New Year's Day, 1986, the national coffers were lighter by almost $3 billion, investors and corporations had received some delightful plums, the financial middlemen had been paid handsomely and millions of dollars of taxpayers' money had made its way to Swiss bank accounts and the pockets of vacationing "ex-patriots."

The SRTC debacle was entirely avoidable. While the extent of the rip-offs was perhaps surprising, the flaws in the program were obvious before it was put into place. And it wasn't just that there were inadequate safeguards against con artists. The more basic flaw was that the measure was constructed in a needlessly complex way that allowed all kinds of unnecessary interlopers to feed off the rich nectar of $3 billion in public funds.

It simply wasn't necessary to structure the mechanism in a way that provided a significant cut for "investors" who put no money at risk, or for brokers, lawyers and accountants who arranged the deals. "It mystifies me that the government takes the most complicated way of doing this," said Jim Finkbeiner, vice-president (tax) of MacMillan Bloedel. Finkbeiner argues that Ottawa could have easily found a simpler system "rather than going through that nonsense of having a broker in the middle."

One such alternative, proposed by MacMillan Bloedel in its 1982 brief to the government, was a kind of "negative tax." Under this proposal, if a research company did not have enough income to take advantage of tax credits, then it could turn in its tax credits to Ottawa in exchange for a refund. The system would essentially operate the same as the SRTC, except without the involvement of middlemen and "investors." The refund could be collectable either in advance or after the research was done, depending on how much control Ottawa wanted to have. Presumably, however, if the refund was collectable in advance, some government body would have to approve the project.

An even tighter system—and really the most logical—would have been to put the money under the control of a government department or council, to be doled out in the form of grants awarded on the merits of a project. Scientists or economists or business representatives could have evaluated the projects and chosen the most promising areas of research for Canadian industrial development.

This kind of approach was very much out of favour in Ottawa, however, where the mood of the times was—and still is—to reduce government control over private enterprise. Mickey Cohen himself explained the attitude to the public accounts committee: "In the case of the SRTC, the deliberate policy decision was made by the government of the day to try to treat the R & D credit more like a conventional tax measure and less like a [grant] program . . . to make it easily accessible, to keep bureaucrats out of it, to avoid the pre-certification."

Champions of this approach, such as Mathieson from McLeod Young Weir, always resort to the unproven theory that the private sector is automatically more efficient at administering programs than the government. Yet it is hard to imagine a more badly run program in every sense than this one, in which the private sector was virtually given free rein. The private sector proved highly efficient at taking advantage of the measure, but the results, for Canada at least, were disastrous. No matter what the shortcomings of bureaucrats, it is hard to imagine a bureaucracy approving a $22 million grant to a company proposing to study the difference between red-and-white and black-and-white cows, or a $5 million grant to a twenty-eight year-old computer researcher who couldn't make it through a beginner's course.

Private sector executives may be efficient at running their own enterprises, but they have a clear conflict-of-interest in administering programs of which they are the beneficiaries. The experience with SRTC unfortunately illustrates that, in far too many cases, they will take as much as they can get and let the public interest be damned. "I don't think there was anyone involved [in the quick flip deals] who didn't feel a bit twitchy," said one lawyer who participated in several. Twitchy or not, the financial community—including members of most of the country's top law, accounting and investment firms—milked the cow for all it was worth, even after the government tried to shut down the program.

Perhaps the clearest indication of the cynicism of those involved in the deals was their insistence on taking their cut up front. While Ottawa was extending enormous trust to them to supervise the transactions, they apparently didn't have the slightest trust in the people for whom they were setting up deals. By demanding payment up front, before anybody left the boardroom, the brokers, accountants, lawyers and "investors" were making sure that, if the research company owner ended up in Hong Kong or Brazil, at least he wouldn't have *their* money in his pocket.

To say this is not to suggest that members of the business and financial community are any greedier or more dishonest than other members of society. Overall, their scruples are probably about the same. The difference is that Ottawa has traditionally been prepared to give the business and financial community far more leeway and, consequently, far more opportunity to take advantage of government largesse.

Compared to its protests against other over-spending by Ottawa, the business community has expressed little criticism of the $3 billion SRTC disaster. Andrew Kniewasser, president of the Investment Dealers' Association, dismissed criticisms of the program with the simple rejoinder: "You try things. Some things don't work well enough." Would Kniewasser and others have been so forgiving and willing to experiment if the government had, for instance, set up a self-assessing welfare system without any effective controls? Imagine the outrage from business if Ottawa had frittered away $3 billion by allowing poor people to claim unlimited benefits up front without any guarantee these individuals would still be in the country when the government asked for an accounting.

The sheer volume of the money lost through the SRTC program is staggering. Needless to say, $3 billion would have paid for a lot of daycare centres or hospitals or schools or accommodation for the homeless. Or, what about research? Simply the *interest* on that amount would have been enough to increase the annual funding of all university research in Canada by sixty percent.

The loss of the $3 billion added a huge chunk to the national debt. With the deficit-obsessed Tories now firmly entrenched in Ottawa, the $3 billion that vanished with the SRTC program meant one thing for sure—a lot of ordinary Canadians were going to have to pay a lot more tax.

This is the sorriest episode in Canadian tax history. But it is important to note that is was not a bizarre departure out of step with other tax programs. Although it perhaps allowed for more abuses, the SRTC program reflected a point of view that dominated tax policy in Ottawa. That point of view—which argues that the tax laws should be loose enough to give the investor a little room—was the philosophical underpinning of the SRTC program and of countless other schemes which saved well-to-do investors large sums of money over the years. Certainly that was the view of the man who, probably more than any other individual, has shaped Canadian tax law over the past two decades—Mickey Cohen.

CHAPTER TEN

Mickey Cohen: Courtier In The Cosy World Of Tax

"You ought to obey your Prince in all things that tend to his Profit and Honour. . . . I would therefore have our Courtier . . . adore the prince he serves above all other Things, and in every minute Circumstance endeavour to please him."
—from Castiglione's *The Courtier*, 1531

It was a rainy day in Windsor, Ontario as Paul Reichmann and Mickey Cohen, shielded under umbrellas, made their way across the elegant courtyard of the Hiram Walker building. Windsor, home of Chrysler Corporation, is a city more associated with car parts than courtyards. But the old Hiram Walker Building on Riverside Drive is an exception. Its graceful ivy-covered entrance and manicured garden suggest an old-world elegance, reminiscent of New York's Upper East Side or London's Mayfair district. The gracious setting was a perfect backdrop for the immaculately dressed Reichmann, who presides over one of the wealthiest families in Canada and, indeed, the world. It was the spring of 1986 and Reichmann had just purchased Hiram Walker, bringing the lucrative distillery business into his family's sprawling $20 billion corporate empire. Cohen was walking a few paces behind him.

As president of Olympia and York Enterprises Limited, the Reichmann's chief holding company, Cohen was a key figure in the family business. He was Paul Reichmann's top official, his corporate architect and manager, trusted to oversee the family empire and supervise the delicate task of passing power from one Reichmann generation to the next. These are enormous responsibilities—responsibilities for which the Reichmanns hand picked Mickey Cohen. In many ways, he is the perfect man for the job. Highly intelligent, smooth and street-smart, Cohen is the ultimate chief of staff, the loyal servant at the top, dedicated to understanding his master's wishes and delivering them. He is the trusted knight in the prince's court, the one chosen to walk within a few paces of his master. To Cohen, Reichmann is simply "Paul."

Being this close to power is of course nothing new for Mickey Cohen. Less than a year earlier, when Cohen was deputy minister of finance in Ottawa, he was a regular visitor in the office of Prime Minister Brian Mulroney, or "Brian," as he is known to Cohen. Half a decade earlier, Cohen was deputy minister of energy and faithfully implemented Pierre Trudeau's national energy program—the nationalistic plan that was anathema to Mulroney's Tories, as well as to the oil industry. But Cohen glided easily between the Trudeau and Mulroney administrations, applying himself with equal loyalty to both. And he now oversees oil giant Gulf Canada for the Reichmanns. Serving such diverse masters as Trudeau, Mulroney and Reichmann is a task that might faze some. But Cohen does it with dexterity.

His dexterity springs partly from his cool-headed detachment, his lack of passion. "I don't think Mickey falls in love," says one who knows him. "Or to put it in the business vernacular, he doesn't get a hard-on. He doesn't fall in love with other people's ideas—or his own. He doesn't have that intense passion." Cohen is as free from passion and intensity as Allan MacEachen and Ian Stewart were gripped by them. Without that passion to serve a cause, a belief or a dream, one can move easily between masters, even dissimilar masters with different—and conflicting—goals. "He has no sense or feel or respect for policy as such," said one observer. Another commented: "After watching Mickey for a couple of years, I wonder what he believes in. He never seemed to have a set of principles of what the tax system should do."

He has a clear sense, however, of how power operates. And he likes being close to it. Perhaps no one knows and understands power better than the courtier, the man who serves the prince. From a modest background, Cohen rose to serve three princes, three of the most powerful men in the country. He also spent nearly a decade presiding over the tax system, making him the individual most responsible for the formation of recent tax policy in Canada. And the effect he has had on the shape of Canada's tax laws largely reflects his sense of how his masters' interests would be best served, rather than of how the tax system could best serve the country. He is the ultimate servant of the prince, the courtier in the cosy world of tax.

Mickey Cohen was born into a lower middle class family in New Jersey in 1935. His sister and brother were much older and Mickey seemed almost like an afterthought. His father, Percy, was a sweet but passive man, almost totally absent from Mickey's childhood. The family moved to Toronto when Mickey was seven, and Percy Cohen worked as a men's clothing designer for Tip Top Tailors. Mickey's mother, Rose, was strong-willed and complex.

At an early age, Mickey became competitive and achievement-oriented, largely under the tutelage of his brother Gordon. Fourteen years older, Gordon took a keen interest in honing the competitive instincts of his younger brother, spending time with him, teaching him athletic skills and, most important, instilling in him a sense of the importance of achievement. It was a lesson that Mickey absorbed like a sponge. Gordon was the first of a series of mentors in Mickey's life. In a sense, Mickey was always the golden boy, always the bright young man with the potential to make something of his life, the kind of person people like to take under their wing.

The Cohen family lived in a duplex on Bathurst Street, just outside the ritzy neighbourhood of Forest Hill, where it was not uncommon for a teenage boy to receive a car on his sixteenth birthday. Cohen, of course, did not. But he fit in well at Forest Hill Collegiate. It was a competitive place, and Cohen was always near the top of his class, sometimes coming in just behind Annette Oelbaum, who later became his wife.

At the University of Toronto, Cohen and Oelbaum were part of a lively, witty group of intellectuals who would talk and debate endlessly in the junior common room at University College. They would discuss articles they'd read in intellectual journals, talk about literature they were studying or rail against the horrors of McCarthyism, which was in full swing in the United States. Cohen majored in philosophy and excelled in the world of ideas. In one course, he wrote an essay on the intricate philosophy of Immanuel Kant, for which he received an A+++++++++, as well as a note from the professor saying that he wished *he'd* written it.

But, unlike some of his friends and associates, Cohen was always cool and detached. Many of the crowd he knew at university—including Oelbaum, Alan Borovoy, Stephen Lewis and Gerry Caplan—were passionate about issues and became heated in debate. But Cohen was never drawn in like this. He was always the broker, the one who could see both sides of an argument. To him, the world of ideas was for the mind, not the heart. He certainly had none of the commitment to social change that had, for instance, characterized the early years of Allan MacEachen. And while the junior common room at University College was a hotbed of debate, it wasn't an activist centre like the extension department of St Francis Xavier University.

Cohen's relationship with Oelbaum was also more intellectual than passionate. But, after years of intellectual rapport both in and out of the classroom, a strong bond had developed between them, and to many they seemed like the perfect couple. They were married in their early twenties, and Cohen was welcomed warmly into the Oelbaum family. In a sense, this seemed like the family he should have been born into. Annette's father was one of five Oelbaum brothers who had, in one generation, built up a large fortune in the paper and real estate businesses. They were active in the Jewish community, donating large sums to local causes. One of the five brothers, J. Irving Oelbaum, even worked full-time as a community worker, while being on the family payroll. As a result, they had considerable prestige within the Jewish community, enjoying a reputation for business acumen and decency that was a precursor of the image later enjoyed by the Reichmanns. The Oelbaums were *haute bourgeoisie* at its best. And they valued achievement. Although he was only the son of a tailor, Cohen's brilliant mind and hard-working ways made him a perfect fit for this prominent and respected family.

Cohen found an important mentor in Harry Wolfson, a brilliant economist who had studied under John Maynard Keynes in England and had worked for the Rothschilds in the Middle East. Wolfson and his wife Rose had a cosmopolitan, intellectual bent that was still rare in Toronto in the 1950s. In the midst of the staid, bourgeois atmosphere of Forest Hill, the Wolfsons turned their home every Sunday afternoon into the closest thing Toronto had to a Parisian salon. They would invite over friends and sit around and discuss ideas—everything from world politics to the future of technology. Mickey and Annette Cohen, although considerably younger than the Wolfsons' friends, became regulars at the Sunday gatherings. And Mickey Cohen was a favourite of Wolfson's, someone Wolfson clearly thought was destined to do big things in the world.

Cohen's considerable intellectual abilities were complemented by a highly personable manner. He had an easy-going style that made him pleasant to deal with. Although he was smart, he wasn't pretentious or arrogant. He smiled and joked and laughed a lot. People liked him. Somehow, the friendly name "Mickey" seemed to suit him perfectly.

With his analytical, unpassionate nature, Cohen was a natural for tax law. After graduating from Osgoode Hall Law

School in 1960, he became a tax and securities lawyer and, in 1965, a partner in the firm Goodman and Carr. He managed to complete his masters of law while working as a lawyer, becoming the first at Osgoode to accomplish such a feat. Like many tax lawyers, Cohen liked the intellectual puzzle of tax. Tax laws and the issues surrounding them presented an interesting analytical challenge, not unlike the challenge of unravelling Kant.

Cohen's reaction to the Carter Commission report in the late 60s was similarly analytical. It wasn't Carter's vision of a fairer tax system that particularly interested Cohen. It was Carter's logical intellectual mode. Cohen thought Carter had handled some complex tax questions well, and he was one of the few to speak favourably of the commission's work at a conference held by the Canadian Tax Foundation. As for Carter's call for full taxation of capital gains—a recommendation that had scandalized conservative elements within the business and tax communities—Cohen didn't have strong views one way or another. It was all just part of an interesting intellectual debate to him.

Cohen soon ended up in the midst of that debate when he became one of several professional tax advisors to the Commons committee examining the government's 1969 white paper on tax reform. It was an interesting time for a tax lawyer to be in Ottawa, and Cohen was fascinated by the whole process—both the tax issues involved and the political manoeuvring. The Liberal government was anxious to get its reform legislation passed into law after years of dithering. Since Liberals held a majority on the Commons committee, the government could control the committee's agenda and recommendations. Essentially, the government was using the committee to come up with a compromise tax reform package, incorporating enough of the progressive elements of the 1969 white paper to please the public but still catering to the voracious demands of the business community. It was a classic cut-and-paste job, involving the kind of deft political skills that were to become Cohen's trademark in later years. It also brought him into close contact with an important man inside the Finance Department, Jim Brown.

Brown, head of tax policy, was impressed with Cohen. So, as Brown prepared to return to his accounting firm in Toronto, he picked Cohen as his successor, asking him to join the department, with the understanding that he would be promoted to the rank of assistant deputy minister for tax policy when Brown departed. It was an extraordinary offer. The job was the top-ranking tax policy position in Ottawa, and the thirty-four-year-old Cohen would be leap-frogging over experts who had been in the department for years. With his marriage on the rocks in Toronto, there seemed to be little reason not to accept. Cohen had found a timely mentor in Jim Brown.

As assistant deputy minister, Cohen showed an incredible knack for surviving in—and quickly gaining control of—a complex bureaucracy. "He turned out to have almost an extraordinary feeling for how government operates," says Arthur Drache, a tax lawyer who served under Cohen at Finance in the 70s. "I don't know anybody who could come in from outside and so quickly adapt to how things get done in Ottawa." Drache recalls that Cohen could handle problems with other departments usually just with a quick phone call to the appropriate high-ranking official. He had an uncanny ability to control meetings. "Mickey at a meeting was an absolutely astonishing thing," said Drache. "He could take control of a meeting even where a lot of people there were senior to him."

Cohen quickly gained a solid hold over tax policy. The new deputy minister, Simon Reisman, knew little about the subject. Reisman, who was later to handle Canada's free trade negotiations for the Mulroney government, had come to Finance when the tax reform process was already well underway, making it even more difficult for him to get a handle on the enormously complex field. But Cohen had a handle on it.

And Cohen, like Reisman, was new at Finance, part of the new Reisman team. Reisman could count on Cohen to be his lieutenant in the tax field. The two men became close friends, and Reisman became another in the long line of mentors.

But if Cohen easily made friends among those above him, his breezy style went down less well with the tax experts he now oversaw. They tended to be concerned with things like the structural integrity of the tax system—keeping the system tight and neutral and focussed on revenue-raising. They generally shunned the use of tax breaks as a way of channelling aid to particular groups or sectors, since the breaks destroyed the neutrality of the system and increased the opportunity for tax avoidance.

Their rigid approach had little appeal for Mickey Cohen. He was less concerned about keeping things tight and neutral than with winning support for the government's tax policies. The way to win support in the tax field, of course, was to relax things a little, let the taxpayer breathe a bit. As far as Cohen was concerned, what was needed wasn't rigid implementation of the tight new tax rules, but a little loosening up all over, the creation of a little breathing space.

This concept of "breathing space" became a central theme for Cohen. "[He] had a philosophy which I think was absolutely crucial to the successful operation of tax policy and which unfortunately nobody else has," says Drache, a good friend of Cohen's. "And that is a theory which he called 'breathing space'. And his belief was that if you draw the net too tight people will cheat." Cohen argued that it was better to leave the rules loose enough so that people could lop a little tax off at the margins, rather than impose a system so rigid they would be driven to great lengths to avoid tax, hiding their income underground or offshore. He insisted it was psychologically important for the taxpayer to feel he'd gotten away with a bit, that he'd managed to keep a little from the government.

Cohen's commitment to loosening things up resulted in considerable relaxing of the tax rules governing corporate reorganizations—changes that saved corporations hundreds of millions of dollars in tax. It also resulted in loosely structured measures like the Registered Home Ownership Plan (RHOSP). The RHOSP provided tax breaks for people saving for their first house, a group that included some relatively low-income earners. But the measure was designed so loosely that a big part of the benefits ended up going to those with high incomes. Since the RHOSP was a tax deduction rather than a credit, the benefits increased as income increased. Furthermore, the measure was so full of holes that even families who already owned houses could take advantage of it. They would simply transfer the house into the husband's name, allowing the wife to save under the RHOSP plan for *her* first house. "I wasn't a dummy when I drafted that," said Drache. "My instructions were: we don't want something that is so tight that only a limited number of people can use it." As a result, the measure was draughty with holes. It ended up being too costly to the government and was eventually discontinued.

Indeed, most of the changes made in the name of increasing "breathing space" primarily benefited those with high incomes. For the most part they involved relaxing the tax rules governing investments, corporate taxation, stock options and personal holding companies. This provided considerable benefit to anyone with investments or corporate income, and little or none to the typical wage-earner.

The creation of all this breathing space had important implications for the national treasury. When Health Minister Marc Lalonde went to cabinet in 1975 with a proposal for a more comprehensive low-income supplement program that included tax relief for the working poor, Finance Minister John Turner resisted the scheme, arguing that the government couldn't afford it. In a sense he was right. With all the

money Ottawa had been losing through tax breaks, there
wasn't a great deal left. Cohen played a key role in the
Finance Department's efforts to resist the low-income supplement, facing off against Al Johnson, who was then deputy
minister of health and welfare. In a classic bureaucratic duel,
Cohen outmanoeuvred Johnson, and the scheme was eventually abandoned. There wasn't enough money, it seemed, to
provide a little breathing space for the working poor.

Cohen's skills won him promotion to the rank of deputy
minister of industry. From there he was elevated to deputy in
the more prestigious department of energy, where he was
charged with implementing one of Trudeau's pet projects, the
national energy program (NEP). Perhaps what was most remarkable about Cohen's stint at Energy was how he managed
to emerge from it unscathed. The oil patch and the government of Alberta vented their fury over the nationalization
package on Energy Minister Marc Lalonde and senior assistant deputy minister Ed Clark, Cohen's junior, despite
Cohen's clear involvement in the scheme. "Mickey's like an
eel," recalls Lalonde. "You can't grab him. He always slips
between your fingers."

In fact, Cohen's lack of trouble over the NEP was no
surprise. He and Ed Clark had a strategy of playing "good
guy, bad guy" in their negotiations with Alberta. Clark, who
was young and tough, would take a hard line, bombarding the
Alberta negotiators with numbers and arguments to back up
Ottawa's case. Then Cohen would come in as the nice guy,
apparently friendly and casual, and take them out for dinner.
He would even laugh at the anti-French jokes cracked by one
of the Alberta negotiators, though he personally found the
jokes distasteful. Cohen's approach essentially was to suggest
that he was on Alberta's side, that he agreed the province had
been raped and pillaged by Ottawa over the years, but that as
long as the province's negotiators refused to budge there was
nothing he could do to right the balance. If he went back
empty-handed, he'd get nowhere with his political bosses.

They had to give him some ammunition. Cohen was so persuasive that the strategy worked, and gradually Alberta made more and more concessions.

Perhaps Cohen's charm is part of the answer. He lacks the abrasive style of other powerful Ottawa bureaucrats, such as Reisman and Robert Bryce, deputy minister of finance before Reisman. Cohen was always smooth and convincing, adroit at handling people. In many ways, Cohen was really a marketing man, a master at marketing himself and whatever ideas or schemes he was promoting. In fact, Cohen may have been most effective as a salesman. "Give him a piece of [dirt] and he'll sell it—and get a fantastic price for it," said one observer. "He's one of the most persuasive people I've ever met."

If Mickey Cohen was a believer in "breathing space" in the 70s, that inclination was only intensified in the 80s, when he returned to Finance as deputy minister. It was the fall of 1982, and the department was still reeling from the beating it had taken over Allan MacEachen's November 1981 budget. That budget had taken aim at Cohen's breathing holes in an attempt to restore some tightness and neutrality to the tax system. The political heat over the MacEachen budget seemed to vindicate Cohen's looser approach or, at least, to suggest that it was politically safer. Now Cohen was back, clearly in the driver's seat this time, and the concept of breathing space returned with a vengeance.

Cohen's appointment as deputy minister marked the first time that a tax specialist had held the top departmental job at Finance. Finance deputies were traditionally economists who had to rely on subordinates to oversee tax policy for them. But Cohen knew the tax system and the history of tax changes intimately, having been responsible for a good many of them. Furthermore, the new finance minister, Marc Lalonde, knew less about the tax system than had many of his predecessors. As a result, unusually large power over tax was concentrated in the hands of the deputy. Furthermore, Lalonde trusted Cohen implicitly. The two men had worked together before, as minister and deputy minister of energy during the NEP period, and Lalonde had requested Cohen be appointed his deputy when he moved to Finance.

For his part, Lalonde believed his mandate at Finance was to continue the retreat from the 1981 budget. MacEachen had already withdrawn some of his own measures, but the cabinet and caucus wanted to go further. "There was still a fair amount of flak about the 81 budget," recalls Lalonde. "You know, how could the government and the minister of finance gracefully exit from some of the proposals or even decisions that were contained in that budget without too much political damage being done? . . . The prime minister was of the view that the government should not appear to back off easily or just let the minister of finance sink." But Trudeau did favour a further retreat, according to Lalonde. "So he decided to make it in the context of a general cabinet shuffle. Then a new minister of finance could proceed much more easily with changes."

With Lalonde clear in his commitment to retreat, Cohen swung into action. In no time, he had come up with a number of measures to appease the business community. The resulting transformation of Marc Lalonde was striking. Once a reformer, who had fought for a low-income supplement in the mid-70s and had brought in the interventionist national energy program, Lalonde was now lavishing tax breaks on business in a style not seen since the days of John Turner's generous spree. Lalonde denies that there was any change in his philosophy, just a change in the times and an unexpected growth in the government's deficit as a result of falling oil prices. "We were in a situation where the government could not add to permanent social programs for the simple reason that we didn't have the revenue."

But in his first budget in April 1983, Lalonde gave up plenty of revenue by handing out an assortment of tax breaks and credits for corporations and investors, leaving business spokesmen practically tongue-tied with praise. "I think the entire Canadian population should look on this with some confidence," announced a beaming Roy Phillips, executive director of the Canadian Manufacturers' Association.

Tucked away in that April 1983 budget, barely noticeable in the crowd of new tax breaks, was a paper outlining the idea for the Scientific Research Tax Credit. Cohen played a key role in shaping the SRTC into its final, unfortunate form. The concept had been fostered and promoted by Glenn Jenkins, assistant deputy minister of tax policy. But Jenkins and those under him who had done the technical work had pushed for a different design to the program. As outlined in the last chapter, the whole purpose of establishing the program had been to find a way to channel R & D tax benefits to companies that had no tax liability. To achieve this objective, Jenkins and his officials proposed a refundable scheme that would let such companies collect cash refunds from Ottawa.

But Cohen opposed the refundability idea. It meant that Ottawa would end up writing refund cheques, which was akin to giving out grants. With a growing deficit, the Liberal government was trying to scale back its grants. No such restraint was being applied, however, to the benefits delivered through the tax system. And business people generally preferred this option anyway, since it gave them—not a bunch of bureaucrats—control over how government subsidies would be spent.

With Cohen's insistence that refundability was out of the question, Jenkins and his officials turned back to the tax system for the answer. They came up with the scheme of allowing research companies to *sell* their tax credits to someone else. This opened the door to the quick flip—with all its associated problems.

The "breathing space" philosophy also played a role in shaping the SRTC disaster. As he had done with other tax measures, Cohen insisted that his officials not make the tax break so tight that it couldn't be widely used. As a result, all kinds of safeguards that could have been put in place were not. Virtually no legal responsibilities were placed on the purchaser of the tax credit or on the lawyers, accountants and brokers involved. Huge pots of government money were made available with almost no restrictions. Within no time, breathing space had turned into heavy panting.

It was a while before the full extent of the SRTC disaster became well known, and by then Cohen was no longer at Finance. As with the politically sensitive NEP, Cohen had moved on before things really got hot, truly Canada's teflon man.

With the arrival of the Conservative government in Ottawa in September 1984, Mickey Cohen's charmed life in the bureaucracy seemed at an end. His association with Liberal administrations went back as far as 1971, and, like most long-serving senior bureaucrats, he had become identified with key Liberal policies. And Cohen was even more political in temperament than most deputies, with a reputation for astute political judgment. All this seemed to tie him in with the Liberals—the kiss of death in Brian Mulroney's Ottawa.

But while Cohen was intensely political, he was not a Liberal. Indeed, he wasn't wedded to any particular philosophy or party. He had served the Liberals faithfully in their interventionist mood, but had switched to a more free-enterprise approach when the political winds blew that way. Now he was quite prepared to serve the Tories in their commitment to impose a stronger free-enterprise stamp on the bureaucracy. "He identifies completely with whoever he is working for," says one who has worked with him.

Mulroney understood this about Cohen, perhaps because Mulroney was a bit this way himself. Despite his occasionally strong ideological rhetoric, Mulroney was from the beginning a compromiser, more ambitious and achievement-oriented than he was committed to a particular philosophy. To the extent that they were ideological, both men leaned to the right and felt at home among businessmen and investors. But neither of them was a dedicated conservative. What really interested them both was success, and here their interests meshed nicely. Mulroney was a prince in need of a smart and effective courtier; Cohen was an accomplished courtier in search of a prince.

Bringing Cohen on to his team was one of the first things Mulroney did in forming a new set of players to run Ottawa. He called in Cohen shortly after taking office, even before appointing his cabinet, and asked him to stay on as deputy minister of finance. Cohen indicated that he would, but only if he had the prime minister's full confidence. After being at the top in the Liberal administration, Cohen had little desire to work his way up in a new Tory dynasty. Mulroney made it clear that he had absolute trust and confidence in Cohen, despite rumblings in Conservative ranks that Cohen was a Liberal partisan. Inspired by Mulroney's strong expressions of support, Cohen set out to prove his loyalty to the new prince.

Cohen also had the confidence of Michael Wilson, the new finance minister. He had developed a good relationship with Wilson in 1979 when they had briefly worked together during the Clark government. At that time, Wilson was minister of state for international trade, and Cohen reported to him as part of his job as deputy minister of industry. The two men had got along well and kept in touch after the Tories lost power.

Now, as Cohen set to work redesigning fiscal policies in the Tory image, he was faced with a difficult dilemma. Mulroney very much wanted to remain popular. He loved the groundswell of approval that had swept him to power. The traditional way for governments to maintain popularity was to give things away, to reduce taxes. But the Tories had inherited a huge national deficit and the business community was howling for deficit reduction, putting tax increases rather than decreases on the immediate agenda. As the new government prepared for its first budget in the spring of 1985, it was confronted with the bleakest set of options—cutbacks, belt-tightening, tax hikes. It was a grim and unpleasant business, not at all the sort of budget that a prime minister desperately seeking approval wanted to present to the people who had just crowned him.

Mulroney was determined that, deficit or no deficit, the budget wouldn't be all bleak. Mixed in with the tax hikes— which the government would do its best to disguise—Mulroney insisted there be a few bright spots, a few crowd-pleasers. There was no shortage of possibilities. In their bid to get elected, the Tories had promised all sorts of things to farmers and fishermen and small businessmen. Now they could simply deliver on some of these promises. But they couldn't possibly afford to deliver on all of them, and sorting out which ones to go for and which ones to drop could be politically messy. The whole thing could end up looking like a hodge-podge of giveaways without a coherent theme.

There was another idea, an idea championed by Cohen. And that was to replace all the promised tax breaks and giveaways with one big, generous tax break; to replace all the bells and whistles on the Christmas tree with one big star at the top. And that star would be a tax exemption for capital gains. Cohen was convinced that this was the perfect solution. The exemption would be enormously popular with farmers, investors and small businessmen—three very noisy and demanding interest groups. Rather than dividing up its largesse into little packages to be spread around, the Mulroney government could give out one big highly visible prize.

Cohen set about selling the idea with all his charm and enthusiasm. He was convinced that a star was better than a tree full of ornaments, and that the capital gains exemption was the perfect star. It fit so neatly with the Tory emphasis on entrepreneurship. And Brian Mulroney was just the person to sell it. A self-made man, Mulroney liked to wax eloquent on the merits of free enterprise and individual initiative. Now here was something bursting with that spirit, something that would prod the private sector and grab the headlines, something that would be seen as a generous and imaginative inno-vation—Mulroney's innovation. It was tailor-made for Mulro-ney, the perfect adornment for the new prince, cleverly crafted by his loyal courtier.

Indeed, if there was any lingering feeling that Cohen was a closet Liberal—big or small "l"—that notion died with Cohen's fight for the capital gains exemption. The idea was more Tory than the Tories themselves. It would even please the political dinosaurs in the Investment Dealers' Associa-tion.

The association had kept up its fight against the tax on capital gains long after most investors had abandoned what appeared to be a lost cause. Led by Andrew Kniewasser, the loud, brassy president of the association, some elements within the financial community were sufficiently persistent on the subject that, in 1980, then deputy finance minister Ian Stewart had felt a need to respond to them. He had had his tax experts examine how other western countries taxed capital and wealth. Their detailed study showed that Canada's taxes in this area were lighter than those of other western nations. Abolishing the capital gains tax would only make the Canadian tax system even more biased in favour of capital, and would place an even heavier tax burden on wage and salary income, the report concluded. Stewart considered that the report put the issue of capital gains to rest once and for all. Finance Minister Marc Lalonde subsequently introduced a system to index capital gains, protecting them from inflation. That was as far as the Liberals were prepared to go on the capital gains front.

But now, as Cohen toyed with the idea of introducing a capital gains exemption, the experts inside the tax policy branch were horrified. Removing the tax on capital gains would bring back all the problems that had led to the estab-lishment of the Carter commission more than twenty years earlier. It would revive all those devious schemes that tax practitioners had dreamt up to transform various forms of income into tax-free capital gains. The forgotten art of surplus stripping was sure to make a comeback. To prevent the situation from getting out of control, there would have to be a large number of restrictions, thereby adding considerable complexity to the tax laws. For the tax experts in the department, an exemption was a huge step backwards from the goals of simplicity, efficiency and neutrality. It did violence to all the basic tax principles they had worked to promote.

It was also such a blatant giveaway to the rich that even relatively conservative experts within Finance were rankled. The 1980 department study had made a compelling case against dismantling the tax on capital gains, demonstrating clearly that capital gains were heavily concentrated among high-income earners. More recent department data verified this trend. Among taxpayers claiming capital gains in 1983, the average gain for those with incomes under $25,000 was $2,100, whereas the average gain for those with incomes over $100,000 was $220,000.

Furthermore, the new data showed that about 50 percent of capital gains claimed were made from real estate investments. Not only did real estate investment do little to create jobs, it had the negative effect of driving up land and housing prices, making both housing and rental accommodation even more expensive.

But Cohen was set on the idea and managed to sell it to Wilson and Mulroney. Wilson was, after all, a former investment dealer himself. He had been a member of Andrew Kniewasser's association and, at one point, chairman of its Ontario district. To Wilson, the capital gains exemption had a certain intellectual appeal as an effective means of stimulating investment. Certainly, given a choice between a Christmas tree full of ornaments and a star at the top, Wilson was drawn to the star.

It was Mulroney, however, who really got caught up in Cohen's excitement about the idea. Mulroney could see it as the perfect centrepiece of Conservative policy, the ultimate symbol of the Tory desire to liberate the entrepreneurial spirit in Canada. It was the kind of thing that he could see himself selling, something positive in a budget otherwise stingy and glum. Mulroney and Cohen spent hours discussing it, getting fired up about the political possibilities. In making his pitch, Cohen argued that there would have to be a lid on it, restricting the amount of capital gains that could go tax-free. Otherwise, it would result in far too much revenue loss for the government. Cohen had in mind a lifetime capital gains exemption somewhere in the range of $100,000 to $300,000. In the end, it was Mulroney who bumped it up to $500,000.

But the measure didn't turn out to be the big political winner that Mulroney and Cohen had expected. Although the prime minister had planned to go out selling it personally, he never really got the chance. Within two weeks of the budget, a storm broke over another item—the move to de-index the old age pension. Almost overnight, the government was on the defensive and remained there throughout the summer, as the de-indexation crisis was followed closely by the even bigger scandal over rancid tuna. And from that point, one scandal just kept turning into another. Meanwhile, the new capital gains exemption was passed into law, and many well-to-do Canadians quietly enjoyed their new gift.

In many ways, Mulroney and Wilson may not have fully appreciated the consequences of their decision to introduce the exemption. Although they certainly had a general idea that the main beneficiaries would be those with high incomes, they probably didn't realize how pronounced that trend would be. Wilson, for instance, had not seen the department's new data showing how heavily the benefits were skewed towards the rich. And since neither Wilson nor Mulroney had tax backgrounds, they were largely unaware of the enormous complexity the capital gains exemption would add to the tax system. Likewise, they may have been unaware that the measure would encourage real estate speculation and provide impetus for exotic new tax avoidance schemes.

Yet all these problems were well known to Cohen. He knew

the issue of capital gains inside out, from his familiarity with the Carter report and his involvement in the review of the 1969 white paper, not to mention his years overseeing tax policy in the department. Mickey Cohen knew as well as anyone the problems a capital gains exemption would pose from a tax policy point of view. But with his astute political sense, he also knew the advantages it could offer to a government trying to win approval from small businessmen, farmers and investors —the backbone of Tory support. Whatever concerns Cohen may have had about the soundness of the tax system, these clearly ranked below his primary goal—serving up a policy coup for his new master.

Five months later, Cohen was serving in yet another court— the court of the Reichmanns. His departure from Finance barely a month after the May 1985 budget and quick re-emergence in October as the top gun in the Reichmann empire raised eyebrows in government and financial circles. Throughout the previous spring, the Reichmanns had been courting Cohen. At the same time they had been asking his department for tax concessions that would save them hundreds of millions of dollars in their takeover of Gulf Canada. When Cohen's new job with the Reichmanns became official, he felt the need to come forward and say that he had had no involvement in the government's consideration of the Reichmanns' tax matter. "I never gave any advice, never met the Reichmanns, never gave cabinet any advice, and abstained," Cohen told *The Globe and Mail* in October 1985. "The department was involved in the deal, both above me and below me, but not me."

In fact, Cohen was somewhat involved, although he signed nothing. He was first approached by the Reichmanns about the job in February. He reported the offer to Mulroney and Wilson. The following month, Cohen approved a Finance Department memo addressing the question of whether the government should make the concessions sought by the Reich-manns.

Basically, the Reichmanns wanted access to more generous tax write-offs in their takeover of Gulf. Gulf's oil and gas assets had already been depreciated for tax purposes before the takeover bid. But the Reichmanns wanted, as part of their takeover, to be able to depreciate these assets for tax purposes all over again. And at a higher value. They wanted to "bump up" the value of the assets from their book value to their market value; that is, to the amount the Reichmanns were planning to pay for them. This would give the Reichmanns substantially larger tax write-offs, making the takeover more attractive.

The Mulroney government wanted the Reichmanns to take over Gulf, thereby delivering a key portion of the oil industry into Canadian corporate hands. But while the cabinet was interested in accommodating the Reichmanns' tax requests, it did not want to appear to be making special concessions to one of the richest families in the country. This raised the question of how best to make the concessions without any apparent favouritism.

There were basically four ways to give the Reichmanns what they wanted. One possibility was for Ottawa to simply give them a grant. Or, in a similar move, the government could grant the Reichmanns a specific remission order, decreeing, in effect, that they could pay the reduced tax burden they requested. Such an order was really a special government dispensation allowing a specific tax concession to a specific taxpayer. It was almost like a grant.

A third possibility was for the government to change the legislation to permit more generous tax write-offs in cases like this. Elements in the business community had been pushing for this change for some time, but Finance had always resisted.

The fourth possibility was for the Reichmanns to accomplish the enriched write-offs on their own initiative by using a complex tax deal known as the partnership bump. (On Bay Street, it was known as the Little Egypt Bump.) Although existing tax law did not permit the kind of enriched write-offs

the Reichmanns were seeking for a *company*, it did permit
them in the case of a *partnership*. So if the Reichmanns teamed
up with a partner firm, they could conceivably get access to
the rich tax advantages.

Inside the tax policy branch of the Finance Department,
there was opposition to the last two possibilities. Certainly,
officials did not like the idea of changing the law, which would
just open the door for other companies that wanted what the
Reichmanns were after. There was also strong opposition to
the idea of having the Reichmanns use an exotic and complex
deal like the Little Egypt Bump, because such schemes made
a mockery of the tax laws. Therefore, the first two options
were the only ones that the officials considered reasonable
from a tax policy point of view. If the cabinet wanted to make
such a huge concession to the Reichmanns to achieve some
desired goal, the thinking went, then it should do so in the
most direct manner—in the form of a grant or a remission
order.

Officials in the tax policy branch drafted a memo to Finance
Minister Wilson making this point strongly. The memo went
up, through the department's normal chain of command, to
Deputy Minister Cohen for approval. (The tax policy officials
did not know, at this point, that the Reichmanns had approached Cohen about the possibility of his working for
them.)

When the memo arrived on Cohen's desk in early March,
he disagreed with its strong opposition to using a tax deal.
Cohen was inclined to favour a tax deal. Certainly, from the
cabinet's point of view, the tax deal was by far the most
attractive of all the options, since it was the only one in which
the government would not seem to be actively helping the
Reichmanns. The first possibility—a grant—was simply out of
the question. Under no circumstances would the government
want to be seen handing over a grant for hundreds of millions
of dollars to a company controlled by one of the richest
families in the country. A remission order posed the same

problem. It would appear to be an awfully generous conces-
sion and would smack of government favouritism towards the
Reichmanns. A change in the legislation—on the eve of the
Gulf takeover—would also look like preferential treatment for
Reichmanns.

But the tax deal option seemed politically safe. If the Reichmanns were to use a clever tax deal like the Little Egypt
Bump, the matter would be largely out of the government's
hands. The Reichmanns would simply be exploiting existing
tax law. Of course, the government would have to be a bit
involved, since the Reichmanns would undoubtedly want an
advance ruling from Revenue Canada indicating that the deal
was within the law. (Without such a ruling, the whole deal
became much more risky for the Reichmanns, because Revenue could decide to disallow the tax benefits after the Reichmanns had purchased Gulf.) Still, the granting of an advance
ruling wouldn't implicate the government that much; Revenue
would simply be ruling on existing tax law, not creating
something special for the Reichmanns.

The memo was sent back to tax policy officers for redrafting
so that a less negative view of the possibility of a tax deal would
be presented to Wilson. "I think it was more a matter of
the presentation of the information, the balance of the memo,
not the technical content of the memo," recalls David Weyman, who, as assistant deputy minister, ranked directly below
Cohen in the department's chain of command. "It was just
perhaps to leave it more balanced, or open—I can't remember
on that score. I'm sure it [was] a matter of guidance from him
[Cohen], that he felt that sort of tone should be changed."

In its redrafted version, the memo was more balanced. It
still opposed a change in the legislation, but it left the door
open to the possibility of using a tax deal. Cohen agreed with
the revised memo and although he would normally sign such a
memo going to the minister, he had Weyman sign this one.
"He saw it," said Weyman, "and at least as deputy, he didn't
want me to be sending a memo to the minister that was out of

step or out of line or that he didn't agree with. I mean, he was the deputy.''

Cohen also apparently advised his officials to contact Davies, Ward and Beck, the Reichmanns' law firm, to let them know that the government preferred that they use a tax deal. At least one telephone conversation on the matter took place between Weyman and David Ward, of Davies, Ward and Beck, although Weyman says that Ward initiated the call.

For Cohen, however, the memo had triggered concerns about his further involvement in the matter. He notified his officials that he no longer wanted to be informed about further developments. He told them that years before, when he was a practising lawyer, he had had legal dealings with the Reichmanns—which was true—so he wanted to avoid any further involvement in a matter affecting them. His uneasiness may also have been due to the fact that he knew the Reichmanns personally, having met them through his former wife's family.

The Cabinet continued to take an active interest in the Gulf takeover and the tax concessions sought by the Reichmanns. The issue involved several departments and led to at least one emergency evening meeting of Wilson, Energy Minister Pat Carney, Revenue Minister Perrin Beatty and Industry Minister Sinclair Stevens. The group decided that Revenue Canada would give the Reichmanns an advance ruling on the use of the Little Egypt Bump in their takeover bid.

The Bump had been used in other situations before, most notably by Petro-Canada in its takeover of Petrofina. But in that case Revenue Canada had declined to give an advance ruling on the Bump's legality. Under the cabinet's order, however, Revenue Canada gave an advance ruling in the Reichmanns' case. It consulted with the Justice department and concluded that the Bump fell within existing law. The result was a tax saving for the Reichmanns of more than $500 million.

Shortly afterwards, the Finance Department changed the

law in a way that specifically prevented the Little Egypt Bump from being used in this way in the future. The Reichmanns had got in just under the wire.

Castiglione provided such useful insight into the proper comportment of a sixteenth century courtier that his book's popularity quickly spread from Florence to other parts of Europe. Thomas Hobbes even translated it for the English market in 1588. It addressed all sorts of vexing questions: Should the courtier dance in public? Was it proper for him to mix with the staff in the Prince's private chambers? Should a courtier smile in a familiar fashion to a Prince he has already been introduced to? How important was it to win jostling matches? What should the courtier do if the Prince just wanted to have a casual conversation? ("Let him divest himself of his Gravity, defer talking of Matters of Moment and Importance to another Time and Place, and give himself entirely up to such pleasant Conversation as may be agreeable to his Sovereign, that he may not give the least Impediment or Obstacle to such Relaxation.")

Alas, Castiglione never addressed the question of how to advise the prince when there is a conflict between what is good for his rich subjects and what is good for the rest of his people. Clearly this wasn't a pressing issue for courtiers in sixteenth century Florence. And in a modern democracy, the issue should be resolved at the polls. These days, people should simply vote for the prince who will best serve their interests, and since there are more common people than rich people, the common people should get their way. But of course, the world is far more complicated than that, especially the world of tax. Since the rich wield far greater power and influence than their numbers warrant, they end up playing a much larger role in the formation of tax policy.

This poses a real dilemma for the courtier. He can easily become caught between the interests of the majority and those of a small, powerful minority. The powerful minority will scream and squawk endlessly if it doesn't get its way in tax matters, making life extremely difficult for the prince. On the other hand, the public at large is generally confused, disorganized and ill-informed and will probably not make much fuss if the powerful minority gets its way, even when it hurts others. If the courtier is trying to serve the interests of the prince, what is he to do?

What if certain powerful groups want a generous tax credit for R & D, for instance, or an exemption for capital gains, or a general loosening up of the laws that force them to contribute large amounts to the national treasury? And what if these groups have shown tremendous skill in the past in making life difficult for princes they don't like? Isn't it in the best political interests of the prince to appease these powerful groups, especially when the rest of the population doesn't seem to notice?

Of course, the courtier may not feel caught in a dilemma at all. He may believe that what is good for the powerful interests also happens to be good for the people. According to this theory, generous tax credits for the rich help everyone in the long run. This, as we've seen earlier, is the view espoused by the rich.

Cohen appeared to share this view. Certainly, he was comfortable with the rich and the powerful; life had been good for him in their company. Despite his humble origins, he had spent much of his life surrounded by power and wealth. He twice married into wealthy families. When his marriage to Annette Oelbaum broke up in the early 70s, he married Judith Loeb, heiress of a grocery store fortune. He is now, of course, closely linked with the Reichmanns. "He likes money," says one close observer. "He likes rich people. He's not without a social conscience but he always says . . . 'I'm not guilt-ridden about the poor. I'm sorry the world has poor people. But I don't spend a lot of my life worrying about that. I think the world would be better off if there were more rich people.' "

It is always tempting for the courtier—and the prince—to accommodate the powerful few. It takes strength and courage to do what Ian Stewart and Allan MacEachen did in the November 1981 budget—buck the establishment and bring in tax changes because they are *fair*, not because they will please the powerful minority. Both men paid an enormous price for their stand. It destroyed Stewart's brilliant career in the civil service and MacEachen's dreams of becoming prime minister.

Cohen, on the other hand, did not buck the establishment. Indeed, he did a great deal to remake the tax system more to the liking of the establishment. He did much to provide "breathing space" for the rich. In doing so, he served his political masters well, if keeping them out of hot water is the measure. And he certainly did well himself. While Stewart is still struggling to put his shattered career back together, Cohen is walking within a few steps of one of the world's richest men, calling him "Paul."

CHAPTER ELEVEN
Deficit Mania: How Ottawa Raised Taxes For Everyone But The Rich

*"Taxes are distinctly disagreeable burdens, and so there is
a constant striving to place them on the backs of others."*
—Louis Eisenstein

On the long, warm evening of May 23, 1985, Jake Epp kept
waiting for the storm that never came. With the bright lights
of the TV cameras whirling around the Parliament Hill lobby
in the commotion of budget night, Epp was ready for the
barrage of pointed, difficult questions that seemed inevitable.
As minister of health and welfare in Brian Mulroney's Conservative government, Epp had been carefully briefed by
officials in the prime minister's office about what to say. It
was the new government's first budget and the prime minister desperately wanted things to go well.

It wasn't going to be easy. The budget was sure to be
highly controversial. Most controversial of all, the government expected, would be its plan to remove the full inflation
protection from the old age pension. Under the plan, pensions would only be indexed to inflation above 3 percent a
year. This would cause a considerable erosion of the value of
pensions over time—a development that would dramatically
reduce Ottawa's costs in providing for the elderly. By the end
of the decade, this de-indexation measure alone would save
$1.6 billion a year. It was a crucial part of the government's
plan to reduce the federal deficit.

But the measure also could get the government into a lot of
hot water. The details of it were spelled out in the budget

documents, and some four hundred reporters had just spent the day locked up inside the convention centre at the Westin Hotel poring over those documents, looking for things that would make juicy headlines. Some bright reporter or TV commentator was bound to do the arithmetic and figure out that the de-indexation was going to cost an impoverished widow $360 a year in pension benefits by 1990. And when that happened, reporters were going to have some tough questions for the government. Jake Epp, the man responsible for overseeing the welfare of senior citizens, was going to have his work cut out for him.

Aides in the prime minister's office were anticipating trouble and, the night before the budget, had mapped out a strategy for damage control. "I said—along with a lot of other people—that the storm was going to come over pension de-indexation," said one of those aides. "We got Jake Epp out and told him: we know it's going to hit the fan and we want you to be ready."

The night of the budget, Epp was fully briefed and braced for the onslaught. He made himself readily available outside the House of Commons, where reporters gather to put questions to politicians leaving the House after the budget speech. But reporters and TV cameras crushed around Wilson and Mulroney and opposition critics. Nobody seemed much interested in talking to Epp.

"This one went right by the media. It floated right by," recalls the aide. "We were all looking at each other wondering when the penny was going to drop."

For days the penny just kind of dangled in the air, as officials in the prime minister's office held their breath, bewildered by the silence.

"I got to the stage," said the aide, "where I was thinking, holy geez, we're going to get away with this!"

When the penny finally did drop the following week, it set off an explosion that rocked the prime minister's office and sent shock waves through the new government. In the Commons, Liberal and New Democrat MPs zeroed in on the devastating impact of the new measure, which could cost an elderly person $1,500 over the next five years. Three senior citizens' groups came out strongly against the change. Inside the Tory caucus, there were rumblings of dissent as former cabinet minister Allan McKinnon promised to fight for full pension indexing. The Manitoba legislature unanimously approved a resolution calling for the return of indexing, and similar sentiments were expressed by several Maritime premiers. Many Canadians expressed horror at what seemed to be a mean-spirited gesture towards the most vulnerable members of society. Indeed, Mulroney's own mother called him and questioned what he was doing.

Even the business community began to feel the heat. For the past several years, business groups had been pressing Ottawa to reduce the deficit. Nobody had been more vocal on that subject than Tom d'Aquino, the glib spokesman for the Business Council on National Issues. The BCNI had welcomed the new government for beginning the process, while pointing out that it had not gone far enough.

But now, as the storm gathered over pension de-indexation, the BCNI was lying low. The BCNI's position, stated publicly in a policy paper on the deficit the previous summer, was that deficit reduction should not be done on the backs of the poor. On the 10th of June, Canadian Press reporter Eric Beauchesne contacted d'Aquino and asked him if the pension de-indexation didn't violate the BCNI's position that the poor should be protected. It was a good question, and it put d'Aquino in a very awkward position. The last thing he wanted to do was attack the government for a deficit-reduction move after he had been so adamant about reducing the deficit. Besides, maintaining good ties with the government was crucial to d'Aquino if he wanted to be effective in Ottawa. And d'Aquino, who had once worked in the prime minister's office under Pierre Trudeau, had already had enough trouble distancing himself from his Liberal past in the eyes of the Tories.

But the other option was fraught with problems as well. To endorse the de-indexation measure would put the BCNI on the discredited, unpopular side of the issue and would shatter the BCNI's carefully nurtured image as a council of socially concerned business leaders. Besides, the BCNI had stated clearly that deficit reduction should not be done on the backs of the poor, which was what this measure did. Above all, the BCNI's credibility had to be protected. D'Aquino took a deep breath and told Beauchesne that pensions for the elderly poor should be fully indexed. The country's leading business group had just jumped off the sinking ship.

Another call by the reporter yielded more results. Roger Hamel of the Canadian Chamber of Commerce echoed d'Aquino's sentiments as he tried to distance his organization from the government's unpopular measure. Geoffrey Hale from the Canadian Organization of Small Business had already expressed some concern about the lack of protection for the lowest-income pensioners.

When Mulroney saw Beauchesne's article printed on the front pages of newspapers the next day, he was shocked and furious. While he had grown increasingly isolated in the last week, the prime minister had taken for granted that at least the business community could be counted on for support. Now, here was d'Aquino, the most militant of the deficit slashers, chastising Ottawa for reducing the deficit on the backs of old people! "These were the turkeys who were telling us: if it moves, cut it; if it breathes, shut it down," said a close Mulroney aide. "What a bunch of chicken-shit artists. One little nibble and they just ran for cover."

And d'Aquino had not even had the common decency to contact Mulroney and let him know the attack was coming. The prime minister had to read the press to find out he'd lost one of his key allies. Even official enemies like Dennis McDermott, head of the Canadian Labour Congress, didn't do things like that. McDermott would phone Mulroney and let him know before he publicly took a shot at him. That way a relationship of mutual respect—even trust—could be maintained, despite political differences. This kind of trust mattered tremendously to Mulroney, who valued loyalty above almost anything. And now, in the first full-blown crisis of the new administration, the prime minister needed loyalty more than ever. "We were up to our ass in alligators," recalls the Mulroney aide.

For Finance Minister Michael Wilson, the desertion of the business community was perhaps even more devastating. One of Wilson's strengths was his connection to Bay Street, and Mulroney had counted on his finance minister to deliver the support of business. Up until now, Wilson had performed this task admirably, and relations between business and Ottawa were better than they'd been in years. The Mulroney government had been positively coddled by business. Bay Street felt it had one of its own boys running the country's fiscal policy. Yet none of the business leaders had even bothered to contact Wilson and let him know the bombshell was coming.

The day the article appeared, Wilson had a prearranged meeting with a number of business groups in his office. As he entered the room, the look on his face made it clear that the session was not going to be pleasant. The finance minister could be brusque and direct at the best of times. Now, he was livid. He had come directly from a meeting with the prime minister about the crisis. As he faced the small group of men sitting tensely in his office, Wilson's anger was palpable. He berated them for their disloyalty, their failure to stand by the government after it had delivered the deficit reduction they had long demanded.

Roger Hamel bore the brunt of Wilson's anger. Of the three business spokesmen quoted in the article, only Hamel was at the meeting. For at least five minutes, Wilson harangued Hamel for his betrayal, pounding his desk at times to underline his anger.

"And if you tell the press I've chewed you out over this, I'll deny every god-damn word," said an enraged Wilson.

His message apparently got through to Hamel, who communicated nothing to the press, except for a statement he made that evening supporting the government's deficit strategy.

But the damage had been done. For the Mulroney government, the desertion of the business groups was the last straw. The prime minister was not going to risk his political neck to achieve the agenda of an ungrateful business community. Wilson still wanted to hold firm, but Mulroney had reached the conclusion there was no way the government could win this one. The best the Tories could do was cut their losses, eat humble pie and retreat.

But there was still about a week to go before Parliament recessed for the summer. If Wilson stood up now and renounced the pension de-indexation, the Opposition would taste blood and go after other measures in the budget. It was crucial, for the sake of the new government's credibility, that the whole budget not be unravelled. The spectre of the Liberal government's humiliating retreat after the 1981 budget haunted Mulroney. He decided that pension de-indexing must go, but not until the end of the session. They would just have to wait.

For the prime minister and his closest advisors, these were agonizing days, as the controversy continued to dominate the news. From the window of his office in the Centre Block on Parliament Hill, Mulroney would look out over the demonstrators, knowing he was going to meet their demands but not yet able to tell them. "It was horrible," said an aide, wincing at the memory.

On June 27, five weeks after the budget was first unveiled, Wilson announced in the House that pensions would continue to be fully indexed. Mulroney said that his government had "violated the rule of fairness" and essentially apologized. Despite the biggest majority in Canadian history, the Conservatives had made a major retreat less than a year after taking office.

For many in the government, Tom d'Aquino was the chief

villain in the whole saga. Certainly, his relations with the government soured drastically after that and remained jaundiced for months. D'Aquino rejects the notion that he "betrayed" the Mulroney government, although he acknowledges that this is how the government perceived it. He argues that the "de-indexation debacle," as he calls it, reveals clearly the independence of the BCNI. It should put to rest forever any lingering notion that Ottawa is in the pocket of the BCNI or vice versa, d'Aquino insists.

There is some truth in this. Clearly, the BCNI and the government had a major confrontation. Nevertheless, the Tories' sense of betrayal sprang partly from their conviction that the BCNI was solidly in their camp. There is also some truth in d'Aquino's contention that the BCNI simply stuck to its guns. It had in the past stated that the poor should be protected in any deficit reduction measures. D'Aquino insists that it should have been clear to the Tories that the BCNI would not support across-the-board de-indexing (without exemptions for the poor). "You don't have to be a genius to conclude that across-the-board de-indexing with no exemption for anybody is totally inconsistent with what we said about deficit reduction not affecting the elderly poor," d'Aquino said. "You'd have to be dumb not to make that connection."

Dumb or not, the Mulroney government apparently did not make the connection, and was genuinely surprised when the BCNI announced its objections. Still, it should be noted that for all d'Aquino's insistence on protecting the poor, he never murmured a word of protest about the de-indexation until the reporter called him in the middle of a raging controversy over the measure. In the weeks before, d'Aquino kept whatever concerns he had about the poor to himself. Had d'Aquino simply not picked up on the significance of the measure, just as the press had missed it? No, d'Aquino insists he spotted it right away, when the budget was released. "Was I struck by it? Yes, I was struck by it," he says. "Yes, because it was totally inconsistent with the advice that we'd given the government. The moment I saw it, I immediately saw trouble. No question about that."

Yet, d'Aquino admits he made no public statement about it, nor did he contact the government to privately express his concerns—a move that could have communicated disapproval without publicly embarrassing the Tories. D'Aquino even admits that he probably would have never voiced any objections, had the reporter not called. Indeed, he had praised the government for its deficit reduction strategy before the budget and had urged that further inroads be made against the deficit. It is easy to understand how press reports of his criticism came as something of a surprise to the prime minister.

D'Aquino paid a high price for his perceived disloyalty. His influence with the new government was sharply reduced. Long after the crisis, his name still evokes unusual cynicism among some Tory aides, who point to his Liberal past and who go out of their way to suggest that some businessmen within the BCNI contacted the government to contradict d'Aquino and voice their support for the de-indexation measure. The aides refuse to supply any names, however.

Certainly, for many months, Mulroney and Wilson were cool towards d'Aquino and others they felt had betrayed them. In a rare show of pique, Wilson decided to do some deficit reduction on the backs of corporations. The day of the de-indexation retreat, he announced that the 5 percent surtax on corporations would be extended another year. In the prime minister's office, the surtax was quickly dubbed the "Tom d'Aquino tax."

Mulroney's first full-blown crisis had come over deficit reduction—an issue that had become the central theme of his government even though he had barely mentioned it during his election campaign.

Instead, the aspiring prime minister ran frantically around

the country promising everything people wanted to hear, most notably "jobs, jobs, jobs." Deficit reduction was no more a part of Mulroney's campaign talk than was deep sea fishing or lawn bowling. All the polls indicated the electorate was far more concerned about unemployment than the deficit. Politicians noted this and focussed their campaign talk on the problem of unemployment. Ironically, John Turner, who had taken over as prime minister after Trudeau, spoke constantly about the deficit. Despite the advice of aides who saw that the issue wasn't appealing to the public, Turner persisted. Within a few months, he was unceremoniously kicked from office by the voters.

Turner's focus on the deficit reflected the business community's preoccupation with the issue that summer. The end of the Trudeau era had raised some expectations that finally deficit reduction might be put on the political agenda. The BCNI was calling for an immediate deficit cut of $5 billion. For business, the Tories definitely appeared to be the best shot. Although Mulroney sounded like a profligate spender in his campaign speeches, business was not worried. It gave generously to the Tory campaign and prayed for an end to Liberal rule.

Despite its public silence on the issue, the Conservative party had been interested in going after the deficit for some time—a fact that had been communicated to business leaders. Led by Wilson, Don Mazankowski and others, the Tory caucus for several years had considered the size of the deficit a key issue. At the same time, the Tories' own polling firm, Decima Research, consistently told them the public didn't give much of damn about it. "It was a great frustration that Wilson and others faced," said a highly placed Tory official, "how to campaign on an election platform for less government expenditure," something the public apparently didn't want to hear.

The Tories knew they had to proceed cautiously for other reasons too. The Conservative party had come to be distrusted by millions of Canadians as the party which had dumped two of the most decent, sincere men in Canadian politics—Robert Stanfield and Joe Clark. And a good part of that distrust had focussed on what the Tories might do in the field of social policy. Party strategists knew many Canadians feared that right-wing elements in the Tory caucus would come to control Mulroney and start dismantling social programs. Mulroney's promise during the election campaign that universal social programs were a "sacred trust" was a deliberate attempt to allay those fears.

Clearly, then, Mulroney's overwhelming victory in the September 1984 election could in no way be interpreted as an endorsement of a serious deficit reduction strategy. In fact, to the extent that taxes and fiscal policy were an issue during that summer campaign, the message given out was an entirely different one. The one tax issue during the campaign—the promise of a minimum tax on the rich—arose unexpectedly and slapped business and investors right in the face.

In April, *The Globe and Mail* ran a front-page story about the fact that some 239 Canadians earning more than $250,000 had paid no income tax in 1982. The story was really just an update of information about high-income tax avoidance that had been contained in the MacEachen budget and largely ignored by the press at that time. But the NDP saw the tax avoidance of the rich as a good issue for the upcoming election and called for a minimum tax in the party's platform. As part of the NDP's campaign, the idea attracted no particular interest; the NDP was always talking about the unfairness of the tax system. But a curious turn of events propelled the idea briefly onto centre stage and then, inexorably, into the campaign platforms of the other two parties.

NDP leader Ed Broadbent raised the issue during the televised leaders' debate in July. Right there, in front of millions of voters, Broadbent was challenging the other two leaders to defend a system that allowed some wealthy individuals to pay no tax. The issue went to the heart of the fairness of the tax system. To defend it would be to place oneself solidly on the side of the rich. Mulroney was also aware of polls which showed that a large majority of Canadians felt strongly that the rich were not paying enough tax.

If so many Canadians felt the rich weren't shouldering their fair share of tax, what would they think of a political leader who seemed content to allow some rich people to pay no tax at all? Mulroney was in a real bind. To hem and haw and promise to look into the situation would appear evasive to the millions of viewers. A decision was needed immediately, right there on national television. Abruptly, Turner endorsed the minimum tax. Now it was Mulroney's turn.

The idea did not fit at all with Mulroney's personal inclinations. Certainly he had been well aware of the NDP campaign promise for a minimum tax but had shown no interest in endorsing it. Now, on national television, what choice did he have but to endorse the idea? Was he going to play into the hands of those who tried to portray the Tories as the party of the rich? Mulroney mustered the appropriate outrage. It was unfair that a high-income person not pay a minimum tax, he suggested. Too vague. The question came back again. This time, Mulroney sounded more forceful: "But in response to your direct question, should anyone in this country of wealth and substance not pay tax, the answer is no. Yes, he should pay tax and it should be a handsome tax reflecting the kind of advantage he gets out of the country." Broadbent's manouevre had pressured both Turner and Mulroney into endorsing a position that their party donors would consider an outrage.

In fact, Mulroney hadn't exactly committed himself to a minimum tax, and in the following weeks the Conservatives tried to backtrack. His campaign officials told the press that Mulroney was committed to tax fairness but that a minimum tax was just one possible option. That made him appear evasive, however. Even if he hadn't technically promised to bring in a minimum tax, that was certainly the impression he'd left during the televised debate. In response to continuing media questions, Mulroney clarified that he was in fact committed to the tax.

Having made that promise clearly, Mulroney was obliged to deliver on it when he achieved office. But having said nothing about the deficit during the election campaign, the new Conservative government nevertheless felt free to elevate it to its Number One priority. The policy bore the unmistakable stamp of the new finance minister, the no-nonsense investment dealer who brought to the job a determination to implement some of the long-held beliefs and dreams of the business community.

Michael Wilson had Bay Street in his blood. His father had been president of National Trust and, like other blue-blood boys in Toronto, Wilson had been educated at Upper Canada College. Before entering politics in 1979, he had been a bond expert for Dominion Securities, where he rose to be executive vice-president. He absorbed the values of the business community and brought with him to Ottawa a distinctly Bay Street point of view. With his square face and firm jaw, he even looked the part. "You phone central casting and say, send me a banker, and in walks Wilson," joked one Tory insider, who nevertheless insisted that, on a personal level, Wilson wasn't nearly as stern and dour as he looked. "Although if I wanted to go out on a toot, I'm not sure he's the guy I'd call."

Wilson was known as a relentless squash player, who on occasion showed up scratched, pieces of his skin dangling from his face. For about six weeks once he walked around with a large scrape on his forehead from a particularly vigorous game. Off the court, he was equally relentless and single-minded in pursuit of a goal.

Wilson signalled his direction at Finance clearly with the appointment of right-wing Bay Street insider William Mackness as his special advisor. Mackness took a leave from his job as vice-president and chief economist of the Bank of Nova

Scotia to serve in the Finance Department. The banker enjoyed a special status within the department; indeed, he was not really within the department at all but reported directly to the minister. Although he was relatively unknown to the general population, Mackness was widely known in business circles, where for years he had been expounding on the dangers of the deficit and the need to channel more money to corporations.

For Mackness, the central problem with the Canadian economy was "undercapitalization," by which he meant that Canadian firms needed more capital. There was a "desperate need" to increase their capital, Mackness had told a meeting of the Toronto Board of Trade in November 1983. The banker estimated that Canadian firms needed about $20 to $25 billion more capital in order to regain their health and start creating jobs.

But where does one get $20 to $25 billion? Predictably, Mackness looked to the tax system. "As long as Canadian industry is so perilously undercapitalized there should be little or no taxation of earnings that are reinvested in the capital base," he told the Board of Trade. Essentially, Mackness wanted to create huge new tax exemptions for those making investments.

Interestingly, Mackness alluded to the fact that investors were concentrated in middle- and upper-income groups. For some people this might have raised troubling questions. For Mackness, however, this was really a "practical matter." Since these were the only people capable of investing, then they should not be so heavily taxed.

This of course was the traditional plea of business and investors for more tax breaks. But Mackness, and other right-wingers, added a new rider. It was not enough for Ottawa to do as it had done throughout the 1970s—give more to business while still providing social programs to ordinary Canadians. This was what caused big deficits. Rather, Mackness and others wanted significant cuts in social programs for ordinary

Canadians. He argued that money spent by Ottawa on social programs was not available for investment in Canadian business. Therefore, he suggested, "reduce public sector consumption in line with taxes foregone." In other words, reduce the money government spends (on social programs) by an amount equal to the amount of revenue given up to the investment community. Put more simply: take money from social programs and give it to business.

Mackness's views were extreme, but Wilson was sympathetic to their basic thrust, as his first budget was soon to reveal. However, Wilson faced a major problem. Although he wanted to start slashing the deficit, the public had little interest in deficit reduction. The attitudes of the public would simply have to be changed.

What was needed was a massive public relations campaign identifying the deficit as a cancer threatening Canada's future. Mulroney was supportive, in principle at least. Although not personally obsessed with the deficit, his pro-business outlook and his keenness to maintain business support made him sympathetic to corporate concerns. In practice, however, Mulroney was inclined to be cautious, fearful of doing anything that might diminish his popular support. But talking about the deficit was easy, a harmless way to test out the issue's marketability.

In speech after speech, Mulroney and Wilson began trumpeting the evils of the deficit. The press picked up enthusiastically on the new theme of "belt-tightening" coming out of Ottawa. Commentators and editorial writers seemed to agree that Canadians were living beyond their means. The party was over, it was frequently said. Articles about the deficit sprang out of nowhere, full of huge multi-billion dollar numbers. Commentators started asking if the government had the "courage" and "political will" to do something about the situation.

Only two months after its election, the new government produced an economic statement that showed its fervour for deficit reduction and restraint. Four billion dollars was to be slashed from government spending, including assaults on the unemployment insurance program and the CBC. Wilson also hinted that he was interested in paring back some of the really big-ticket items, such as family allowances and old age pensions.

The economic statement caused surprisingly little controversy and was generally well received by commentators. Emboldened, Wilson ventured a little further. In a speech in Vancouver in late November, the finance minister suggested that the government could no longer afford social programs for the middle and upper classes. That came perilously close to saying Mulroney's "sacred trust" was no longer sacred.

Wilson's comments set off a minor controversy, which was a forerunner of the ugly battle over pension de-indexation the following spring. In the fall controversy, Ottawa had simply raised the possibility of cutting back universal social programs. When the prime minister was repeatedly reminded of his "sacred trust" commitment, he retreated, saying in effect that his government was really just thinking out loud. Six months later, Wilson got the go-ahead to put some of these thoughts into practice; although this time the government was a little more sly. Instead of cutting back universal social programs directly, it reduced their indexation, so their value would diminish slowly and, hopefully, unnoticeably over time.

If Mulroney hoped the public wouldn't notice this cut in benefits to the elderly, he was certainly well aware of it himself. Some officials had argued, in fact, that the de-indexation of old age pensions should be accompanied by a measure to protect the elderly poor. Basically, this could be done by providing added benefits for those receiving the Guaranteed Income Supplement, an additional monthly pension paid to the poorest pensioners. This idea had been pushed by Ed Clark, the former negotiator in the Alberta energy talks who was now at the Treasury Board. Clark's idea had support among Finance officials. But Mulroney said no.

The crisis that followed was perhaps inevitable. In many ways it revealed what the new Conservative government was all about. The Tories were eyeing the large social safety net that successive Liberal governments had put in place during the postwar decades. Canadians had become accustomed to Ottawa's extensive spending. It meant well-financed public facilities, aid to underdeveloped parts of the country, accessible post-secondary education and universal health care. It also meant special support for anyone with children, for the old, the poor, the handicapped, the unemployed.

The wide array of programs and services had made Canada a relatively egalitarian society. While Canada ranked well below many European countries in terms of social assistance, it provided for considerably more of the basic needs of its citizens than did the United States, where the individual was generally left to get by on his own. Canada's social welfare system was really a social leveller, in that it attempted to bring everyone up to a certain minimum standard of living—using money raised through the tax system.

But the business community and the new Conservative government were now insisting that the "party" was over. What it meant by this was that the country's social programs had become too generous, that the net was too thick and too wide. Why for instance did a bank president need to receive a baby bonus? Why did a retired millionaire need an old age pension cheque each month?

While these situations had a certain absurdity about them, the purpose behind the questions involved far more than simply removing government benefits from the crowd in Rosedale and Westmount. Although the debate was always framed in terms of wastefulness of channelling aid to the rich, what was really at issue were the subsidies that went to the millions of Canadians who belonged to the middle and lower middle classes. This vast majority wouldn't starve without them, but the wide range of benefits these ordinary Canadians enjoyed had been part of what had guaranteed them a basically comfortable, secure life. This comfort and security was the "party" which business, government and the media now declared "over."

Essentially, the business community and the Conservatives wanted to replace this whole social welfare system with a much more narrowly targeted one. The truly needy would be cared for in the new Tory world. No one would freeze or go hungry. But anything much beyond that was not the government's responsibility. It was the individual's. The vision of Canada as a series of interdependent communities where the strong helped out the weak and everyone had a right to a decent standard of living was now "impractical" and "unrealistic," part of yesterday's feast.

This transformation was to be brought about in the name of fiscal responsibility, getting the country's balance sheet back in order. It wasn't that the Tories were mean-spirited or liked making people's lives less comfortable. They simply had no choice, if the country were to have a future. It was a pretty tight argument, but it didn't tell the whole story. In fact, it missed a key element. What the Tory's deficit-reduction campaign was really all about—as the May 1985 budget made clear—was the redistribution of Canada's resources from the middle class to the rich.

In the bundle of budget documents released on May 23, 1985, deficit reduction was elevated to the level of a national crusade. The income taxes of millions of Canadians were going to rise significantly as a result of the budget—something that hadn't really happened in more than a decade. For a prime minister obsessed with remaining popular, it was a daring move.

But inside the "lock-up" on budget day, journalists reading through the package of documents were struck immediately by the tax increases aimed at the rich. It was hard not to notice them, since they virtually leapt off the page. The budget appeared to be hard on the fat cats. There was a temporary surtax for high-income earners as well as for large corporations and banks, and there were plans for a minimum tax for the rich. Reporters commented to each other that Ottawa was going after the well-to-do.

In fact, these initial impressions were misleading—and deliberately so. Mulroney had insisted that the budget appear to be fair, and so the budget papers and the accompanying press releases drew attention to and made much of the few limited tax increases aimed at the rich. The minimum tax, to which the Tories were at best reluctant converts, was played to the hilt, presented as if it were central to the Tory philosophy. An entire fifty-two page paper outlining possible options for such a tax accompanied the budget. Michael Wilson said in his speech that night that Canadians felt frustrated when some high-income individuals paid little or no tax. "I share this frustration," he said, looking firmly committed to changing the situation.

But the special surtaxes on high-income individuals were only temporary. A chart in the budget showed that Ottawa would collect an extra $550 million from the high-income surtax in 1986-87, after which the tax would disappear. Furthermore, it would only apply to one's existing tax burden. If high-income people were able to reduce their taxes through all the traditional methods, they would pay the surtax only on their small tax burden. The rich who paid no tax would pay no surtax. It was as simple as that.

So, despite the fanfare, the rich hadn't really been singled out to pay more tax. Indeed, the biggest single revenue-raiser in the budget, which attracted relatively little attention, was the de-indexation of the entire personal income tax system. This reversed John Turner's 1973 decision to index the tax system so that individuals would not face higher taxes just because inflation had bumped them into higher tax brackets. Under Wilson's new modified indexation plan, indexation would only click in for inflation above 3 percent. If inflation ran at 3 percent or more, as seemed likely, Canadians were going to find themselves continually bumped into higher tax brackets, facing bigger tax bills.

This de-indexation was a dramatic move. It was a massive

tax grab that would keep growing over time as taxpayers' inflation protection was eroded by 3 percent a year. Government figures showed that in the year 1990-91, this change alone would bring in an extra $4.3 billion in taxes. Plans to limit the indexation of the old age pension and the family allowance in the same way would save the government $2 billion that year as well.

The other key method for raising new revenue was a startling increase in the federal sales tax—a hidden sales tax applied at the manufacturer's level and generally passed on to consumers. By increasing the rates and extending the tax to consumer goods previously exempted, such as candy and pet food, the government planned to collect an extra $3.2 billion in sales taxes by the year 1990-91.

These changes—the sales tax increases and the de-indexation measures—were the heart of the government's deficit reduction strategy. Together, they meant Ottawa would be collecting an extra $9.5 billion a year from Canadians by the end of the decade. Although the budget pointed to the surtaxes on high-income earners and corporations as part of its deficit reduction strategy, these taxes imposed a small extra burden, particularly since they were scheduled to disappear almost as soon as they appeared.

Essentially, the middle and lower classes were going to shoulder the burden of deficit reduction. The de-indexation of the income tax system would affect those in every income bracket. But, as with the high-income surtax, many well-to-do individuals would be able to avoid the increases. If they were sheltering much of their income through the use of various tax breaks, then they were already paying little tax. The de-indexation measure would hit them no harder than low-income people paying the same amount of tax.

The de-indexation of old age pensions and family allowances was also particularly hard on low-income individuals. Although these programs provided the same universal benefits for everyone, regardless of income, the relative effect on the poor and the middle class would be much greater. The new de-indexation would erode the old age pension by $360 in 1990-91—a minor difference for a retired millionaire, for instance, but a significant setback, for say, an elderly woman barely able to support herself and her cat on a meagre yearly pension.

The sales tax increases were also regressive. As noted in earlier chapters, sales taxes hit lower income earners harder because these people spend a high proportion of their incomes. High-income earners actually spend more in dollar terms, but their spending is a smaller proportion of their incomes.

And if these measures weren't tough enough on the middle- and low-income groups, there was more. In an almost completely overlooked move, the budget quietly did away with the "federal tax reduction"—one of the few tax breaks that had benefited those with incomes under $40,000 by allowing them to reduce their tax by up to $100 per family. Long after the surtaxes on high-income individuals, large corporations and banks were to disappear, the elimination of the federal tax reduction would keep hurting low-income individuals. By 1990-91, when the high-income surtax was to be long-gone, Ottawa would be collecting an additional $695 million a year from those with low incomes, due to the elimination of the federal tax reduction. So, although the language in the budget papers tried to convey the opposite, the middle and lower classes were the real losers in Ottawa's war on the deficit.

Indeed, there was another measure in the budget which was puzzling to anyone who took the Tories at their word. For months the government had spoken of little else than the need to cut the deficit. This budget had endlessly extolled the virtues of deficit reduction. Yet right here on its pages was a measure that flew in the face of any serious deficit reduction strategy. At a time when Ottawa was adding significantly to the taxes of ordinary Canadians as part of a nation-wide crusade against the country's debt, the government was proposing a move that would *reduce* taxes dramatically for the rich. It was proposing to give up more than $1 billion a year by exempting capital gains from tax (up to a lifetime limit of $500,000). For some Canadians, the party was just beginning.

In his budget speech, Wilson waxed almost lyrical when he talked about his plan to allow individuals to receive capital gains tax-free. He spoke of encouraging "risk-taking" and allowing Canadians to "enjoy the rewards of those efforts." No mention was made about the fact that the benefits went largely to the rich or that the new measure was bound to drive up housing prices by increasing real estate profits.

Wilson justified the capital gains exemption almost entirely in terms of the need to create jobs. Yet the exemption was so untargeted that it was hard to believe that all, or even much, of the money was going to end up in job creation. The budget specified that all capital property would qualify for the exemption: that meant profits from the sale of yachts and jewellery and fine art and real estate, as well as from stocks. Even property owned outside Canada—a condominium in the south of France, a vacation home in the Bahamas—would qualify for the exemption. University of Toronto economist Richard Bird noted that when he sold his cottage he would now reap a tax-free capital gain. "That will be nice for me," he said. But as a way of creating jobs? "It's just silly."

The new measure even went beyond what the Investment Dealers' Association of Canada had called for. The association had urged that the tax be removed only from capital gains made on the sale of stocks. But Andrew Kniewasser, president of the association, was only too pleased to see the government go further. He argued that by extending the exemption to all capital gains, Ottawa was inducing Canadians to pull their money out of other types of investments and put it into stocks. "It opened up tremendous pools of locked-in capital," he says. "There was then and there still are all kinds of people sitting on useless condominiums or yachts or necklaces. . . . Now they have an opportunity to sell those god-damn things and put them into equity investments." On the other hand, what was to prevent these people from simply re-investing their profits in other useless condominiums or yachts or necklaces, which would provide the same tax rewards?

And those rewards were nice. The exemption, which was to be phased in over five years, would provide a lifetime tax saving of up to $125,000. The exemption would even apply to investments made in the past. Owners of commercial buildings that had appreciated in value over the years, for instance, could sell those buildings and receive the gain tax-free.

The business community was delighted. One company even took out a small ad in *The Globe and Mail* to express its gratitude to Wilson. "On behalf of all Canadian entrepreneurs, I thank the Honourable Mr Michael Wilson for the budget that has given us our 'dignity' back," said the advertisement by Diemaster Tool Incorporated. The ad didn't explain why giving someone a tax break gave him dignity. Was paying tax undignified? What must these people think of wage or salary earners, who pay so much tax?

The fact that the capital gains exemption would add an extra $1.2 billion to the annual deficit seemed unimportant to the business community. The same people who squawked constantly about the size of the deficit were unperturbed when the deficit was enlarged in order to put money into their pockets. Indeed, by including a huge tax break for the rich among its stringent deficit-reduction measures, the Mulroney government gave itself all the credibility of a father who tells his children he can't afford to buy them bicycles—and then goes out and buys himself a Porsche.

As the Mulroney government's second budget approached in the winter of 1986, deficit mania reached a fevered pitch. Business commentators were constantly interviewed about the seriousness of the situation. Political reporters, columnists and editorial writers accepted as fact that there was little choice but to trim the deficit and declare the picnic over. People who didn't even realize they had been enjoying a picnic started to believe the picnic was over.

With the budget set for February, the Canadian dollar went

into a sharp slide in January, plunging below 70 cents U.S.
The Bank of Canada responded by raising Canadian interest
rates to encourage short-term foreign capital to stay in the
country. Business commentators concluded that the dollar's
decline resulted from the fact that international money traders
and investors had lost all confidence in the Canadian economy
because of Canada's deficit. The only way to restore confidence and bring interest rates down? Reduce the deficit.

While the media pondered how far deficit reduction would
have to go to restore international confidence, there was another point of view that was receiving no attention. Many
academic economists looked at the situation and concluded
that the dollar's decline had little to do with the deficit. Rather,
they argued, it appeared to be the result of speculation by
international money traders, who were betting the dollar
would fall, largely because of declining oil prices. Furthermore, they pointed out that the measures in the previous
budget were already going to be taking a huge chunk out of the
deficit over the next decade or so, and no further restraint was
needed.

This was certainly the view of Data Resources of Canada, a
prominent economic forecasting firm owned by New York-
based Data Resources Limited. Tom McCormack, the Canadian firm's director of economics, argued in the company's
pre-budget newsletter that Ottawa had already gone far
enough with deficit-reduction and that anything further would
seriously aggravate the unemployment situation. "The elimination of the deficit—while achievable in short order—is ob-
tained only at the cost of a considerable decrease in real output
and employment," McCormack said. Data pointed out that
Ottawa had already made major inroads against the deficit,
most notably with the de-indexation of the personal income
tax system introduced in the May 85 budget. This measure
alone, McCormack said, meant that Canadians would be paying an extra $15.3 billion a year in personal income taxes by

the year 2005. "Many observers are not aware of this important result," he noted.

This wasn't surprising, since the media had all but ignored it. The media had become so caught up in the deficit-reduction crusade that there was little room for alternative points of view, even when they were coming from mainstream economists. The Data Resources analysis received barely a mention among the flood of hyped-up deficit stories. Would Wilson take the deficit below $30 billion or wouldn't he? Did he have the political will or didn't he? The speculation was endless as the deficit drama droned on. There was apparently little room for irrelevant stories asking whether or not he *should* take the deficit below $30 billion.

On budget day, February 26, Wilson showed he had the political will. The budget, he said, would bring the deficit below $30 billion, to $29.5 billion. There were some expenditure cuts, although not in universal social programs. The bulk of the deficit reduction again was to be accomplished through tax increases. There was another 1 percent rise in the federal sales tax, bringing it up to 12 percent. There was also a general 3 percent surtax imposed on all taxpayers. (The high-income surtax, due to expire at the end of the year, was not renewed.) Together, these measures would raise an additional $2.7 billion a year by the end of the decade. As in the May 1985 budget, Wilson had turned to the middle class to carry the load of deficit reduction.

The 3 percent surtax would hit everyone. But, as with the de-indexation of the tax system, the effect on the high-income earner might not be as punitive as appeared at first glance. The chart in the budget indicated that the surtax would increase the tax bill of a single taxpayer earning $20,000 a year by $74 in 1987, whereas a single taxpayer earning $100,000 would pay an additional $786. While this was true in theory, it would rarely be the case in practice. The $20,000-a-year individual would certainly end up paying $74 more. But most individuals

with incomes of $100,000 were able to claim special invest-
ment tax breaks or were using tax avoidance schemes. Since
the surtax was applied to their tax bill and many of them were
able to reduce their tax bills considerably, their surtax would
be correspondingly small. It would certainly be smaller than
$786.

The budget did, however, contain one new measure that
would hit the investor. It raised the tax rate on dividend
income from 25 percent back to 33 percent, where it had been
before it was lowered in the March 1977 budget. By restoring
the higher dividend tax rate, Wilson restored the "integration"
of the tax system, so that income received directly by an
individual was taxed at the same rate as income received
through a personal corporation. In the future, there would be
little incentive to set up personal corporations as a way of
avoiding tax.

The business community generally approved of the budget,
although there was some grumbling about the higher tax rate
on dividends and some dissatisfaction that the deficit reduction hadn't gone further. Media commentators generally
voiced approval. At his press conference the night of the
budget, the most persistent question Wilson faced was why he
had not taken a bigger bite out of the deficit. And on the CTV
program "Question Period" that week, Wilson was again
grilled primarily on the deficit, with most of the questions
focussing on why he hadn't gone further. Roy MacGregor, a
columnist for *The Ottawa Citizen*, briefly asked about the
increased tax burden for the ordinary Canadian, and then the
questioning returned to the more familiar terrain of deficit
reduction.

But while the budget largely won praise for the Tories, its
harsh line on the deficit would exact a price from Canadians,
as the government knew. Internal Finance Department calculations indicated that the defict-reduction measures in the
budget would dampen job growth in the country considerably,
by taking money out of people's pockets and reducing

consumer demand. Indeed, even as reporters were studying the budget in the lock-up, a senior government official was giving an internal briefing on the negative growth effects of the budget. William White, a top official of the Bank of Canada who was on loan to the Finance Department, told the closed-door session of Finance officials that the budget would reduce the growth of the economy by about 0.3 to 0.4 percent—a reduction that would mean 40,000 fewer jobs than would otherwise be created. The budget made no mention of this.

Although the rhetoric in the Mulroney government's first two years focussed on deficit-reduction, there was actually far more going on. Allan Maslove, director of Carleton University's School of Public Administration, suggested that Wilson's May 85 budget was more noteworthy for its redistribution from the middle class to high-income groups than for its deficit reduction. To some extent, the deficit was being used as a rationale to reduce the scope of the welfare state, to remake Canada more in the image of the United States, where the social safety net provides only the most basic necessities.

This was apparently what lay behind the government's new emphasis on targeting benefits to the very poor. Helping the very poor was, of course, a laudable objective. But for the Mulroney government, it was coupled with an overall reduction in the amount of benefits, and an elimination of benefits from many people who were, if not very poor, at least poor. What the government did was enrich benefits somewhat at the lower end, while cutting them off completely after a certain income threshhold—a very low income threshhold.

For instance, in the February 1986 budget, the government introduced a federal sales tax credit for the very poor. The measure was meant to compensate for increases in the federal sales tax in both that budget and the previous budget. The tax credit provided $50 for each of two spouses in a family, plus $25 for each child. But in order to qualify, a family had to be very poor indeed. An individual earning just over $18,000 *and supporting a spouse and four children* would be too well-off by the government's standards to qualify for the tax credit. Yet such a family was well below the poverty line, as defined by Health and Welfare Canada, for just about every city in the country. The Finance Department was effectively setting its own poverty line, and setting it much lower than the department charged with overseeing the health and welfare of Canadians.

Furthermore, even the very poor—the ones supposedly targeted for extra help—would also end up worse off. The sales tax credit introduced with such fanfare would not fully offset the increases caused by the new sales tax rates. A family of four with an income of $10,000—very poor by anyone's standards—would in 1987 qualify for a sales tax credit of $150. But, as a result of the sales tax increases in the Mulroney government's first two budgets, this family would end up paying an estimated $353 more in higher sales tax. So, even with the $150 credit, the family was losing $203.*

In the crucial area of child tax benefits, Ottawa was also weaning many low- and middle-income earners away from government support. To begin with, it removed the full index-ation of family allowance payments so that the value of the payments would be eroded each year through inflation. It also restructured the child tax credit and the child tax exemption in ways that reduced the benefits at the higher end of the income scale and, at least in the case of the credit, enriched the benefits at the lower end. Yet, as the years passed, the new enriched benefits would be restricted to a poorer and poorer group, since the income threshold—set at $23,500 in 1986—was not indexed. An income of $23,500 in 1986 was barely skirting the poverty line. By 1990, with inflation eroding the value of money, an income of $23,500 would certainly be well below the poverty line. (That is, Health and Welfare's poverty line.) So, as in the case of the sales tax credit, the changes made

---

*Statistics from the National Council of Welfare.

to child benefits in the name of targeting benefits more specifically to the very poorest families, still left those poorest families worse off.

This revamping of the child tax benefits would save Ottawa a great deal of money. By 1990, the de-indexation of the family allowance alone would save $400 million, according to the government's own figures. The combination of these three changes in child benefits would cut government support for families by a total of $555 million a year. Although the changes were being made in the name of targeting benefits more effectively towards the truly poor, they also had the effect of eliminating or reducing benefits for many low-income families who were anything but well-off. With the money saved, Ottawa was going to reduce the deficit—and the tax burden on investors.

The government was of course reluctant to come out and say this, fearing the public might not be keen on the change. But its outside supporters were not always so careful, and sometimes their candid comments revealed that they knew this prescription would hurt some Canadians far more than others.

Such was the case with a speech made by Bill Macdonald the day after the May 1985 budget. Macdonald, a senior tax lawyer at McMillan, Binch and a longtime activist against tax reform in the late 60s and early 70s, was close to the new government.

In his post-budget speech to a seminar of businessmen, lawyers and accountants, Macdonald endorsed the government's new direction, although he complained that the deficit-reduction measures didn't go far enough. Macdonald was attuned to the political realities, however. He knew the difficulty of prescribing such harsh medicine in a democracy, where voters can avoid taking the medicine by simply voting governments out of office. He feared that this popular dislike of harsh medicine might shake the government's resolve. It came down to a question of "political will." Macdonald was really asking: Did the new government have the guts to force deficit-reduction down the throats of unwilling Canadians?

Then, in a "final comment," he made a most interesting observation. "Despite the progressive feature of the temporary surtax [on high-income individuals]," he said, "*the main burden of the budget seems likely to fall on the middle and lower middle classes*" (italics added). This was an amazing admission for someone who supported the budget. Macdonald went on to point out that the de-indexation of the tax system "will build in automatic real tax increases for the lower middle and middle classes that will become quite considerable over time." This fact raised some concerns in Macdonald. But apparently not because it seemed unfair to be sticking it to the less-well-paid members of society. Rather, Macdonald feared this might result in some "heavy political water for the government" which would further diminish its political will. The only problem with forcing deficit-reduction down the throats of unwilling Canadians was that they might fight back.

Those pesky voters can ruin the best-laid plans of government, it seems.

CHAPTER TWELVE

Michael Wilson And The Hijacking Of Tax Reform

"It's unconscionable that they pay so little tax."
—**Donald Blenkarn, Chairman of the House of Commons finance committee, commenting on the fact that two Bronfman companies paid no income tax in 1986—a situation that is unlikely to change under Michael Wilson's tax reform**

On a paper napkin in a Saskatoon hotel room, one of the prime minister's top aides scrawled four words that spelled out the dilemma facing the Mulroney cabinet. It was July 1986, and the inner cabinet, which included the sixteen most powerful ministers, had chosen Saskatoon as a suitable western spot in which to map their future course and figure out how to regain popularity with the Canadian public. South of the border, the United States was about to lower its tax rates in what looked like a very popular move—a move that was attracting considerable interest in the cabinet. Yet this was far from the course Ottawa had been pursuing. For the past few years, the Mulroney government had been raising taxes. And the Finance Department was now deeply involved in a plan to replace the existing federal sales tax with a whole new comprehensive sales tax that threatened to do the unthinkable—impose a tax on food.

After the day's formal session, a small group of the prime minister's aides were meeting informally with the urbane deputy minister of finance, Stanley Hartt. Bill Fox, the prime minister's earthy press secretary, was arguing that the new sales tax Hartt had outlined to the cabinet ministers in

Saskatoon might be sound and sophisticated policy, but it would never sell in Perth, Ontario. On a napkin he wrote two words—"Tax reform"—and then, right beneath, another two words—"Food tax." He then turned to Hartt and asked pointedly: "Which side do you want to be on?"

Fox's little napkin memo neatly summed up the government's vexing problem. For some time, Finance Minister Michael Wilson had been keen on bringing in the revised sales tax in order to correct some of the problems in the existing sales tax and to greatly extend the government's taxing power. By restructuring the sales tax and broadening the number of goods and services subject to it, Ottawa would have a lethal weapon in its war against the deficit. Every tiny increase in the sales tax rate would generate billions of dollars in revenue in a way that would be largely invisible to the consumer—by taxing the product as it moved through each stage of the production chain. It was no wonder similar taxes in European countries had been branded "cash cows." For Wilson, the new sales tax—whether it was called a value-added tax or a business transfer tax—was the answer.

But, as Fox was suggesting, it didn't fit that well with popular notions of "tax reform." Tax reform had long been associated with the idea of removing the special privileges of powerful interest groups in order to create a fairer system. But sales taxes were widely known to be unfair; they were known to hit hardest against those with least income.

The government knew it would have trouble selling the public on a revamped and enlarged sales tax, even if there were special tax credits to compensate those at the bottom end. The Finance Department insisted that for the new tax to be workable it would have to be comprehensive, hitting pretty well all goods and services. This meant people would be paying tax on a whole new range of things, from haircuts to drugs to dental bills. And the tax would probably have to apply to food as well, leaving the Tories open to charges that they had about as much grasp of the problems of the poor as did Marie-Antoinette when she discovered that eighteenth century French paupers had no bread. Worse still, while Marie-Antoinette may have seemed insensitive suggesting the poor eat cake instead, the Mulroney government wanted to tax cake as well. Clearly, the government was going to be faced with a daunting task if it tried to sell "tax reform" in one breath and a "food tax" in the next.

This dilemma was not lost on cabinet ministers, who had felt the public's angry reaction only a year earlier when Wilson had attempted to remove the full inflation protection from old age pensions. "The antennae went up, very early on," said one insider. In particular, concerns were expressed by the red Tories in cabinet—David Crombie, Flora Mac-Donald and Joe Clark. With the Opposition parties poised and ready to pounce, wasn't the government just handing them the perfect election slogan: "Here's the government that brought you the food tax."

The debate raged on for months inside the cabinet and among the prime minister's aides and advisors. What finally emerged in June 1987 was a solution designed to let the government have it both ways: proceed with plans for an expanded sales tax, but don't implement it before the next election. In the meantime, reduce income taxes a bit in the name of "tax reform." If everything worked according to plan, the government could have its cake—and tax it too.

So while the sales tax was slated for a post-election date as Stage II of tax reform, attention focussed on how best to turn Stage I into an attractive pre-election give-away. Above all, the Tories felt the need to shake their long-standing image as the friends of big business and the rich—an image that had been enhanced by the Mulroney government's earlier budgets. Tax reform would have to at least appear to hit these groups.

And this certainly was how things appeared on June 18, when the tax reform proposals were unveiled. But the reality turns out to be a little different.

On the corporate side, the tax reform is surprisingly gentle. In fact, it came as a welcome relief to the business community, which had been expecting much harsher medicine. The basic thrust of the corporate reforms, as in the personal income tax reforms, is that tax breaks will be trimmed or eliminated in exchange for lower tax rates—a trade-off that seems to please most industries. The combined federal-provincial corporate tax rate is to be lowered from 46 to 38 percent. This amounts to a substantial drop, particularly as many corporations are beginning to show the first large profits since the recession of the early 80s. Altogether, the reform is supposed to raise corporate taxes by $5 billion over 5 years, or about $1 billion a year.

This may sound impressive, but it should be seen in perspective. In fact, it will not even increase the share of corporate tax to the level it was at when the Tories took office. In 1984-85, corporate income taxes accounted for 20.3 percent of Ottawa's major revenues—close to a historic low. (They made up 26.2 percent of revenues in 1975-76, for instance.) Under the Tories, the corporate share sank lower still, so that corporate income taxes were only contributing 16.4 percent of major revenues in 1986-87. Under the white paper proposals, Ottawa estimates that the corporate share will only rise to 17.2 per cent—still below the level it had sunk to when the Tories came to power.

Besides, much of this increase will disappear after five years. That's because the most significant tax hikes are due to changes in the capital cost allowances which enable companies to depreciate machinery at fast rates. What the change essentially amounts to is a one-time increase in tax revenue as companies move to a system of slower write-offs. After five years, once the change has been fully phased in, no additional corporate revenue will be collected. The government revenue projections, however, only look five years ahead.

All in all, the business community was anything but displeased with the corporate tax changes. Unlike the outpouring of rage that had greeted earlier tax reform efforts, all was calm and even cheerful on the business front after the release of the white paper. The following week, Stanley Hartt flew to Toronto and met for several hours with a high-powered group of executives from the Business Council on National Issues. They responded by releasing a strong statement endorsing the "broad thrust" of the white paper.

The business community was particularly pleased that Wilson had decided not to bring in a minimum corporate tax, as the United States had done in its 1986 tax reform. Wilson himself seemed to be providing ample reason for such a tax. He noted that in 1983 some 110,000 *profitable* firms—including some very large companies—had paid no income tax at all. A minimum corporate tax would have forced some tax out of these artful dodgers. But Wilson decided against it, arguing that the corporate tax breaks he planned to eliminate would generate sufficient revenue. By his department's own calculations, however, his tax reforms will still leave roughly 25,000 of these profitable firms paying no income tax as a result of special tax breaks.

Among the group of companies enjoying tax-free status in 1986 were some of Canada's most profitable corporations. Hees International, a holding company for the sprawling corporate empire of Edward and Peter Bronfman, was one of those corporations, as was another Bronfman holding company, Carena-Bancorp Incorporated. Yet these two had combined profits of $111.3 million that year. Don Blenkarn, chairman of the Commons finance committee, was shocked by these numbers. As he told Jacquie McNish of *The Wall Street Journal:* "It's unconscionable that they [Hees and Carena-Bancorp] pay so little tax."

And the Bronfmans were not alone. A number of prominent Canadian firms managed to go tax-free in 1986, on profits ranging in the tens of millions of dollars. Alcan Aluminium Limited, for instance paid no income tax on a profit of $220 million (U.S.); in fact, Alcan chalked up a credit of $32 million to reduce its future taxes. And Brascan Limited, with its massive resource and manufacturing interests, also avoided income taxes entirely that year, despite a profit of $186 million. It qualified for a credit of $2.3 million. Xerox Canada, a subsidiary of the U.S. photocopy giant, reported a profit of $115 million, but paid no income tax and ended up with a $10 million credit. Real estate developer Cadillac Fairview had a profit of $95 million, paid no income tax and managed to qualify for a credit of $12.4 million. The list goes on.

Leonard Shifrin was at first perplexed by his own lack of enthusiasm for Wilson's reform package. As a social activist in the 70s, Shifrin had talked the government into setting up the National Council of Welfare and had served as its first director. In more recent years, he had switched to journalism, writing newspaper columns that pushed for social reform and a more progressive income tax system. Now, here in the tax reform lock-up, he was faced with a set of proposals that accomplished one of the key things he had long pushed for—the replacement of tax deductions and exemptions with tax credits. Since deductions and exemptions allow bigger savings for those in higher tax brackets, the move to a system of flat credits—which offer the same dollar benefits for everyone—is highly preferable. Still, Shifrin was unhappy, and with good cause.

As Shifrin noted, Michael Wilson had heeded the advice of welfare activists and moved to a system of credits, but he had done so as part of a package that nullified the gains of this move. The whole point of moving to credits is to allow low-income people to receive the same tax savings as high-income people have received on a wide range of basic tax breaks such as the basic personal exemption, exemptions for a spouse and dependent children, and the deduction for tuition fees. But along with the move to credits, the government was also proposing reductions in tax rates that would provide greater benefit for those at the upper end. It was hard to see exactly where the money was going, but somehow the poor and middle class weren't ending up with a bigger share.

Indeed, it is interesting to see how Wilson proposed to divide up the $3.1 billion that he was taking out of the income tax system. The bottom group, which included 26 percent of all households, would receive only $257 million—a mere 8 percent. The top income group, however, which included only 2 percent of all households, would receive $379 million—12 percent.

But the government was selling the white paper as a progressive reform. It offered up a carefully prepared set of numbers that showed the package would make the system fairer—if only slightly. In fact, the relative tax burden borne by each income group would be virtually unchanged.

And all this should be seen in the broader context of what the Mulroney government had already done on the tax front. Although the white paper did little to redistribute the tax burden, earlier Wilson budgets, as we have seen, had done some significant redistribution—with the poor and the middle class being made to shoulder a heavier burden. By keeping the tax reform relatively neutral within tax brackets, Wilson was essentially allowing the status quo to be maintained—a regressive status quo that he had established himself.

Of course this regressive trend wasn't documented in the massive statistics contained in the tax reform documents. But the National Council of Welfare, which operates under the auspices of the federal department of health and welfare, used government numbers and a sophisticated computer model to show that the poor and middle class had suffered significantly during the Mulroney administration and that the tax reform didn't even bring them back to where they'd been.

This trend was particularly strong among the poor. A one-earner family of four, with an income of only three-quarters of the poverty line, would pay $191 more in income tax as a result of tax reform than it would have paid if the Mulroney government had not made any changes to the tax system. And while the government claimed it was raising the threshold at which low-income people had to start paying tax, in fact, the threshold was lower (using constant dollars) than when Mulroney came to power. For instance, before the Mulroney government's first budget, a one-earner family of four would start paying tax once its income reached 76.4 percent of the poverty line. After tax reform, such a family would start paying tax when its income reached only 71.9 percent of the poverty line. Furthermore, the situation for low-income families would get worse over time, since tax credits were not fully indexed to inflation. By 1991, this typical family would start paying income tax when its income reached only 67.3 percent of the poverty line.

And the tax savings the rich would enjoy as a result of the tax reform were likely to be bigger than the government was letting on. Wilson's figures were misleading because they failed to take behavioural changes into account. While there are few ways low-income people can alter their behaviour to adjust to the new measures, the rich have more manoeuvring room. So, for instance, if the tax shelters are removed from investments in films and MURBs, high-income investors will simply find new tax shelters.

Indeed, the *Financial Times* was quick to predict that tax shelters for investments in power generating stations would soon be the new rage. Up until then, there hadn't been much interest in the way the fast write-offs for power stations could be used for tax sheltering, because investors had been so accustomed to other tax shelters, according to lawyer Jay Shepherd, a partner in the Toronto firm of Blaney McMurtry Stapells. Shepherd, who is best known for doing the legal work on the SRTC deal studying the difference between red-and-white and black-and-white cattle, told the *Times* that power projects would likely become popular when the better-known tax shelters were scaled back.

Yet the government statistics simply assume that the rich will continue to invest in films and MURBs and just pay the higher taxes—even though the government knows this is not likely to be the case. Indeed, Wilson has given the rich plenty of time to rearrange their affairs before the new measures come into effect.

And while the government stressed that it was cutting back tax breaks, most of the breaks affected were ones that had been particularly beneficial to the middle class. By converting deductions and exemptions to credits, for instance, the government was seriously cutting back the tax breaks that had helped the middle class, such as the basic personal exemption, the exemptions for dependent children and employment expenses. While higher income earners benefited as well, these measures were proportionately more important to middle-income earners.

High-income earners are more concerned about special tax breaks for saving and investment. And here the tax reform was more gentle, trimming rather than slicing and phasing in rather than abruptly removing. The higher RRSP contribution limits are to be phased in more slowly, but, as planned, the limit will eventually reach $15,500 a year—a level that will only benefit those able to *save* this amount per year.

The tightening of the tax break for capital gains was also not severe, particularly in light of how much this tax break had already been enriched by the Mulroney government. Instead of only half of capital gains being included in income for tax purposes, two-thirds were to be included in 1988 and three-quarters after 1990. But the punitive effect of including more of capital gains in income was diminished by the fact that the top marginal tax rate would be dropping.

Also, the $500,000 capital gains exemption was retained for farms and small businesses. There was virtually no criticism of this costly decision, even though it is an ineffective way to subsidize farmers and small businesspeople since it benefits them only when they sell their operations. Surely it would be far wiser to help these individuals while they are in business—indeed help them stay in business—not just reward them when they retire or decide to abandon their efforts.

For all other capital gains—and real estate and yachts and jewellery would continue to qualify—the exemption was to be limited to $100,000. But $100,000 is still extremely generous. This is certainly a far cry from Carter's call for capital gains to be treated like all other forms of income.

Another crucial tax break for high-income earners is the right to deduct interest costs on funds borrowed for investments. Allan MacEachen had encountered severe resistance when he attempted to tamper with this one in 1981; indeed, he recalls it as being the most hotly protested of all the measures in his controversial budget. There was wide speculation that Wilson would cut off this deduction as part of his tax reform, especially since the U.S. tax reform had eliminated it. But Wilson left it largely intact—a move that is highly beneficial to investors.

Had Wilson wanted to seriously reduce tax breaks that benefited the rich, he could have for instance converted these last three tax breaks—RRSPs, capital gains and interest deductibility—to credits as well. This way, he would have applied the same principle to these tax breaks that he had applied to others; that is, that the value of the tax break would be worth the same to people in all income brackets. But with the tax breaks that the rich really care about, no such egalitarian principles applied.

Of course the government never even considered removing or cutting back many of the tax breaks that most aid the rich. The exemption for capital gains made on the sale of one's house confers a far larger benefit on the rich than the poor, as we saw in Chapter One. If the government was serious about limiting tax benefits for the rich, it could have begun by capping the tax savings allowed on the sale of a house, so that profits above a certain point would be taxable.

Instead it kept fully in place a tax break that offers almost no benefit to low-income people and enormous benefit to the rich, and drives up housing prices in the process.

And, of course, Wilson made no moves to bring back the estate tax—the most progressive tax of all. A popular argument against taxing inheritances is that the revenue to be gained is trivial. But when the estate tax was removed in 1971, it was collecting more than $125 million a year. Had it been left in place, it would likely be collecting close to $1 billion a year today, due to inflation and the growth in wealth. Its re-instatement would produce more than enough revenue to remove all of Canada's poor from the income tax rolls. But the possibility of bringing back the estate tax was never seriously entertained in the months of government agonizing over how to broaden the tax base.

When examined closely, Michael Wilson's tax reform isn't really a progressive tax reform at all. In the end, each income group ends up shouldering roughly the same burden as it did before. The real tax reform lies down the road—in the form of the revised sales tax—and it's inevitably going to hit the middle class hardest.

Indeed, Wilson's tax reform hasn't really caused the government to veer from its agenda, except perhaps to throw out a quick and highly publicized income tax reduction to bolster its election hopes. From the beginning, the Mulroney government has been moving towards a much heavier emphasis on the sales tax—the most regressive kind of tax. Since it came to power in 1984, it has increased corporate taxes by only 8 percent, the income tax by 45 percent and the sales tax by a whopping 67 percent. And this trend towards sales taxes will become still more pronounced in the second stage of tax reform.

Interestingly, the move to tax credits appears to be a key part of the government's strategy. It allows Ottawa to target benefits to those at the bottom, while removing them from those in the middle. This is, of course, the same thinking that lies behind the idea of ending universal social programs. If those at the bottom can be protected, then the middle class is fair game. With an extended system of tax credits in place to protect the disadvantaged—and ward off charges of unfairness—the Mulroney government will be able to crank up a huge new sales tax that will hit the middle class much more severely than the rich.

Despite the progressive gloss, Wilson's proposals promise to take Canadian tax policy in a seriously regressive direction. Dressed up in the lingo of social justice, the proposals threaten in the long run to shift the tax burden significantly —*off* the backs of corporations and the rich. What is going on isn't tax reform at all, it's the hijacking of tax reform.

Indeed, Wilson's reform reflects the neoconservative approach to taxation, an approach which has come to dominate the tax scene in recent years. The changes the neoconservatives envision on the tax front are anything but progressive. In fact, they go in exactly the opposite direction, relieving the tax burden on the rich and shifting it down the income ladder. Traditional tax reformers, who sought progressive change, have been pushed from the scene. It is now the neoconservative tax agenda that is presented to us as "tax reform."

Wilson's reform is, in many ways, the culmination of a process that began in the late seventies, when a new generation of economists began pushing for the elimination of tax breaks. They used much of the same rhetoric as the traditional tax reformers, but their concerns were different. It was "efficiency," not "fairness," that primarily concerned them. They argued that tax breaks should be eliminated because they caused economic distortions: since tax breaks are available for some investments and not for others, investors often make decisions on the basis of tax—rather than market— considerations. The economists also argued that greater efficiency could be achieved through tax cuts for the rich. They maintained that high tax rates on those with high incomes killed incentive and therefore impaired economic efficiency. It all sounded very scientific.

These arguments appealed to business and high-income earners. The same people who had vehemently rejected Carter's plea for the removal of tax breaks suddenly found much merit in the idea when it was linked to an overall reduction in their tax burdens. In the neoconservative version of tax reform, the elimination of tax breaks became inextricably linked with significantly lower tax rates for those at the top.

As this approach became part of the political agenda in the eighties, the neoconservatives took an even bolder step. They proposed shifting the emphasis away from income taxes entirely and onto consumption taxes. This, the economists argued, would encourage saving. But the key difference—the one that isn't stated—is that a consumption tax is almost inevitably more regressive than an income tax.

The neoconservative version of tax reform is reflected perfectly in the tax reform proposals put forward by the Business Council on National Issues in 1986. As mentioned in Chapter Seven, those proposals urged a reduction in the top tax rate, a greater reliance on the sales tax and increased tax incentives for savings, along the lines of RRSPs. The BCNI of course went to considerable trouble to dress up its proposals as progressive.

The similarity between the BCNI's proposals and Michael Wilson's reforms are striking—right down to the progressive veneer. Wilson dropped the top rate and moved to a greater reliance on the sales tax. While he didn't increase the incentives for savings, he did maintain the enormously generous $15,500 annual limit for RRSPs—a move that flew in the face of his own rhetoric about cutting back on special tax breaks. No wonder BCNI president Tom d'Aquino was so pleased with Wilson's reform. It has pushed Canada's tax system in the direction that d'Aquino, the business community and the neoconservative economists have long wanted to go.

It was somehow fitting that a final tribute to the Carter commission report, twenty years after its release, turned out to be a rather intimate affair. In addition to some of the key principals from the tax reform period—Harvey Perry, Douglas Hartle, Edgar Benson, Robert Bryce—the conference at Osgoode Hall Law School last spring attracted mostly academics and members of social reform groups. The huge community of tax practitioners, whose prosperous careers revolve around the tax system, was barely represented. Although tax practitioners turn out in droves for the highly technical sessions of the Canadian Tax Foundation's annual conferences, they apparently had little time to engage in a debate about the ideal of a progressive tax system.

It was appropriate that this final look-back and tribute to the Carter philosophy should be held just months before the Mulroney government introduced its own version of tax reform, putting the final nail in the coffin of any Carter-style reform. In the first major attempt to reform the tax system since the effort that grew out of the Carter report, Ottawa has opted to turn its back on the ideals of the Carter commission. Carter rejected the notion that income from capital should be taxed more favourably than income from labour, suggesting that all income should be treated the same—a move that would have greatly aided those who work for a living. But Wilson's reforms, despite rhetoric to the contrary, largely preserve the favoured treatment of the holders of capital.

Apart from the central question of fairness, this raises some interesting questions about our public morality. There is a moral order to the world of tax, whether we realize it or not. While taxes should perhaps be seen as part of our civic duty, to be paid cheerfully in exchange for the privilege of living in a civilized culture, in the public mind they have become more associated with punishment. They signal a kind of penalty or indication of disapproval.

Hence, when revenue-hungry governments look for more money their first targets are almost inevitably the popular "sins" of cigarettes and alcohol. And the taxes on gasoline skyrocketed when government sought to discourage or punish energy consumption during the energy crisis. Even our eating habits are scrutinized by the watchful moral eye of the government. If we eat healthy, nourishing snacks like apples or raisins, we can avoid the federal sales tax. If we are driven to candies or other junk foods—potato chips, corn puffs, pretzels, etc.—we face the sales tax.

Similarly, we have come to feel entitled to tax concessions when we are behaving well. So governments have offered tax breaks for homeowners insulating their houses and for corporations installing pollution abatement equipment, as well as for those giving money to charity or putting away money for their retirement. Indeed, one can spare oneself a considerable amount of tax over the years if one sticks to an exemplary, sober sort of life—low consumption, particularly of intoxicating beverages, tobacco products or junk food, slow driving, and lots of charitable giving and responsible saving for the future.

In the midst of this puritanical universe, the preferential treatment accorded capital over labour strikes one as odd. Whatever happened to our Protestant work ethic? Isn't working for a living at least as commendable as insulating one's house, abstaining from alcohol or giving up smoking? Do we really mean to signal our social disapproval to those who live by the sweat of their brow, as opposed to those who merely clip coupons or dabble in commodity futures? W.O. Twaits, former president of Imperial Oil, once questioned whether it was fair to tax the entrepreneur at the same rate as the "drones" in society. In his moral universe, the drones were employees who merely worked for a living. Twaits's view may not be widely shared by Canadians—the bulk of whom would fall into his drone category. But while most Canadians undoubtedly place a high value on the dignity of work, our tax system does not.

Our implicit acceptance of Twaits's moral order is perhaps

best illustrated by the tax treatment of the speculator. In just about everybody's moral universe, the speculator is a bad guy. He buys up land—or shares or gold or currency—for the sole purpose of holding it for a short period of time and then selling it at a significant gain. Speculators drive up prices and contribute little to economic growth, and governments have traditionally shown their disapproval of such behaviour through the tax laws.

Thus, in the United States, investors who sold stock too quickly were considered speculators and their gains did not qualify for the lower rates applied to other capital gains. Similarly, Canada denies preferential tax treatment to capital gains made through land speculation, and a great deal of Canadian court time has been devoted to the question of separating a legitimate capital gain from a speculative one. If the gain is found to be speculative, it is taxed as regular income. The speculator's punishment then, is to be treated as badly by our tax system as the ordinary working person is!

Even current language has come to reflect this departure from the work-ethic mentality of earlier times. Journalist Tom Walkom, writing in *This Magazine*, has nicely captured the way the media language of today reflects a Twaits-style view of the world:

> When I was a kid in South Porcupine, a creative person was an artist, an interior decorator or someone who worked for the CBC. And a risk-taker was a person, such as a hard-rock miner or steeplejack, who paid high life insurance premiums. No more. The creative person is now the capitalist; the risk-taker, someone who risks money. When the government says it is committed to rewarding risk-takers, it doesn't mean it will give bonuses to hard-rock miners. It means it will give tax breaks to anyone who has capital.

But perhaps the ultimate comment on our tax system's bias

towards capital over labour is our failure to tax inheritances. Although the estate tax fits into the category of taxes on capital, it is, in some ways, in a class by itself. The usual arguments used to justify low taxes on capital are even more unconvincing when applied to the inheritance tax.

The general argument against high taxes on capital, for instance, revolves around the theme that we do not want to destroy the motivation of the rich to invest their capital. But once the investor has died, he can surely no longer be motivated. Some argue that the rich will be discouraged *before* they die if they know large amounts of their money will be taken in taxes *after* they die. But how far can this argument go? Do we have to cater to the motivation of the investor not only now but on into eternity? Will the investor lose his will to invest if he fears that his children or grandchildren or great-grandchildren might face high taxes decades from now?

Certainly, if we use the criterion of ability to pay, inheritances are an ideal thing to tax. To begin with, only the very well-to-do are affected. Carter argued that inheritances should be taxed in the hands of the heirs, and on the basis of how much the bequest increased an individual's income and therefore his ability to pay, just as surely as if he had earned income from a job.

But in fact he did not earn the income from a job; he did not *earn* the income at all. It was nothing more than a windfall, a lottery-like prize for being born into the right family. In a reasonable moral scheme of things, we might expect inheritances to be taxed at higher rates than regular income, reflecting our greater respect for those who *earn* what they receive. Surely the very minimum we would expect is that inheritances would be taxed at least as heavily as regular income—the eminently fair and neutral solution recommended by the Carter commission. But instead, we do just the opposite. We actually treat inheritances more favourably than regular income, so favourably in fact that we don't tax them at all. Are we not then setting up a dreadful double standard, an ultimate insult to those who win their money the hard way and whose only lottery winnings will probably be in the $5 to $10 range? Hartle comments: "The idea that earned income accords an ability to pay taxes but that bequests do not seems to me utterly perverse."

Indeed, this tax break flies in the face of some of our most cherished notions about democracy and our political system. The doctrine of equal opportunity is about as deeply embedded as our political values go, and one would be hard put to find a politician who did not endorse it. Even an ultra-conservative like Ronald Reagan pays lip service to the idea that everyone should at least start out with the same chances. As Reagan once said of the United States: "We offer equal opportunity at the starting line of life, but no compulsory tie for everyone at the finish."

Of course neither Canada nor the United States offers anything approaching real equality of opportunity for its citizens. The circumstances of one's birth and upbringing determine all sorts of crucial factors that limit or expand one's horizons. But for our tax system to actively exacerbate these inequalities—by taxing earned income heavily and inherited income not at all—seems hypocritical, to say the least. The race is going to be uneven enough. Do we really want to let a small group of citizens start half way to the finish line?

Of course, even with an inheritance tax, the children of the wealthy would still inherit enough money to get a substantial head start. But how much is enough? After being given every opportunity from birth and the bulk of their parent's fortune, are they not well enough situated to begin the race? Is it really necessary to compound the favouritism by sparing them completely from tax on their inheritances—tax they would have had to pay if they'd received the money from a weekend job in the local grocery store?

And in our value-ridden tax system, what message are we communicating by this huge tax exemption? Judging by the enormity of the tax break offered, inheriting money must be

an even finer activity than investing, giving to charity, installing pollution equipment, insulating your home or eating nourishing snacks. Working for a living, on the other hand, is down
there with drinking, smoking, speculating and eating pretzels.
But whose moral universe is this anyway?

The Carter commission, in its relentless pursuit of neutrality, was opposed to the very idea of a tax system embodying
these sorts of moral judgments. The notion that "a buck is a
buck is a buck" meant, among other things, that the government wasn't going to pass judgment on how that buck came to
be in the taxpayer's pocket. What mattered was that it was
there and that it gave the taxpayer a certain command over
available resources. We ignored Carter's advice, however, and
our tax system does reflect moral values. But, oddly enough, it
doesn't seem to reflect the values of the majority of Canadians,
who appear to have a strong belief in the work ethic. In the
twisted moral universe of our tax system, the worker is deni-
grated, buried under a mountain of tax. It is the heir and
heiress who receive our highest tribute—tax-free status.

A century ago, the wealthy feared that the imposition of an
income tax and the extension of voting rights to the unproper-
tied classes would inevitably lead to the plunder of the great
fortunes. At the time, their fears probably seemed quite reasonable, if a little exaggerated. Why wouldn't the have-nots, at
the very least, want to shift the tax burden off their own backs
and onto more amply endowed backs? But it didn't happen
that way. And decades later, when the Carter commission
conducted an exhaustive five-year probe of the tax system,
Carter concluded that the system so favoured the wealthy that
there were grounds for a revolution in Canada. Now, we are in
the process of consolidating all the benefits won by the rich
over the years, dressing them up in a new package and calling
it tax reform.

It is the particular genius of our modern system that all this
has happened while appearing not to happen. In fact, this is

the only way it could have happened. If the middle and lower classes had actually understood what was going on, it's unlikely they would have been so acquiescent. But, as we have seen, they have been poorly informed, even misinformed. They have been kept at arm's length from the decision-making process with assurances that they could not possibly understand the complexities; they have been bored to death by a highly technical approach that is enough to make anyone's eyes glaze over; and they have been downright led astray by arguments that suggest their own self-interest—indeed their only hope of employment—lies in enriching the rich.

Here then lies the real problem of tax reform: the confusion of the public. The Carter commission provided an astonishingly detailed blueprint for a progressive tax system, and one that would have gone far towards meeting the long-sought-after goals of neutrality and simplicity, as well as fairness. A real made-in-Canada solution, admired even abroad. So much of the work has already been done. If we were really interested in a progressive tax system, we could start by adopting Carter's simple concept of treating all income the same and taxing it at genuinely progressive rates.

But the rich have declared that option closed, out of bounds. And so we are now engaged in a massive national debate on the future of our tax system—a debate in which the most important question in taxation is off limits. Like the U.S. tax reform, the first stage of Wilson's tax reform is essentially neutral within tax brackets; that is, each economic group or "class" will end up bearing the same portion of the national tax burden as it did before tax "reform." Is it any wonder that, while the current reform has captured the rapt attention of pundits and tax experts, it has produced widespread *ennui* out there among the public?

In fact, what is going on is anything but boring. We are in the midst of revising how our national pie is to be divided. But, those directing the revision—the business community, the tax experts and the politicians—have already decided what size the pieces will be. Once the second stage of the tax reform is in place, the share of the nation's resources enjoyed by the middle class will almost certainly be smaller than it is today. At this point we should be urgently debating whether this is how we want the pie cut. Only by refocussing the debate in this way and by including everyone with a vested interest—every Canadian who pays tax—can we stop the rich from serving themselves an even larger slice.

SELECT BIBLIOGRAPHY

Arnold, Brian J., McNair, D. Keith and Young, Claire F.L. (eds.) *Taxation of Corporation and Shareholders* (Toronto: Carswell, 1986).

Baldwin, Robert, *Wealth and Taxation*, unpublished paper, Dec. 1980.

Baldwin, Robert, "The Case Against the Write-off of Capital Costs," *Canadian Taxation*, vol. 1, no. 3, 1979.

Beach, Don, "Silence should be golden in the art of tax planning," *Financial Times*, Nov. 12, 1984.

Benson, E.J., Minister of Finance, *Proposals for Tax Reform* (Ottawa: Queen's Printer, 1969).

Bossons, John, "Economic Overview of the Tax Reform Legislation," *Report*, Twenty-Third Tax Conference, 1971, Canadian Tax Foundation.

Brean, Donald J.S., *International Issues in Taxation: a Canadian Perspective* (Toronto: Canadian Tax Foundation, 1984).

Brooks, Neil "Current Tax Reading," *Canadian Tax Journal*, vol. 34, no. 3, May-June 1986

Brooks, Neil, "Taxation of Closely-Held Companies: The Partnership Option and the Lower Rate of Tax," *Australian Tax Forum*, volume 3, number 4, 1986.

Brooks, Neil, "Making Rich People Richer" *Saturday Night*, July 1981.

Bucovetsky, Meyer, "The Mining Industry and the Great Tax Reform Debate" in A.P. Pross (ed.) *Pressure Group Behaviour in Canadian Politics* (Toronto: McGraw-Hill Ryerson, 1975).

Bucovetsky, Meyer and Bird, Richard M., "Tax Reform in Canada: A Progress Report" *National Tax Journal*, vol. XXV, no. 1.

Business Council on National Issues, *The Federal Deficit: Some Options for Expenditure Reduction*, Ottawa, Aug. 1984.

Business Council on National Issues, *Social Policy Reform and the National Agenda*, Ottawa, Dec. 1986.

Business Council on National Issues, *Taxation Policy in Canada: A Report on the Task Force on Taxation Policy of the BCNI*, Ottawa, Oct. 1986.

Canada, Department of Finance Department, *Analysis of Federal Tax Expenditures for Individuals*, Nov. 1981.

Canada, Department of Finance, *A Review of the Taxation of Capital Gains in Canada*, Nov. 1980.

Canada, Department of Finance, federal budgets.

Canada, Department of Finance, *Government of Canada Tax Expenditure Account* (Ottawa: 1979).

Canada, *Report of the Auditor General of Canada to the House of Commons* (Ottawa: Department of Supply and Services, 1985).

Canada, *Report of the Royal Commission on Taxation* (Ottawa: 1966).

Canadian Tax Foundation, *The National Finances* (Toronto: Canadian Tax Foundation).

Carmichael, Edward, *Tackling the Federal Deficit* (Montreal: C.D. Howe Institute, 1984).

Carter, Kenneth LeM., "Canadian Tax Reform and Henry Simons," *Journal of Law and Economics*, vol. XI, Oct., 1968.

Cherry, Zena, "Sparkling garden party given for Loblaw head," *Globe and Mail*, Sept. 9, 1986.

Coady, Moses, *The Man from Margaree*, edited by Alexander F. Laidlaw (Toronto: McClelland and Stewart Limited, 1971).

Doman, Andrew, "The Effects of Federal Budgetary Policies 1978-80 on the Distribution of Income in Canada," *Canadian Taxation*, vol. 2, no. 2, 1980.

Dowler, Robert, *Housing-Related Tax Expenditures: An Overview and Evaluation* (Centre for Urban and Community Studies, University of Toronto, 1983).

Drache, Arthur, *Canadian Tax Treatment of Charities and Charitable Donations*, 2nd edition (Toronto: Richard De Boo Limited, 1980).

Economic Council of Canada, *Road Map for Tax Reform* (Ottawa: Canadian 1987).

Eisenstein, Louis, *The Ideologies of Taxation* (New York: Ronald Press, 1961).

Ferguson, Jock, "Firms had no qualms about unsavory clients" *Globe and Mail*, Dec. 29, 1986.

Ferguson, Jock, "Convicted bomber spends and parties" *Globe and Mail*, July 26, 1986.

Flemming, Harry, "Allan J. MacEachen, politician," *Atlantic Insight*, May 1980.

Foster, Peter, *The Master Builders* (Toronto: Key Porter Books Limited, 1986).

Francis, Diane, *Controlling Interest* (Toronto: Macmillan of Canada, 1986).

Galt, Virginia, "Banks Escape Unscathed from Wilson's Tax Reform Moves," *Globe and Mail*, June 20, 1987

Gardner, Robert, "Tax Reform and Class Interests: The Fate of Progressive Tax Reform, 1967-72," *Canadian Taxaton*, vol. 3, no. 4, 1981.

Gau, George W. and Wicks, Anne P. "Impact of ARP and MURB Programs on the Vancouver Housing Market." (Unpublished paper, available at the Centre for Urban and Community Studies, University of Toronto, 1982).

Gillespie, W. Irwin, *In Search of Robin Hood* (Montreal: C.D. Howe Research Institute, 1978).

Globe and Mail, "Noranda shelves plans, blames Carter report" April 19, 1967.

Globe and Mail, "Anvil Mining reverses view on effects of Carter report" Report on Business, Sept. 6, 1967.

Gordon, Walter, *A Political Memoir* (Toronto: McClelland & Stewart, 1977).

House of Commons, *Minutes of Proceedings and Evidence of the Standing Committee on Public Accounts*, respecting the Scientific Research Tax Credit Program, 1985 and 1986.

House of Commons, *Eighteenth Report* of the Standing Committee on Finance, Trade and Economic Affairs, Respecting the White Paper on Tax Reform, Oct. 1970.

Hulchanski, J. David, "Tax Costs of Housing" *Policy Options*, vol. 6, no. 5, June 1985.

Johnson, Jim A. "Tax Expenditures for Business Investment: Their Effectiveness and Their Beneficiaries," *Canadian Taxation*, vol. 1, no. 3, 1979.

Krever, Richard, "The Origin of Federal Income Taxation in Canada," *Canadian Taxation*, vol. 3, no. 4, 1981.

Ladner, Peter, "Fast Lane through the Loopholes" *Monday Magazine*, Sept. 5, 1984.

Lewis, David, *Louder Voices: The Corporate Welfare Bums* (Toronto: James Lewis & Samuel, 1972).

Little, Bruce, "Cohen Joins O & Y" *Globe and Mail*, Oct. 17, 1985.

Lundberg, Ferdinand, *The Rich and the Super-Rich* (New York: Bantam Books).

MacIntyre, Linden, "The lonely stranger who is finance minister," *Saturday Night*, May 1980.

MacDonald, Leslie T., *Taxing Comprehensive Income: Power and Participation in Canadian Politics 1962-72* (Ph.d. thesis, Carleton University, Ottawa, 1985).

MacQueen, Ken, "Submarines and Deceit" *Maclean's*, Feb. 3, 1986.

Mathieson, Kenneth and Maika, A. Peter, "Investment Aspects of R & D Tax Incentives from the Perspective of an Investment Dealer" *Report*, Thirty-fifth Tax Conference, 1983, Canadian Tax Foundation.

Matziorinis, Kenneth N., "Tax Incentives for Capital Investment: Tax Stimulus or Tax Relief" *Canadian Taxation*, vol. 1, no. 3, 1980.

McCall-Newman, Christina, *Grits* (Toronto: Macmillan of Canada, 1982).

McFetridge, Donald G. and Warda, Jacek P., *Canadian R & D Incentives: Their Adequacy and Impact* (Toronto: Canadian Tax Foundation, 1983).

McKnight, William, Minister responsible for housing, *Consultation Paper on Housing* (Ottawa: January, 1985).

McNair, Mac, *The Senate Banking Committee Hearings*, unpublished paper, Osgoode Hall Law School, 1983.

Motherwell, Cathryn, "Achieving tax reform no easier elsewhere," *Globe and Mail*, June 5, 1987.

National Council of Welfare, Government of Canada, *Giving and Taking: The May 1985 Budget and the Poor*, Ottawa, July 1985.

National Council of Welfare, "What to Look for—and Look out for—in Tax Reform," Ottawa, June 1987.

National Council of Welfare, "Working Poor Canadians Hit by Tax Increase," Feb. 1987.

Newman, Peter C., *The Canadian Establishment* (Toronto: Seal Books, 1983).

Olive, David, "What's Gone Wrong with the Reichmanns?" *Report on Business Magazine*, Dec. 1986.

Pen, J., "A Parade of Dwarfs (and a few Giants)" in J. Pen, *Income Distribution* (Allen Lane the Penguin Press, 1971).

Perry, David, "Fiscal Figures; The Cost of Indexing the Federal Income Tax System" *Canadian Tax Journal* (Toronto: Canadian Tax Foundation, 1985).

Perry, J. Harvey, *Background to Current Fiscal Problems* (Toronto: Canadian Tax Foundation, 1982).

Perry, J. Harvey, *Taxation in Canada* (Toronto: Canadian Tax Foundation, 1984).

Pitts, Gordon, "Tax reform hot again," *Financial Post*, May 24, 1986.

Rashid, A., *Characteristics of High Income Families*, (Ottawa: Statistics Canada, 1986).

Ratner, Sidney, *Taxation and Democracy in America* (New York: John Wiley & Sons, 1967).

Robertson, J.R. "The Use of Tax Evasion and Tax Avoidance by Multinational Companies: A Canadian View" *Canadian Tax Journal*, vol. XXV, no. 5, Sept.-Oct. 1977.

Salutin, Rick, "The case for universality" *Canadian Business*, July 1986.

Salyzyn, Vladimir, *Canadian Income Tax Policy: An Economic Evaluation* (Toronto: CCH Canadian Limited, 1986).

Sandford, Cedric, *Wealth Tax—European Experience: Lessons for Australia* (Canberra: Australian National University).

Senate of Canada, *Proceedings* of the Standing Committee on Banking, Trade and Commerce on the Government White Paper "Proposals for Tax Reform," Ottawa, 1970.

Sinclair, Clayton, "Housing's Bull Market" *Financial Times*, April 13, 1987.

Shortell, Ann, "Who's the Richest of them all?," *Financial Post* Moneywise Magazine, Feb. 1987.

Sidenius, Derek, "Tax debt crushes R & D firm," Victoria *Times-Colonist*, April 20, 1985.

Statistics Canada, *Survey of Consumer Finances*, 1970, 1977, 1984, (Ottawa).

Sikeman, H. Heward, "Ability to Pay Revisited," *Report*, Fifteenth Tax Conference, 1961, Canadian Tax Foundation.

Surrey, Stanley S., *Pathways to Tax Reform* (Harvard University Press, 1973).

Tafler, Sid, "Inventor plans to generate jobs, power," *Globe and Mail*, April 9, 1984.

Tamagno, Ed, "Comparing Direct Spending and Tax Spending" *Canadian Taxation*, vol. 1, no. 4, 1979.

Thompson, A.E. John, *Taxation of the Life Insurance Industry and Cooperatives: the Post-Carter Evolution*, paper presented at the Annual Lecture Series 1986-87 of Osgoode Hall Law School, March 1987.

Wolfe, David, *Politics of the Corporate Income Tax in Canada*, paper presented to the National Conference of the Canadian Centre for Policy Alternatives, Ottawa, Jan. 1982.

Wolfson, Michael, "The Bequest Process and the Causes of Inequality in the Distribution of Wealth" in James D. Smith (ed.) *Modeling the Distribution and Intergenerational Transmission of Wealth* (University of Chicago Press, 1980).

Walkom, Thomas, "Torytalk" *This Magazine*, vol. 18, no. 6, Feb. 1985.

Walkom, Thomas, "The Brain Behind the Budget," *Globe and Mail*, Nov. 10, 1981.

Waddell, Christopher, "Petrocan deal to cost millions in lost taxes," *Globe and Mail*, Aug. 17, 1985.

Watkins, Lyndon, "Big Yukon deal positive reaction to Carter report" *Report on Business, The Globe and Mail*, Aug. 30, 1967.

Wilson, Michael, *Tax Reform 1987*, (Ottawa: Department of Finance, 1987).

Wong, Jan, "Elite Group of 20 Gets Early Peak at Tax Paper," *Globe and Mail*, June 17, 1987.

INDEX

Abbott, Douglas, 107
Alcan Aluminium Ltd., 79, 186, 335
Algoma Central Railway, 168
Aluminium Company of Canada, 184
American Express Canada Inc., 80
Antoniou, Andreas, 257
Anvil Mining Corp., 157
Argus Corp., 128
Arviv, Harold, 251, 252
Asselin, Judge D'Arcy, 78
Association of Canadian Foundations, 56
Atlantic Sugar Refineries, 168
Auld, Douglas, 66

Baldwin, Ged, 214
Bank of Canada, 324
Bank of Montreal, 168
Bank of Nova Scotia, 104, 168, 186
Bata family, 31
Bata, Thomas, 39
Battle, Ken, xviii
Beach, Don, 109
Beatty Perrin, 269, 298
Beachesne, Eric, 304, 305
Beauvais, Emile A., 139, 144, 149
Beith, Robert, 268
Bell Canada, 60
Benesh, John, 190
Benson, Edgar, xxxv, xxxvi, 158, 167, 177, 181, 197, 344
Bird, Richard, 66, 179, 322
Birks Jewellers, 89
Black, Conrad, 39, 218
Black, Montegu, 39
Blaney McMurtry Stapells, 338
Blenkarn, Don, 31, 335

Bond, Arthur, 55
Borden, Robert, 20
Borovoy, Alan, 278
Bossons, John, 42, 68, 152
Bouchard, Rejean, 262
Bourassa, Robert, 37, 167
Brascan Limited, 336
Brazilian Light and Power Co., 128
British American Oil Company, 156
British Columbia Forest Products, 131
Broadbent, Ed, 311-312
Bronfman family, 31, 331
Bronfman, Charles, 39
Bronfman, Edgar, 37
Bronfman, Edward, 173n, 335
Bronfman, Peter, 173n, 335
Brooks, Neil, xiii, 87n, 92
Brown, Colin, 86, 166
Brown, Jim, 155, 159, 162, 167, 196, 197, 281
Brown, Robert D., 100, 105, 137, 154
Bruton, Len, 257, 258
Bryan, William Jennings, 24, 30
Bryce, Robert, 154, 162-164, 167, 197, 285, 344
Bucovetsky, Meyer, 179
Bulloch, John, 164-166, 193, 232-233
Burton, E.G., 129
Burton, John, 182
Business Council on National Issues, xiv, xxix, 100, 103, 185-192, 195, 196, 304-309, 310, 335, 343
Bussieres, Pierre, 268

357